THE GUINNESS

-PETER-
-CLAYTON-

JAZZ

-PETER-
-GAMMOND-

COMPANION

GUINNESS BOOKS

References

The following books which are frequently referred to in the text are identified simply by the name, or initials, of the author or authors as follows:

Chilton *Who's Who of Jazz* by John Chilton. 375p. London: Macmillan, 1985 (revised edition).

Collier *The Making of Jazz* by James Lincoln Collier, 543p. London: Macmillan, 1978.

Feather *The Encyclopedia of Jazz* by Leonard Feather. 527p. London: Quartet Books, 1984; also supplements and *Encyclopedia of Jazz in the Sixties/Seventies.*

Gold *A Jazz Lexicon* by Robert S. Gold. 363p. New York: Knopf, 1964. Up-dated as *Jazz Talk* (1975).

Panassié *Dictionary of Jazz* by Hugues Panassié & Madeleine Gautier. 288p. London: Cassell, 1956.

R & S *New Orleans Jazz* by Al Rose & Edmond Souchon. 362p. Baton Rouge: Louisiana State University Press, 1984.

Stearns *Jazz Dance* by Marshall & Jean Stearns. 464p. New York: Macmillan, 1968.

Townley *Tell Your Story* by Eric Townley. 416p. Chigwell: Storyville, 1976.

W & F *Dictionary of American Slang* by Harold Wentworth & Stuart Berg Flexner. 766p. New York: Crowell, 1975.

Editor: Beatrice Frei
Design and Layout: Alan Hamp

© Peter Clayton & Peter Gammond and Guinness Publishing Ltd, 1986, 1989

First published in hardback, 1986
Revised and updated edition, 1989

Published in Great Britain by Guinness Publishing Ltd,
33 London Road, Enfield, Middlesex

Typeset in Times
by Input Typesetting Ltd, London
Printed and bound in Great Britain by
The Bath Press, Bath

'Guinness' is a registered trade mark of Guinness Superlatives Ltd.

British Library Cataloguing in Publication Data

Clayton, Peter, *1927–*
    The Guinness jazz companion.—2nd ed.
    1. Jazz. Encyclopaedias
    I. Title II. Gammond, Peter III. Clayton, Peter, *1927–*. Jazz A–Z
    785.42'03'21

ISBN 0–85112–362–7

Introduction

FOR a long time we resisted any suggestion that we should add, by even so much as a word, to the plethora of printed information and opinion that now exists about jazz. We felt that the only person with the remotest chance of offering anything new would be someone with a limitless private income, with access to a record, tape and book library so vast that it required a separate building to house it, and with the inclination to visit every city in which jazz has established healthy roots. Yet the nagging feeling persisted that there was still one more way of presenting the known facts and – with a little luck – one or two new ones as well.

Leaving aside for a moment the minutely detailed discographies which are perhaps unique to jazz studies, the bulk of jazz literature tends to take one of three main forms: the biographical dictionary, like Leonard Feather's *Encyclopedia of Jazz* or John Chilton's *Who's Who*; the general jazz history, along the lines of James Lincoln Collier's *The Making Of Jazz* or Joachim Berendt's *The Jazz Book*; and the single person biography typified by Ian Carr's penetrating study of *Miles Davis*.

All three categories to a greater or lesser extent reflect the fact that jazz history is largely a matter of fitting into their correct places the names of the people who have played the music. But we should not forget that jazz also has its geography, its placenames, its venues, its landmarks – real and metaphorical – its shrines, movements, artefacts and language. That seemed to leave room for something resembling a *What's What* rather than a *Who's Who* – a book where the main concern would would be to tell the enquirer about the Apollo Theater, explain what a stop chorus is, try to put gospel song into its context, define hip and its predecessor hep, unravel the long history of the Lindy Hop, point out that there is another meaning to the word chart which has nothing to do with the Top Forty.

It is an approach which leads to what looks like anomalies. Chu Berry, a splendid but historically overshadowed saxophone player, has an entry; Miles Davis, a trumpeter of incalculable importance, has not. That is because the newcomer to jazz might well read or hear about this 'Chu' without having the foggiest notion of who or what is being referred to. He or she can go straight to Chu and break the code immediately. Miles Davis, on the other hand, has the sort of aura which has carried his name well beyond the confines of jazz, and is usually referred to in such a way that the reader or listener is not left mystified for long.

Thus it is that Bix gets an entry – under Bix, and not his surname, Beiderbecke. The reason is twofold. First, although it was his true name and not a nickname, 'Bix' on its own can crop up in page after unbroken page of text, or in whole minutes of speech, without any further elucidation. Second, Beiderbecke's short life generated an extraordinary volume of myth and legend, so it is the Bix legends that are the subject of the entry rather than the man himself. The same applies to Buddy Bolden and several others.

Occasionally a musician's (or other person's) name will be followed by his or her dates, but most of the time it will not. These parenthetical dates appear where that person's activities have a direct bearing on the pursuit, movement or place being described in the entry. If we are writing about Washboard Bands, for example, it is useful to have Jimmy Bertrand's dates of birth and death there, for they help to place the washboard bands – the small pond in which Bertrand was a big fish – in their chronological context. When a musician's name is not followed by the relevant dates, they will usually be found in a separate alphabetical index.

Apart from such special cases, the way the book functions should be self-evident. There are ommissions. We found a long while ago that if we read everything there was to read about jazz, there would be no time left to hear any, or to write anything but notes to the milkman. No reference book would be complete without errors and omissions, and the average user would in any case feel thwarted if he were denied the chance of catching the authors out. Whatever happens, we hope you find it far easier to read this book than we did to write it.

PG & PC

Authors

PETER CLAYTON was born in the Deep South of London in the days when the tram still held sway. In fact, swaying was the thing it did best, and among his earliest memories are the lurching views to be had from the crow's nest of a No. 58. He learned to read from the labels of 78 rpm records, which was not good for his sight but did wonders for his speed. After a dare-devil career in public libraries and a few long-playing years with the Decca Record Company he moved, thanks to a series of well-planned accidents, into broadcasting in 1962; since when listeners to BBC domestic radio and the World Service have been regularly trying to switch him off. Since 1964 he has written an entertainment column for the *Sunday Telegraph*. With Peter Gammond he has written *A Guide to Popular Music, 101 Things, Know About Jazz* and *Fourteen Miles on a Clear Night*; their latest joint title is *Bluff Your Way in Jazz* and they collaborated on a BBC series on the Musical Theatre.

PETER GAMMOND was born on the North-West frontier. Eventually, after a period as a mercenary in the Far East and a mendicant in Oxford, he came to London in search of work, ending up at Decca where he bumped into Peter Clayton. Leaving Decca by request in 1960 he became Editor of the *Gramophone Record Review* in 1965 and Music Editor of *Hi Fi News & Record Review* 1970–80. Since the 1950s Peter Gammond has kept up a steady stream of books, starting with *The Decca Book of Jazz* and continuing with *Duke Ellington, Bluff Your Way in Music, One Man's Music, Scott Joplin and the Ragtime Era, Music on Record, Schubert, The Magic Flute, Music-Hall Songbook* – some thirty books in all, including those with Peter Clayton mentioned above; the latest being *Bluff Your Way in Golf* and *Class*, and books on Ellington and Recorded Opera. At present he is working on *The Oxford Companion to Popular Music* and a song-cycle.

Abadie's New Orleans downtown café at the corner of Marais and Bienville Streets. Regular group there was Richard M. Jones's Four Hot Hounds, sometimes with King Oliver or 'Wooden' Joe Nicholas.

Ace in the hole The title of at least three songs: one by Cole Porter (1941), another, much performed by traditional bands, by Mitchell & Dempsey, and a third by Louis Pannico and Elmer Schoebel. The phrase was a once fairly common American expression meaning 'something in reserve', 'something up one's sleeve', and almost certainly derives from cards where, in most games, the ace is unbeatable. In their different ways, the text of the Porter and the Mitchell and Dempsey songs make this clear. The Porter lyric includes the lines: 'Just in case, always have an ace/In some secluded but accessible place'. Paradoxically, in games of dice, the ace is the side of the cube with only one pip, and is therefore low in value. It is this suggestion of smallness which gives us the phrase 'to come within an ace of' achieving something – to miss it by a very small margin.

Ace is also common slang, much used amongst musicians in USA, for a dollar bill, so used since *c.* 1935. As a verb: 'to ace' is to be owed a favour by doing one, especially, in the musical world, by getting someone work or a date.

Across the tracks It often happened that the railroad would divide the better-off part of an American town from the poorer (often black) quarters. Hence the term 'across the tracks', thus applied to a poor or unacceptable person. A phrase used beyond the jazz orbit but particularly well known in the Duke Ellington title *Across the track blues*. It's most widely celebrated use in song is probably in connection with the *Two little girls from Little Rock* (from *Gentlemen Prefer Blondes*) who come from the 'wrong side of the track'.

Action From the common use of the word, as 'where the action is', the act of something exciting happening in music, when it's 'all happening'.

Ad lib A piece of spontaneous improvisation, something done off the cuff, made up as it goes along. Not specifically jazz, being similarly used in classical spheres, from *ad libitum*, but probably more widely practised in jazz than in classical spheres where no one is supposed to.

Afro-, Afro-American Most of jazz history is based on the assumption that the jazz spirit, the blues tradition, and the rhythms of jazz were an inheritance that the African slaves brought from Africa with them. The way these elements intermingled with the characteristics of European music to produce jazz in the form in which we recognize it today is discussed elsewhere under the heading of **Jazz**. One of the leading black writers on jazz, Le Roi Jones, has said (in *Blues People*): 'blues could not exist if the African captives had not become American captives . . . most of the black people who were freed from formal slavery in 1865 *were not* Africans. They were Americans.' Jazz was created by people who were born in America and whose African culture was as much as 200 years or more behind them.

The embryonic forms of jazz, such as ragtime and early Dixieland were, apart from those general rhythmic characteristics that make jazz different from other

5

music, not especially African. Four-square rhythms, European forms and harmonies predominated, and jazz – like minstrel music before it – owed as much to white folk music as it did to black. It could be argued that the true, that is the most Afro, of all jazz, should logically have developed in Africa and not America.

Le Roi Jones goes on to point out that, in fact, it was in those areas *away* from the American mainland where people of African origin settled – places like Haiti, Brazil, Cuba, Guyana, the Caribbean and West Indies generally – that the most Afro-oriented music was and is to be found. These are all areas where black culture was far less diluted or dominated by the white. While most jazz can be loosely identified as an Afro-American music to some degree, the Afro element only re-emerged with strength when the blues came to be heard in a very forceful form (as in much of the rhythm-and-blues-based pop music) and in the jazz that developed after the 1940s when the complicated cross-rhythms of African music began to supplant the hitherto steady 4/4.

All things Afro have become rather emotively loaded. Black culture has emerged in its own right and is admired; but black social emancipation has taken slower steps. Most pop musical manifestations are heavily Afro, and too unfettered by far in spirit and action for some conservative white taste. Use of the word or prefix 'Afro-' (with its political overtones) is inevitably weighted for or against. Perhaps only in the jazz world is the fascinating balance of cultures looked at with truly objective interest.

Books: *The Music of Black Americans* by Eileen Southern. 552p. New York: Norton, 1971. *Black Music* by Le Roi Jones. 221p. London: MacGibbon & Kee, 1969. *Black Music in the United States: an Annotated Bibliography* by Samuel A. Floyd & Marsha J. Reisser. 234p. New York: Kraus, 1983.

Afro-Jazz In a sort of looking-glass image of all said in the previous entry, Afro-Jazz became, in the revolutionary years of the 1940s, the popular urban music of southern Africa; an imposition in reverse of Euro-American jazz and swing idioms on African folk styles. In the 1940s it was widely known as Kwela and was purveyed by local bands mainly playing penny whistles or flutes, guitars and single-string basses. Kwela derives from a Zulu word meaning to climb and there was obviously a suggestion that such music was socially a notch above the unmodified native product. It developed mainly in Johannesburg, where it was interestingly often referred to as 'jive'; and later spread to Rhodesia, Nyasaland and elsewhere in South Africa.

Afterbeat The beat or beats that come after the main (or down) beat. The terms here are not specifically jazz owned, clearly deriving from the European conducting tradition of marking the main beats with downward movements, the weaker with cross or upward beats. The point is, though, that many kinds of jazz achieved their lift (as did the Viennese waltz) by an emphasis on the second or afterbeat in 2/4 time. It was very much a feature of the swing era rhythms that were laid down by such drummers as Cozy Cole, Gene Krupa and Chick Webb. Also referred to, logically, as the upbeat, offbeat and sometimes backbeat.

After hours Referring to those times when the paid stint of work in the club or dance-hall is over and the musicians can relax and blow as and when they like, generally in the clubs where jazz musicians gather and, suitably refreshed, can continue into the small hours. The time for many a jam session. An after-hours joint – any establishment remaining open later than the rest, and thus a place of resort for musicians wanting to jam.

Aircheck, airshot A recording of a jazz (or other) performance taken from a radio or television programme. Such recordings are generally made illegally (according to the regulations in most Western countries), but have led to the release of much valuable and interesting

Outline map of the south-eastern states of America showing the names principally associated with jazz.

When they brought the band—lemonade!

Cartoon that neatly sums up the musicians' traditional relationship with alcohol. (Drawing by Reg Harrison, *Melody Maker Dec. 1929*)

material on smaller jazz labels. The practice obviously has its shadier side as extensive pirating in this manner has often deprived many musicians of their rightful rewards.

Album A term that arose in 78 rpm-record days when multiple-record sets or collections of records were housed in stout albums with record pockets inside (rather like photograph albums) and much was made of this sales gimmick. They also happened to be ideal for record storage. In the LP era when such sets tended to be boxed, the word was soon taken over to mean an LP record in its sleeve, the multiple variety being categorised as double-album, etc. 'Latest album' simply refers to somebody's latest LP issue. This usage began in the US, but is now practically universal.

Alcohol The stuff, according to many a legend, on which jazz musicians' engines run. The music itself has tended to encourage the idea over the years, with titles ranging from *Sloppy drunk blues* through *Gin mill blues*; *Knockin' a jug*; *I keep drinkin'*; *Wine-o-baby blues*; *Drunken spree*; *Last call for alcohol*; *Gimme a pigfoot and a bottle of beer*; *Cocktail swing*; *Straight no chaser*; *Hit the bottle*; *Mug of ale*; *Plastered in Paris*; *Beer drinking woman* to *Whisky fool*.

There are numerous indirect references also, incorporating words which are one remove away from drink itself – honky tonk for instance, American slang for a low-class saloon – hence *Honky tonk train blues* and *Honky tonk blues*. By further extension one arrives at generic terms, Honky-tonk piano and barrelhouse piano, signifying the percussive and thus loud piano styles prevalent in bars and saloons. These styles, along with boogie-woogie piano, are generally considered to have developed in the way they did because of the need to cut through the noise habitually made by the customers. In other words, their form is thought to have been dictated by their function. That seems reasonable enough, but it is unwise

simply to repeat that theory without pausing to consider that it might be the result of the historian's habit of rationalizing after the event. Be that as it may, the fact that places where liquor was sold should give their names to styles of playing is extremely important as a clue to the cause and nature of the jazz musician's supposed drinking habits. Jazz is perhaps unique among the 20th-century arts in that it largely developed, and has mostly been played, in places where alcohol – legal or otherwise – was part of the stock-in-trade.

From its earliest days jazz accompanied dancing, eating and drinking. When Prohibition – the Volstead Act – became part of American law in 1920 (in spite of President Woodrow Wilson's attempt to veto its passage), most adult Americans decided to break the law and carry on drinking. What they drank was anything from smuggled genuine Scotch whisky to paint-thinners, and traffic in alcohol, good or bad, was in the hands of gangsters. Swiftly the gangs took over most of the premises in which drink was sold, which meant, perforce, that entertainment, especially jazz, was run by the mobs. The most famous Syndicate-run establishment was The Cotton Club in New York, but the same thing applied to most of them. Practically every jazz musician who played anywhere of importance in America between 1920 and 1933, when the Volstead Act was repealed, therefore worked directly or indirectly for the gangsters. He also tended to drink a great deal; the stuff was almost at his elbow – indeed it was pressed upon him by admirers – it was plentiful, and swallowing it was among the social accomplishments of the day. Many were over-achievers in this respect, the most celebrated of them being Bix Beiderbecke, who died of its effects at the age of 28 in 1931.

To this day, in spite of concert hall and theatre performances, by far the larger percentage of live jazz takes place in clubs and bars of one sort or another, and practically every jazz musician with a drink problem has atributed it to the ready availability of a literally stunning array of alcoholic beverages.

British traditional jazz, like Music Hall before it, almost grew up in public houses, and cultivated its own beerily cheerful image. Nonetheless, several of the major venues in which it was played, like the Humphrey Lyttelton Club (now 100 Club, 100 Oxford Street, and still offering jazz) had no drinks licence in those days, and the hilarity was generated entirely by Coca Cola and enthusiasm. An endearing characteristic observed among British jazz musicians – and it doubtless exists elsewhere – is that they will, wherever possible, do their drinking on premises other than those where they happen to be working. During intervals between sets they are almost invariably to be found round the corner or across the road.

Algiers Loosely described as a district of New Orleans. Lying across the Mississippi River opposite the Vieux Carré, it remains 'an oddment – an exotic' (*Fodor*). Known locally as Old Algiers or Algiers Point, it is still a 'sleepy Delta village' and as independent as Quebec, although annexed by New Orleans in 1870. Birthplace of Henry 'Red' Allen (1908–67) and immortalized in his *Algiers stomp*.

Alligator Familiar terms, greetings, descriptions, and so on based on animals, have been common in jazz. Alligator, or more often 'gator, was one such term, an early name (*c.* 1930s) for a jazz (especially swing) enthusiast, one who was hep.[1] Usually abbreviated to 'gator' or 'gate'. The phrase 'see you later alligator' became popular in the rock era,

and a song-title. Also used as a name for a jitterbug in the 30s.

The most famous composition utilizing the word was probably Fats Waller's *Alligator crawl* but it turns out to be a totally non-descriptive piece with no clear connection with the word. And, in fact, the tune, composed in 1927, was initially called by its creator *House party stomp* and, later, *Charleston stomp*. It was its original publisher, one Joe Davis, who decided on its copyright title. The sheet music in certain editions takes the title literally and has a drawing of an alligator on the cover. Also *Alligator blues* (John Hyman); *Alligator hop* (King Oliver).

W & F also define it as a 'mildly disparaging' word for a white jazz musician used by Negro jazzmen in New Orleans *c.* 1915 and after.

All-in The equivalent of the classical *ensemble* or *tutti* – all playing together. But particularly applied, as in Chicago jazz, to the all-out final chorus that traditionally rounded off the number after a string of solos. Also occasionally another name for a jam session.

Apex Club Nightclub on 35th Street in Chicago. Originally called The Nest. Jimmie Noone played there from 1926 to 1928 and celebrated it in his *Apex blues*.

Apollo Theater This important resort of entertainment in Harlem, New York (at 253 West 125th Street, between Seventh and Eighth Avenues) was originally Hurtig and Seamon's Music Hall. It acquired the name Apollo the year before it was taken over in 1935 by Frank Schiffman and Leo Brecher – who had previously run the Lafayette Theater – but it was in their regime that it became one of the key locations in black entertainment. Even under its old management, the first Apollo show had featured Benny Carter's orchestra, and from then on almost every American jazz and swing band – black and white – of any importance appeared there, as did the black singers, dancers and comedians. The Harlem Opera House, just down the

---

[1] In the documentary film *Bix*, made by Brïgitte Berman (1982) it was suggested that alligators was the name given to the fans who crowded round to listen rather than dance because they were like alligators leaving the river to bask on the bank.

Anita O'Day, in her autobiography *High Time, Hard Times*, credits Cab Calloway with the coining of alligator for fan in the early 30s.

block from the Apollo, was also owned by Schiffman and Brecher, and it was there rather than at the Apollo itself that Ella Fitzgerald won a Wednesday Amateur Night contest. The process by which history is transmuted into legend has already been at work in this instance. Jervis Anderson's detailed book – *Harlem, The Great Black Way, 1900–1950* (Orbis, 1982) – is the source of the Harlem Opera House version, which goes on to say that on the strength of that win Ella was later booked by the Apollo, and that it was there that the bandleader Chick Webb spotted her, took her on as vocalist and thus launched her career. That account differs markedly, however, from the one generally repeated in programme and sleeve-notes. In these the location of Ella's win is commonly given as the Apollo itself. This is firmly refuted in *Showtime at the Apollo* by Ted Fox (New York: Rinehart & Winston, 1983; London: Quartet, 1983) which relates how she was spotted at the Harlem Opera House – yet another minor variation – by Bardu Ali (who actually fronted the Webb band). Ali immediately arranged for her to audition for Chick Webb, at the Savoy, the following day.

One thing is clear: the Apollo, like the Savoy Ballroom, was one of those places where the shrewdness of the management and the dedication and discrimination of the patrons combined to guarantee that the entertainment to be found there was the best of its kind. It therefore became an important way-station in an artist's climb to the top, and confirmed an artist's status once the top had been reached. To quote Jervis Anderson: 'Harlem recognized almost no popular entertainer until he or she had appeared and excelled at the Apollo'. A few names will suffice to indicate the kind of acts – from the jazz point of view – that the Apollo put on: Duke Ellington, Billie Holiday, Andy Kirk & His Clouds of Joy, Count Basie, Jimmie Lunceford, Claude Hopkins, and great dancers like Bill 'Bojangles' Robinson, the Nicholas Brothers and Honi Coles. The Apollo

stayed in business a long time by keeping abreast of Harlem's musical tastes. In the 1950s, early rhythm and blues found a home there, ousting the old vaudeville set-up in which the bands or the important singers had been merely the climax of a show which included jugglers, comics and animal acts, and bringing in the 'r-and-b revue' – one singing act after another. In the 1960s (admission still $1.25 to $1.50) James Brown became a superstar there; in the 70s, there would be black artists like Dionne Warwick and Smokey Robinson. In fact it was while Smokey Robinson was on stage there that a shooting incident occurred in which one member of the audience was shot dead, towards the end of 1975. The Smokey Robinson show saw the week out but less than a month later the Apollo was dark. Since then the Apollo has tried sporadic re-openings, managing to keep going with mainly black pop acts for a time in 1978–9. The latest, uncompleted plan, is for it to become a whole entertainment complex, including recording and video-filming facilities. Whatever happens, it can never again be the place which set the standards for the world's entertainment merely by catering to the leisure needs of its own surrounding community.

Apple, Big Apple (1) The Big Apple was one of those many party dances which proliferated during the public-dancing craze years of the 1920s and 1930s. It first appeared in New York, *c*. 1935 and had a brief period of popularity in England *c*. 1937/8. Its name seems to have no connection with the city's nickname (2), but was derived from the Big Apple Club in Columbia, South Carolina where the dance was invented. It has been described as a 'swing square dance', a combination of square-dance and truckin'.

(2) The Apple has been used as a general slang name for any large town or city, but the Big Apple has been a fairly widespread nickname specifically for New York City. The name possibly derived quite simply from the famous apple of the

R·A·C

One of the names frequently associated with the Apollo, often inaccurately – the singer Ella Fitzgerald who rose to fame with the Chick Webb band. (Drawing by Richard Cole from *Gramophone Record Review*)

HERE'S A HOT ONE!

LOUIS ARMSTRONG
THE RED HOT TRUMPETER

NEW RHYTHM-STYLE RECORDS

R462
Louis Armstrong's Hot Five
AINT MISBEHAVIN'
coupled with
TIGER RAG
Trumpet Solo by Tom Dorsey

NEW RHYTHM - STYLE RECORDS TO BE ISSUED SHORTLY

R510 { No. 7. Fifty-seven Varieties. *Earl Hines. Piano Solo.*
No. 8. Bugle Call Rag. *Fox-trot* Eddie Lang's Orchestra.

R511 { No. 9. Shivery Stomp. *Fox-trot.* Frankie Trumbauer's Orchestra.
No. 10. Prayin' the Blues. *Jimmy Dorsey. Clarinet Solo.*

PARTHE

THE HOT FIVE AGAIN

PARLOPHONE
EXTENDED PLAY 45 R.P.M. RECORD

LOUIS ARMSTRONG

Advert as Armstrong was exciting the jazz collectors with his famous Hot Fives and Sevens in the 1920s. (*Melody Maker*, Dec. 1929)

The same recordings have been re-issued countless times since and still sound as fresh as ever. (Sleeve: Parlophone (EMI Records))

Garden of Eden, a symbol of forbidden temptation, which was how New York, or any big city, appeared to the aspiring jazz musician of early days, viewing it from places of lesser largesse.

Perpetuated in various songs and jazz numbers including *Forty-Seventh Street jive*, as sung by June Richmond – 'He's going to the Apple to live on Lenox Avenue . . . but I'm staying right here, 'cos 47th Street will do'. Also the starting point, one presumes, for Charlie Parker's theme *Scrapple from the Apple*, scrapple being described in American dictionaries as a sausage-like preparation containing a high proportion of minced pork.

New York was also familiarly referred to as Gotham – a name derived from the English village, near Nottingham, whose inhabitants were noted for their foolishness, as told in the 16th-century book *Merry Tales of the Mad Men of Gotham.*

Arcadia Ballroom Situated at 53rd Street on Broadway, Manhattan, New York. Opened in 1924, it was a regular venue for white, and later, black bands in the 1930s. Frankie Trumbauer organized a band to play there in 1925 which included Bix Beiderbecke.

Archer Street Street in Soho, London, between Great Windmill Street and Rupert Street where traditionally musicians in search of a job gathered. On Mondays this short thoroughfare became impassable to ordinary traffic. The offices of the Orchestral Association and many agents and managements were situated there at one time. Celebrated in *Archer Street drag* by George Chisholm (b. 1915). Subject of an amateur film shot by pianist/trumpeter/arranger Denis Rose (a key figure on the early British bebop scene) and shown on BBC-2 TV in December 1985 under the title of *The Street*. The film was actually a composite of Denis Rose's original early 50s 8mm footage and shots of present-day reaction to it of some of the musicians shown in it: Ronnie Scott, Benny Green, Johnny Roger, Flash Winstone and others.

Archer Street jazz Contemptuous revivalist enthusiast's term for the pseudo-jazz, slick but unfeeling, in their opinion, as played by the professional Archer Street/Tin Pan Alley musicians, for example, Harry Gold and his Pieces of Eight, Sid Phillips and his Band, Joe Daniels and his Hotshots, etc. They were assumed to be cashing in on the jazz boom for purely financial reasons. Furthermore, they played in tune, a source of great irritation to revivalist extremists.

Armstrong legends One of the great names of jazz. Helped to lead it from the streets of New Orleans to world acceptance. There are not too many untidy legends about Armstrong because he wrote his own story down and offered fairly clear (though debatable) facts. The only point that seems to be in some doubt is the actual date of his birth, which he gave at 4 July 1900. Some would place it a few years earlier, most probably in 1898. Even 4 July seems to be an invention (Collier).

He was born in New Orleans, in a street one block long in the heart of a tough area known as 'The Battlefield' between Gravier Street and Perdido Street. Armstrong always referred to it as James Alley, but a photograph clearly shows it as 'Jane Alley'. The house (No. 719) was demolished in 1964.[1] At the corner of the street was Funky Butt Hall where Bolden played. Armstrong was put in the Waifs' Home after firing off a gun in the street in a moment of exuberance. There he learned to play bugle and cornet and earned the nickname of Dipper or Dippermouth. (See also **Satchmo**.)

Later, while working for the C. A. Andrews Coal Company, loading and driving a cart from 7 am to 5 pm (*Coal cart blues*), he would spend his evening working in a honky-tonk. He was helped and encouraged by Joe 'King' Oliver, whose place he took in the Kid Ory Band

---

[1] At the time it was reported as being 'at 2723 Jane Alley, off South Broad Street'.

when Oliver went to Chicago to play at the Lincoln Inn Gardens. In 1922 Oliver sent for Armstrong to join him as second cornet in his Creole Jazz Band. And thus the national, and eventually international fame of Armstrong began. He died at his home in Corona, New York on 6 July 1971.

In the 1950s an area of some sixteen acres was demolished in the middle of New Orleans, north of North Rampart Street and east of the old Storyville area, to the great sorrow and indignation of the preservationists who saw many of the famous jazz-associated landmarks like Economy Hall and Hopes Hall disappearing for ever. After the demolition the area lay barren for many years while its future was discussed. Eventually it was turned into a park which was dedicated on 15 June 1980 as the Louis Armstrong Park, a fitting memorial to the city's greatest jazzman.

Books: *Swing That Music* by Louis Armstrong. 144p. New York & London: Longmans Green, 1937. *Satchmo: my Life in New Orleans* by Louis Armstrong. 240p. New York: Prentice-Hall, 1954; London: Davies, 1955; Jazz Book Club, 1957; etc. *Louis Armstrong: Roi du Jazz* by Robert Goffin. Paris: Seghers, 1947; as *Horn of Plenty*, New York: Allen, Towne & Heath, 1947. *Louis Armstrong* by Albert McCarthy. 86p. London: Cassell, 1960; New York: Barnes, 1961. *Louis: the Louis Armstrong Story, 1900–1971* by Max Jones & John Chilton. London: Studio Vista, 1971; New York: Little. Brown, 1972; London: Mayflower, 1975; etc. *Louis Armstrong: a Biography* by James Lincoln Collier. New York: Oxford University Press, 1984; London: Michael Joseph, 1984; London: Pan Books, 1985.

Art Ensemble of Chicago Avant-garde experimental jazz group which gradually evolved in the late 1960s, growing out of the Association for the Advancement of Creative Musicians founded by pianist Muhal Richard Abrams (b. 1930) in 1965. With Roscoe Mitchell (b. 1940) and Joseph Jarman (b. 1937) playing the whole gamut of wind instruments, Lester Bowie (b. 1941) mainly trumpet and flugelhorn, Famoudu Don Moye (percussion). The group plays an immense array of instruments, in a variety of styles, ranging from free or energy music to pastiches of most of the forms through which jazz has evolved,

producing a sort of modern equivalent to the music of Charles Ives. The group first came to Europe in 1969 and created a sensation in the intellectual spheres of jazz-making. They have made a prolific number of recordings. Their stage appearances involve much theatricality in terms of visual presentation.

Asman's Jazz Centre Jazz record shop founded in 1953 by jazz writer and collector James Asman (b. 1914) at 23a New Row, St. Martin's Lane, London. Asman for a short time ran two other shops, one at Camomile Street, the other in Cannon Street, both in the City of London, but these were merely 'precautionary' premises, acquired at a time when the New Row Shop was under threat of redevelopment. That threat receded and the original shop marches on into its fourth decade. In the 1980s James Asman has produced a number of LPs by British musicians of the traditional persuasion (Wally Fawkes, Keith Nichols and others) for the American Stomp Off! label.

Atlanta The largest city (*c.* 500 000 inhabitants) and State Capital of Georgia. Situated in Fulton County, it was the location of many famous blues recordings made by Columbia in the 1920s and 30s. W. C. Handy wrote his *Atlanta blues* following a concert there with his band in 1916. Armand J. Piron and Clarence Williams were supporting artists and Handy's daughter Katherine was making her debut as a singer. The visit was highly successful and the band extended its stay in Atlanta to a week. The lyric of *Atlanta blues* appropriately includes the immortal 'make me a pallet on the floor' line.[1] One of the main streets in the black downtown district, Auburn Avenue, has also been celebrated in jazz, as has Bell Street.

Atlantic City New Jersey seaside resort. According to Willie 'The Lion' Smith,

[1] In some catalogues *Make me a pallet on the floor* and *Atlanta blues* are treated as interchangeable titles for the same song.

most of the top jazz men from New York and the eastern states would try to find jobs at coastal resorts during the hot summer months. Atlantic City was a favourite, having its own tenderloin section known as 'The Line', where such clubs as The Boat House, Charlie Reynold's, The Elephant Café and Kelly's Café flourished and offered seasonal employment.

Aunt Hagar Celebrated in *Aunt Hagar's children (blues)* written by W. C. Handy (1873–1958) in 1921 in Brownlee's Barber Shop in Chicago. He completed the song there and then and it was tried out the same night by Tate's Orchestra in the Vendome Theater. Aunt Hagar is derived from the biblical character Hagar who was handmaiden to Sarah, Abraham's wife. In the Bible areas of the South blacks sometimes referred to themselves as 'Aunt Hagar's children'. This was one of Handy's most sincere tributes to his people, inspired by hearing a woman singing to herself as she hung up the washing, wondering where her 'good ole use-to-be' was.

Austin High School Chicago primary college (still operating) in the Austin district of north-west Chicago, just north of the Washington Boulevard, where five young jazz enthusiasts happened to coincide in 1922. All except Bud Freeman, who played the clarinet, C-melody sax from 1923 and tenor sax (from 1925) were originally violinists, but having become interested in jazz they changed to something more appropriate

– Jim Lanigan to piano, Jimmy McPartland to cornet, Dick McPartland to banjo and Frank Teschemacher to alto saxophone. In jazz histories they have always been referred to as the Austin High School Gang or Group, but they never actually worked under that name. They began playing at tea-dances arranged by the parent-teacher association. Opposite to the Austin High School there was a café called the Spoon and Straw that had a coin-operated phonograph on which they heard a record of the New Orleans Rhythm Kings playing *Tin Roof blues*, which gave them some idea of the direction they wanted to go in. Playing regularly at the Lewis Institute, they met drummer Dave Tough who introduced them to trombonist Floyd O'Brien. Teschemacher now took to the clarinet, Jim Lanigan to string-bass. They started to play under the name of the Blue Friars, found a manager in Husk O'Hare who decided to call them the Red Dragons. Eventually, in 1925, when the original Wolverines disbanded, they became known as Husk O'Hare's Wolverines.

Avalon Wherein 'I lost my heart', is a seaside holiday resort and harbour in Santa Catalina Island, off Long Beach, California.

Ax, axe A musical instrument, especially a horn of some kind, and more specifically a saxophone. The term was introduced in the 1940s. An abbreviated form of battle-axe, similarly used.

Baby Nickname generally applied to the younger or youngest where two or more of the family were active in jazz; best-known 'Baby' Dodds (1898–1959), christened Warren, youngest of a family of six and younger brother of John M. 'Johnny' Dodds (1892–1940). General term of endearment used since *c.* 1900 of a girl; latterly has come to be used of almost anybody.

Baby doll An attractive young girl. Implies, generally, one who is kept as the mistress of an older well-to-do man. The more innocent meaning was probably intended in the well-known song *Broken doll* (1916) – 'You called me Baby Doll a year ago', giving it the benefit, but the Bessie Smith *Baby doll* (1926) carried rather more innuendo.

Back To play in a supporting role, to play riffs or other fill-ins behind a solo. More generally, a band playing behind a singer or soloist; backing group.

Back Bay A once prosperous district of Boston, Massachusetts situated on the inner harbour. Used in the titles *Back Bay boogie* and *Back Bay shuffle*.

Backbeat see **Afterbeat**

Back o' Town The area in New Orleans which lies north of Rampart Street. The section which lies south of Rampart Street on the river is known as Front o' Town.

Bad One of the commonest of the inverted jazz slang words – now meaning good to extreme – excellent, wonderful. It extended its meaning in this general use from being a musicianly term of approbation meaning well-played or arranged in an appropriate and tasteful way. Thence entered the cool jargon, exemplified by W & F as 'the ultimate understatement'. The baddest of all, i.e. the very best, would be referred to as 'the worst', although 'baddest' is in quite common use.

Bad health The state one is reduced to by anybody who can do something better than oneself. 'The bands at the Savoy would swing you into bad health', would express a musician's admiration (and chagrin) at finding that the bands at the Savoy Ballroom could outswing and outplay the band that he himself was in. The term may well exist outside the jazz musician's argot, but it is certainly most frequently heard when musicians converse, and appears often enough in jazz literature to justify its inclusion here. A sentence, already creaking under the burden of other slang expressions, makes clear use of it in Rex Stewart's book, *Jazz Masters of the 30s* (Collier Macmillan, 1972): 'Willie, these are the bimbos that I told you I heard out in the Windy City, and you can bet a man that they can get off on them horns and blow a "Boston" that will swing you into bad health.' Rex Stewart continues obligingly 'a Boston was a real get-off'. Quite.

Bag Amid a plethora of general slang meanings, bag in a jazz or pop music context denotes either a musician's personal style or an entire genre of performance. 'He's into a blues bag now' would indicate that the musician referred to had begun to concentrate on the blues. It seems to have come into use in the late 1950s, and by 1965 it had filtered far enough down into vernacular American speech for the blues/soul performer James Brown (b. 1928) to have a hit record with *Papa's got a brand new bag*.

Bags Nickname of vibraphonist Milt Jackson (b. 1923). When used, this curious name always appears on its own, as in the title *Bag's groove*. He is either 'Bags' or Milt Jackson, never 'Bags' Jackson. According to Milt Jackson's own account, it dates from the monumental bags which appeared under his eyes the day after he celebrated his demob from the US armed services. Sounds too good to be true but must be accepted owing to lack of evidence to the contrary. Jackson played in the Modern Jazz Quartet during its entire existence from 1952 to its sporadic reincarnations in the 80s.

Baker's Keyboard Lounge in Detroit, Michigan, USA, claims to be the world's longest running jazz club, having operated in the same location since the father of the present owner, Clarence Baker, opened it in 1934. Pianists have tended to predominate, but many other attractions, among them John Coltrane, Art Pepper,

A Red Nichols arrangement of the 1920s. (*Melody Maker*, Nov. 1928)

As revived by a best-selling Danny Kaye recording in the 1950s. (Music: Francis, Day & Hunter)

The bamboula as seen by artist E. W. Kemble in 1885. (*Century Magazine* 1886)

Adverts following the banjo's rise to popularity from USA in the catalogue of Elias Howe (established in Boston in 1840) and the British equivalent of the 1920–30 period.

Wynton Marsalis and Clifford Brown, have been booked into Baker's. Two so-called live recordings have been made there, one by Oscar Peterson in the 1960s and one by Johnny O'Neal in 1985.

Ball As a noun, ball is straightforward and obvious slang for a good time; thus, 'to have a ball'. There is an increasing tendency, however, to employ it as a verb: 'to ball' – 'to have a good time', but in some subtle way suggesting particularly active participation. Like many such words, the pull towards a sexual use for it seems irresistible, and 'he was balling this chick' can – while not necessarily losing the more innocent connotation of simply having a good time – also mean 'he was in the habit of going somewhat further with this young lady'.

Ballad One sometimes suspects that the language of music is entirely manipulated by publicity men. Words are bent to mean whatever it is most profitable for them to mean at any given time.

Originally a ballad (a name which comes from Latin *ballare*, meaning to dance) was, in the Middle Ages, a song to which one danced; which suggests a light and rhythmic nature. By the 16th century the word was used of almost any solo song that was essentially of a simple and folky nature. By the 18th century the word had changed its nature entirely and it was now a name appended to a long narrative song or poem. There followed an age of street ballads and broadsheets that continued the narrative tradition but often added satire or even broad humour as an ingredient.

In its next incarnation the ballad had become something akin to an operatic aria – a sort of watered down, simplified version but equally sentimental and caressing and it was now mainly known as the drawing-room ballad, catering largely for those comfortably-off middle-class people who possessed a piano and entertained themselves with amateur playing and singing. The professional ballad concerts of the period were glorified demonstrations mounted by publishers and designed to plug the sheet music.

Not so very different was the ballad in Tin Pan Alley days, during which time it continued to be the slower, more sentimental type of commercial popular song. One sub-division of the ballad category, emerging during the 1930s, was the torch-song, invariably dealing with unrequited love.

Even into the rhythm-and-blues and pop and rock eras the concept of the ballad has persisted. The old 32-bar form may be less in evidence, but slow numbers, usually referred to in the trade as 'ballads', and certainly ballad-like in intent, are often to be found on even the heaviest rock albums.

Ballin' the Jack A dance step or series of dance steps that Perry Bradford remember seeing as early as 1909 though it may go back further still. Became a formulated dance in the hands of the black professionals and was put into musical form in 1913 by Chris Smith and Jim Burris, when it was published in Harlem and became a success in the *Ziegfeld Follies of 1913*. The writers usefully incorporated the old dance instructions into the lyric:

First you put your two knees close up tight,
Then you sway 'em to the left, then you sway
   'em to the right.
Step around the floor kind of nice and light,
Then you twist around and twist around with
   all your might.
Stretch your lovin' arms straight out into
   space,
Then you do the Eagle Rock with style and
   grace.
Swing your foot way 'round then bring it
   back.
Now that's what I call Ballin' the Jack

The dance was considered rather rough and lowdown before it was given social grace by Danny Kaye. The twist part of the dance, probably the source of the modern twist, was a pelvis-rotating movement sometimes known as the Georgia grind. (See also **Eagle Rock**.) The phrase 'ballin' the jack', according to one authority, derived from railroad sources, 'jack' being a locomotive in Negro slang and 'balling' meaning to get rolling – to go or work fast.

Baltimore The sixth largest city in the USA, a major port of Maryland with a population of *c*. 950 000. Built in 1729 and named after a family who founded Maryland in the early days of America's history. The *Baltimore buzz* was one of those dances concurrent with the *Ballin' the Jack* craze; composed by Perry Bradford in 1913.

Bamboula Originally the name of a drum of African origin, the bambala, transmuted through West Indian usage to bamboula. Classified as a 'tambour à friction' (Chauvet) and hence sometimes wrongly referred to as a tambourine, it was an instrument of the tom-tom variety with a skin of some kind stretched over each end of a cylindrical body, tapped or rubbed by the fingers or palms. Similar drums would have been used in the West Indies and in Southern USA. As a dance, the bamboula is one of several, all deriving from African dances, variously modified in the West Indies – Babouille, Bamboula, Calinda, Chacta, Congo, Counjaile, Juba and Voodoo are the best known – but the Bamboula seems to have been the one most frequently danced by the black slaves at their weekly gatherings in Congo Square, New Orleans. There it was seen and heard by the Creole composer Louis Moreau Gottschalk[1] (1829–69) who wrote a piano piece based on the dance.

Band The name 'band' for a jazz ensemble was a natural takeover from the military and brass band world. The New Orleans marching bands, playing for parades, weddings, funerals, etc., had annexed the military band instruments, trumpet, trombone, clarinet, sousaphone (a more portable version of the tuba), drums, performing in the early ragtime, cakewalk style. So the collective term

---

[1] Gottschalk was a Creole in the original dictionary meaning of the word.

'band' continued into jazz history as being descriptive of the small, mainly brass and woodwind, group (with piano and guitar/banjo added) e.g. The Creole Jazz Band, the Original Dixieland Jazz Band, the name generally identified with smaller groups. The term 'big band' came into jazz parlance in the 1920s, used of any such group that doubled up on its instruments and moved toward arranged jazz. The word 'orchestra' has always had a slightly more pretentious ring to it, through its classical associations, and perhaps also suggests a band with strings attached. Even so it was used of some jazz ensembles at a very early date, not only of big bands, but of small groups, probably mostly those which played for white society functions, e.g. the Wolverines Orchestra, where orchestra sounded better-class than band. Many of the early New Orleans groups liked to call themselves orchestras. The distinction, however, remains loose and irrational; but it is generally taken that a band would be playing small group jazz, whereas an orchestra something larger and perhaps in the swing style. Many jazz groups use neither term, either employing a collective name: Loose Tubes, Juggernaut, Art Ensemble of Chicago, Nucleus, Midnite Follies, District Six, Boss Brass, Brotherhood of Breath – or title which indicates their number: Hot Five, Hot Seven, Dektette, Tentette, Five Pennies, Twelve Clouds of Joy, Dozen, Half-dozen.

Band Box (1) Night club in Kansas City on 18th Street, run by a lady called Lucille and more fully known as Lucille's Band Box, where Kansas City bands like Moten's once played.
(2) A musician's haunt at 161 West 131st Street between Seventh and Lenox Avenues in Harlem. A second floor club, it contained rehearsal and social rooms and was popular as a late jamming place in the 1920s. Later it became the premises of an undertaker.

Band man The sort of musician who is reliable and useful in the ensemble; not

necessarily a brilliant soloist but in demand as a sideman. One who plays for the band rather than for himself.

Band-within-a-band When bands grew to an average size of between 14 and perhaps a score of members during the swing era, it became a common practice for smaller, self-contained units to form within them. This fulfilled several purposes, chief among them the varying of the texture of the music at dances, concerts and broadcasts (and on record) and the desirability of allowing musical individualists the chance to escape the stringent disciplines of the more formal arrangements. It was the equivalent of letting the dog go for a run in the park. Most big bands fielded smaller contingents, the best known being the Benny Goodman Trio and Quartet – though in their original form neither was made up entirely from regular members of the band, since pianist Teddy Wilson and vibraphonist Lionel Hampton (b. 1909) did not normally function as parts of the full Goodman orchestra. The Bob Crosby Band had its Bob Cats, Tommy Dorsey had a Clambake Seven, Artie Shaw fronted his Gramercy Five (Gramercy, incidentally was a New York telephone exchange in the days before all-figure telephone numbers). The Shaw small group was additionally famous, in its first recorded manifestation (1940), for using a harpsichord – played by Johnny Guarnieri – instead of a piano. In the light of that it is worth mentioning that there is also the term 'chamber jazz' which is not fully interchangeable with the music of the band-within-a-band. The Goodman Trios and Quartets created a very definite form of 'chamber jazz' which a unit like the Bob Cats, with its looser format, did not.

The Count Basie Sextet which worked in the very early 50s, and the Woody Herman small band of 1949, were not bands-within-bands, but more strictly speaking two manifestations of the bandleader-without-a-band at a period when public taste and the economic climate were unfavourable to bigger organizations.

Banjo The banjo was not only a basic instrument of jazz right from the start but its characteristic sounds and rhythms might well have had an early influence on how jazz emerged, particularly in the syncopated rhythms of ragtime. Banjo teams and banjo solos were a dominant feature of the minstrel entertainments which flourished in the mid-1800s, and the first flavourings of ragtime can be sensed in the banjo accompanied songs that were then in vogue.

It is likely that the banjo derived from a similar African instrument (still in use today) known as the banja, banjar or banza. Early stringed instruments were made in imitation of these by the black slaves in America, using half a gourd with a piece of sheepskin nailed over it as the soundbox. Such instruments have been reported as being in use in America around 1770, and even earlier in the West Indies. The banjo was developed commercially in America soon after this and had become a popular instrument by the 1840s. The early models sometimes had an open-backed soundbox, sometimes a closed one on the gourd principle, four or five strings and a plain fingerboard like a violin. Instruments with fretted fingerboards came in around 1870 and were often referred to as zither-banjos.

The typical 19th-century banjo, with a vellum head stretched over a circular frame and metal strings, achieved a sharp, twangy tone that was far more percussive than the guitar's sound and made it an ideal accompanying instrument, almost an adequate rhythm section on its own. Solo instruments had an extra string added and virtuoso players achieved remarkable dexterity. In its varying forms the banjo found a natural place in the folk-dance ensemble. Moving from plantation music-making to the professional minstrel show it was there in the 1890s as a natural part of the emerging jazz styles, its syncopated sounds clearly helping to form the music to some extent.

Jazz histories often appear to suggest that all early jazz players used the banjo and that the guitar came in later as a more sophisticated alternative. While this may have been true in the ragtime-cum-Dixieland styles, the guitar, more flexible and less dominating, would almost certainly have been the instrument more frequently used by blues singers and in the more earthy kinds of jazz. What seems to have happened is that for a time in the early days of acoustic recording the banjo's sharp tones reproduced better so that many guitarists were forced to use the instrument until the refinements offered by electrical recording came in. The banjo was the most frequently recorded instrument in the pioneer days of the phonograph a decade or so either side of 1900. It was generally favoured in New Orleans jazz because its sharp tones cut through the hubbub of collective improvisation when a guitar's softer tones would have been lost; but it was not employed as exclusively as the revivalist insistence on using the banjo might suggest. The only photo of the pioneering Buddy Bolden band, for instance, taken *c.* 1905, shows a guitarist rather than a banjoist in their rhythm section. Once electrical recording and the use of microphones made it possible to amplify individual instruments, those who originally used banjos, or had been forced to do so for acoustical recording purposes, made a wholesale abandonment of the unsubtle banjo. The point is that many were returning to the guitar rather than taking it up for the first time.

Very few of the early banjo-players in jazz made much of a lasting mark until they were able to take a more flexible part in the proceedings as guitarists. Prominent amongst these were such as Johnny St. Cyr, banjoist with the Oliver and Armstrong bands and white musician Eddie Lang in the Chicago-based groups. The change from banjo to guitar within the big bands happened sometime around 1930, the date when, for instance,

Fred Guy of the Ellington band appears to have made the switch.

The early minstrel-style banjo with its busy solos was occasionally exploited in jazz as in some of Jelly Roll Morton's Red Hot Peppers recordings. Within the revivalist bands the banjoist is given what is generally looked upon as a sort of light relief or comedy spot. The very nature of the banjo seems to be jaunty and tongue-in-cheek, its tone not conducive to any great depth of feeling; so that, on the whole, the instrument's influence on jazz developments, after its initial contribution to the formation of the style, has been slight. Its main role has been to provide a clean and emphatic rhythmic backing that some consider essential both in the playing and recording of traditional jazz.

Barbecue A sexually attractive young girl (W & F). Knowing this helps those who thought it was merely an occasion to eat sausages in the open air to appreciate the import of the Louis Armstrong number *Struttin' with some barbecue* (1927); strut – meaning to dance.

Bari, barry Abbreviated slang for baritone-saxophone, in use since 1930s.

Barrelhouse A popular name for a low-class, usually black, drinking dive where beer, wine and home-brewed brandy were served at a crude bar, straight from the barrel. Also functioned as betting shops and for other illicit trades. The music there, generally performed on a knocked-out piano, tended to be primitive, pounding and loud and became known as barrelhouse music. Also loosely applied to instrumental jazz of the crude early New Orleans variety; but usually confined to the piano style. An almost interchangeable name was honky tonk, but that had a more specific meaning. Jess Stacy recorded a genteel but driving impression of the music in his *Barrelhouse* (1935).

Basin Street A well-known street in New Orleans which was once part of the segregated Storyville district, the eastern boundary of the red-light district and the location of some of the most expensive and luxurious sporting-houses. It got its name from an 18th-century canal that terminated in a basin near where the Municipal Auditorium stands today – but which was filled in during the early 1900s. With the virtual demolition of Storyville after its closure, most of the old Basin Street disappeared, though the name has been perpetuated on a thoroughfare in the same area.

The name will linger on for ever in jazz history and in the strains of Spencer Williams' *Basin Street blues*, written in 1923. Originally it was a number with two basic sections – a 16-bar theme said (Panassié: *Dictionary of Jazz*) to have some affinity with Liszt's most famous *Liebestraum*, and a 12-bar blues theme. The introductory 'Won't you come along with me to the Mississippi' was added for the Charleston Chasers' recording in 1931 by Glenn Miller and Jack Teagarden.

Battle see **Cut**

Battle-axe Early musicians' slang for a musical instrument; generally referring to one of the front-line wind instruments. Now more commonly shortened to ax or axe.

Beale Street Famous thoroughfare in Memphis, Tennessee (originally Beale Avenue), which was named after a Mayor of the City. Runs east–west to where the Wolf River joins the Mississippi.

Immortalized in W. C. Handy's *Beale Street blues* which was written in 1916, with the name adjusted for the sake of poetical symmetry, and which, romantically, lists all the attractions of this hub of entertainment. In grateful respect Memphis now has a Handy Park and a W. C. Handy Theatre. The *Beale Street Dip* (commonly referred to as The Dip) was a dance in vogue *c.* 1912.

Books: *Beale Street Where the Blues Began* by George W. Lee. New York: Ballou, 1934. *Beale Street Sundown* by George W. Lee. New York:

House of Field, 1942. Also: *Beale Street, USA* – Booklet issued by the City of Memphis Housing Authority (nd) and reprinted by Blues Unlimited, Bexhill-on-Sea.

Bean Early nickname of saxophonist Coleman Hawkins (1901–69). He was more generally known as Hawk during his successful days. According to West Indian-born alto saxophonist Louis Stephenson, who knew Hawkins in Europe in 1937, the name Bean derived from Hawkins' alleged parsimony, usually expressed in the words 'I haven't a bean'.

Bear **(1)** General American slang meaning 'remarkable', 'first-rate', 'great' or (W & F) a 'humdinger'. Became a common phrase in connection with the music of the quasi-ragtime era of the mid-1900s, extending to the 1920s, frequently in the form of 'it's a bear', as in *Everybody's doin' it* (Berlin) (1911), etc.
(2) Mainly outside jazz is occasionally used as a synonym for 'beast', i.e. an ugly girl, *c.* 1955.
(3) About 1935–40 it sometimes switched usage to a derogatory sense, from the craze for rhyming slang at that time – being rhymed with 'nowhere'. One who was playing a bear, was doing nothing useful or remarkable, getting nowhere.

Bearcat A fairly generalized American slang term or name applied to a strong and aggressive person, especially a slogging sort of boxer. It is based on the mammal of that name (a she-bear, known to fight ferociously in defence of its young). A famous Kansas City fighter was known as 'Bearcat' Wright. The nickname was also given to saxophonist John Overton Williams (husband of Mary Lou Williams) by Ben Webster because Williams liked to shadow-box in an imitation of the above-mentioned Kansas City pugilist.

Hence it was also applied to a punchy sort of rolling bass figure used in boogie-woogie, exemplified and remembered by Meade Lux Lewis's (1905–64) *Bearcat crawl* (1938). From the same sources:

Bearcat blues (Jimmy Blythe) and *Bearcat shuffle* (Andy Kirk).

Similarly applied to a beautiful, spirited, sexually aggressive young girl.

Beard An intellectual, an egghead; cool, far-out, beat sort of person; even avant-garde; a hipster (W & F). The way-out bop-musicians were the first to popularize beard-wearing in the 1940s which was then a symbol of non-conformity, though now common-place.

Beat The central pivot of all music but particularly emphatic in jazz. Most usually 2-beat or 2/4; less frequently 4-beat or 4/4 (common time). Very occasionally 3/4 or, in modern jazz, more cerebral time signatures.

The downbeat is derived from straight conductor's usage – i.e. the first beat of the bar; the upbeat or afterbeats are the succeeding ones. Used loosely in Tin Pan Alley's *Beat me daddy, eight-to-the-bar* – an unscientific allusion to the boogie-woogie idiom, as used in various popular manifestations of the art in the 1930s. 'Beat me daddy-oh' may well have non-musical connotations.

A fine distinction should be made between beat (the rhythmic pattern) and rhythm which is more the forward movement itself, later categorized as swing. Originally a 'beat' was a loafer or moocher *c.* 1860. Occasional 1935 jive use – beat-out – 'beat out that rhythm', etc.

Also a slang nickname for 125th Street, a main thoroughfare of Harlem, New York – known as The Beat; alternatively as The Drag or The Main Drag.

The word beat rather confusingly started to be used in the early 1960s to designate the 'beat' or drop-out generation, whose philosophy crystallized in the writings of Jack Kerouac. The usage in this context has marked similiarities with the 19th-century 'loafing' and 'mooching' connotations. Further confusion can arise from the almost contemporary employment of 'beat group' and 'beat music' in connection with the rudimentary but loud attempts by young (usually British) musicians to play rock-and-roll.

Beaulieu The grounds of jazz and car enthusiast Lord Montagu's stately home, The Palace House at Beaulieu, Hampshire, England were the setting of a short-lived but fondly-remembered jazz festival in the years 1956–61.

The first, a jazz concert in the garden with receipts shared, was a small affair, suggested by members of the Yellow Dog Jazz Club of Southampton. The leading attraction was the Avon City Jazz Band from Bristol. The festival drew an audience of 400. It suggested possibilities and the next year the Mick Mulligan band was engaged. Some news coverage resulted, including a full page in the *Observer*, and 2000 people attended. By 1959 it had become a national event with 5000 present. The 1960 festival, on the August Bank Holiday weekend, included Acker Bilk, John Dankworth, Tubby Hayes, Nat Gonella, Ronnie Scott and Humphrey Lyttelton and visiting Americans Memphis Slim and Little Brother Montgomery. The festival proved a disaster. Although at least 10 000 people were expected, the police refused to give it adequate surveillance. Troubles arose from the fierce 'trad' and 'mod' rivalry rampant in those days; and from the 330 gallons of draught beer and 24 000 bottles sold at the Montagu Arms. The 'trad' element proved noisy during the Dankworth session resenting having to wait for Bilk. The BBC's scaffolding collapsed under the weight of bodies, the lights failed and the cameras were put out of action. Some peace was restored but a scene of wreckage was left and the village and press alike complained.

In spite of this, a 1961 festival was held with Chris Barber, John Dankworth, Kenny Ball, Mick Mulligan and American singer Anita O'Day in attendance. The tickets were limited to 6000 and the 'mod' and 'trad' events were kept apart. Some 20 000 flooded into the village, however, and caused havoc there. The proceedings were called to a halt on the Sunday and it was sadly announced that

25

no more Festivals would be held. It had been a success artistically but the unruly element had ruined its chances. An attempt to stage something at Belle Vue, Manchester two years later failed; and a Folk Festival at Beaulieu in 1966 was washed out by torrential rain. One more attempt in 1977 failed financially and was the last.

Book: *The Gilt and the Gingerbread* by Lord Montagu of Beaulieu. 232p. London: Michael Joseph, 1967.

Bebop, bop Name under which the new trends in jazz that developed *c*. 1940 first emerged. Alliterative word (meaning broadly 'go, man, go') (W & F), possibly a reflection of the 'arriba' or 'riba' used as a shout of encouragement in the Latin-American bands then in vogue. Partly a vocalization of the typical phrase-ending that was common in the new jazz styling and imitated in the scat vocalizing, e.g. 'hey-baba-re-bop' (first vocalized by Lionel Hampton in 1940) as practised by Gillespie and others. Almost always 'bop' in usage.

Jazz was catching up with serious music in the use of 9th, 11th and 13th chord harmonies and breaking the rock-solid rhythmic patterns of earlier jazz. These innovations were partly a deliberate attempt to make jazz more difficult for the average player on the part of black musicians who (for racial reasons) were being kept out of the lucrative jobs that the 1930s jazz and swing booms had to offer. A pioneer in the new styling was the black guitarist Charlie Christian (1916–42) who was allowed, after some resistance from the leader, to sit in with the Goodman band where he quickly became a sensation with his percussive amplified playing, dissonant notes and blatant use of the diminished 7th chord and flatted 5th. It was a more matter-of-fact and cooler approach to jazz than hitherto and it fascinated the young black musicians who saw it as an escape route from the established conventions – and as a symbolically black music.

Others were reaching the same musical conclusions by different routes: Billy Eckstine (b. 1914) in the Hines band, for instance, which he reorganized in 1944 and therein joined forces with Dizzy Gillespie (b. 1917) from the Calloway band (where he was playing after replacing Roy Eldridge in the Teddy Hill band). Another innovator in the Hill band at that time was drummer Kenny Clarke (1914–85). It was Hill, when he took over the management of Minton's Playhouse in 1941, who helped to bring all these bop elements together by incorporating these musicians into the house band, with others such as Thelonious Monk (1917–82) and Charlie Parker (1920–55) soon becoming involved.

The name bop lasted as long as the music stayed in the rather formalized strain that had been arrived at by *c*. 1942. As modern jazz loosened and broadened, the word bop fell out of current use. The actual emergence of bop on record was delayed by the strike of the American Federation of Musicians which lasted from August 1942 to 1944, thus losing us much of the innovatory history of modern jazz. The first fully-fledged bebop records were those by Parker and Gillespie made for Guild in February and May 1945, utilizing original bop material such as *Groovin' high, Shaw nuff, Salt peanuts* and *Hot house*.

Books: *Inside Be-Bop* by Leonard Feather. 103p. New York: Robbins, 1949; re-issued as *Inside Jazz* – New York: Consolidated, 1959. *Four Lives in the Be-Bop Business* by A. B. Spellman. 241p. New York: Pantheon, 1966; London: MacGibbon & Kee, 1967; New York: Schocken, 1970. (Further titles under **Modern Jazz**.)

Beefsteak Charlie's Popular meeting place for jazz musicians; a restaurant and bar in Manhattan, New York on 50th Street, between Broadway and Eighth Avenue. Latterly the name has been changed to McAnn's Tavern but is still frequented by the fraternity.

Bellevue Hospital Large general municipal hospital in New York at 1st Avenue and 27th Street in Manhattan by the East River. It had special wards for mental and alcoholic cases and was thus much frequented by ailing jazzman. One of its most famous patients was composer Stephen Foster (1826–64), who died there, a penniless alcoholic. It has been celebrated in a jazz number called *Bellevue for you* (Pete Brown, 1944). Also referred to in Jon Hendrick's lyric to *Doodlin'* – 'sent me to Bellevue where I was tested'.

Bells Used in a friendly way as a greeting or an acknowledgment of everything being all right. Possibly derived from the pleasing sound of bells or from the name of a bar well-used and liked by jazzmen, it is said to have been instigated by that great inventor of jive, Lester Young (Gold). It became a regular cool greeting – 'Bells, man'! Lester Young, in answer to most solicitous enquiries, would respond with 'bells' or 'ding dong'.

Bend A deliberately impure tone obtained on a brass instrument either by the lips or by half-valving, resulting in a slight upward or downward variation of pitch. One of the devices that distinguishes jazz from straight playing.

Berklee College see **Boston**

Bibliography It took a surprisingly short time for jazz to acquire the status of an art-form, with the consequent appearance of the attendant literature that art-forms attract.

The first full-length British book to be written about jazz could have been *The Appeal of Jazz* by Robert W. S. Mendl, published in London in 1927. But its title is somewhat misleading as (quite forgiveably in its pioneering time) the author more or less misunderstood what the true nature of jazz was and concentrated most of his wisdom on such subjects as George Gershwin and Paul Whiteman and popular music in general.

The earliest full-length book from America seems to have been Henry Osborne Osgood's *So This is Jazz*, published in Boston in 1926, which missed its target by almost the same margin. But these were early times in which to have acquired any overall

perspective of jazz, and their distorted pronouncements now simply serve to illustrate the early confusions and prejudices – similar to the sort that one can find in *The Melody Maker* and elsewhere in the 1926/7 period. Robert Goffin's *Aux Frontières du Jazz* had been written in 1930 (published 1931/2) but was not translated into English, so that Hugues Panassié's *Hot Jazz*, which appeared in an English translation in 1936, was the first book to spread the true gospel with any sort of insight.

Jazzmen, edited by Frederic Ramsey Jr and Charles Edward Smith appeared in 1939, the first book to dig out the musicians themselves and to try (it claimed) 'to tell of something that really happened'. Unfortunately, the memories of some of the musicians interviewed were already somewhat vague and Ramsey and Smith, while giving a really well-balanced view of jazz as a whole, published many details that were to form the basis of various perpetuated inaccuracies and misconceptions.

The explosion of jazz literature that followed these pioneering efforts in the 1940s and 1950s was truly remarkable and had a telling effect on the market for jazz records. It seemed that every publisher wanted to have at least one jazz book in his catalogue and some were compiled hastily in response to the demand. It was not until more recent times that the more scholarly assessments began to appear. See **Discography, Histories, Dictionaries & Encyclopedias**.

Following the rule that books beget books, the subject was soon well enough covered to merit its own bibliographical studies. The first substantial bibliography of jazz was Alan P. Merriam's *A Short Bibliography of Jazz* published in *Music Library Association Notes* in 1953 and in separate form in 1954. In that year the Bulletin of the New York Library also published *The Literature of Jazz: a Preliminary Bibliography* by Robert George Reisner. This was updated in 1959. Most of the early efforts were simply lists. The first critical bibliography was Donald Kennington's *The Literature*

A page showing the 1959 activities at Beaulieu. (*Lord Montagu's Beaulieu Scrapbook 1952–1977*)

Was the title right or wrong this time in this publication of it by a Morton expert? (Music: R. J. Carew, Washington DC)

THE FAMOUS

BIG FAT HAM

by

FERDINAND J. MORTON

Characteristic
PIANO SOLO

ARRANGED BY
J. LAWRENCE COOK

Published by R. J. CAREW
818 Quintana Place, N. W.
Washington 11, D. C.

Charlie 'Yardbird' Parker in his heyday. (Photo: James J. Hagsmann, Gale Agency, Inc.)

Of Jazz published in 1970 and covering around five hundred books and selected periodical articles. The fullest bibliography to date is *Jazz Bibliography* by Bernhard Hefele (Munich 1981) which has 6600 entries.

Bienville Street Street in the Storyville district of New Orleans that ran parallel to Canal Street. Named after Jean Baptiste le Moyne, Sieur d'Bienville, the French colonial administrator who founded the settlement that became New Orleans in 1718. His brother, who led the original expedition toward the Mississippi area, Pierre le Moyne, Sieur d'Iberville, was likewise celebrated in Iberville Street.

Biff To muff a high note on a brass instrument. Not exclusively jazz but occasionally used by all musicians.

Big Apple see **Apple**

Big band jazz Term used to describe jazz played by almost any band that had got beyond New Orleans dimensions and had more than one instrument of any category, e.g. a saxophone section. By normal standards they were never that big, maybe 15 or so at most. The term was used in a slightly derogatory way at times to suggest a band had strayed from the righteous path, but later returned as a widely used synonym for swing or even dance music and is thus used in the titles of several books on this area of jazz activity. People who describe themselves as big band enthusiasts seldom apply the term to latter-day manifestations of it, even though, for example, a Gil Evans band or a 1980s Gerry Mulligan band might use a similar number of players.
Books: *Big Band Jazz* by Albert McCarthy. 360p. London: Barrie & Jenkins, 1974; New York: Putnam, 1974. *The Big Bands* by George T. Simon. 537p. New York & London: Macmillan, 1967; rev. 1971, etc. *The World of Big Bands* by Arthur Jackson. 128p. Newton Abbot: David & Charles, 1977. (See also **Swing**.)

Big Bear Tavern A roadhouse in Redwood Canyon, near Oakland, California, across the bay from San Francisco. West Coast traditionalists regularly had jam sessions there after hours in the 1930s and it was some of these who formed the nucleus of the Lu Watters Yerba Buena Jazz Band in 1940. They recorded a *Big Bear stomp*.

Big butter and egg man A phrase descriptive of the rich farmers from the Midwest who came to Chicago and other cities to do business and spent their leisure time in the saloons, clubs and brothels. Almost a country cousin to the sugar daddy. The song *Big butter and egg man*, by Cliff Friend and Joseph Santly, has been much recorded and is extremely popular among traditional bands.

Big Chief Nickname of Russell More (1912–1983), trombonist and vocalist, one of the small handful of American Indians in jazz, born on a reservation near Sacaton, Arizona.

Big Foot Ham A Jelly Roll Morton title, immortalizing a black vaudeville comedian known as Hamtree Harrington, whose costume included an oversize pair of shoes. Composed in 1923 and recorded that year, it often gets listed as *Big Fat Ham* (perhaps considered more logical). The issue is also confused by Morton's alternative title (not necessarily his idea) *Ham and eggs* (1928 recording). 'Big Foot' was a nickname also given to Bob Zurke (1912–44) for a time when he had his leg in plaster.

Big house Slang name for a prison; especially applied to the infamous New York State Penitentiary, Sing Sing.

Big John's A Harlem bar that was particularly favoured by jazz musicians, including members of the Duke Ellington, Fletcher Henderson and other big bands in the 1920s and 30s. Situated at 2243 Seventh Avenue near the Lafayette Theater, the proprietor was John Reda in whose honour the Henderson orchestra mixed a *Big John special* (1934).

Big T Familiar name for the great trombonist 'Jack' Weldon Leo Teagarden (1905–64), the T standing as much for Texas, where he was born, as for Teagarden. His younger brother Charles (b. 1913) was likewise known as Little T. Jack was also known as Big Gate.

Big 25 A club on Franklin Street (now Crozat Street) in New Orleans that was a popular haunt of jazz musicians from *c.* 1902 onward. It was demolished in 1956 and is now a car park.

Bird Shortened form of 'Yardbird', the nickname of the great alto-saxophonist Charles 'Charlie' Parker (1920–55). Said to be given the name because he always referred to chickens as yardbirds. Probably the only jazz musician to have figured in urban graffiti; within hours of his death, the words 'Bird lives!' are said to have appeared on walls in the New York subways.

Birdland New York nightclub at 1678 Broadway in Manhattan. It was named after Charlie 'Yardbird' (or 'Bird') Parker who played there at its opening in 1948 and thereafter. Owned and managed by Morris and Irving Levy. The name is perpetuated, and spread beyond the jazz world, in George Shearing's attractive composition *Lullaby of Birdland* (1952), and in Joe Zawinul's *Birdland*.

Birmingham A city of *c.* 350 000 inhabitants in Jefferson County, Alabama, which has industrial affinities with its English namesake. Surprising that there aren't more blues dedicated to the British one. Not a jazz centre, though Erskine Hawkins (b. 1914) and a few others came from there, but crops up in several titles. A suburb known as Pratt City also occurs in titles.

Bit Small, minor or isolated part of a jazz engagement. Sometimes similar to gig. Derives from the theatre usage – a bit part, a small acting role.

Bitch Something difficult to achieve or perform, applied to music and jazz from *c.* 1935. Thence applied to one who was capable of handling such matters, did impossible things on his instrument. Uttered in admiration.

Bix legends Of all jazz legends, Bix Beiderbecke (1903–31) has remained one of the most legendary, to use a word entirely in its perverted popular way. He was not strictly legendary at all, being very factually born in Davenport, Iowa on 10 March 1903, he became a legend partly by dying young, partly by the sheer uniqueness of his jazz contribution. Jazz encourages an individuality of tone not tolerated in straight music, but distinctive as they are, some of even the greatest jazz musicians do not achieve the individuality that Bix Beiderbecke had. Although sadly often heard among inferior or unsuitable musical company, his tone had a ringing, bell-like quality, at the same time poignant and sad, and his solos have a poetry that defies logic. He clinched his place in jazz history by dying of pneumonia at the age of 28 on 7 August 1931 – his demise much hastened by an excessive addiction to alcohol.

Although most reference books say that he was christened Leon Bismarck Beiderbecke and later nicknamed 'Bix', it appears, according to his own family (though not supported by a certificate) that he was actually christened Leon Bix. The truth seems to be that his father was named Bismarck Herman Beiderbecke and that *his* nickname was Bix, which was later conferred, as a formal name, on the future cornettist. The first book to saddle him with the full name of Bismarck was probably the equally legendary *Jazzmen*; this unfounded assumption has been copied ever since with bold confidence. Some simply presumed that 'Bix' was a nickname, and gave it the dubious dignity of quotes.

Bix started on piano at the age of three and would often play the instrument throughout his career. He took up the cornet at the age of 14 – playing it left-handed for the first eight years. He came to fame with the Wolverines in 1923.

Beiderbecke was said to have got some of his first inspiration from the 'legendary' white trumpet player Emmett Hardy (1903–25) whom he heard in Davenport, later modified by his admiration for Armstrong, Tommy Ladnier and Joe Smith. Bix was one of the few white jazzmen to gain a real following among black musicians. It has been suggested, (with his piano piece *In the mist* (1927) as a prime example) that: 'like the Creoles, he was influenced by classical composers, particularly Debussy. Maurice Ravel was a close friend and from him Beiderbecke learned a sense of order and purpose that was instilled into the burgeoning canon of jazz'. (Ellington was similarly credited with Debussy leanings which he hotly denied.) It was with such 'legendary' material to hand that the eminently fictionally styled '*Bix: Man and Legend*' by Sudhalter, Evans and Dean-Myatt (quoted above) betrayed its otherwise commendable to desire to get the facts straight – as in the question of his name. It lost itself in too many wild flights of fancy in the shape of imagined dialogue and description. For example: during a Whiteman recording in 1928, Trumbauer is said to have pointed out to Bix 'an expensively dressed, bearded man, obviously not American, who had entered and was standing with a group of Victor officials listening to the music.

'Say, Bix, any idea who that is?' Trumbauer's smile betrayed immediately that he knew something Bix had better know, too, and fast. 'Nope. Looks French to me.'
'Very astute, old boy. That's Maurice Ravel.' Maurice Ravel. Bix gulped. Ravel, whose music he all but worshipped.
'Oh, my God,' said Bix. 'It really is.'

Apart from this dialogue, reported as if it had been taken down in shorthand at the time, Ravel had not worn a beard except for a short period, *c.* 1902, though he does appear to have dressed quite well. The 'close friendship' seems to be wishful thinking as they probably only chatted briefly once.

Much of Bix's mellifluous tone is attributed to his playing the cornet, a shorter, wider-bored instrument than the trumpet, with a softer, mellower sound.

Far from his being unhappy playing in the Paul Whiteman Band, as often suggested the truth seems to be the very reverse; all he was unhappy about was his slowness as a reader compared with the technically flashier instrumentalists mainly hired by Whiteman. He was given prominent solo work (including the cornet part in Gershwin's *Piano Concerto*) and appears to have looked forward to his jobs with Whiteman who, for the first time, paid him a high salary (one of the highest in the orchestra). He had, in fact, played in far inferior ensembles when his solo efforts still stood out.

It is interesting to note that, throughout 1927, the *Melody Maker* insisted on calling him Bix Bidlebeck.

Books: *Bix Beiderbecke* by Burnett James, 90p. London: Cassell, 1959; New York: Barnes, 1960. *Bugles for Beiderbecke* by Charles H. Wareing & George Garlick. 333p. London: Sidgwick & Jackson, 1958; Jazz Book Club, 1960. *Remembering Bix* by Ralph Berton. 428p. New York: Harper & Row, 1974; London: Allen, 1974; *Bix: Man and Legend* by Richard M. Sudhalter, Philip R. Evans & William Dean-Myatt. 512p. New Rochelle: Arlington House, 1974; London: Quartet, 1974.

Black and tan A slang name for a mulatto (a person of mixed black and white parentage) – the word deriving from the Spanish for mule, hence one of a mixed breed and tawny colour. In England applied to an animal with black and brown amongst its colourings, or a drink that was a mixture of porter (stout) and ale, *c.* 1850, later of mild and bitter. It was presumably the first USA alternative that Ellington had in mind in his *Black and tan fantasy* (1927). No connection with the Black and Tans, a term used by the Dublin Irish to describe British troops during the unrest there in 1921.

Black and Tan Orchestra Jazz band led by cornettist Buddy Petit (1897–1931) in the 1920s in which Edmond Hill played from 1921–3.

Black Artists Group Avant-garde jazz

group founded in St. Louis in the late 1960s, on similar lines to the Art Ensemble of Chicago, employing a wide variety of instruments and intuitive ensemble to produce some extraordinary textures.

Black beauty An Ellington composition dedicated to the glamorous black vaudeville artist Florence Mills, who appeared in several famous Negro revues and died on 1 November 1927 at the age of 26, shortly after a triumphal tour of Europe. She may also have been the original inspiration of Ellington's *Sophisticated lady*. *Black beauty* was one of two tunes (the other was *Swampy river*) recorded by Ellington for his first ever *solo* piano recording in 1928.

Black berry Familiar slang name for a Negro used in the 1930s and thereabouts in revue and band titles.

Black Betty A leather whip used in Southern prisons.

Black Bottom A dance (or dance movement) well known among black dancers in the early 1900s, probably originating in Atlanta, Georgia, and as old as the hills according to one casual reminiscer. It probably first became widely known through the minstrel shows. Perry Bradford's *The Original Black Bottom*, published in 1919, was an up-dated version of his own *Jacksonville rounders dance* (also known as *Pimps walk* and presumably based on the original *Black Bottom*) written in 1907.

The Black Bottom eventually became a white society craze, ousting the Charleston in popularity, when it was danced by Ann Pennington in George White's *Scandals of 1926* to music supplied by DeSylva, Brown and Henderson. She acknowledged that she had learned the dance steps from a black dancer called Freddie Taylor (Stearn's *Jazz Dance*). The name is descriptive of the original basic movement which involves a slapping of the buttocks. The 1926 song's suggestion that the dance originated in the mud-flats of the Swanee River should not be too literally accepted, though it is said to be named after the black waterfront area of Black Bottom in Nashville, Tennessee.

The name was also perpetuated in Jelly Roll Morton's classic jazz number *Black Bottom stomp*, written in 1925 (first published as *Queen of Spades*) and recorded by his Red Hot Peppers in 1926.

Black Hawk Restaurant Chicago establishment that featured jazz orchestras in the 1920s and 30s. The Coon-Sanders orchestra played there in 1924 and 1926 and later the Bob Crosby band was resident there 1938/9.

Blackstick Occasionally encountered as a term for the clarinet. Possibly used a great deal more than the oft-quoted but slightly synthetic 'liquorice stick'. Bechet recorded *Blackstick* in 1938.

Blackstone's Record Shop Jazz record shop, the 'only decent one in New Orleans', run by Orin Blackstone whose four-volume discography *Index to Jazz* (first published by *The Record Changer* 1945/8; later by Blackstone 1947-50; repr. (in one volume) Greenwood Press, 1978) has always been highly regarded. A Dobell's of New Orleans, where enthusiasts and musicians could meet.

Blanche Touquatoux Name given to a 'creole' (i.e. light-skinned) girl who tries to pass herself off as a white person. Celebrated in a popular 'Creole' song that was recorded by Kid Ory in 1945. It is not known for certain whether it was based on a real person or not; but considered likely.

Blindfold Test A term which, like *Desert Island Discs*, started as the title of a quite specific ritual, and came to be used for the idea in general. The *Blindfold Test*, conducted by the British-born jazz historian and writer Leonard Feather began to appear in *Metronome* in 1946, and from 1951 onwards in *Downbeat*. The principle is simply to play a record

33

to a listener (in the original *Blindfold Test* usually a musician) without telling him or her anything about it. The correct arrival at the performers' names is of lesser concern than, to quote Feather, 'the eliciting of an honest reaction to the music'. The blindfold is a metaphorical one, a verbal way of indicating that the participant is denied the luxury of preconceptions. Jazz record enthusiasts are wont to spring these tests on their friends at the slightest provocation.

Block chords A style of piano playing in which both hands simultaneously play chords: effective in small doses but obviously has its limitation in the lack of variation thus achieved. One of its first exponents was Milt Buckner and others who have used it have been Jimmy Jones, George Shearing and Erroll Garner.

Blow, blowing To play a musical instrument, but especially to play jazz. Not confined to wind instruments but applicable to any, e.g. piano, guitar, drums. Commonly used from well before 1920 in jazz circles. More recently it has come to imply not only playing but playing well, to be 'really blowing'. Blowing – the act of playing jazz or a jazz instrument. A 'blowing cat' is a jazz musician in 1950s parlance. 'Blow' has various other general slang meanings some of which have moved over into jazz, slightly modified by the jazz meaning, as in 'to blow one's cap' or 'to blow one's top', to go mad, but in a jazz sense, to get really sent. Likewise 'to blow up a storm' – to play jazz in an exciting and activating way. 'Blowing' session: a name often given to the sort of free-wheeling playing, with the minimum of restriction and arrangement, for which the Blue Note label was celebrated in the 1950s and 60s.

Blow for canines To play high-register notes on a trumpet; a fairly synthetic term, but occasionally used. Alludes to the ability of dogs to hear notes at a pitch far above normal human hearing. In view of that fact it is interesting to note that one of the best-known canine blowers,

William Alonzo Anderson, was nicknamed Cat.

Blue Generally see under Blues, but used in the singular to mean a) a very dark skinned Negro; b) the sky, hence Heaven; c) (rare) to play the blues or to perform in a bluesy manner.

Blue-blowing Refers to music-making on such non-legitimate 'wind' instruments as kazoo, jug or common-or-garden paper-and-comb; especially the latter. Hence the band that featured one of the best paper-and-comb blue-blowers in the business, William 'Red' McKenzie (also as vocalist) was known as The Mound City Blue Blowers.

Blue Book *The Blue Book* was the famous, or infamous, directory of the New Orleans tenderloin district, printed by the authorities for the guidance of visitors, and on sale at the railway station, in Storyville bars or from any disreputable newsagent, price 25 cents. It carried adverts for all the leading sporting-houses.

Blue Devils Jazz group formed in 1925 by members of the Billy King band, a touring unit that generally played in theatres. Jimmy Rushing joined them in 1927 and then the pianist Bill Basie (later 'Count'), a fugitive from another show band. Bennie Moten took over the group in autumn 1929 when it became his Kansas City Orchestra, but still recording as the Blue Devils under the leadership of bassist Walter Page (1900–57), making *Blue Devil blues* in November 1929. Within this set-up much of the emergent Kansas City style was created, later perpetuated by Basie and others.

Blue Goose Occurs in various titles either in reference to (a) a bus company in Michigan, (b) an area in any city where black people live.

Blue Monday Specifically the Monday before Lent, the last chance to have a celebration; more generally any Monday spent in dissipation by those whose weekend excesses had made them incapable of working. Blue Monday parties held in coloured areas of American cities went on after the club working hours on Sunday and often carried on throughout the day. Used as the name of an early one-act opera by George Gershwin.

Blue notes, blues notes Referring to those notes of the scale which are frequently flattened (or semi-flattened) in producing typical blues-oriented jazz phrasing and harmony, namely the 3rd, 5th and 7th notes.

More loosely, any note that is given a flattened intonation.

Blue Rhythm Band Originally known as the Coconut Grove Orchestra when first formed in 1930. Fronted by Louis Armstrong for a time. Irving Mills took over the management in 1931 and it then generally became known as the Mills Blue Rhythm Band, though it was always available to play and record under any name. In 1932 it was led by Baron Lee and for a time was billed as Baron Lee and the Blue Rhythm Band. By 1937 Lucky Millinder was in charge and a number of fine recordings were made under his name. The Blue Rhythm title was dropped in 1937. The peak years of the band were 1931–2, with a resurgence during the last years when such players as Charlie Shavers, Harry Edison, J. C. Higginbotham, Billy Kyle and Hayes Alvis were in the line-up.

Blues The name, and associated expressions like 'to feel blue', 'to have the blues', are not particularly Negro in origin. The adjective 'blue' has actually had many connotations, such as, in near contradiction to our present use, 'constancy', as in 'true blue'. It has also implied dissipation as in the celebration of Blue Monday – the Monday before Lent; and 'obscene' – 'blue' jokes, films etc. All these uses arose after about 1840. In the sense that the jazz world uses 'blue' (or now 'blues') to imply a mood of depression, low-spirits, sadness, the word

actually dates back to *c.* 1550 (according to the *Oxford Dictionary*) and was particularly used in the phrase 'to look blue' rather than 'feel'. Only in modern times has the noun been commonly amended to 'blues' (used thus both in a singular or plural sense) e.g. 'singing the blues', 'feeling the blues', 'a fit of the blues'.

It is now impossible to pinpoint the time when the term was first verbally appended to a tune title. Songs of that nature were in general currency in the early 1900s. The first piece of music to be published with 'blues' in the title in the jazz sense (there were early pieces such as *The Richmond blues* which referred to military uniforms, as worn in the Civil War) is said to be *Baby seals blues* published in St. Louis 3 August 1912. Hart Wand's *Dallas blues*[1] was published in Oklahoma on 6 September 1912 and W. C. Handy's *Memphis blues* on 28 September. Abbe Niles in *Blues: An Anthology* (1926) claims that *Memphis blues* had been played by various bands for some three years prior to this. Before *c.* 1910 the various work-songs and folksongs from which Handy derived his formalized blues compositions were probably in the blues form, but no one had thought to add the name blues to them.

Niles proposes *Joe Turner* (*blues*) as the prototype 'modern' blues, but it is impossible to establish with finality how the blues fell into the 12-bar form that is commonly associated with it now. Probably many of the early black folk songs were not in this form. Any suggestion that the four bars added at the end of the normal eight is a sort of coda is contradicted by the harmonic sequence – four

---

[1] *Baby seals blues*, an intriguing name, turns out to be, more correctly, *Baby Seals' blues*. It is not a very bluesy number, more a popular song, and was written and published in St. Louis by a vaudeville comedian called Arthur 'Baby' Seals who was one of a duo, Seals & Fisher, who were billed as 'the klassy, kooney, komedy pair'. Samuel B. Charters dates it as coming after *Dallas blues* and suggests it was written after Seals had heard this number in the south-west, though the publication date (as given above) suggests differently. Bessie Smith later used some of the words and the melody in her *Preachin' the blues* (1926).

Bix Beiderbecke when a
member of the Paul Whiteman band
c. 1929. (*Melody Maker*)

The greatest of the classic blues singer
Bessie Smith (1895–1937) in 1925.
(Photo: courtesy of Albert McCarthy)

One of the leading exponents of boogie-woogie, Pete Johnson (1904–67) and samples of his recordings. (Sleeves: Top Rank and Vogue)

bars tonic, two bars sub-dominant, two bars tonic, obviously needing to be resolved by two bars dominant and two bars tonic. It would seem to be putting the cart before the horse to suggest that anyone deliberately contrived this form. It is probable that the music came second, being moulded to the three-line verse that was commonly used, the first line always being repeated. There is no way that this can fit to an eight-bar pattern comfortably. What is more reasonable to claim is that *Dallas blues* helped to establish the 12-bar form simply by putting it into print.

The basic 12-bar outline has become the structure of most blues of all periods. As with all formal, but simple and pliable, structures, the art is to move away from and bend them without losing touch. Various practitioners have tried such ways as moving to the mediant rather than the tonic chord in the seventh bar – a feature of many modern blues. A similar effect can be obtained by delaying a harmonic change, e.g. maintaining the sub-dominant basis of bars five and six through bar seven, and only changing to the tonic at bar eight. Examples of this are to be found in the traditional *Frankie and Johnny* and in Duke Ellington's *Creole love call*; or the sub-dominant can be re-introduced briefly in the final two bars as in *Mamie's blues*.

It is hardly surprising that all the blues experts are, in the end, as unhelpful in explaining these matters as in pinpointing any historical facts concerning them. All that can be said, as with any folk phenomenon, is that is just happened that way. The first occasion that anyone strummed a 12-bar blues, and the idea caught on, could have been at any time in the dim and distant past of black history.
Books: a basic list from the numerous books on the subject of blues.

The Country Blues by Samuel Charters. 288p. New Orleans: Charters, 1959; New York: Rinehart, 1959; London: Joseph, 1960; Jazz Book Club, 1961; New York: Da Capo, 1975; etc.

The Poetry of the Blues by Samuel Charters. 112p. New York: Oak Publications, 1963; pb. Avon Books, 1970.

The Bluesmen; the Story and the Music of the Men

Who Made the Blues by Samuel Charters. 223p. New York: Oak Publications, 1967.

Listen to the Blues by Bruce Cook. 263p. New York: Scribner, 1973; London: Robson, 1975.

Blues and Gospel Records 1902–42 by Robert M. W. Dixon & John Godrich. 765p. London; Storyville, 1969; New York: Stein & Day, 1970.

Recording the Blues by Robert W. M. Dixon & John Godrich. 112p. London: Studio Vista, 1970; New York: Stein & Day, 1970.

Blues from the Delta by William R. Ferriss. 112p. London: Studio Vista, 1970; New York: Stein & Day, 1971.

Blues: an Anthology edited by W. C. Handy & Abbe Niles. 180p. New York: Boni, 1926; rev. as *Treasury of the Blues*. New York & London: Macmillan, 1972; etc.

Urban Blues by Charles Keil. 231p. Chicago & London: Chicago University Press, 1966; etc.

Blues Records 1943–1966 by Mike Leadbitter & Neil Slaven. 381p. London: Hanover, 1971; New York: Oak, 1971.

The Devil's Music: a History of the Blues by Giles Oakley. 187p. London: BBC Publications, 1976.

Blues Fell This Morning by Paul Oliver. 336p. London: Cassell, 1960; New York: Horizon, 1961; London: Jazz Book Club, 1963.

Conversation with the Blues by Paul Oliver. 217p. London: Cassell, 1965; New York: Horizon, 1965; London: Jazz Book Club, 1967; etc.

Screening the Blues by Paul Oliver. 294p. London: Cassell, 1968; London: Oak Publications, 1970.

The Story of the Blues by Paul Oliver. 176p. London: Cassell, 1968; Barrie & Rockliff, 1969; Penguin, 1969; etc.

Ma Rainey and the Classic Blues Singers by Derick Stewart-Baxter. 112p. London: Studio Vista, 1970; New York: Stein & Day, 1970.

Blues shouting A swing-era style of blues singing much associated with Kansas City, growing up as an adjunct to the big band and generally performed with band backing. A declamatory, uninhibited way of singing the blues as compared to the more introspective traditional manner. Well-known leading exponents were Jimmy Rushing (1902–1972), best remembered for his work with the Moten and Basie bands; Big Joe Turner (1911–1985) and Jimmy Witherspoon (b. 1923) who made his name with Jay McShann's Kansas City band before starting a considerable career on his own. In Witherspoon's case the shouting element has been modified over the years. The style was an interim link between the early blues and the rhythm-and-blues activities of early pop days.

Blues Unlimited Journal of the Blues Appreciation Society published in England since 1963. A duplicated discographical magazine, it covers all forms of Negro blues, gospel music and rhythm and blues from 1920 onwards. Also has a unique column on Cajun music. It contains discographical material as well as book and record reviews, biographies and general articles on the blues. Distributed worldwide. An equivalent magazine in the USA, *Blues Research* (founded 1959), a subsidiary of *Record Research*, covers a similar field.

Bo bo A dance popular in the early days of jazz, hence such a title as *Georgia bo bo* recorded by Lil and Louis Armstrong in 1926.

Bobby sox Ankle length white socks, fashionably worn by the teenage girls who followed the music and film crazes of the 1940s. Hence, known as bobby-soxers.

Bojangles Nickname of the famous black tap-dancer/entertainer William 'Bill' Robinson (1878–1949), honoured thus in Ellington's piece of the same name in 1942. Not to be confused with the *Mr. Bojangles* in Jerry Jeff Walker's famous (and very good) song of that name; if based on a real person at all, the dancer in the song was a very different character from Bill Robinson.

Bolden legends Charles 'Buddy' Bolden (1877–1931), being of that generation of pioneer jazz musicians who came too early to be documented or recorded, has been showered in legends from the very start of jazz writing. There were very few facts available and the Bolden background was handed down to several generations of jazz writers and readers by way of *Jazzmen* and other early books; and through the uncertain (or sometimes deliberately misplaced) memories of such veterans as Bunk Johnson (1889–1949), who took the liberty of moving Bolden's as well as his own birth-date in order to suit his claims

to have played with the Bolden band. Johnson said that he joined Bolden in 1895 when Bolden was between 25 and 30, which would place Bolden's birth date between 1865–70. In fact, the official records show that Bolden was born on 6 September 1877. Bunk Johnson gave his own birth date as 27 December 1879, but the researcher Lawrence Gushee and others have found evidence that it was probably ten years later in 1889. So the likelihood of having played with Bolden in 1895 (when he was six and Bolden eighteen) seems much less probable and 1905 is feasible – although Bunk did claim he was in 'short pants' at the time. Others have refuted the claim that he ever played with Bolden at all. Bassist George 'Pops' Foster (1892–1969) says that Johnson was in the Superior Band at this time and was not generally seen around until *c.* 1908. Nor is there any evidence of Bolden's band with a second cornet in it.

Another Bolden legend perpetuated by *Jazzmen* and hence others, was that Bolden was a barber by trade and added to his income by editing a 'scandal-sheet' called *The Cricket*. He is often referred to (in Sweeney Todd-like terms) as 'the barber of Franklin Street' and is described as gathering his orchestra together 'in the back room of his shop to try over a few new tunes for a special dance at Tin Type Hall'. There was no evidence that he was ever a barber. But the story was still being repeated as late as 1967 in Martin Williams' *Jazz Masters of New Orleans* where he is referred to as 'a local barber'. The truth seems to have been that he was often to be seen hanging around certain barbers' shops, including one run by his friend Louis Jones, who supported the contention that Bolden was not himself a barber. Williams endorses the scandal-sheet legend including an embellishment that tells how he got his titbits from a local policeman as well as his regular customers. Everybody else connected with Bolden, as mentioned above, however, denies the existence of the publication; certainly no copies have ever been unearthed or recorded. Russell, discussing the basis of the legend in *Jazzmen*, later admitted that it was probably 'a figment of someone's imagination'. Nor, incidentally, was there any such place as Tin Type Hall. The above legends were gently put to rest in a well-researched book *In Search of Buddy Bolden*, by Donald M. Marquis, published in 1978. If someone now comes up with a copy of *The Cricket*, we should all have to reconsider our verdicts.

The book goes on to examine the next legend, which concerns Bolden's supernatural powers as a trumpeter. We have, of course, no recorded evidence of Bolden's power or capabilities as a player. There are no ways of assessing his reputed skills but it does seem likely that he was a forcefully expressive player who had a great deal of influence on the shape that New Orleans jazz took and was an early example to many subsequent cornet players. His legend-builders seem to have gone a little far. Jelly Roll Morton, habitually a great enhancer of stories, called him 'the most powerful trumpet player I've ever heard', and goes on to describe how 'on a clear night' he could be heard playing at Lincoln Park 'ten or twelve miles from the centre of Town'.[1] This is partly explained by the fact that the journey to Lincoln Park, by public transport, may have been about six miles (but possibly seemed longer, the way such journeys do). The actual distance, as the local crows flew, was probably nearer to two miles. Which is still a long way for a trumpet to be heard. The New Orleans *Times-Picayune* added its own mite to the story in 1940, when they said that he could be heard from town while 'playing across the river in Gretna'. Perhaps, on a still night, in the bowl-like situation of New Orleans, sounds travelled inordinately well.

The only bit that is got more or less right is that he died in a 'lunatic asylum', namely the Insane Asylum of Louisiana

at Jackson, where he was admitted for a second time (aged 39) on 5 June 1907, categorized as an alcoholic and of filthy habits. Even here the writers in Ramsey and Smith's *Jazzmen* insist he was listed as a barber. In fact his first committal document lists him as a musician, the final one amends it simply to 'Lab' (a labourer). The implication is that his insanity was brought on by excessive alcohol and there seems little doubt that it was a contributory if not exclusive factor. He died in the Parker Medical section of the hospital (after 24 years in the Jackson Institute) on 4 November 1931, aged fifty-four. There was no press coverage and very few attended his funeral. The exact location of his grave (plot No. C-623) in Holt Cemetry is unknown.

The Bolden picture. To add a subject for detailed debate, the only actual photograph of Bolden is one with his band, probably taken *c*. 1905. Belonging to valve-trombonist Willie Cornish (the original copy has since been lost), it has been reproduced in various places with a caption stating it to be from 1895 (the information again provided by Bunk Johnson who said it had been taken just before he joined the band). Making the usual adjustment of ten years (reinforced by the known ages of some of those included) the general assumption now seems to be that it dates from 1905. Finally, however, in farcical keeping with the Bolden legend, there is even a doubt that the picture was originally printed the right way round. The photo included Jimmy Johnson (string bass), Bolden (cornet), Willie Cornish (valve trombone), William Warner (C-clarinet), Jefferson Mumford (guitar – an interestingly early use of the instrument) and Frank Lewis (Bb clarinet). If the picture was as printed it leaves the clarinettists and trombonist apparently fingering their instruments the opposite way round to the usual. If, however, it is reversed the bass-player and guitarist are made to appear left-handed. Bolden, to be totally unhelpful, holds his cornet flat in the palm of his hand. It almost seems that

---

[1] The authors of the present book helped to swell the legend by entitling an early joint book *Fourteen Miles on a Clear Night*, basing this on the story as it was then accepted.

they were trying to confuse the issue. Even their jackets are not buttoned up, nor are any buttons visible. Only Frank Lewis provides a clue by wearing some sort of lapel button which one would normally expect to find on the left. If this is a correct assumption then the reversed version is the correct one with the bass and guitarist holding their instruments left-handedly (perhaps for the convenience of the photographer) – though neither were said to be of this ilk. Books: *In Search of Buddy Bolden* by Donald M. Marquis. 176p. Baton Rouge: Louisiana State University Press, 1978.

Bombs Sudden accentuated loud use of the bass drum; an over-indulged habit with many drummers of the 60s in imitation of a fashion set by Kenny Clarke. (See also **Explosion**.)

Bone Commonest musicians' slang for a trombone.

Bone orchard A cemetery. Likewise bone-yard, which is also applied to a hospital. Encountered in blues lyrics and the occasional title, e.g. *Bone orchard blues*.

Boogaboo or **bugaboo** An article of superstition that is thought to bring bad luck or failure. Or simply the fear of failure. Jelly Roll Morton wrote his *Boogaboo* in 1928.

Boogaloo A later adaptation of boog (*c.* 1941), itself an adaptation of boogie-woogie. The black discothèque-style dancing of the 1960s. *New York Spy* on Small's Paradise: 'Here you can see the real boogaloo, the Philly dog, the jerk, the truck.'

Boogie-woogie A piano style that came to the notice of the world at large in the 1930s. Before that it had enjoyed a good 10 years of underground existence, and had an even longer ancestry in various kinds of early jazz and specifically in the barrelhouse piano music that preceded it. Usually employed a 12-bar blues harmonic sequence with the right hand

improvising over a repetitive figure in the left. Various exponents invented different left-hand boogie figures and patterns ranging from the simple habanera-type bass of Jimmy Yancey (also widespread among blues pianists from New Orleans) to the muscle-straining pounding of Meade Lux Lewis's *Honky-tonk train blues* recorded in 1927. In early boogie-woogie style performances the piece would usually be designated a blues (as above) or a stomp as performed by Jimmy Blythe and his Barrelhouse Five and other groups. Clarence 'Pine Top' Smith brought his boogie-woogie to Chicago in 1927 and is generally credited with being the first player actually to use the term as part of a title, in his *Pine Top's boogie-woogie*, recorded in Chicago in 1928. The music assumed craze proportions for a while in the 1930s, popularized by such players as Albert Ammons and Pete Johnson, and during this period there were many swing band arrangements which took advantage of the riff-like bass for maximum propulsion.

Willie 'The Lion' Smith said that the first pianist he heard using the 'walking' or 'boogie' bass was a southern player known as Kitchen Tom in Atlanta. His *Kitchen Tom rag* was full of boogie figurations and Smith claims he heard him play it in 1914. The style seems to have materialized in the lower Mississippi River area before being brought to the barrelhouses of the cities. It is said to derive from certain guitar accompaniments to the blues and began to flourish in Texas, in towns west of the Mississippi *c.* 1910 to 1920, finally reaching commercial maturity in Chicago.

The even eight quavers of many boogie figures led to its designation as 'eight-to-the-bar' music in its Tin Pan Alley period.

Pinetop's performance of his own boogie, with its spoken comments, suggests that it was originally thought of as a dance accompaniment. The physical nature of that sort of dance demanded a name with some kind of sexual connotation, as in many jazz dances, and it probably derived from the Southern slang terms 'boogie' – a prostitute, or 'boogie-woogie' – secondary stage of syphilis. Later, after the piano craze was over. boogie became a general term for jazz, or simply as a verb to enjoy oneself – thus used in the pop music scene.

Book A band's repertoire, charts, library of arrangements.

Boot To play an instrument in a forceful, 'kicking' manner; to play energetically and excitingly and thus 'boot' others into action. The ascription of a 'booting' tone seems especially to have been applied to saxophonists, hence a common nickname of 'Booty' or 'Boots'.

Bop see **Bebop**

Bop City A New York night club in Manhattan, on Broadway and West 49th Street, opened in 1948 and a haunt of modern jazz musicians.

Bossa Nova Literally the 'new bump' or 'style'. Based on Brazilian rhythms such as the samba (hence its alternative name of jazz samba), it started a fashion for jazz with Latin-American rhythms in the early 1960s.

Two pairs of musicians were largely responsible for its importation into North America. First, Californian saxophonist Bud Shank and Brazilian guitarist Laurindo Almeida returned from a tour in Brazil in the late 1950s bringing with them several jazz-tinged sambas for which no separate name as yet existed. Then, in 1962, tenor saxophonist Stan Getz and guitarist Charlie Byrd similarly returned from Brazil, this time bringing with them some of the elegant compositions of Antonio Carlos Jobim (in particular *Desafinado*), Joao Gilberto and others. Many of these were true bossa novas, and the term came into immediate use. An early bossa nova hit, which became a standard, was *The girl from Ipanema*.

Boston (1) Large city and seaport with a population of *c*. 700 000 in Massachusetts, USA. A name known to all students of American history in connection with the Boston tea-party of Massachusetts Bay where, on 16 December 1773, three whole shiploads of tea were dumped into the harbour as a protest against British taxation. This was one of the events that led up to the American War of Independence 1775–81.

A rather high-class city, 'the home of the bean and the cod, where the Cabots speak only to Lowells and the Lowells speak only to God', and the birthplace of Harry Carney (1910–74) and cornettist Ruby Braff (b. 1927). It is also the home of George Wein (b. 1925), the creator of the Newport Jazz Festival, who mounted his first apprentice jazz presentations in Boston. Another of Boston's claims to fame is the presence there of the Berklee College of Music, the best-known permanently established centre for jazz tuition in the world, founded in 1945 as Schillinger House.

(2) A social dance, originally a modern version of the waltz which, *c*. 1903, introduced new 'walking' steps to simplify the dance for the amateur. The new walking steps, like the foxtrot, were to revolutionize ballroom dancing and Boston style became, briefly, a synonym for all such trends; as in the Boston two-step.

(3) A hot solo (slang term) as in *B sharp Boston*; a real 'get-off', in the sense of being inspired. (See **Bad health**. See also **Comp**.)

Bottle party A British invention of the 1930s, designed to circumvent the stringently-enforced licensing laws, and relevant here because where there's drinking, there's bound to be dancing, and music to dance to was invariably supplied, in the 1930s, by live musicians. They were not all jazz musicians by any means, but since, by definition, a musician wanting to play jazz in Britain between the wars *had* to be a dance-band musician, much after-hours jazz was to be heard in the smaller bottle party 'clubs'.

The bottle party was ostensibly a private function. The proprietor was the 'host', his customers were his 'guests'. No drink was sold on the premises – that had all been ordered beforehand by the intending 'guest' from a convenient nearby wine merchant, who would keep it until required. Payment for admission was disguised as the 'guests'' contribution towards the expenses of the night's entertainment.

Bounce A jazz number played in a lively, jumpy tempo, full of buoyant energy. Verb or noun. Attached to many titles, particularly in the Swing era – e.g. *Jersey bounce*. No connection with the usual slang usage of 'bounce' – to throw out; more with the non-slang 'bounce' as of a ball.

Bourbon Street New Orleans thoroughfare in the French Quarter originally named after the French royal family (likewise the parallel Dauphine Street); but perhaps more appropriately associated with the much admired drink consumed there in considerable quantities. Originally an elegant residential street, but as the city spread it became a street of sporting houses, pleasure haunts and cafés and slightly sleazy in a Soho way. A great attraction for tourists. The French Opera House, once a social and cultural centre of New Orleans (built in 1859, burnt down in 1919) and venue for the Mardi Gras Balls, stood on the corner of Bourbon and Toulouse Streets. Celebrated in several jazz numbers.

Bo-weevil, bo-weavil or (correctly) boll-weevil Small insect of the beetle variety which lays its eggs in cotton bolls which are then devoured by the grubs. The first major plagues of the weevil occured *c.* 1892, gradually spreading from Texas into the southern States (the insect is frequently referred to as the Texas boll-weevil) and thus became a symbol of economic failure and disaster that much affected the lives of the southern blacks. Often mentioned in blues lyrics, e.g. Ma Rainey's *Bo-weevil blues*.

Box **(1)** An occasional, old-timers' slang word for piano. Rarely if ever heard now, but to be found in one or two early vocabularies of jive-talk. Willie 'The Lion' Smith uses it in his book *Music On My Mind* (Macgibbon and Kee, 1965): 'Phil Harris used to like to sit in on drums at The Nest and used to like to have me playing the box'.

Another slang word for the piano occasionally used (more in white jazz circles) is 'eighty-eight' or '88 – from the usual number of keys on the instrument. *Down Beat*-type jargon mainly.
(2) A guitar or similar stringed instrument. Also applied to the accordion, sometimes referred to as a 'box of teeth' (W & F) but more generally as a 'squeeze-box'.
(3) A rather obvious synonym for square, i.e. a person who knows nothing about jazz, is hooked on straight music or has old-fashioned ideas. The opposite of hip.
(4) A freight box, hence the American 'box-car', the equivalent of the English 'goods van', much used as a cheap means of travel by the hobo element and eloquently termed a 'sidedoor pullman car'. Common mode of transport for itinerant blues musicians, and thus frequently referred to in their songs.

Box-car see **Box (4)**

Bracknell Festival South Hill Park, Bracknell, Berkshire in England became the home of a largely 'modern', post-Parker, jazz festival in 1975 which included free jazz and other improvised music. It was publicly funded, mainly by the Arts Council, Southern Arts and various local councils. Bracknell's prime mover was John Cumming, who worked for the South Hill Park Arts Centre and who guided the festival through ten years of adventurous programming and artistic success. Held over a midsummer weekend in an attractive house and its grounds, it also did quite well in terms of attendance figures, though ticket revenue was never sufficient to pay for the event. In 1984, it is said to have lost about £28 000, and in spite of promises of larger financial support the management of

The Bolden photo of *c.* 1905 – see under **Bolden legends**

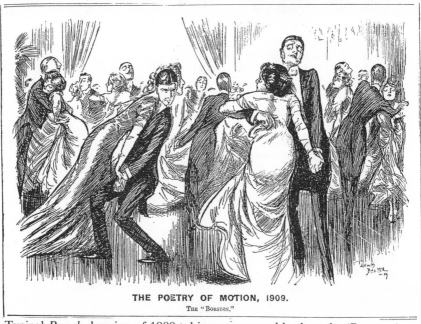

THE POETRY OF MOTION, 1909.

The "Borston."

Typical *Punch* drawing of 1909 taking an amused look at the 'Borston'.
(Drawing by Baumer, *Punch*, Feb. 1909)

The ever-pressing need for more volume and less capacity as responded to by the 'Stroh' (amplified) bass of the 1920s. (*Melody Maker*)

South Hill Park declined to sanction the planned 1985 weekend. In 1985 therefore a similar type of event was mounted at Pendley Manor, Tring, in Hertfordshire, a pleasant enough but less suitable venue. In 1986, however, it was announced that the festival would resume in its old venue in Bracknell. In the past Bracknell has commissioned new, extended works from a number of British musicians, among them Stan Tracey, Graham Collier and Trevor Watts.

Bread American slang for money, generally associated with the swing era jive of the mid-1930s and the hip talk of the bop period. Thus associatively applied to one who supplied the bread – namely the employer or, in jazz, the bandleader. Long bread means a large amount of money and small bread (or crumbs) a meagre amount. Interchangeable with 'loot'. Occasionally the word 'green' is used, encouraged by Dave Frishberg's song about money, *Long Daddy Green*.

Break An improvised passage, a sort of short cadenza, taken by a solo instrument or a section of instruments while the rest of the band are quiet for a few notes or bars. It was yet another of Jelly Roll Morton's claims that he had originated the idea of the break in jazz, and certainly his music is liberally sprinkled with them. Even in his piano writing there are passages that can only be described as breaks where the accompanying left hand is silent for a bar or so while the right hand plays a linking flourish. Morton went so far as to say: 'without breaks . . . you can't play jazz', seeing them as a sort of 'musical surprise'. This is not literally true, of course, but it is very much an effect that has become one of the hallmarks of jazz-styled playing. An alternative name is lick.

Breakdown A fast, swing jazz number or an energetic dance. Also used, mainly in the dance sense, in country and folk music circles. It figures in several jazz titles: *Munson Street breakdown*; *Chicago breakdown*; *Central Avenue breakdown*. The very earliest uses of the word in the 'dance' connotation seem to have been in American rural areas as far back as 1820.

Breakfast dance A dance usually held on a Sunday morning from about 7 to 11 a.m. as a continuation of whatever had been going on the Saturday evening before. Popular in Harlem in the 1920s, they became a regular feature of some of the smart clubs there, notably at Casper Holstein's Lenox Club at 625 Lenox Avenue which was also known as the Breakfast Club. The Liberty Inn in Chicago among others was also so named. Duke Ellington celebrated the phenomenon in his *Breakfast dance* (1930).

Bricktop Nickname for the popular red-haired coloured singer and dancer Ada Beatrice Queen Victoria Louise Virginia Smith (1894–1984) who was a popular favourite in Chicago in the early 1920s. Later, in New York, she helped to find Duke Ellington one of his first Harlem engagements. She went to Paris *c*. 1930 and opened a famous night club 'Brick-tops' at 66 Rue Pigalle in Montmartre that became a favourite haunt of visiting American jazz musicians and writers, as did her second club known as the Big Apple at No. 52. She died on 31 January 1984 at the age of 89.

In interviews she gave in London (PC) in the late 1970s Bricktop was very forthright in her rejection of the word 'black' to describe Afro-Americans. Being light-skinned herself, and having spent almost her entire life in the years when 'black' was faintly pejorative, she preferred 'Negro' and 'coloured', words which fashion and usage have now put out of court.

Bridewell City prison of Chicago at 26th Street and California Avenue. So regularly frequented by the jazz fraternity that it was popularly known as the 'Band House'. One of its famous visitors was Mezz Mezzrow who spent six months there in 1919 for carrying a gun.

Bridge Most popular songs and jazz numbers are based on four 8-bar sections, the first eight being repeated then followed by a different, linking eight that leads back to a final repeat of the first eight; the form generally being A-A-B-A. This third B section is known as the bridge section or passage, or alternatively as the middle eight, or, quite frequently in jazz, as the release. Similarly channel, in use since *c.* 1945 in modern circles, a linking passage between two themes.

Bright boy A fair-skinned Negro.

Brittwood Bar The Brittwood Bar and Grill was a popular nightclub in Manhattan, New York, from *c.* 1932–42, featuring bands led by Willie Gant and Frankie Newton. Situated at 594 Lenox Avenue.

Broadhurst Gardens Undistinguished road in West Hampstead, North London, remembered in British jazz (and other musical) history as the location of the Decca recording studios in the good old days of the industry, from the late 1930s to the middle 60s. A *Broadhurst Gardens blues* was recorded by George Chisholm in 1944.

Broadway Main entertainment street of New York, running the entire length of Manhattan Island with the theatres and clubs mostly between 42nd and 59th Streets.

Brooklyn Items with this name in the title could either refer to the residential and industrial area of New York City at the south-western end of Long Island connected to Manhattan Island by the 5989-ft (1825 m) Brooklyn Bridge (opened in 1884); or a small town in Clair County on the fringes of East St. Louis on the eastern banks of the Mississippi.

Brown A light-coloured Negro. Brown sugar – an attractive girl of this kind. A brown betty, however, is a dessert made with apples, bread, butter and sugar. *Bubbling Brown Sugar* was the title of

the stage presentation which in the mid-1970s launched the vogue for shows about the recent past of black entertainment, particularly in Harlem. Similar shows have been *Aint Misbehavin'* (built round songs associated with Fats Waller) and *One Mo' Time* a brilliant evocation of black vaudeville as presented at the Lyric Theater, New Orleans, in the mid-20s.

B sharp Jokey musicians' name for the key of C. As in *B sharp boston*.

Bucket of Blood A favourite fashionable name for many nightclubs in the 1920s.

Bucktown A resort area in Jefferson Parish on Lake Ponchartrain on the northern fringes of New Orleans, next to West End. Now swallowed up in the general spread of the city. Mainly a rough sort of district inhabited by commercial fishermen, it is largely remembered in jazz history for the Bucktown Tavern (sometime known as Martin's Café), the first building over the bridge across 17th Street from West End.

It was a regular venue for jazz musicians during the 1920s. The New Orleans Rhythm Kings played there and bands led by the Brunies family. Remembered in Morton's *Bucktown blues* (1924) and other titles. Such bands as the Bucktown Five also perpetuate the name.

Buffalo City and port on Lake Erie in New York State, population *c.* 550 000, which people 'shuffled off to' in the popular song title.

Bull fiddle A slang name for the double-bass.

Bull's Head Perhaps the best-known public house jazz venue in Britain. Facing the River Thames in the south west London suburb of Barnes, it celebrated 25 years of jazz presentation, 7 days a week, in 1985. It has been a regular spot for almost every noteworthy British jazz musician, and has also booked many American artists, including Jimmy

Album of Cake Walks issued around 1903 at the height of its British popularity.
(Music: B. Feldman, London)

Ed. W. T. Kirkeby (1891–1978), founder of the California Ramblers. (Photo: *Jazz Journal*)

High-blowing trumpeter William 'Cat' Anderson, Ellington sideman for many years. (Photo: P. Spinks, Manchester)

Witherspoon, Sal Nistico, George Coleman, Lanny Morgan, Mundell Lowe – names picked at random from literally dozens. The jazz activities were started by the licensee Albert Tolley in 1960, and are continued by the present incumbent, Dan Fleming.

Bump A dance movement in which the pelvis is thrust forward in a sexually suggestive manner. Also known as 'the bumps'. Found in such titles as Morton's *Tanktown bump* and *New Orleans bump* (both 1929), stomp-like pieces that would have been used for such dancing.

Bunk A load of cobblers, boloney, untruths, exaggeration, in general use during the 1920s, deriving from an earlier English verb meaning to cheat. It is tempting to believe that 'Bunk' Johnson was thus jocularly known because of his tendency to exaggerate and embroider. Christened Geary, he preferred to give his name as William or Willie. He had an embarrassing tendency to fabricate both jazz history and his own life story which the editors of *Jazzmen* did not know when they asked him to supply some background details. He told them, among other things, that he had been born in 1879, simply in order to support his historical claims, but research now favours New Orleans, 27 December 1889 as his place and date of birth. Henry Ford is supposed to have said 'history is bunk'. A British Bunk Johnson Society is run from Westcliff-on-Sea and has its own Purist record label.

Bunny Popular name of Rowland Bernart Berigan (1908–42), a neat substitute for a somewhat pretentious name and (as with Johnny 'Rabbit' Hodges) a reflection on his size.

Burgundy Street Runs north-west from Canal Street in the French Quarter of New Orleans. It was originally known as the Rue de Craps, so named by a wealthy gambler whose estate covered that area. Celebrated in the popular *Burgundy Street blues*, recorded by many New Orleans bands and especially associated with George Lewis who recorded it several times. When spoken or sung, the stress is always on the second syllable of Bur*gun*dy.

Burn To play with intensity and impact, also to play well and efficiently. The word 'cook' is similarly and frequently used.

Businessman's bounce Derogatory term, used by those hipped to the real thing, for commercial dance band music; the smooth Lombardo kind of commodity aimed at tired businessmen, or a monotonous two-beat for dancing (Gold).

Buster There were several Busters in jazz. Two were Buster Harding, pianist and arranger (1917–65) and clarinettist Buster Bailey (1902–67). In English parlance it is a friendly sort of nickname given to anyone whose surname begins with B (or any other letter). One American lexicon tells us that Buster is slang for a born failure; but it is hardly likely it was used in this spirit in the jazz world. Knowing the American fondness for strip cartoons, and in view of the way strip cartoon characters have invaded the American language, a connection between any American 'Buster' and the cartoon character Buster Brown, an engagingly mischievous figure created in the early 20th century, does not seem too remote. It was Buster Brown's dog, Tiger, after all, which inspired the title *Sic 'em, Tige* ('sic 'em' being the equivalent of 'seek them' or 'seize him').

Busy Playing in an energetic, unstinting sort of way (drummers); or using a lot of notes, almost to the point of over-indulgence (others).

Butt A word for the human rump by no means confined to jazz usage, but prominent enough in two jazz contexts to be worth of inclusion here. One is *Buddy Bolden's blues* which incorporates the lines: 'I thought I heard Buddy Bolden say/"Funky butt, funky butt – take it away" ' (funky in this instance meaning 'filthy, smelly'). The other is in the slang name Funky Butt Hall for a New Orleans public dance hall (in some books identi-fied as the Masonic Hall) of low and malodorous repute.

C Cryptic reference to cocaine.

Café To distinguish it from the rather low-key English use of the word café (originally from the French word – and thus a coffee house), the Americans tend to apply it to what we would more often call a club and the sort of place where musicians would find regular work. Generally a place (e.g. Kelly's Café in Atlantic City) with a bar at the front and a room behind with tables for eating, a modest stage and a piano for entertainment or a small band for dancing on a limited floor. Very much places where jazz developed as a music for dancing.

Café Society A nightclub which Barney Josephson (1902–88) opened at 2 Sheridan Square in New York's Greenwich Village in 1938. It became known as Café Society Downtown when he opened another club, to be known as Café Society Uptown, at 128 East 58th Street. They were among the first racially integrated clubs and Josephson did much to encourage the talents of such singers as Billie Holiday, Lena Horne and Sarah Vaughan. The term 'café society' had originated in the Prohibition years of the 1920s to describe the society-cum-racketeer set who frequented such clubs.

Cajun Another name for the descendants of the Acadian people – the French-Canadians of Acadia who settled in south-west Louisiana in the late 18th century, after the English had taken over their country in 1713 and renamed it Nova Scotia. They had been told to swear allegiance to the King of England and renounce their Roman Catholic faith or leave. Many left and settled finally along-side the Mississippi River, thus becoming sort of country cousins of the New Orleans Creoles. Cajun country is an area of 22 parishes, centring on Lafayette, west of Baton Rouge, and such towns as St. Martinville (where the Acadian House Museum is situated), New Iberia and Loreauville. The Cajun language, almost pure old French, has led to a distinctive brand of folksong close to the creole variety. Cajun music was deftly exploited by the composer Virgil Thomson, as the background score to Robert Flaherty's film *Louisiana Story*. (See **Zydeco**.)

Cakewalk A social dance that started as one of the regular weekend amusements on the plantations, done originally to the jig-like, banjo/fiddle music of the time which induced a high-spirited strutting sort of step, usually done by couples, prancing side-by-side. It was thus described: 'The Cake Walk came into vogue around eighteen-eighty in the South. It originated in Florida where, it is said, the Negroes got the idea from the Seminole Indians. These consisted of wild and hilarious jumping and gyrating steps, alternating with slow processions in which the dancers walk solemnly in couples'. Benevolent plantation owners, to encourage their workers in this harmless exercise, would present prizes for the best couples, which traditionally became a large cake usually cut and shared with the other participants. The men would dress in long-tailed coats with high collars, the women in frilly gowns, aping, so it is suggested, their white society superiors and even quietly taking the mickey. From Florida the dance soon spread to Georgia, Virginia and the rest of the south, eventually to New York and the world where it became a highly competitive activity along the early lines.

The cakewalk era is closely intertwined with the ragtime era, the ragtime strains being found in the kind of music that was used for cakewalking with many pieces that were loosely called rags in the early days being more of a cakewalk nature. The cakewalk was probably earlier and would have pre-dated 1880 suggested above. It was possibly the seed from which ragtime grew, rather than the reverse. Such pieces as *Walking for dat cake* by David Braham had already emanated from Tin Pan Alley by 1877. The cakewalk arrived in Europe before 1908, when Debussy wrote his *Golliwog's cakewalk* and was very popular in England, particularly in the North with its clog-dancing traditions. George Formby Sr. recorded *At the cakewalk last night* in 1910. W & F suggest that 'take the cake' was an expression in use around 1840, so the origin of the dance could be even earlier.

California Ramblers Early white group playing in the formative 'big band' style with a degree of arrangement and much section work. Played in a corny dance idiom, basically Charleston style, but kept a good jazz flavouring through the varying presence of such players as Red Nichols, Tommy & Jimmy Dorsey and Adrian Rollini, whose bass-saxophone gave the band much of its distinctive flavour. Formed in 1920 and managed by Ed W. T. Kirkeby, later to become Fats Wallers' manager, they became one of the most polished and popular bands of the period. They played for many years in their own roadhouse, the Ramblers' Inn, just outside New York, and recorded prolifically between 1921–8 under their own and various other names such as the Goofus Five, University Six, Birmingham Babies.

Calliope A mechanical organ made up of whistles activated by steam and operated from a keyboard. It was popularly used on the old Mississippi steamboats, though more as a separate means of music making. Like the similar fair organs, some were small and mobile and used as street instruments while some of the larger models, as installed on the boats, were large and elaborate. The legendary Fate Marable (1890–1947) was one of the calliope's few well-known exponents. He held the post of entertainment manager to the Streckfus Line boats and employed in his various bands many later well-known jazz musicians, including Louis Armstrong.

Camel Walk One of the many 'animal' dances popular *c*. 1917–25, in which the humped position of the back essayed an imitation of the camel.

Camp meeting A religious gathering held in the open air or in a tent. Popular event in rural America in the late 19th century. *At a Georgia camp meeting* is the title of a classic cakewalk written by Kerry Mills in 1897.

Canal Street Main thoroughfare and shopping centre of New Orleans and perhaps the most famous of all jazz streets, running from the Mississippi River (where a ferry crosses to Algiers Point) north-west toward West End on Lake Pontchartrain as far as the City Park Avenue. It divides the Uptown American section of New Orleans from the older Downtown French part of the city. This unofficial boundary is acknowledged by a wide raised concrete strip down the centre of the broad street (where the street cars run) which is referred to as 'neutral ground'. The scene of many parades and jazz activities in the heyday of New Orleans jazz. Celebrated in *Canal Street blues* first recorded by King Oliver in 1923 and by many since.

Canary When used in a jazz or other musical context (as opposed to a criminal one, where it means an informer, a grass – the allusion is to 'singing') a canary is a female singer with a band. It is worth adding that the word appears to be more of a journalist's concoction than a true piece of jazz argot. Another term for a female singer, logically, is a 'chirp', also used verbally. Yet another is 'thrush'. See also **Chick**.

Cannonball (1) Nickname of Julian Adderley (b. 1928), alto/soprano saxophonist, leader and composer. He acquired the nickname, it is said, as a corruption of Cannibal, a name given to him while still at school in deference to his impressive appetite. An alternative version suggests that the rotundity of his figure as a youth earned him the Cannonball title. Much of his working life was spent as leader of a vigorous late-bop quintet (embracing also a mild form of jazz-rock towards the end) usually including his cornet-playing brother, Nat. He achieved considerable fame during nearly two years he spent with Miles Davis – part of the time alongside John Coltrane, in 1957–9. Cannon (a frequent shortening of the nickname) had a very engaging public persona, compered the quintet's appearances extremely well and usually humorously, and got through to a somewhat larger public than 'modern' jazz was wont to do.
(2) General nickname for any long-distance express train; cf. *Cannon Ball blues* by Morton (1926).

SS Capitol One of the most famous of the Streckfus Line riverboats sailing up and down the Mississippi from New Orleans to Memphis and St. Louis. During the winter it was docked at St. Louis. It was used mainly for excursion trips and had nightly dancing to an eight to ten-piece orchestra. The musicians might be hired anywhere along the river but after *c.* 1918 mainly came from New Orleans thus providing regular employment for many later well-known jazz players. Pianist and caliope player Fate Marable led the band during the 1920s and it was on his recommendation that the company hired a musician. It was hard work, with long hours, bringing in some $28.00 a week (about half of what a good musician could earn in New Orleans) but the surroundings were

pleasant. Amongst those taken on by Marable during his musical directorship were Manuel Perez, Louis Armstrong, Johnny St. Cyr, Baby Dodds and Pops Foster. The band operated under such titles as The Capitol Harmony Syncopators or Marable's Cotton Pickers Band.

In later years Marable moved to other boats of the Streckfus Line, working with them until 1940. Other leaders took over, such as Dewey Jackson, A. J. Piron, Sidney Desvignes and Walter 'Fats' Pichon who was there well into the 1930s. The famous boat was finally retired and demolished in 1942. These musical activities did much to ensure interchanges of ideas and styles, New Orleans men going to Memphis, Memphis innovations coming to New Orleans, and so on. (See also **Riverboat**.)

Capitol Palace A 'large and fancy club' (cf. Willie 'The Lion' Smith) located in a basement in Harlem between 139th and 140th Streets in the 1920s. It had a pool room upstairs and dance-floor downstairs and was a popular Prohibition drinking spot, specializing in 'top and bottom' – a mixture of gin and wine.

Carnegie Hall Famous concert hall in New York on Seventh Avenue and West 57th Street, financed by the philanthropist steel magnate Andrew Carnegie (1835–1919) and opened on 9 May 1891, with Tchaikovsky conducting a programme of his own music. Like the equivalent Albert Hall in London it has mainly served classical music but has also become a sort of mecca of jazz (and other) respectability; it is a kind of growing-up qualification to have a Carnegie Hall concert. An important one was the Paul Whiteman concert in 1924 that introduced Gershwin's *Rhapsody in blue*. The Benny Goodman concerts in 1938 marked the apotheosis of the swing era and not only introduced big band jazz there but cavorting in the aisles. The Ellington Band first appeared at Carnegie Hall in 1943.

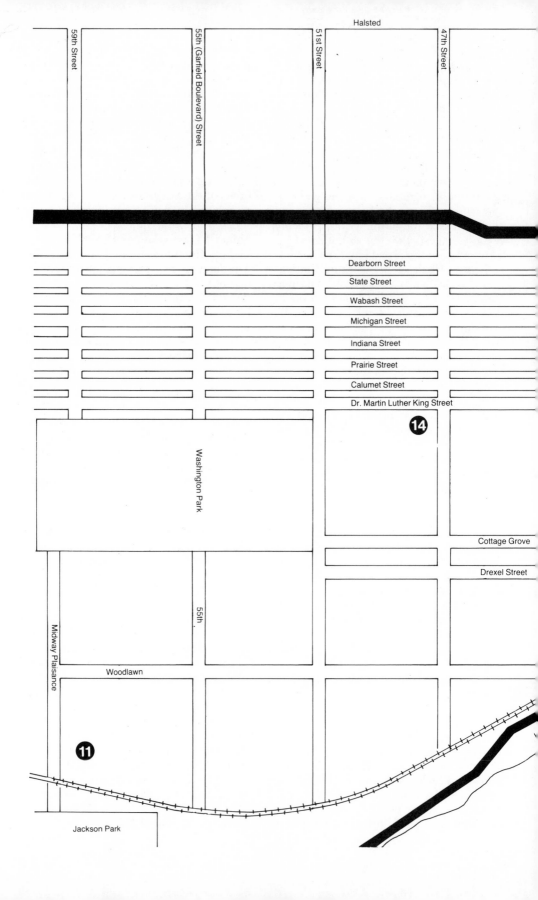

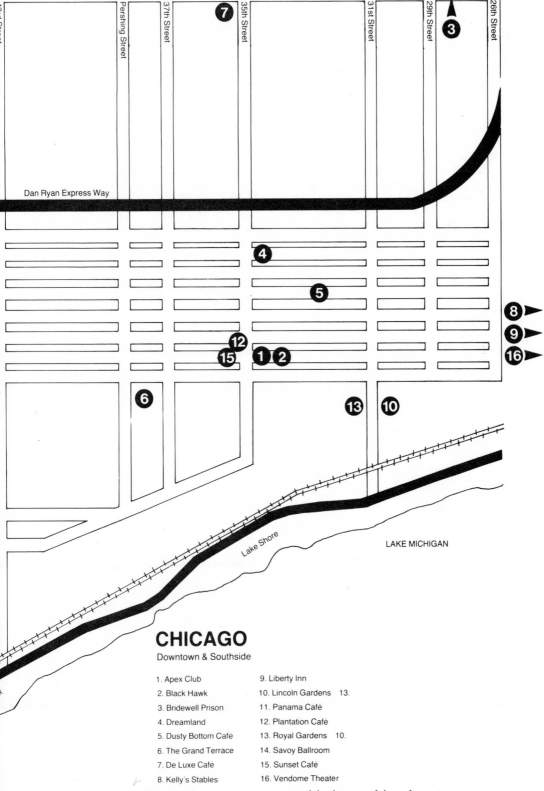

CHICAGO
Downtown & Southside

1. Apex Club
2. Black Hawk
3. Bridewell Prison
4. Dreamland
5. Dusty Bottom Café
6. The Grand Terrace
7. De Luxe Café
8. Kelly's Stables
9. Liberty Inn
10. Lincoln Gardens   13.
11. Panama Café
12. Plantation Café
13. Royal Gardens   10.
14. Savoy Ballroom
15. Sunset Café
16. Vendome Theater

Map showing some of the main names perpetrated in jazz and jazz haunts.

Carve see **Cut**

Casa Loma Literally 'house on the hill' in Spanish. It came into jazz via a Canadian venue of that name, which booked a Detroit-based band, The Orange Blossoms (a Goldkette unit), as its resident orchestra. The band changed its name in preparation for the move but the Casa Loma never actually opened, leaving the orchestra with a title but no work. It kept the one and quickly found the other, since it was proficient if not inspired, vigorous if not original (it was obviously modelled to a large extent on the Jean Goldkette band), and soon built up a large college following. By late 1929 the Casa Loma band was in New York, where it made its first records. The orchestra was a little stiff, but it could swing on occasion, and its machine-like precision was, of course, much appreciated by white dancers. That, and the presence of several competent jazz soloists (especially clarinettist Clarence Hutchenrider) won the band a strong following, and it is still fondly remembered by many older jazz enthusiasts as a kind of prototype swing band.

Casey Jones see **Railroads**

Cat (1) A jazz musician, or practically any man, when spoken of by a jazz musician. Thus 'Wingy' Manone, in 1941, recorded a number called *Stop the war, the cats are killing themselves*, the cats in that instance being the soldiers. It was thus clearly in regular jazz use by at least the late 1930s. W & F imply that it came in from the Negro stream of the American language (a suggestion that feels somehow 'right'), while the glossary in Mezz Mezzrow's book *Really The Blues* (Secker and Warburg, 1946) makes it plain that in Mezzrow's circle at least it was a word incorporating a degree of approval: 'a *regular* fellow,' says Mezzrow (or his co-author Bernard Wolfe).
(2) Nickname of trumpeter William Alonzo Anderson (1916–81), probably given in the above spirit of commen-

dation for his prowess in the Ellington band and elsewhere. 'Cat' Anderson himself tells us that he earned the name when, being a pugnacious boy, he had a reputation for fighting like a cat.

Celeste Not a common instrument in jazz owing to its delicate, bell-like tone. Mechanically, it is like a small piano, with the hammers striking thin, tuned metal bars. Meade Lux Lewis made very effective use of one to record *Celeste blues*. He appears simply to have come across the instrument in a studio, and decided to use it. There are other isolated instances, including at least one occasion when Memphis Slim played celeste with his right hand, and piano with his left. Has occasionally been used in arranged jazz as a tone colour.

Central Avenue There must be many of these, but among those celebrated in jazz is the one in *Central Avenue breakdown*, named after a main street in Los Angeles which runs through the coloured area of the city. Another is a street of the same name in Dallas, Texas.

Chamber Music Society of Lower Basin Street A radio Dixieland band and programme popular on NBC in the 1940s. Although the jazz standard was often low, it did much to educate the public into jazz and introduced a number of big names of the past, like Jelly Roll Morton and of the future, like Lena Horne. The band of varied personnel was led by an English trumpeter Henry 'Hot Lips' Levine and the announcements were done in the most phoney radio style imaginable.

Channel see **Bridge**

Charleston (1) Second largest city and seaport of South Carolina, population *c.* 70 000. When first established in 1670 it was known as Albemarle Point but was renamed Charles Town (later Charleston) after King Charles II in 1671.
(2) It was after James P. Johnson had written a piece in honour of the city

called *Charleston, South Carolina* in 1923 with its intriguing stop-time rhythms that a dance was appended to it which was popular amongst Negroes. The official step with its intriguing vitality gradually developed with Johnson's new *Charleston*, which was a hit of the show *Runnin' Wild*, a black revue which toured America in 1923. The dance was then introduced by Ned Wayburn, who claimed to have invented the popular steps, in the *Follies* at the Amsterdam Theatre in October. The dance bands began to take it up around 1925. It was again performed as a revue number at the Hotel Metropole in London in early 1925. Sensing its potential, Annette Mills and Robert Siel gave a demonstration of the steps in July and this seems to have sparked off the craze which lasted until about 1927 when it was superseded by the newly discovered Black Bottom and finally the quickstep. (Charleston cymbals – see **High-hat**.)

Chart(s) **(1)** In pop music the Charts are the regularly published lists of best-selling records. At present chart is also a verb: *I want you back* by the Jackson 5 'charted' in 1969. A pop record which reaches No. 1 on any given chart is often said by a semi-literate pop press to be a 'chart-topper'.
(2) Chart in jazz usage is a written-out arrangement for any number of performers, though obviously the larger the band, the greater the need for such passages of formal arrangement. A band's library of charts is its book or pad. An arrangement not written down but agreed upon verbally or made familiar by usage is a 'head arrangement' frequently abbreviated to 'head'.

Chase, chase chorus A feature of a performance where two players or two instrumental groups alternate short phrases of a few bars, each succeeding player or group trying to equal or excel the last, thus building up an intriguing sequence and cumulative excitement.

Chenil Galleries Venue much used by the Decca recording team (their main jazz recording studio *c.* 1929–34) in Kings Road, Chelsea and scene of many historic British sessions. A useful adjunct was the Six Bells public house nearby whence there was something of a stampede at the end of sessions.[1]

Chestnut Street Street in downtown St. Louis, Missouri. What happened there between 18th and 19th was revealed by Charlie Barnet in 1939.

Chicago Industrial city in Illinois, USA, the second largest in the country, situated at the south-west corner of Lake Michigan on which it has a 26-mile (42 km) waterfront. Population *c.* 3 550 000. It is generally nicknamed the Windy City, not because of the amount of jazz blown there but because of the cold east winds that come in from the lake during the winter months. Its main entertainment centre is situated in the downtown area, south of the Chicago River, where some of the famous street names celebrated in jazz are Dearborn, State, Wabash and Calumet. The area is familiarly known as The Loop because it lies within a large loop of the elevated railway.

Being the railway centre of the USA and a central market for grain, livestock and meat, as well as an industrial centre (cars, etc), it was a rich target for the early jazzmen who left New Orleans both before and after the closing of Storyville in 1917. It was the centre for much jazz activity *c.* 1919 to 1930, both by native and imported musicians; after which jazz tended to move on to New York and elsewhere. Famous black musicians who continued their early careers in Chicago included King Oliver, Freddie Keppard, Tommy Ladnier, Louis Armstrong, Jimmie Noone, Jelly Roll Morton and Johnny Dodds. Many famous early jazz recordings were made there.

---

[1] The title *Six Bells stampede* may have been inspired by just such an exodus on the day in 1932 when the photographer arrived late for a session picture. No band being available, the leader was taken with a band entirely made up of studio personnel and Decca staff, later captioned 'Spike Hughes and his Orchestra'. This was used in innocence in *The Decca Book of Jazz* (1958), p. 257.

Among the jazz haunts (see below) that became celebrated in the heyday period were the Apex Club, the Grand Terrace, the De Luxe Café, the Beehive, Plantation Café, the Royal Garden, Savoy Ballroom, the Sherman Hotel and the Sunset Café.

Chicago jazz What became known specifically as Chicago-style jazz was that which was an early copy and adaptation of the New Orleans style, played by young white musicians from the Chicago area and nearby. It had a similar line-up but there was a growing tendency to move toward a string of solos with a riff backing, sandwiched between statements of the theme in beginning and ending all-out ensembles, rather than maintaining collective improvisation throughout. This gave a clearer ground for the individual to make his mark and is to be observed on records made by such groups as the Chicago Rhythm Kings, the Friar's Society Orchestra (which became the New Orleans Rhythm Kings), the Wolverines and the McKenzie and Condon Chicagoans which included such musicians as Jimmy McPartland, Floyd O'Brien, Bud Freeman, Pee Wee Russell, Joe Sullivan, Jess Stacy, Eddie Condon and George Wettling. The purest Chicago style is perhaps to be found on the recordings made under Wettling's name in 1940.

The saxophone became more prominent in Chicago jazz, occasionally replacing the trombone or clarinet and there is a developing solo style, often moving toward a slightly cooler and more experimental idiom. (See quote under **Cool**.) Some musicians on the fringes of Chicago jazz, such as Bix Beiderbecke and Gene Krupa, soon moved into other spheres; others, like Mezz Mezzrow and Muggsy Spanier, manifested more of the New Orleans element in their playing. The difference between these early styles was never of profound significance and the changes were gradual, with jazz, if anything, following the trends set by powerful individuals like Armstrong and Hawkins rather than any group identity.

Perhaps the most significant thing was the gradual move toward a rather more arranged approach, which was to lead to the swing era.

In more recent times a vastly different music has come out of Chicago, emphasizing an astonishing blend of theatricality and improvisational spontaneity. First came the AACM (Association for the Advancement of Creative Music), then the Art Ensemble of Chicago. In both of these, Lester Bowie (pron. Boo-ie), a fine trumpet and flugelhorn player, was a key figure. Other members of the Art Ensemble, mostly born in Chicago, are Muhal Richard Abrams – piano and other instruments; Malachi Favors – bass and percussion; Joseph Jarman (who moved to Chicago while very young) – saxophones and percussion; and Roscoe Mitchell – saxophones and percussion. In that they do unorthodox and unexpected things, often with frightening intensity and enormous dramatic elaboration, they are an avant-garde group, but the term avant-garde is itself faintly old fashioned in jazz circles, and there is nothing old fashioned about the Art Ensemble. The AEC came together in 1969, spending much of its first two years in France, and is still an active and influential band.

Another Chicago-born musician connected with AACM and, from time to time, with the Art Ensemble, is the saxophonist and bass clarinettist Anthony Braxton. He is one of the most controversial figures of all, having cleverly divided the critics into opposing camps, one saying he doesn't play jazz, the other claiming that he does. The truth is probably that sometimes he does, sometimes he does not. He has a tendency to identify his compositions not by titles but by little geometric diagrams, making life for radio presenters even harder than it is already.

Chick (1) Familiar slang name for one of the female sex. Starting from the universal synonym of bird, the imaginative variants are many in number. Chick seems to have been popularized in jazz circles, notably Harlem, in the mid-

1930s. It has the merit of suggesting that the lady in question is attractive, lively and young – hence, pretty hip. Unlike hen or crow. Conversely a 'hip chick' generally referred to a girl who was somewhat snooty in character. A jazz lexicon published in 1957 was titled *For Cool Cats and Far-Out Chicks*.
(2) Friendly nickname for anyone who is small, the best-known bearer being the talented drummer and bandleader William Henry Webb (1909–39) who was very small and deformed owing to tuberculosis of the spine.

Chimes A set of tuned metal tubes, struck by a mallet, which give a bell-like chiming tone; a regular feature of the classical percussion section. Occasionally used in jazz, notably by Sonny Greer in the Ellington bands as in *High Life* (1929). In *Ring dem bells* (1930), however, the chiming is credited to one Charlie Barnet. Also refers to a chiming figure; King Oliver's *Chimes blues* attempts a chiming effect in the brass. Piano players also produced a ringing effect called *The Chimes*, and it has been said (Panassié) that when a pianist played 'the chimes' it was a hint that he was in pressing need of a drink and one should be brought to him.

Chippie A prostitute, dance-hall hostess, female bartender (professionally), or simply a promiscuous female. Term in use from *c.* 1915 – see Armstrong in *Satchmo* (1934) – 'Around the honky-tonks on Liberty and Perdido life was the same as in Storyville except that the chippies were cheaper'. Also, the simple, easily removable dress that such ladies wore. Rather dubious nickname of dancer/singer Bertha Hill who worked in Chicago with many famous jazzmen from *c.* 1925–1942.

Chirp see **Canary**

Chittlins or chitterlins Forms commonly taken by the word chitterlings, which are the small intestines of certain animals prepared – usually fried – as a food.

References to them occur in titles and lyrics, which is hardly surprising, since chitterlings, a cheap source of nourishment, were a favourite dish at rent-parties, which were occasionally actually called 'Chittlin struts' or 'Chittlin dances'. *Chitterlin' strut* occurs as a title, as does *Chittlin' rag blues*. Slim Gaillard, some of whose songs are little more than menus set to music, has a *Chittlin' switch blues*.

Chocolate A show-business euphemism for brown-skinned or black, pertaining to Negro entertainment. A popular adjective in the 1920's and 30s, used as in the black revue title *Hot Chocolates* (1929) with music by Fats Waller. There were numerous bands called the Chocolate Dandies (see below); and chocolate crops up in several titles, e.g. *Harlem chocolate babies on parade* (James P. Johnson); *Chocolate shake* (Ellington).

Chocolate Dandies The Chocolate Dandies was originally another name for a band that emerged from the McKinney's Cotton Pickers. Both titles sound embarrassing these days, but in the late 1920s 'Chocolate Dandies' was a distinct improvement over 'Cotton Pickers'. The same nucleus of talented black musicians, with such guiding spirits as either Don Redman or Benny Carter behind it, recorded *That's how I feel today* and *Six or seven times* for Okeh in 1929. The personnel then was Rex Stewart, Higginbotham, Redman, Carter, Coleman Hawkins and Fats Waller.
Various groups functioned under this title with overlapping lineups, e.g. Buster Bailey's Seven Chocolate Dandies; and it was used on and off, mainly for recording groups, up to about 1946. Oddly enough one of the earliest usages seems to have been by a band in which Don Redman was the only chocolate amongst such players as Tommy and Jimmy Dorsey, Frank Teschemacher and Frank Signorelli in 1928. The French issued it as by The Little Aces.

Chops Literally the lips, and thus, quite logically, the embouchure of the player of any wind instrument. In actual use, however, the possession of chops is extended to performers on all instruments. A pianist may be said to have good chops if he or she can execute difficult passages with accuracy and apparent ease. There is also a hint of stamina in the word, good chops implying the ability to play long as well as efficiently. The word 'fangs' has sometimes been used in the same way.

Chorus In musical terms, the repeated, catchy part of a song reiterated after each verse; but, in jazz, more frequently applied to the passage of 8, 16 (or so on) bars taken by a soloist – who is said to take a chorus.

Chu One of the controversial nicknames of jazz. It is now generally agreed (see Chilton and others) that the nickname given to Leon Berry (1910–41) was properly Chu, given to him by a fellow musician because at the time he sported a goatee beard and a moustache and looked very oriental, very like, indeed, Chu Chin Chow, from the British musical of that name. Mr Berry himself confused the issue, however, by appearing in a photograph in the 1930s, wearing a sweater emblazoned with the word CHEW, upon which evidence several authorities plumped for this spelling. The matter was further confused by Spike Hughes, who knew him well in New York, and consistently spelt it Choo. All these options still exist, but most people settle for Chu.

Chuck Standard American corruption of forename Charles, for example Gentry, Peterson, Mangione, Domenico.

Clambake, clam A specialized form of picnic where clams are baked for the same social purpose that meat is barbecued. Hence a party of some kind, a good time for all. Not easy to pinpoint, but for a brief period around 1940 or so clambake was sometimes used as a journalistic name for a jam session; this being reinforced by the existence of The Clam-

bake Seven, a dixieland unit which was Tommy Dorsey's version of a band-within-a-band.

In jazz circles, in about 1952, the word took on a more derogatory meaning of a session or jam session that was disorganized, unsuccessful; hence the shortened clam – a misplayed note or, as a verb, to play such a note (Gold).

Clarinet A woodwind instrument which first appeared in recognizable form at the very end of the 17th century, the major modifications thereafter generally relating to the system of keys employed (e.g. the 'simple', 'Albert' and 'Boehm' systems). The clarinet most often encountered is a Bb instrument (the one generally used in jazz); others are in A, C (Tony Coe, has built an entire, distinctive style on the use of the C clarinet) and Eb, and there are alto, bass and contrabass forms. The clarinet was an essential part of the traditional jazz ensemble from the earliest days (*c.* 1895) typically supplying an obbligato part above the trumpet lead; also an agile solo instrument which relatively soon produced a crop of brilliant exponents: Johnny Dodds (1892–1940), Jimmie Noone (1895–1944), Sidney Bechet (1897–1959), Albert Nicholas (1900–73), Omer Simeon (1902–59). It was carried to virtuoso heights by such 1930s swing band leaders as Benny Goodman (b. 1909) and Artie Shaw (b. 1910); Woody Herman (b. 1913), though not of virtuoso standard also became identified with the clarinet and developed a very personal style.

With the coming of the modern jazz era, the clarinet fell out of popularity, remaining mainly a revivalist or mainstream instrument. Buddy de Franco (b. 1923) came closer than most to adapting it to the needs of bebop, and he remains practically alone in successfully continuing in this vein. Avant-garde jazz, 'free' jazz, 'energy music' have had little use for the clarinet, but Eric Dolphy (1928–66) discovered the remarkable possibilities of the bass clarinet, which he used to disturbing effect in his own wildly exciting version of post-Parker jazz in the late 1950s and early 1960s. Anthony Braxton (b. 1945) has also made much use of the bass clarinet in his own unorthodox music.

Classic As in all arts, a term used in a loose but mainly praising sense to imply a recording that has become acknowedged as a lasting masterpiece – a jazz classic; or a period when certain forms and styles achieved their most perfect manifestations, e.g. classic blues; also, a song or item that has become a standard in regular use.

Cleanhead Nickname of alto-saxophonist and singer Eddie Vinson (1917–88); a plain description of his clean-shaven Kojak-like cranium.

Clef Club A musician's club formed, with the prime purpose of being an agency to represent and promote coloured musicians and performers, by James Reese Europe (1881–1919) in 1910. It was not, as some film makers have supposed, an actual club, but it ran its own members' Clef Club Orchestra which had its inaugural concert at the Manhattan Casino (later the Rockland Palace) at 155th Street and Eighth Avenue in May 1910. In 1914 they presented a programme of 'Negro' music at Carnegie Hall. The main object of the Clef Club was to get work and fair pay for Negro musicians in difficult days. At that early date most of what the Clef Club Orchestra played would not have been *echt* Jazz. The large orchestra that performed at Carnegie Hall in 1914, for example, was made up of eleven banjos, eight violins, one saxophone, one tuba, thirteen cellos, two clarinets, two baritone horns, eight trombones, seven cornets, two string basses, timpani and five drummers; all this acting as a backing to thirty pianists who performed on ten pianos. (From *Jazz: a History of the New York Scene* by Charters and Kunstedt.) It must have been an interesting sound.

The club's administrative HQ was originally at Newton and Walnut Streets in Louisville, Kentucky, then at 9th and Walnut Streets which later became the offices of the local branch of the American Federation of Musician's Unions.

It was not actually the first attempt to organize black musicians as the New Amsterdam Musical Association of New York had been formed in 1906 with a similar purpose, though it was more concerned with serious music-making and excluded syncopated music from its activities.

James Reese Europe (b. Mobile, Alabama, 22 February 1881) was the first black bandleader to become well known in America. After musical training he went to New York in 1904 and became MD of a touring revue *Shoo Fly Regiment*. After a period as teacher and accompanist, he became aware of the difficulties of black musicians and got himself involved in the organization of the Clef Club in 1910 and in the promotional activities mentioned above. Jealous rivalry as a result of these activities led him to leave the Clef Club and to form a new organization, the Tempo Club in 1914. From 1913 he had become closely associated with the pioneer dancing team of Irene and Vernon Castle, leading their backing orchestra and helping to pioneer the introduction of the foxtrot. In 1913 he was the first black bandleader to make a recording having signed a contract with Victor Records. In 1917, when the USA joined World War I, Europe enlisted and was asked to form the 369th Infantry Band (popularly known as the Hellfighters) and went to France on a triumphant tour. Europe continued the band after the war touring America and recording extensively for Pathé. He was all set for new triumphs and an important role in publicising black music, when America was shocked to hear that Europe had been stabbed to death by a drummer in his band, Herbert Wright, whom he had cause to reprimand, on the night of 9 May 1919.

Clinker Deriving from a technical slang term, applied to unwanted noise on a telephone line, it became similarly

61

The
BUESCHER
True Tone
Saxophone Family

THE musical importance of the Saxophone family can best be shown by contrasting its history and development with those of other families of musical instruments.

When Antonius Stradavarius, of Cremona, Italy, perfected the instruments of the Violin family, three centuries ago, the whole structure, technique and instrumentation of music underwent a change.

First came the Violin, then the String Quartet— Violin, Viola, Violincello and Bass Viol. From the String Quartet developed the Symphony Orchestra, which sprang into existance everywhere during the eighteenth and nineteenth centuries.

Music became immeasurably more popular than it had ever been before.

To-day we are in the midst of a new musical era. Again instrumental music is being revolutionized. This time by a reed instrument, and by the very first reed instrument perfected in America.

The BUESCHER Saxophone Family consists of E♭ Soprano, C Soprano, B♭ Soprano (straight and curved models), E♭ Alto, C Melody, B♭ Tenor, E♭ Baritone and B♭ Bass, having a collective compass of nearly five octaves, a range sufficient to meet all the requirements of musical composition and expression, and satisfy the demands of players.

Easy to Play Easy to Pay

WRITE FOR ILLUSTRATED FOLDER AND PRICE LIST,

AND PARTICULARS OF OUR HIRE PURCHASE SYSTEM.

Telephones :
GERRARD
3418—3419

Clifford Essex & Son.

15ᴬ GRAFTON STREET, NEW BOND ST. LONDON. W.I.

Telegrams :
"TRIOMPHE
LONDON"

This 1920s advert usefully shows the comparative size and shape of the saxophone family, including the C-melody (4th from right). (*Melody Maker*, Feb. 1928)

This card can be used as a Post Card for mailing. See reverse side.

Closed Sundays

★

Per Person

2 50

MINIMUM

EDDIE CONDON
presents Nightly
Walter Page - Bass
Edmund Hall - Clarinet
John Windhurst - Trumpet
Cutty Cutshall - Trombone
Gene Schroeder - Piano
Cliff Leeman - Drums
Eddie Condon - Guitar
INTERMISSION — RALPH SUTTON (at the piano)
JAM SESSIONS EVERY TUESDAY
Closed Sundays

Souvenirs of Condon's in its flourishing days at 47 West 3rd Street in 1953.

applied to a squeak or other extraneous noise produced by a reed player. Widened to mean any error, a false or bum note. Widened even further, beyond the bounds of music, to mean anything that falls flat or happens in error. The original term is said to derive from clinker – a large cinder, the end result of a piece of coal that didn't burn well.

Club Eleven Jazz venue in London at Mack's Rehearsal Rooms, 41 Great Windmill Street, which opened in 1948 providing a centre for the modernist faction and its supporters, the British equivalent of Minton's.

It took its title from the fact that it was founded by eleven people: Harry Morris, the only non-musician, but a great enthusiast and the real organizer of the club; Ronnie Scott, John Dankworth, Johnny Rogers, Hank Shaw, Tommy Pollard, Lennie Bush, Tony Crombie, Bernie Fenton, Joe Muddel and Laurie Morgan. The ten players split into two groups. Ronnie Scott on tenor led Rogers (alto), Shaw (trumpet), Pollard (pno), Bush (bass), Crombie (drs); Dankworth (alto) had Fenton (pno), Muddel (bass), Morgan (drs). To that group was added Leon Calvert on trumpet, while Flash Winstone was often around as comic, compere, and alternative drummer to either group.

In due course the club, with a number of changes in its resident musical personnel, moved to premises at 50 Carnaby Street (this was about fifteen years before the rest of the world came to hear of that unremarkable thoroughfare). Inevitably the pioneering spirit evaporated, there were differences of opinion over the actual running of the club (jazz musicians are not good businessmen), and in April 1950 came a raid by the Vice Squad, resulting in half a dozen musicians being charged with drug offences. Advertising in the music press under the name Club Eleven ceased at that point, but a month or two later the Copacabana opened at the same premises, apparently involving all the same people. This final lease of life under the new name lasted until September 1950.

C-melody saxophone Latecomers to jazz might be puzzled by references to the C-melody saxophone, a popular instrument at one time, and the one on which multi-instrumentalist Frankie Trumbauer (1901–56) made a considerable contribution to jazz history. It appears to have been the sole survivor into the 20th century of several non-transposing saxophones in Adolphe Sax's original series which filled the gaps between the alternating Bb and Eb models throughout the range. It has been suggested by Jim Hol, the most wittily readable of Sax's biographers, that, since the military bands were almost the only users of the saxophone in the 19th century, concentrating exclusively on the Bb and Eb members of the family, the rest – except the C-melody – simply withered for lack of customers. Fundamentally, the C-melody is a tenor in C; it was relatively easy to play, and figured among the instruments offered for sale in Sears, Roebuck's Mail Order Catalogue. In fact in 1916 Sears, Roebuck began pushing it somewhat, suggesting that it had caught on among home players. This may well have been thanks to the extremely skilled use of it in vaudeville by such performers as Rudy Wiedoeft (1893–1940). Whatever the reason, it seems to have led quite a successful existence well into the 1920s, at the end of which decade, of course, home entertainment was already becoming more passive and the sales of all instruments for home use were starting to suffer. Frankie Trumbauer's use of the C-melody saxophone in jazz is of two-fold importance. First, he produced a beautiful sound in its own right, a lovely 'floating' effect not unlike that achieved in the 1950s and onwards by Paul Desmond (1924–77) on alto; secondly, he was acknowledged by Lester Young (1909–59) as a major source of inspiration in the creation of Lester's unsurpassed, consummately elegant sound on tenor.

Cold in hand In use in US black communities, particularly during the 1920s, to mean broke; having no money. It appears as a title in Bessie Smith's famous record of *Cold in hand blues* (1925). In the introductory verse of the song, there's a suggestion that the phrase might imply that the person so afflicted perhaps had only him- or herself to blame for being hard up, rather than external circumstances: 'I got a hard-workin' man;/the way he treats me I can't understand/He works hard every day/'n' on Sat'day he throws away his pay./Now I don't want that man/'cos he's done gone cold in hand.'

Collectors The recognition of recorded jazz as a collectable commodity grew rapidly in the 1925–35 decade. Stephen W. Smith in *Jazzmen* names some of the earliest recognized American collectors as a group from Princeton University which included Wilder Hobson and John Hammond. Charles Edward Smith (co-editor of *Jazzmen*) wrote an article on jazz collecting for *Esquire* in 1934 – probably the first on the subject. The best years for collecting were between 1935 and 1945, when awareness of the possibilities was heightened by the discovery of the unknown. Those were the days, in England, when black label Brunswicks were like gold-dust. The advent of the LP and wholesale compilation of early masterpieces and rarities has now made collecting less of an adventure and more of an offshoot of affluence. (See also **Discography**.)
Book: *Your Jazz Collection* by Derek Langridge. 162p. London: Bingley, 1970.

Collett's see **Ray's**

Combo Abbreviation of combination. A group of musicians, especially (in the 1930s) a dance orchestra. Later (from *c.* 1940) seems to have been increasingly applied to small three- or four-man units, probably a soloist and a rhythm section. A modern jazz term rather than traditional, but now heard less and less.

Come on, come-on In regular use everywhere for an inducement, an enticement, almost invariably to spend money, and in no need of elucidation in that sense. But it occurs in the title *Comin' on with the come on*, a famous record (1938) by Mezz Mezzrow, and in the glossary to Mezzrow's book *Really The Blues*. 'Come on' is there defined as 'give a terrific performance; be superb'. It is doubtless that which he was implying in one half – perhaps both halves – of his title.

Commercial A term used in an almost entirely derogatory sense by jazz writers and enthusiasts; if not by musicians who are never averse to making a little cash as a side-product of art. To brand a musician or band as commercial inevitably implies a dilution or degradation of the music, a concession to the accepted bad taste of the general public who are only prepared to pay for jazz if it comes in a popularized form. Thus, for example, Louis Armstrong was adjudged guilty of commercialism when, in the 1930s, he counted on his fame to get away with working with inferior bands, appearing in corny films and relying more on his clowning and singing than on his trumpet playing which, it must be said, remained immaculate and unique – and art.

Commodore The Commodore Music Shop at 136 East 42nd Street in Manhattan, New York, was opened by Milt Gabler in 1926, and by the 30s had become one of the world's best-known jazz record shops and something of a social centre for the more traditionally-minded New York jazz fraternity. From 1938 to 41 there was also a branch at 46 West 52nd Street. In 1938 Milt Gabler, who was an executive with the American Decca Record Company (he produced many of the historically important and immensely successful Louis Jordan records), started his own Commodore record label, one of the very first exclusively jazz, independent outlets. For his first session he used the band that was playing at Nick's (then just across the street from the shop; it later moved to Seventh Avenue, at 10th Street, in Greenwich Village), and from then on Eddie Condon was at the centre of many of the Commodore recordings. Other artists who figured prominently in the Commodore catalogue were Bobby Hackett, Miff Mole, Jess Stacy, Lee Wiley, Wild Bill Davison. Some of Gabler's records were unusual in that they were 12-inch 78s, a relatively uncommon format for jazz at the time. Many of the Commodore sides, both 10- and 12-inch, began to reappear on LP compilations in the 1980s as Commodore Classics.

Comp To provide a piano, guitar, etc. accompaniment in a basic vamp manner, alternating bass notes in the left hand with chords in the right. In America referred to as a boston, deriving from the sort of 3/4 accompaniment that would have been played when a Boston waltz was demanded from jazz players usually rooted in 4/4. A steady, basic sort of accompaniment such as guitarists and banjoists would provide. Now also applied to more sophisticated modes of accompaniment.

Concerts by the Sea see **Lighthouse**

Condon's Club, Eddie Condon's Club founded by the guitarist and band organizer Eddie Condon (1905–73) who was an influential figure in the early days of Chicago jazz and was the name prominent in the McKenzie and Condon Chicagoans, deemed by some to be the finest purveyors of pure Chicago style. Opened in December 1945 at 47 West 3rd Street in Manhattan, it featured the kind of jazz that its owner had always been associated with and became an important revivalist stronghold. It moved to 56th Street in 1958 and in 1967 to 144 West 54th Street. After Condon's death in 1973 the club continued as a memorial to his name but eventually the 'old four-storey brownstone' in which it was housed was torn down to make way for a skyscraper. The last survivor of the jazz clubs that

flourished on or around 52nd Street, when midtown Manhattan was the postwar jazz capital of the world, closed in 1985; and seems unlikely to stage a revival.

Congo Square Popular unofficial name for a plot of open ground in the old city of New Orleans to the north-west of North Rampart Street where it is intersected by St. Peter, Orleans and St. Ann Streets. It was originally known as Circus Square. Now known as Beauregard Square, it is a part of the Louis Armstrong Park complex and is overlooked by the Municipal Auditorium which was built in the 1930s.

In the pre-Civil War days, as far back as the late 17th century, it was a place where slaves were allowed to spend their half-day off on a Sunday, dancing there to the insidious beat of their inherited African style music. It is seen, historically, as a pivotal point where jazz was evolved and one of the main reasons for New Orleans being regarded as the birthplace. What went on there was certainly a source of inspiration to such pioneer composers as Louis Moreau Gottschalk (1829–69) and W. C. Handy (1873–1958) who both, in their formative years, heard the bamboula there.

The primitive spectacle attracted many visitors, especially at the time of the Mardi Gras festivities, but it was strongly disapproved of by puritanical elements in the New Orleans hierarchy. In 1768 a law was passed forbidding slaves to dance in public squares on Sundays and on other religious festival days until all evening services were ended. In 1817 the law was amended to allow dancing on Sundays – but only until sundown and in designated places. The only such designated place was Congo Square. In 1819, one observer remembers seeing 500 to 600 Negroes there, dancing in circular groups with slow, sad movements of the feet, to the accompaniment of two drums and stringed instruments, the women chanting. Writing in 1819, the architect B. H. B. Latrobe found the spectacle 'brutally savage' yet 'dull and stupid'. By

1945 the puritans had triumphed and the dancing in Congo Square ceased, though, until 1941, it was still the centre of the Mardi Gras celebrations.

Connie's Inn Large and popular night-club in New York's Harlem, next door to the Lafayette Theater, of the kind that catered for white society with black entertainment, the main competitor of the Cotton Club in the 1930s. Opened and run by the brothers Connie and George Immerman. It was not, like so many clubs, controlled by gangsters but the proprietors probably had some arrangement with the Madden gang (who ran most establishments in those parts) that assured their immunity from inter-ference. The elaborate shows at Connie's Inn rivalled those of the Cotton Club and they had a particulary big success with the revue *Hot Chocolates* (1929) with music by Fats Waller and Harry Brooks.

Conway Hall A hall in Red Lion Square, London, headquarters of the South Place Ethical Society, which in the 1950s was the venue for weekly concerts by the Humphrey Lyttelton band and of other jazz and folk activities. The Conway Hall concerts are fondly remembered by many grey-haired jazz enthusiasts. It was also used occasionally for recording.

Cook A jazz musician is said to cook or to be cooking, or to be a cooker, when inspiration is flowing well and – equally important – the momentum of his playing (together with that of the whole band, ideally) has an irresistible and 'inevitable' feel to it. In group terms, 'to gel' wouldn't be a bad translation. Musicians called Cook come as a godsend to dreamers-up of album titles – thus any record under saxophonist Junior Cook's name is almost bound to use it in some punning fashion. Booker Ervin likewise attracted the attention of the name-givers, who came up with the clever 'in' title of *The Book Cooks* for an album made by him in 1960.

Cook's Ferry Inn Public house in Angel Road, Edmonton, North London, a shrine of British revival jazz where the Cleveland Jazz Club met and the Freddy Randall band played every Sunday evening in the late forties and the fifties.

Cool Somewhere along the way, some-body decided that the most apt adjective for early jazz was 'hot', in the sense of hot-blooded, exciting, emotionally charged (especially that last, since 'hot' did not necessarily imply at a rapid or hurried tempo). A hot style was partially achieved by a strong vibrato, punchily rhythmic phrasing and a fiery tone. As jazz matured, players arrived on the scene who no longer wished to rely upon purely physical excitement and who gave conscious thought to the actual musical principles on which jazz rested. Inevi-tably, this gave rise to a cooler – that is, more considered – approach, and prod-uced a Lester Young in contrast to a Coleman Hawkins (at least in his earlier days). With the advent of so-called modern jazz, where harmonic and struc-tural ideas partly took over from the excitement of warring counterpoint over simple, emphatic rhythms, a cooler, quieter, often vibratoless tone became the desirable norm. 'Cool' as a label seems first to have been applied – though probably not by the performers them-selves – to the modifications to bebop made, consciously or otherwise, by West Coast musicians, who tended to be better schooled in the musically academic sense. It quickly became a vogue word, taken up by such maladroit users as the adver-tising copywriters, who pushed it to its limit of meaninglessness in describing a pair of shoes as 'cool as a red-hot trumpet'.

Among musicians themselves, and in their immediate circle, 'cool' became the word to describe the correct manner of behaviour at all times – unruffled, detached, undismayed. In this sense it was by no means limited to the West Coast, and, as a word on its own, came to denote anything that was good, anything that met the approval of the user. It also gave compilers of dictionaries a handy term for narrowing down the currency of a word or phrase; thus W & F can say, of 'Zelda', 'a female square. *Some cool or beat use since c*. 1950'. One may never have encountered the word Zelda before, but it is immediately obvious what group of people would have used it.

As with many another, the word 'cool' has spread its meaning. It still applies in a straightforward and obvious way to certain kinds of music, but an ageing hipster might yet say to you, as you depart, 'Stay cool', when all he means is 'Goodbye'.

Coon see **Negro**

Co-op bands; co-operative bands Name given to bands organized and administered by its playing members who then appoint or elect a leader to front the group. One of the best known of these was the Casa Loma Orchestra. It was a widespread practice during the swing era and many well-known name bands, for example the Bob Crosby Orchestra, were, in fact, run on these lines. The principle has been revived recently by the 20-piece British band Loose Tubes, a joyous assembly of young musicians formed in 1985.

Corn (n), corny (adj) Music that is considered trite and gimmicky in its effects, over-sentimental, old-fashioned, melodramatic, or obvious; anything that the sophisticated listener considers unworthy of his taste. The origins of the phrase go back to the 1930s when it was applied to the dated styles of hill-billy music, country music of a rustic nature, hence cornfed – shortened to corny. Came into general musical usage *c*. 1940; but then, as it obtained more general currency, was not used so much in jazz circles. One who played or indulged in corn was known (also outside music) as a cornball.

Cornet In the early days of jazz, supporting the contention that many of the instruments used were picked up cheaply from the discarded equipment of

Civil War bands, the cornet would certainly have been more accessible and cheaper than the trumpet, which is much less used in military and brass bands even today. It was generally assumed by writers attempting to trace the course of early jazz that most pioneer 'trumpeters' used the cornet; a regular source of discographical wrangling concerned what was being used and when. In fact, most of the early players did start out on cornet and then switched to trumpet to take advantage of that instrument's extra brilliance; or simply because it looked better.

The cornet, for matters of identification in photographs, is a shorter, fatter instrument with a wider bore; the valves are much closer to the player's face, making the instrument very comfortable to handle. The valved cornet (*cornet à pistons*) was introduced in the 1820s in Paris by a maker called Halary. He provided an instrument that was both mellifluous and flexible, a welcome alternative to the trumpet, which was generally played in a traditionally ceremonial, brazen way. The vital difference, to the player, is the deeper cup of the mouthpiece which makes the cornet less fatiguing and more flexible; hence its popularity in brass bands. Gradually, as trumpet technique improved, jazz players tended to switch back to the more penetrating and brilliant trumpet tone. Both are B-flat instruments with similar ranges, and it is often difficult, particularly in older recordings, to detect the difference by ear. The trumpet remained the 'classical' instrument (though cornets are often used as well), but in more popular fields, where its tonal and melodic characteristics were appreciated, the cornet became immensely popular – particularly among the brass bands, which produced a number of virtuoso players; and hence, by descent, in early jazz. The cornet retains a broader, warmer, fatter sound which may give the impression of less agility though there is no technical foundation for this. In spite of its being a physically short instrument, the cornet can, in photographs, be mistaken for a trumpet, because an extra mouthpiece length (shank) is often used. The famous photograph of Beiderbecke in 1924 holding his cornet in front of him shows an instrument that looks quite like a trumpet, with only the shorter bell proving final identity. In fact, some jazz players used the 'trumpet-cornet', a streamlined instrument that looked more like a trumpet, e.g. Nick la Rocca in the ODJB.

Louis Armstrong is listed as playing cornet until *c*. 1925 and the majority of players who made the change did so round about that time. There were some, however, who continued to find the cornet more suited to their style and conceptions; among them, notably, Bix Beiderbecke, Muggsy Spanier and Rex Stewart. Even into the modern jazz period there were players like Nat Adderley who have liked its qualities, and who switched to it from trumpet *c*. 1950.

Ruby Braff went back to the cornet after hearing his first records on trumpet. Thad Jones likes to play cornet, as do Kenny Wheeler and Marc Charig. Wild Bill Davison plays, and Alex Welsh played, the hybrid referred to as a trumpet-cornet.

Corrigan Hop Not, as you might expect, a dance, but a tune, which exists in a number of recorded versions, to celebrate (or perhaps to make fun of) an accidental exploit. In 1938 an airman named Corrigan set off to fly from New York to Los Angeles. By an error, which seems too great to be possible, he somehow contrived to fly 180° off course – in other words he flew east instead of west and his hop ended not in California but Ireland. After almost half a century the whole escapade still defies belief but at least it called into being a sprightly jazz number.

Cotton Club The most famous of the New York nightclubs of the 1920s and 30s, it was at 644 Lenox Avenue on the northeast corner of 142nd Street in the Harlem district of Manhattan. Originally a dance hall that was part of the Douglas Casino and Theater complex, it was rented in 1920 by the heavyweight champion Jack Johnson who turned it into an intimate supper club called the Club Deluxe. It had little success until it was taken over in 1922 by a syndicate of bootleggers headed by the notorious Owney Madden as an outlet for their illicit wares, and the name was changed to the Cotton Club.

In spite of name and situation, the Cotton Club catered for a white audience, only the entertainment being black. Originally, under the management of Walter Brook (one-time producer of *Shuffle Along*), the entertainment was mainly imported from Chicago, basically a fast-moving revue based on the Ziegfeld model. There was a grand opening in January 1923 with a slick and professional show. The club now flourished, dubbed the 'Aristocrat of Harlem' and a distinguished audience flocked there. It was closed by the Federal Court in 1925 for violation of the Prohibition laws, opening again three months later, under new management. The resident band up to then had been Andy Preer's Cotton Club Syncopators, but Preer died in 1927 and the club looked around for a prestigious new band. Jimmy McHugh, writer of much of the Cotton Club revue material, suggested Duke Ellington's orchestra, then resident at the Kentucky Club near Times Square; but the job was offered to King Oliver who turned it down for financial reasons. An audition was held and Ellington got the job anyway, opening there on 4 December 1927. The Cotton Club shows were frequently broadcast, featuring such stars as Ethel Waters, 'Bojangles' Robinson and Adelaide Hall; and it now became the most prestigious nightspot in New York. Ellington stayed there until 1930 during which time the 'whites only' rule was relaxed to let in a few affluent coloured people. Cab Calloway then took over with his 'hi-de-ho' Missourians and made his reputation there.

The Club suffered some decline during the worst of the Depression in 1932 but was booming again by 1933 when Ethel Waters was the big attraction. At last

The most famous song from the Connie's Inn *Hot Chocolates* of 1929. (Music: Lawrence Wright)

A good view of the cornet in the capable hands of one of its greatest adherents, Rex Stewart (1907–67). (Photo: Chadel)

The Aristocrat

of

Harlem

The Famous

COTTON CLUB

Lenox Ave. & 142nd St.

presents

Dan Healy's

new fall revue

"It's the Blackberries"

with

Special restricted music by

Jimmy McHugh & Dorothy Fields

Phone reservations:

Bradhurst 7767 - 1687

Souvenir of the famous Cotton Club in 1929.

Prohibition was repealed in December 1933, the club thereby losing some of its illicit glamour. Cab Calloway left in 1934 and was replaced by Jimmie Lunceford. By this time many of the rivals to the Cotton Club had moved to more lucrative downtown areas and the Cotton Club planned to do the same. The Harlem premises closed on 16 February 1936 and the club moved to a site previously occupied by the Palais Royal on Broadway and 48th Street. It continued, pricier than ever, to present its glamorous revues, in 1936 featuring Bojangles with the Cab Calloway band back again. Ellington returned in 1937 with Ivie Anderson and the Nicholas Brothers, and again in 1938 with a one-legged dancer called 'Peg-Leg' Bates. Bill Robinson and Calloway were again featured in the 1939 show and Louis Armstrong made his first appearance there in the autumn.

Eventually the club began to run into financial difficulties and was finally closed for good on 10 June 1940. There were several revivals of Cotton Club revues at other venues in subsequent years. The Cotton Club era was recalled in the 1976 show *Bubbling Brown Sugar* which took its name from the club's 1930 show. A film *The Cotton Club* (1985) mixed the show-business and gangster warfare elements in a colourful and imaginative way.

Books: *The Cotton Club* by Jim Haskins (New York: Random House, 1977); *Night Clubs* by Jimmy Durante & Jack Kofoed (New York: Knopf, 1931), etc. (See also under **New York**, **Harlem** and other clubs.)

Cotton Pickers see **McKinney**

Count Noble nickname given to William Basie (1904–1984) by a radio announcer. Basie himself claimed that this happened about 1935–6, during the then recently formed Basie band's regular broadcasts from the Reno Club in Kansas City. This, however, leaves unexplained the title *The Count*, recorded by Bennie Moten's Kansas City Orchestra in 1930, by which time Basie had been in Moten's band for a year. It is a strong possibility that it was actually an announcer at WHB in Kansas City, from which station Basie broadcast some organ solos in 1930, who elevated plain Bill to the jazz aristocracy. Perhaps 'Count' came into regular use only when he joined the hierarchy of bandleaders, where one Duke was already firmly established. Bill Basie certainly had plenty of experience behind him by 1935/6, particularly in Walter Page's Blue Devils and Bennie Moten's band. He'd been a boyhood acquaintance of Fats Waller (three months his senior) and had learned from him enough in the early 20s to be playing in a Waller-like style. Over the years he refined this by removing more and more notes, so that the fully developed Basie manner was largely a matter of highly-charged rhythmic spaces.

Whether or not they provided Basie with a nickname, the Reno Club broadcasts were important in another respect. It was a relay from there which the influential enthusiast John Hammond picked up one night on his car radio; and it was largely a result of Hammond's urging that the Basie band moved to New York in late 1936.

Basie started his own club in New York, Count Basie's at 2245 7th Avenue at 132nd Street in Harlem. Such musicians as Kenny Dorham, Wild Bill Davis, Eddie 'Lockjaw' Davis and Stanley Turrentine could be heard there as well as the Count himself when in town. Favourite hangout for jazz musicians, black and white, who came to jam there after hours.

Country blues The blues in their natural folk-music state of uncultivation. As in all genuine folksong the singers do not attempt to prettify or regularize their art; they are only concerned with what they have to say about their human plight and the musical style is rough, poignant and functional. Also known as Rural Blues. It must be assumed that much country blues singing was done unaccompanied. The use of the guitar, however, was widespread, and many blues performers from rural backgrounds attained virtuoso status within the limits of the genre. Big

Bill Broonzy and Muddy Waters both began as country bluesmen and ended as internationally known celebrities. Muddy Waters (whose real name was McKinley Morganfield) almost personifies the migration of the blues from the country to the city – especially Chicago – and was a key figure in the evolution of guitar-dominated rhythm-and-blues and, ultimately, rock music. (See also **Blues**.)

Cow Cow Familiar name given to blues pianist Charles Davenport (1895–1955). His well-known 'train' blues, originally known as *Railroad blues*, had an extra part tacked on one night describing how the switchman climbed onto and travelled upon the cow-catcher on the front of the locomotive. He was quoted as singing: 'Nobody here can do me like Papa Cow Cow can do'. The name stuck. The piece became *Cow Cow blues* and Charles became Cow Cow Davenport.

Crane River Jazz Band Formed by British fundamentalist trumpeter Ken Colyer (b. 1928) in 1948, who took the name from a trickle of water in west London known as the River Crane. It rises near Pinner in Middlesex (its upper stretches sometimes being referred to as Yeading Brook) and joins the Thames at Isleworth. The band's actual birthplace was the White Hart Hotel in Cranford.

Crazy Adjective that came in with the cool era of jazz; a term of high praise signifying good, unique, outstandingly different, with-it, cool, generally exciting, wonderful, thrilling, satisfying. Use spread from the jazz arena to more general areas since the 1960s. Early use as a book title was in *That Crazy (American) Music* by Elliott Paul in 1957. 'Mad' is also used in the same way; likewise 'wild'.

Creole There has been much confusion in jazz literature over the use of the word 'creole'; to some extent this confusion is generally based upon a misconception, deliberate or otherwise, of its true meaning. It seems to have been fostered by light-skinned Negroes (who liked to be considered a cut above those of darker hue) calling themselves creoles. One who frequently did was Jelly Roll Morton who made much of his French ancestry. In fact, most of them were more correctly mulattos, i.e. of mixed black and European ancestry.

The dictionary definition of a Creole is (*Larousse*) 'personne de pure race née dans les colonies' (about which there is no ambiguity at all). But this has been amended by the *Oxford Dictionary* and others to mean a person born specifically in the West Indies or the Americas and naturalized there but of pure European descent. The OED adds 'also of African Negro race, the name having no connotation of colour'; which does not so much amend *Larousse* as contradict it.

With special reference to the Southern States of America and more particularly to Louisiana and New Orleans, 'Creole' is clearly used to define one who was the child of colonial settlers mainly of French origin. The name derived from 'criollo' – similarly used by the Spanish. So the true Creole (particularly in the eyes of those so describing themselves) was generally a white person of French origin, born in New Orleans or neighbouring Louisiana – the term not being current in other parts of the USA though common in the West Indies.

The matter becomes perplexing, at least to those distant from New Orleans, by the further definition of a creole being possibly of pure African descent. This would, in fact, make most black Americans creole, but the lineage was presumably felt to have changed once there was a generation or two of naturalized American heritage behind it. But this could also apply to white creoles. The main ambiguity arises where inter-marriages (perhaps way back) between those of French and of black origin produced the light-skinned mulatto who would then claim to be a creole, through sharing the creole cultural heritage. The true white Creoles, who founded New Orleans and its distinctive French Quarter (Vieux Carré) were anxious to keep the social distinction between the white creole and the black creole. In jazz usage the creole tends mainly to be the 'café au lait' mulatto, the 'creole of color', who performed and created jazz that was basically New Orleans style but with a distinctive French flavour and often utilizing the old creole songs and melodies. The misconception remains deep-rooted throughout jazz, where the perception of the creole as a light-skinned Negro (of mixed ancestry) is predominant, and the term is so used by such New Orleans experts as Samuel B. Charters (b. 1929) who employs it in the accepted jazz world sense (as Morton did). He quotes the introduction from the book *Nos Hommes et Notre Histoire* by R. L. Desdune (Montreal, 1911): 'I love the Creole of Colour. I love him above all when he speaks my language. He is almost my cousin. What does the color of his skin matter? His father came from Marseilles perhaps, or Bordeaux, my ancestors from Havre: Provence, Guyenne, or Normandy, isn't it still France? . . . No, I have no wish like the down to earth Anglo-Saxon or the narrow Protestant, to pretend that my latin blood could have been corrupted by mixing with the blood of the African.' He clearly accepts the creole of mixed ancestry as a creole, contrary to all dictionary definitions.

The culture of New Orleans (and much of Louisiana) is fundamentally creole: the patois, the music and writing, the cooking etc. New Orleans itself became divided into various areas. South of Canal Street, became known as Uptown, and north of Canal Street as Downtown, the latter being the French (or creole) Quarter, the former the American section. The Downtown area was further divided, with the 'black' creoles mostly residing in the city's 6th and 7th wards, an area bounded on the east by Elysian Fields, on the west by Orleans Avenue, on the north by Broad Street, and on the south by Rampart Street.

Creole Jazz Band Title used by King Oliver for the historic group that he led in Chicago from 1922 to 1924 mainly at the Lincoln Gardens. Loose use of the word creole (see entry above) as few, if any, of its members could be thus categorized.

Crescent City Nickname for New Orleans, in Louisiana, derived from the way the original settlement fitted into an immense bend in the River Mississippi at this point; bounded in the north by Lake Pontchartrain. Although in practice a seaport, New Orleans is a good hundred miles from the river mouth.

Crescent Theater New Orleans theatre in the Tulane-Crescent Arcade off Baronne Street. Famous venue of minstrel shows. See also **Harlem**.

Crow Jim see **Jim Crow**

Cut, also carve These verbs arise from the competitive element in jazz performance, a characteristic absent from most other forms of musical activity. In the informal, yet often deadly serious, jam session, two or more players of the same instrument might find themselves in a trial of improvisational and artistic strength from which one would emerge a clear 'winner'. This result would be decided both by audience reaction and by that inner, instinctive knowledge that an artist has of his own prowess at any given moment. Individual cutting or carving contests have grown less common as jazz has made less and less use of standard themes known by everybody involved. With much latterday jazz being collectively extemporized from the outset, a good deal of the old common ground (e.g. *Sweet Georgia Brown*; *I got rhythm*; *Honeysuckle rose*) has been rejected, and if strangers are to blow together at all, they have to co-operate rather than compete.

Cutting and carving contests have not been confined to jousting matches between individual musicians. Whole bands have been involved, the most obvious instances being those meetings in the streets of New Orleans of two rival bands advertising rival attractions, when, according to legend, the waggons would lock wheels and the bands would lock horns in an encounter which must have relied more on brute strength than musical finesse. *The Battles of the Bands* which took place in the swing era at such ballrooms as the Savoy in Harlem were similarly competitive but one imagines that one band 'carved' another on those occasions with meritorious playing, based on the judgement of an experienced and critical dancing clientele.

Cut in A person who has contributed little or nothing to a composition for a song, yet whose name appears on it as a co-writer, is said to have been 'cut in' on it. The object of course is to 'earn' a royalty which the recipient would not normally be entitled to, such payments usually being a kick-back in disguise. Thus, bandleader X would undertake to record and/or publicly perform W and Y's song provided he got a piece of the action. W and Y agree – they have little choice if bandleader X has a big following – and X is cut in on it, his name for ever after appearing alongside theirs at the top of the sheet music and in parenthesis after the title of the song on record labels. Many bandleaders have done it, and some have had it done to them. It is wise, for example, to treat with a degree of scepticism the frequent appearance of Irving Mills' name alongside Duke Ellington's as the co-composer of some classic piece of Ellingtonia. He was involved in some, to be sure, but as Ellington's very necessary white manager in the late 1920s and for much of the 1930s, he was in a position to exaggerate his contribution. Slightly outside the jazz field, the singer Al Jolson (1886–1950) is said to have sometimes made the cutting in of himself a condition of his agreeing to sing a particular number. Most of the time composers and lyric writers were only too happy to agree, knowing that Jolson's performance was almost a guarantee of the song's success.

Dad, daddy, daddy-o Various forms of address, similar to pops, papa in older form. Dad is common outside jazz. Daddy has the added connotation of a male lover, a provider of the goods; big daddy – a rich one of this variety. Later, in bebop circles, the variants daddy-o, daddy-oh, daddio became more widely used as a term of address, ousting the older, more trad-associated pops. Daddy is further used as a term of adulation or admiration of one who was a leader, progenitor or example, 'the daddy of them all', thus, in more generalized terms, one who could really blow.

Dallas City in Texas, a port on the Trinity River, with a population of *c.* 680 000. Large trade in cotton and oil. In the 1920s and 30s it was a centre of blues recording, with the Columbia field unit particularly active there. Celebrated in one of the earliest published blues, *Dallas blues* by Hart A. Wand of Oklahoma City, in 1912.

Dance Jazz history tends to look, quite naturally, at the music first and then allows that much of it was conceived and played for dancing. The truth is probably that the majority of jazz activities (certainly in the earlier days) were closely linked to dancing and its requirements, and it was often the changing fashions on the dance floor that shaped many of the developments in jazz rather than the other way round. In the beginning, ragtime and the cakewalk were almost totally intermingled and as far back as one can go in jazz history, early bands were providing the music for dances such as the one-step and two-step and all the novelty creations of the time from the Camel Walk to the foxtrot. This was still true of the 1930s swing era which developed partly as an adjunct to the obsessive dancing activities at the Savoy Ballroom and elsewhere, the driving, riffing music being exactly what was required for the Lindy, the jitterbugging crazes and the rest. Only after this period did jazz become totally conceived as an intellectual exercise and as music for listening to.

Beyond the social dancing world and the close combat of the ballroom, jazz eventually provided the material for ballets and a whole world of specialized jazz dance. It is a subject of vast proportions beyond our present scope, so far most notably dealt with in *Jazz Dance* by Marshall & Jean Stearns. 464p. New York & London: Macmillan, 1968.

Date From its common use of an appointment, arranged time, lovers' meeting; more specifically used in jazz and music circles to mean a recording session, in the sense of 'on that date' and also in a more general sort of way, a 'jazz date'. Also used, but probably less so, of any arranged engagement for a club or concert.

Davenport Town in Iowa on the Mississippi with a population of *c.* 89 000; remembered as the place where Bix Beiderbecke was born and immortalized by him in his 1925 recording of *Davenport blues*.

Dawn Club Nightclub in San Francisco situated in Annie Street off Market Street behind the Palace Hotel where Lu Watters came to light in 1946, when his Yerba Buena jazz band headed the West Coast traditional jazz revival. The Yerba Buena band had actually been founded in 1940, but it was not until just after the war that it managed to make its mark.

Dearborn Street Thoroughfare running north to south in the South Side district of Chicago. Its intersections with 29th Street and 35th Street in particular have given rise to jazz titles.

Decca Book of Jazz A comprehensive survey of jazz published in 1958 by the Decca Record Company, in collaboration with Frederick Muller. The volume contained contributions by British critics Jeff Aldam, James Asman, Vic Bellerby, Graham Boatfield, Ernest Borneman, Stanley Dance, Charles Fox, Peter Gammond, Keith Goodwin, Benny Green, Tony Hall, Daniel Halperin, Rex Harris, Raymond Horricks, Burnett James, Gerald Lascelles, Alun Morgan, Francis Newton, Paul Oliver, Steve Race, Brian Rust, Peter Tanner, Sinclair Traill, Mark White and Charles Wilford. Edited by Peter Gammond with an introduction by Mezz Mezzrow. Tony Hall's chapter on early British modern jazz is particularly informative, having been written not long after the events it describes. Charles Wilford's ragtime chapter was written over a decade before ragtime was rediscovered by the general public.

Desdume Mamie Desdume (dates unknown). Blues singer, presumably active in the early 20th century, much admired by Jelly Roll Morton and now remembered for his revival of her fine *Mamie's blues* in a 1938 Library of Congress recording. Also recorded by Louis Armstrong. Morton, in his spoken references to her, pronounced the name Dezzdume, and claimed that this was the only tune she knew. She called it *2:19 blues*. 'Two nineteen done take my baby away'. The 2:19 was a well-known train that left New Orleans daily. It tends to be assumed that 2:19 refers to its departure time, and it is usually written thus. In fact, 219 is the train's running number, the means by which it was identified in the schedules. It was common practice among American railroads to allot odd numbers to trains travelling in one direction, and even numbers to those going the other way (the equivalent of 'up' and 'down') though that fails to explain why the words of this particular blues should continue: '2:17 gonna bring him back some day'.

Detroit City and port, with a population verging on two million, in Michigan, USA, lying on the Detroit River between the great lakes Huron and Erie. Dates back to 1701, when it started as a fur-trading post. In the 20th century it became the world's largest car-manufacturing centre and has been described as a 'lunch-bucket' town, i.e. a place where people go to make money rather than for pleasure. Not, therefore, rich in tourists, so that Detroit made music for itself, most of the jazz coming from its own black community.

Detroit produced a few jazz musicians such as J. C. Heard (b. 1917), Everett Barksdale (b. 1910), Hank Jones (b. 1918), Lucky Thompson (b. 1924), Bob Zurke (1912–44), Milt Jackson (b. 1923) and Donald Byrd (b. 1932). Most of these went elsewhere but Detroit became particularly noted as a centre of urban blues singing from the days of Big Maceo (1905–53) and Sonny Boy Williamson (1912–48) through John Lee Hooker (b. 1917) to the flourishing Motown scene. Motown, a contraction of 'Motor-town', was the creation of the black entrepreneur Berry Gordy and it was the label on which The Supremes, Diana Ross and Stevie Wonder rose to pop fame. A well-known Detroit venue in the 1930s was the Greystone Ballroom where McKinney's Cotton Pickers established their reputation.
See: 'The Detroit Jazz Scene' by Philip Hanson in *Jazz Monthly* (September 1968).

Dictionaries, Encyclopedias and other reference books Until very recently there have been remarkably few standard reference books on the subject of jazz. This has been remedied, since the first edition of this book in 1986, by the appearance of the first really comprehensive reference – *The New Grove Dictionary of Jazz*, edited by Barry Kernfeld. 2 vols. 1000p. London: Macmillan, 1988.

The expense of this volume will still leave readers turning to volumes such as our own for general information and for biographical information to the wide-ranging *Jazz: the Essential Companion* by Ian Carr, Digby Fairweather and Brian Priestley. 561p. London: Grafton Books, 1987. This selectively covers all periods of jazz in a thorough and critical way.

For those whose interest lies mainly in traditional jazz there is:
John Chilton: *Who's Who of Jazz*. 375p. London: Bloomsbury Bookshop, 1972; New York: Chilton Book Company, 1972; 4th edition (pb) London: Macmillan, 1985; New York: Da Capo Press, 1985.

This is an exceptionally thorough work which one now turns to as reliable authority in the names it deals with, especially in its new and up-dated edition. It does, however, deliberately limit its entries to jazz musicians who were born before 1920 so that one accepts that it is basically a trad. reference – nonetheless frustrating when one can, for example, find Thelonious Monk there because he was born in 1917 but not Charlie Parker because he was born in 1920. Considering our position in history and the fact that many not included would either be dead or at least 65, it is to be hoped that Chilton is contemplating the new edition with the qualifying date moved substantially forward. There is also:
Leonard Feather: *The Encyclopedia of Jazz*. 527p. New York: Horizon Press, 1960.
Leonard Feather: *The Encyclopedia of Jazz in the Sixties*. 312p. 1966.
Leonard Feather and Ira Gitler: *Encyclopedia of Jazz in the Seventies*. 393p. 1976.
These three books provide a comprehensive Who's Who, though they omit many of the obscurer early names that Chilton includes. The basic encyclopedia (first published in 1955) has not up-dated but the 'Sixties' and 'Seventies' volumes update all the material that has previously been included in supplements to the original. So that most names can be referred to, except for the very latest.

Columbia—the Snappiest Dance Records

This Month's Star Dance Records

10-inch Double-sided, 3/- each.

4724	Play-Ground in the Sky, Fox Trot / Wherever You Are, Fox Trot	Ben Selvin & His Orchestra. (With Vocal Chorus).
4720	Four Walls, Fox Trot / Baltimore, Fox Trot	Fred Rich & His Hotel Astor Orch. (With Vocal Chorus).
4721	Polly, Novelty Fox Trot / Dawn of Tomorrow, Waltz	Fred Rich & His Hotel Astor Orchestra (With Piano Solo).
4722	I Fell Head Over Heels in Love Fox Trot / She's Got " It," Fox Trot	Fred Rich & His Hotel Astor Orch. (With Vocal Chorus).
4729	Dear, on a Night Like This, Fox Trot / Dream Kisses, Fox Trot	
4730	Can't You Hear Me Say I Love You ? Waltz / I'm Living on Love, Fox Trot	DEBROY SOMERS BAND.
4731	Baby's Wooden Soldiers, Fox Trot / I'm Going Back Again to Old Nebraska, Fox Trot	(With Vocal Chorus).
4746	I Scream, You Scream, We all Scream for Ice Cream, Fox Trot / When the Robert E. Lee Comes to Town, Fox Trot	HARRY RESER'S SYNCOPATORS. (With Vocal Chorus).
4747	Keep Sweeping the Cobwebs off the Moon, Fox Trot / Away Down South in Heaven, Fox Trot	TED LEWIS and His Band. (With Vocal Chorus).
4748	I've Been Longing For a Girl Like You, (For a Long, Long Time), Fox Trot / Everywhere You Go, Fox Trot	PAUL ASH and His Orchestra. (With Vocal Chorus).

COLUMBIA Leadership is shown every month in its New Dance Records. Always a surprise—always full of Novelties. In Columbia you have exemplified at its best the new standard of brilliance secured by the Columbia Electric Recording

Exclusive to Columbia

*Write for New Descriptive List of this month's New Dance Records, and Complete (244 pp.) Catalogue Post Free from COLUMBIA, 102-108, Clerkenwell Road, London, E.C.*1

—and BRITISH to the Core!

Columbia
New process RECORDS
ELECTRIC RECORDING WITHOUT SCRATCH

The dance craze and jazz in the 1920s. (*Melody Maker*, April 1928)

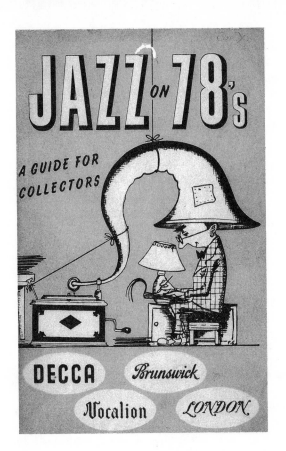

Useful Decca discography published just before the advent of the LP age compiled by P. G. (The Decca Record Co. Ltd)

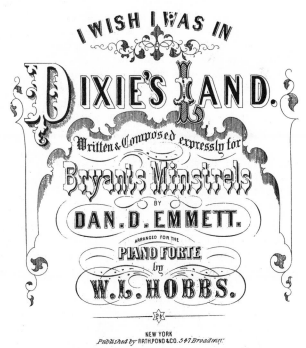

The original issue of the famous *Dixie* song of 1859.

Beyond these there are specialist volumes that go further in coverage of their own areas notably:

Blues Who's Who by Sheldon Harris. 775p. New Rochelle: Arlington House, 1979. Offers good coverage in its field.

For a general musical biographical dictionary that gives good representative jazz coverage the most comprehensive (apart from Grove) is:

Nicolas Slonimsky (ed): *Baker's Biographical Dictionary of Musicians*. 7th Edition. 2577p. New York & London: Oxford University Press, 1984.

Dicty High class; stylish. The word comes into music via its use, early in the 20th century, by American Negro communities. Besides its straightforward meaning, it could also carry the implication of 'assumed airs and graces' and in that form was faintly mocking. As a title word it appears in *The dicty glide*, and in 1923, Fletcher Henderson recorded a *Dicty blues*.

Dig Has almost too many shades of meaning for its own good. It can simply be the imperative 'look at' as in 'Dig that chick over there', the exact equivalent of 'clock that bird over there' in cockney speech. In the sense that that particular form of the use of 'dig' usually implies look-at-with-appreciation, it ties in with 'dig's' main meaning: 'to appreciate'; thus: 'I really dig your music'; 'dig that jive', etc. That links with a third connotation: 'to understand' (since appreciation often implies comprehension): 'We only play here on Tuesdays, you dig?'

Its past tense is the conventional 'dug'.

Dippermouth An early nickname bestowed upon Louis Armstrong likening the dimensions of his mouth to those of a ladle or dipper. Armstrong later acquired the second and much more widely known nickname of Satchmo, which, as an abbreviation of 'Satchelmouth', was almost another way of saying the same thing. *Dippermouth blues*, recorded by the King Oliver band (of which Armstrong was a member) in 1923 was presumably named after him. *Dippermouth blues*, however, was later recorded again by Oliver as *Sugar foot stomp*. In its turn, Sugar foot was the name sometimes given to an impressively good – sweet-footed – dancer.

Dirty Apart from its many slang usages the word 'dirty' used to be applied to a tone that was 'rough, hard, harsh' a 'gravelly' tone. Often increased in instrumental tone by the use of 'growl' and other mutes. The opposite of 'legitimate'. 'Dirt' – a general term for hot, earthy, usually small band, jazz.

Dirty dozens A ritual name-calling game, practised mainly by black town-dwellers, in which the participants heaped insults upon one another in accordance with an elaborate routine. 'Speckled Red', whose real name was Rufus Perryman, made a famous solo piano-and-voice record called *The dirty dozens* (1956) which gives some idea of how it was done – but not much.

Discography Jazz, being a fairly neatly contained subject and holding a wealth of interest in its make-up, personnel, dates and other minutiae, was found worthy of documentation fairly early in its public career. Catering for the truly pernickety jazz fan, jazz discography set a new standard for such studies, in matters of detail and eventual accuracy. This is still unequalled in other fields of musical research, including classical music (except perhaps opera) where recording dates and venues have only been dealt with in comparatively recent times and where detailing personnel is mainly impossible. The word 'discography' to describe this kind of chronicle is first identified by the *Oxford English Dictionary* in the mid-30s.

Discographical listings as an adjunct to periodical articles became common in the 1930s and 1940s. As separate publications or integrated into books or articles, they are now of a vast number and fairly well covered in various bibliographical works. Reasonably thorough is the *International Bibliography of Discographies* by David Edwin Copper (USA 1975).

The first well-known general discography of jazz to appear in book form was Charles Delauney's *Hot Discography*, first published in Paris in 1936. After three editions more or less in its original form, in 1940, 1943 and 1944, it reappeared in 1948 in America as *New Hot Discography*, now a substantial work of 608 pages, and of immense value, though still full of the inevitable innaccuracies and omissions that must beset pioneer works of this nature and which they tend to perpetuate. In England, also in 1936, there had appeared *Rhythm on Record* by Hilton R. Schleman which did not have the same success and is now rarely seen.

Earnest attempts to put as many matters straight as possible came in the promising English *Jazz Directory* whose first A–B volume appeared in 1950. Unfortunately, the task of keeping up with the ever-increasing flow of records, and lack of regular financial backing, left this work stranded at Vol. 6 – Ki-Lo. So it didn't even get to Morton. A proposed yearly extension to this work lasted only one issue in the shape of *Jazz Discography 1958* (published 1960).

The first native American discography in book form was Orin Blackstone's *Index to Jazz* (covering 'hot' records 1917–44) published in four volumes 1945–48. A definitive edition proposed in 1949 under the title *Jazzfinder* only achieved one volume. Discography suffers even more than bibliography by being expensive and time-consuming to compile and print, while the material rewards are infinitesimal.

Working on the basis of these early ventures, more recent discographies have become the standard works, such as Brian A. L. Rust's 2-volume *Jazz Records 1897–1942* (indispensable but limited in scope by his purist traditional view of jazz); Jorgen Grunnet Jepsen's *Jazz Records*, taking up the task from 1943 onwards in numerous volumes and

editions, and giving surprisingly adequate coverage up to 1962, and the 40-volume Belgian *Fifty Years of Recorded Jazz, 1917–67* by Walter Bruyninckx (probably the 'completest' of all). Covering a more specialized area, there was Dixon and Godrich's *Blues and Gospel Records 1902–1942*. As the 'complete' discography of jazz became less and less a practical proposition, the collector has been better served by thorough discographies devoted to single subjects or musicians; but even many of these are not entirely adequate. Such big names as Ellington and Goodman have been well served and the collector interested in lesser figures can usually find at least one, often poorly duplicated, publication somewhere.

The first American magazine to concentrate on discography was *Rag*, first published by the Hot Record Society in 1938.

District, The see **Storyville**

Dixie Dixie or Dixieland became a popular designation for the southern States of America only after the publication of the song *Dixie* which was written by the famous minstrel Daniel Decatur Emmett (1815–1904) in 1859. It was published in the following year and was then generally known as 'I wish I was in Dixie's Land'; sometimes also spelt 'Dixey'. Became immensely popular after it had been used in a show called *Pocahontas* and, having appeared at an opportune moment, was widely used in the Civil War, often played, paradoxically, by the bands of the north. By 1861 'Dixie Land' was a general affectionate name used by the southern blacks for their 'homeland'.

Where Emmett, or anyone else, got the name Dixie is a subject that has been a source of endless and still unended controversy. There have been many explanations. One is that it survived in memory of the Dixie family, still extant in England, some of whom emigrated to the Colonies around 1630 and became influential and well-liked there. Another,

INTERNATIONAL JAZZ CRITICS POLL

August 6, 1959 35¢

down beat®

Complete Newport Coverage

Ellington Wins Critics' Poll, Breaks It Up At Newport

Jonah Jones' Blindfold Test

Plus

Record Reviews

**Ruby Braff
Johnny Hodges
Barney Kessel
Carmen McRae
Lester Young**

Down Beat covers the Newport Festival in 1959. Usual features included the Blindfold Test. (*Down Beat*, Aug. 1959)

perhaps more likely, idea is that it derived from the New Orleans ten-dollar bills which had long been known as 'dixies' from the French 'dix' printed on them. There may seem to be an obvious link between the name and that of the Mr Dixon who became known in connection with the Mason-Dixon Line, a boundary between Pennsylvania and Maryland agreed in 1760 and generally considered to be the symbolic dividing line between the north and the southern slave states; but this seems to be simply coincidental. A later theory has traced the origin to a Negro character (an isolated and therefore noteworthy example) in a play that was known at the time (and would have been to Emmett) who was called Dixie. The matter seems likely to remain unresolved. A full discussion can be found in: *Dan Emmett and the Rise of Early Negro Minstrelsy* by Hans Nathan. 196p. Norman: Oklahoma University Press, 1962; repr. Detroit: Detroit Reprints, 1972.

Dixieland jazz When jazz began to emerge in the early 1900s, Dixieland was a convenient commercial tag for a sort of light-hearted New Orleans cum ragtime style that was the first kind of jazz to be popularized. Confusingly, the early Original Dixieland Jazz Band, which had much to do with the popularization, was a white band; and thereafter Dixieland, as a genre, became associated with white jazz played in the traditional ensemble manner in a cleaned up sort of way that made it suitable for general consumption.

The jazz purists have tried to get the term used in its more correctly derived pre-1919 sense, as a music synonymous with New Orleans style and, therefore, with the original black jazz that emanated from the South or Dixieland. It is used rather more widely in this sense in the USA and certainly in New Orleans jazz circles. But to many it still suggests white jazz, and the revivals of the 1940s tended to perpetuate the error (if it may be so-called – or is it just another case of usage dictating?). The revival of traditional jazz idioms, complete with banjos, pumping tubas and four-square rhythms, was often done under the name of Dixieland, frequently by white bands in such places as Nick's in New York, where it was inevitably referred to as Nicksieland jazz. In the widest possible sense Dixieland now embraces all traditional styles, but there is a clear need for clarification of what one intends when using the name.

Dobell's Famous London jazz record shop; in its peak years of fame known as a 'clearing house for jazz gossip'. At this time it was situated at 77 Charing Cross Road (whence it also issued records on the 77 label) but was moved in 1980 to Tower Street, WC2 (behind the Ambassadors Theatre) as the result of the rebuilding of the west side of Charing Cross Road. It remains one of the best-known specialist shops but not quite so hectically patronized as in its Charing Cross Road days. Founded in 1946 by Doug Dobell (son of a respected bookseller) who started with two boxes of records in the corner of his father's shop. In the 1950s jazz musicians and critics almost crowded out the earnest buyers of jazz (one department) or folk (another) until they overflowed into a wedge-shaped Italian restaurant next door.

Dobell's, inevitably, is no longer unique, several other excellent specialist dealers having sprung up in London and most big towns since the 1950s.

Doc Nickname given to anyone of a slightly studious, serious, bespectacled sort of aspect or nature; one who knows his theory and diagnosis. There have been a large number of Docs in jazz – Cheatham, Cooke, Poston, West and Whitby among them.

Doghouse Musician's slang term for the double-bass. Plucking the strings is referred to as 'slapping the doghouse'.

Dogtown Nickname for the Douglastown area of Long Island on Little Neck Bay. The area was named after a family called Douglas who were famed as dog-breeders.

Dogtown blues was recorded by Bob Crosby in 1937.

Dots Familiar musicians' slang (by no means confined to jazz) for notes or, in general, musical copy. Fairly obvious derivation. As a variant spots is sometimes used, but less frequently since the 1940s.

Double time Occasional device, used by pianists, also in early big band orchestration, where the tempo of a performance appears to be doubled because twice as many notes are being played. As in Morton's *Mr. Jelly Lord*. A device reworked in the Parker and post-Parker eras by athletic, energetic young modernists, especially the saxophone players.

Down Beat Fortnightly American dance band and jazz interest journal started by Maher Publications in Chicago in July 1934. Originally edited by Jack Maher. Like the *Melody Maker* in England, it was initially intended primarily as a magazine for the professional musician, giving its news and views in a suitably colloquial idiom and becoming noted, as did *Metronome*, for its cryptic headlines. Its jazz affiliations have always been stronger than those of *Melody Maker* (which now ignores jazz) and even in these days of jazz fusion and confusion is still largely devoted to the hard core of jazz. Initiated *Down Beat* awards for musical popularity which have always been taken fairly seriously in spite of often quirkish choices. Published a series of *Down Beat* Yearbooks from 1954.

Downbeat see **Afterbeat**

Down home An almost inevitable synonym in USA for down South or Dixieland. Later used widely to cover all phenomena concerned with everything, including racial prejudices, of and about the South. In jazz, specifically, a way of playing that perpetuates the early New Orleans style. *Down home rag* was written in 1935 by Wilbur Sweatman; *Down home blues* in 1921 by Tom Delaney; and 'down home' crops up in several titles of the pseudo Tin Pan Alley jazz variety.

Downtown Almost exclusively an Americanism for the lower part or business section of any city or town. Downtowns that spring to mind, as having jazz connections, are in main centres like New Orleans – in the north of the city; Chicago – the area south of the Chicago River, where the principal entertainment areas are found; New York – the southern part of Manhattan Island (Harlem is Uptown and other areas are designated East Side and West Side).

Drag (1) In jazz, generally a slow tempo number akin to a blues or mooche. So named from a leisurely kind of drum figure that accompanied such numbers. Slow drag has a more specific meaning (see separate entry).
(2) Early 1920s – a dance or dance party (still used in this sense in some circles). This is the usage implied in Morton's *Shoeshiner's drag* (1928).
(3) A versatile word, 'drag' has an immense variety of meanings, some of which drift into jazz. Most commonly, a bore, tedious, unexciting – 'life can be a drag one minute and a solid sender the next' (Louis Armstrong); a real drag. Also: a share of something; influence or pull; a main street; a cigarette (in 1930s specifically marijuana – dragged, meaning drugged – but elsewhere more conventional) or the smoking of a cigarette; 'in drag' – being dressed in the clothes of the opposite sex; a party where such a thing occurs; a girl accompanying a man at a dance; a dull person (as above); a railroad engine, especially of the slow, goods variety; a short race between hotted up cars; a wad of money; etc. Interesting how one word can have such a spread of meanings.

Dreamland Café Chicago jazz haunt that became prominent *c.* 1918 with the arrival of New Orleans jazzmen in the city. It opened in 1917 on 35th and State Streets, and one of its early attractions was a band led by Lawrence Duhé which, part-time, included King Oliver who was doubling at the nearby Royal Garden Café. Oliver then formed a band at the Dreamland Café under his own name in January 1920 – with Honore Dutrey, Johnny Dodds, Lil Hardin, Ed Garland and Minor Hall in its ranks, and thus the predecessor of the Creole Jazz Band. Later, the band there was led by Ollie Powers who had Louis Armstrong playing for him for three months when Louis was between the King Oliver band and his departure for New York to join Fletcher Henderson's Roseland Ballroom Orchestra. By 1925 the orchestra there was led by Lil Armstrong (Hardin) and the manager of the establishment was one Bill Bottoms. She brought Louis Armstrong back from New York to play with her for a while. There was a Dreamland Ballroom in Chicago and also one in Omaha, Nebraska, both celebrated in the 1920s.

Drive The sort of momentum and urgency that a good jazz or swing band achieves when everything is swinging into place over a forceful, flowing rhythm.

Drums The emphatic percussive element of jazz is one of those which clearly distinguishes it from straight music where the rhythm is more often an underlying pulse rather than a feature of the music. Much of the early opposition to, and denigration of, jazz was induced by its 'tom-tom' rhythms. Developing both from the African element and the brass band parade drumming, jazz came in with a drum rhythm at the heart of it.

Once jazz had found its sedentary role in the dance halls and places of entertainment, the drummer's art quickly developed and his equipage or traps became more elaborate, operated by both hand and foot. Early jazz drummers such as Vic Berton (1896–1951), Minor Hall (1897–1959), Baby Dodds (1898–1959), Jimmy Bertrand (1900–1960), Paul Barbarin (1899–1969), Kaiser Marshall (1899–1948), tended to lay down a solid on-the-beat rhythm. A gradual switch to

afterbeat playing and more variation in successive choruses was to be found in the work of such drummers as Zutty Singleton (1898–1975) – one of the greatest of the early practitioners.

The formation of bigger bands, leading to the swing era, made the drummers more prominent than ever with a propulsive rhythm the key to much of the excitement of 1930s jazz: white drummer Ben Pollack (1903–1971); Sonny Greer (1895–1982) who under-pinned the Ellington band with one of the biggest assortment of traps seen till then; Walter Johnson (1904–1977) with Henderson; and others. The essence of big-band drumming is to be found in the work of Chick Webb (1909–39) fronting his own band. From the 1930s on the showy drum solo becomes increasingly (and often boringly) a part of the drummer's role. The emancipation of drummers was continued by such as Dave Tough (1908–48) with Shaw and Herman, Cozy Cole (1909–1981) with Carter and Calloway, Sid Catlett (1910–1951) with Carter and Henderson, Jimmy Crawford (1910–1980) with the Lunceford band. The heights of showmanship (but also a good solid beat) were to be heard and seen (in several films) from Gene Krupa (1909–1973) in his work with the Goodman band and small groups. The art of maximum propulsion with the minimum of hammering was perfected by Jo Jones (1911–85) with the Count Basie band during its first period of greatness. The traditional style of drumming has been kept intact within the work of such as Kansas Fields (b. 1915), J. C. Heard (1917–88) and Buddy Rich (1917–87) – perhaps the most technically awe-inspiring of all drummers.

Part of the changes that modern jazz of the 1940s wrought was to be found in the different rhythmic emphasis of drumming. Rather than the blatant solid regular beat, the modern drummer now found new interest and invention in broken and cross-rhythms that both underlaid the solo phrasing and made the drummer himself more of an intrinsic soloist – the underlying beat now suggested rather than emphasized. A pioneer in this was Kenny Clarke (1914–85) followed by others such as Art Blakey (b. 1919), Shelly Manne (1921–84), Max Roach (b. 1924) and one of the most powerful of all – Philly Joe Jones (1923–85). The biggest forward step in the conception of the drummer's contribution in post-Parker jazz has probably been that inaugurated by Elvin Jones (b. 1927). Working alongside John Coltrane at a crucial period in Coltrane's own development (starting 1960), Elvin brought to the drums the same total onslaught that Coltrane brought to the tenor (and increasingly the soprano) saxophone. It was a foaming rush of percussive sound, barely perceptible as separate strokes, African in its rhythmic complexity if not in its actual style.

Duke Nickname given to Edward Kennedy Ellington (1899–1974) long before he got on the jazz scene. As a boy he was even then an elegant dresser and of lofty, ducal disposition and the name was given to him by his school-friends. Later it was to spark off several contending noble titles – Basie's Count was partly in rivalry. Ellington pointed out in his autobiography that he also had many alternative nicknames used from time to time, such as Otto, Cutey, Stinkpot, Phoney Duke, Wucker, Kid, Apple Dumpling, Dumplin', Dumpy, Macow, Pops, Big Red, Piano Red, Head Knocker, Puddin' and Govey. Jazz history would not have been quite the same had 'Stinkpot' Ellington or 'Dumpy' Ellington been the ones that stuck rather than the respectable 'Duke'. Would the Sacred Concerts have even been contemplated?

Dukes of Dixieland A rather formalized, though lively, Dixieland jazz group led by Frank (1932–74) and Fred (1929–66) Assunto, starting from their New Orleans High School days. On turning professional they played for 44 months at the Famous Door in New Orleans and became widely popular through their recordings (some with Louis Armstrong and other stars) made for Audio Fidelity *c.* 1958/9. These were amongst the first stereo jazz records to be released.

Dusty Bottom Nightclub in Chicago where Albert Ammons (1907–49) often played. Familiarly known as The Bottom.

Eagle Band Early jazz band that flourished in New Orleans from 1900–17. Co-operatively run, it included in its ranks at times such pioneer players as Bunk Johnson, King Oliver, Buddy Petit, Sidney Bechet, Johnny Dodds, 'Big Eye' Louis Nelson, Pops Foster, and Warren 'Baby' Dodds. Took its name from the Eagle Saloon at the corner of South Rampart and Perdido Streets which was their HQ.

Eagle Rock A popular black dance, performed with the arms outstretched like wings and the body rocking from side to side. Originally a dance with religious significance, the high-armed gestures being commonly associated with evangelical traditions and the religious trance. It originated at the Eagle Rock Baptist Church in Kansas City just after the Civil War. It soon spread north and south where it became urbanized into a dance with rather more sexual overtones and more shuffling in its movements. One Charlie Love (1885–1963), cornettist, remembered dancing the Eagle Rock to the strains of Buddy Bolden's band in New Orleans.

The Duke and his orchestra were frequent visitors to Europe.

SEE V PAGE 42

The advent of the stereophonic LP in jazz – Louis Armstrong with the Dukes of Dixieland. (Audio Fidelity Records)

Duke Ellington leads the polls again in the 1956 *Down Beat*.

Complete Results 1956 Readers Poll
December 26 1956
35¢

down beat

Duke Ellington

AUGUST 20, 1956

TIM

THE WEEKLY NEV

JAZZMAN
DUKE ELLINGTON

The first jazzman to have his picture on the front of the influential *Time* magazine (1956). (*Time*, Aug. 1956)

East Coast (jazz) Has never had the currency that West Coast has had as a generic term, but used (mainly by writers) as signifying the opposite kind of jazz; the bluesey, funky hard bop and earthy modern jazz as played by such as Donald Byrd, Kenny Dorham, Art Farmer and Charles Mingus, the latter issuing an album in 1957 under the title of *East Coasting* on the Bethlehem label.

East St. Louis A city that considers itself a separate entity from St. Louis across the Mississippi. It lies at the junction of the Mississippi and Missouri rivers in Clair County, Illinois (population *c.* 82 000). Generally referred to in jazz songs and blues as being the place farthest west and nearest to St. Louis to which it would be safe to hitch a lift on the railroad. Most of the hobos (coming from Kentucky and thereabouts) therefore disembarked here. An unprepossessing industrial town, scene of violent race riots in 1917. Titles: *East St. Louis blues* (Bumble Bee Slim); *East St. Louis toodle-oo* (Duke Ellington). There was also an *East St. Louis blues* (transcribed by W. C. Handy) that came from Kentucky in the early 1900s; a very rudimentary blues that was expanded into a full four-stanza blues (also called *East St. Louis blues*) and recorded by Faber Smith and Jimmy Yancey.

East St. Louis toodle-oo This is the title of a Duke Ellington tune which Ellington himself, tended to announce (and the band played it many times from 1926 onwards) as *East St. Louis toodle-oh*. He said it was intended to be toodle-oh in reference to a popular dance of the 1920s known as the Toddle. It was the Ellington orchestra's theme tune until Billy Strayhorn's (1915–67) *Take the 'A' Train* superseded it in 1940.

Easy rider An adroit and sexually satisfying partner. 'Easy rider struck this burg today' (cf. *Yellow Dog blues*). More innocently, easy rider was sometimes merely the guitar slung over the itinerant guitarist's back.

Economy Hall Popular New Orleans hall, headquarters of the Economy and Mutual Aid Association, opened in 1885 and demolished in the 1940s, situated at 1422 Ursuline Street. King Oliver was among the famous jazzmen who provided the music for dances there. It was irreverently known by the musicians as Cheapskate Hall.

Ellingtonia Such was the longevity of the Duke Ellington band, existing in some form from *c.* 1924 to the death of its leader Edward Kennedy 'Duke' Ellington (1899–1974), and such was its inbred and isolated nature, that it became itself a category within the main body of jazz. Many musicians who graced its ranks hardly ever worked anywhere else and those who did, rarely achieved the same stature as they had under the Ellington banner. Duke Ellington himself was a fine original pianist and an inspired and visionary composer and arranger who created the band's sounds out of the timbres, tones, quirks and styles of his musicians. He therefore tried to keep them as long as possible, by paying them well and establishing a family feeling in the band. Ellington's distinctive jungle style was evolved during the band's residency at the Cotton Club (1927–31), while his acknowledged finest work was from *c.* 1940 to 1950, a decade of unsurpassed achievement. Even after that, when the passage of years began to remove earlier members and the turnover of personnel was inevitably speeded up, classic material still came from Duke and his men, and it remained impossible to confuse the Ellington sound with any other.

Continuity was given to the Ellington band particularly by the long service of such as baritone-saxophonist, reed-player Harry Carney (1910–70) who joined in 1926 and was there to the end. An original genius of an alto-saxophonist, Johnny Hodges (1907–70) was a member from 1928 to 1951 and 1955 to 1970, and even when away from it remained thoroughly Ellingtonian. Charles 'Cootie' Williams (1910–85) was a trumpeter, succeeding the legendary Bubber Miley

(1903–32), who did much to create the Ellington sound of the vintage years. Williams left for twenty years but returned to the fold to help maintain the band's character.

The Ellington trombone-section modelled itself willy-nilly on the growling style of Joe 'Tricky Sam' Nanton (1904–46) who was with Ellington from 1926 till his death; modifications were applied by the sweeter tones of Lawrence Brown (1907–88) during 30 years' service, and the oriental flavours of valve trombonist Juan Tizol (1900–84) were audible from 1929 to 1944.

Drummer Sonny Greer (1895–1982) (a friend of Duke's from adolescent days) provided the staple rhythm of the band from 1924 to 1951 and was never wholly replaced. Wellman Braud (1891–1966) was a founder bass player, but on bass it was the short stay in the band by the revolutionary Jimmy Blanton (1918–42), (tragically ended by tuberculosis), which gave the band its progressive flavour of the 1940s. Blanton, indeed, influenced almost all subsequent bass-players, not merely those who worked for Ellington.

The arrival of Billy Strayhorn (1915–67) in 1938 as Ellington amanuensis, assistant composer-arranger, deputy pianist, added much in general terms to the band's output and special qualities, but so alike was their thinking that it's often hard to detect where one leaves off and the other begins.

Of course Ellington himself, and the distinctive piano style on which his orchestral works were based, was the most permanent key to the band's continuity of creative achievement. The gramophone must remain the most important source of Ellington documentation, as many of the scores, depending on the improvisational resources of the musicians, were rarely finalized or published.

Other prominent Ellingtonians:
Trumpets: William 'Cat' Anderson (1916–81); Harold 'Shorty' Baker (1913–66); Willie Cook (b. 1923); Freddy Jenkins (1906–78); Louis Metcalf (1905–81); Ray Nance (1913–76); Rex Stewart (1907–67); Clark Terry (b. 1920); Arthur Whetsol (1905–40).
Trombones: Tyree Glenn (1912–74); Quentin Jackson (1909–76); Britt Woodman (b. 1920).
Reeds: Harold Ashby (b. 1925); Barney Bigard (1906–80); Paul Gonsalves (1920–74); Jimmy Hamilton (b. 1917); Otto Hardwick (1904–70); Russell Procope (1908–81); Al Sears (b. 1910); Norris Turney (b. 1921); Ben Webster (1909–73).
Guitar: Fred Guy (1897–1971).
Bass: Hayes Alvis (1907–72); Oscar Pettiford (1922–60); Alvin 'Junior' Raglin (1917–55); Jimmy Woode (b. 1929).
Drums: Louie Bellson (b. 1924); Sam Woodyard (1925–88).
Vocalists: Ivie Anderson (1905–49); Ozzie Bailey (b. 1925); Kay Davis (b. 1920); Al Hibbler (b. 1915); Joya Sherrill (b. 1927).

Books: *Duke Ellington* by Barry Ulanov (New York: Creative Age Press, 1946; London: Musicians Press, 1947; New York: Da Capo, 1975). *Mood Indigo* by Dennis Preston (Egham: Citizens Press, 1946). *Duke Ellington: Harlem Aristocrat of Jazz* by Jean de Trazegnis (Brussels: Hot Club de Belgique, 1946). *Duke Ellington: his Life and Music* edited by Peter Gammond (London: Phoenix House, 1958; New York: Roy, 1958; London: Jazz Book Club, 1959; New York: Da Capo, 1977). *Duke Ellington* by G. E. Lambert (London: Cassell, 1959; New York: Barnes, 1961). *The World of Duke Ellington* by Stanley Dance (New York: Scribners, 1971; London: Macmillan, 1971). *Music is my Mistress* by Duke Ellington (New York: Doubleday, 1973; London: Allen, 1974; New York: Da Capo, 1976; London: Quartet, 1977). *Celebrating the Duke* by Ralph Gleason (Boston: Little, Brown, 1975). *Duke* by Derek Jewell (London: Elm Tree, 1977; Sphere, 1978). *Duke Ellington in Person* by Mercer Ellington & Stanley Dance (Boston: Houghton Mifflin, 1978; London: Hutchinson, 1978). *Portrait of Duke Ellington* by Don George; London: Robson, 1982). *Duke Ellington* by Peter Gammond (London: Apollo, 1987). *Duke Ellington* by James Lincoln Collier (New York & London, Macmillan, 1987).

Energy music One of the best of the names coined for the extremely untrammelled, usually completely extemporized forms of jazz that began to emerge in the early 1960s. At first avant-garde was a quite acceptable term for the revolutionary new music of people like Albert

Ayler and Archie Shepp, which appeared to be taking John Coltrane's blizzards of notes ('sheets of sound' as they were already being called in the late 50s) several stages further. But avant-garde has several inherent disadvantages. One is that no manifestation of any art form stays 'avant' for long; as one development succeeds another, either the new thing becomes the avant-garde, requiring a different name to be found for what is no longer new, or the term avant-garde is retained, inaccurately, while a fresh coining has to be made for its successors. The word 'modern' suffers from the same problem.

Another drawback is that the avant-garde of the 60s was not all of a piece. Some of it – the chilly and ascetic experiments of the Jimmy Giuffre Trio, for example – was cerebral and introverted in the extreme, so different from the rest of what was going on that (given the need for *some* kind of labelling) no one category could encompass both. Energy Music has the great virtues, therefore, of being almost self-explanatory, not chronologically restricted, and free of any

hint of qualitative judgment. It is 'free-form' jazz (another useful, workable term for post-bop jazz which kicks over the old harmonic, rhythmic and structural traces) but of a cathartic, vigorous and often passionate kind.

Many listeners consider that it is not jazz at all, and when it is compared with the music of the 20s and 30s, it is easy to hear why. But the fact remains that 'free form jazz' and 'energy music', despite their apparent excesses, could not have come about without all the jazz playing that had gone before, and it is better not to draw a line at all than to draw one in the wrong place.

European Jazz Federation Organization founded in 1969 with the aim of developing 'co-operation amongst all European countries in the jazz field' and the general stimulation of jazz activities.

Explosion A powerfully, markedly dramatic flare-up or emphasized beat on drums or cymbals as a lead-in to a final all-in or excitement building chorus. Any unexpected, heavily percussive outburst.

Face A name sometimes given to drummer Zutty Singleton (1898–1975) at times because of his own habit of referring to others as Face with appropriate adjectives added. 'The faces' is occasionally a way of referring to people of a specific group. A regular follower of jazz might, on casting his eye over a band formed for a particular event and finding it full of the 'right' musicians, say to a companion: 'The band's got all the faces in'.

Fake To improvise, to cover up with something that fits the harmonic sequence and suffices when things have been forgotten or otherwise gone astray.

Sounds slightly derogatory but, in fact, shows a good sense of harmony and improvisatory skills to be able to do it. Also 'fake it' – similar, possibly extended to any improvised solo that keeps things going. Up to *c*. 1925 the verb 'cheat' was also used. In early jazz those who couldn't read music were sometimes referred to as 'fakers'.

Famous Door, The A basement night club in Manhattan, New York, at 35 West 52nd Street, started by Lennie Hayton and others (including Glenn Miller, Jimmy Dorsey and Jerry Colonna) as a club for musicians. There was an actual door which stood on a dais and had been signed by the founders and henceforth acquired many famous signatures. It was opened on 1 March 1935 with a capacity clientele who were entertained by Louis Prima and his New Orleans Gang. It became a fashionable haunt which attracted custom from beyond the musical world and it used some very famous jazz names as entertainment including Bunny Berigan, Teddy Wilson and Billie Holiday. In 1936 Bessie Smith made an appearance there accompanied by the Berigan Band. The club became bankrupt and closed in May 1936.

The name was pinched by a new club which opened at 66 West 52nd Street in December 1937 and inadequately housed many of the famous big bands of the period; it moved to No. 201 in November 1943 but closed down soon after. Another club of that name opened featuring such musicians as Ben Webster, Dizzy Gillespie and Ella Fitzgerald but this only survived for two years. Other clubs in the cities of Baltimore, Boston, Los Angeles and New Orleans have borne the name Famous Door, though none had any actual connection with the original. The New Orleans Famous Door on Bourbon and Conti Streets opened in the 1940s and became a favourite spot with tourists wishing to sample the revival New Orleans jazz as provided by such as Sharkey Bonano and Santo Pecora.

Far out A term not necessarily confined to jazz usage, to describe the activities of the avant-garde, the innovators and experimenters; progressive in a wildly experimental way. Thus used to describe those who indulge in or follow such activities. In a general sense, suggests somebody who has gone way beyond the bounds of normality to achieve new expression, possibly in a trance-like state. Also: 'way out'.

Fat A full and warm tone. A 'fat' sound.

Fatha Unlike the other phoney nobles of jazz – King, Duke, Count, etc – Earl Kenneth Hines (1903–83), jazz pianist supreme, was actually christened that

way. So, in the perverse ways of jazz, he had to have something rather less grand found for him: he became 'Fatha' Hines, an affectionate nickname bestowed upon him by radio announcer/engineer Ted Pearson.

Feetwarmers A popular title for jazz groups in the 1930s, the best-known being the New Orleans Feetwarmers led by Sidney Bechet from *c*. 1932 to 1940.

The suggestion is of a band guaranteed to keep the extremities in rhythmical action, and the name was revived by London trumpeter/author/researcher John Chilton for the small jazz group which has regularly backed George Melly since 1972.

Fewclothes Cabaret New Orleans place of entertainment on Basin Street between Canal and Customhouse Street flourishing *c*. 1902–17. Freddie Keppard played there in 1913 and King Oliver 1915/16.

Fiddle Colloquial name for the violin, but also covering a number of dance instruments such as the small pocket fiddles that would not normally be described as violins. A name used more in country music than jazz, where the dignified name of violin seems to have been preferred.

Fifty-Second Street For roughly a decade from the mid-30s to the mid-40s, 52nd Street in Manhattan was the jazz centre of New York, with numerous night clubs and jazz haunts situated between Fifth and Seventh Avenues. Well-known clubs included the Famous Door, the Onyx and Jimmy Ryan's, known in publicity circles as Swing Street. 52nd Street took over the mantle from 133rd Street, between Lenox and Seventh Avenues, which prior to those dates had a similar plethora of jazz locations and was known as Jungle Alley (cf. Willie 'The Lion' Smith). In view of the Swing Street label it is interesting to note that when Dizzy Gillespie's group – one of the very first to play uncompromising bebop in public –

opened in a club there in January 1944, one reaction of a bewildered public at first was to call it 'Fifty-Second Street Jazz'.

Films Anyone who set out to jot down the number of films they could think of that used jazz as a subject or background might well get stuck after a dozen or so titles. So they would be surprised to find that David Meeker's *Jazz in the Movies* (London: Talisman, 1981) lists nearly 4000 films. In fact, one could well be a jazz collector by accumulating reels of film instead of records; the only disadvantage being that a few great names of the earlier days would sadly prove to be missing.

Jazz will be most widely known on film through certain popularized and highly romanticized biographies such as Universal's *The Glenn Miller Story* (1953), *The Benny Goodman Story* (1955), Republic's *The Fabulous Dorseys* (1947) or the Red Nichols-based *The Five Pennies* (1959). But they are best served by those films that feature actual jazz or swing groups in a story or setting where they are incidental to the plot (jazz-slanted or otherwise) such as *Hollywood Hotel* (1937) (Goodman band), *Stormy Weather* (1943) (Fats Waller, etc), *Birth of the Blues* (1941) (Teagarden, Dorseys, etc), *Girl Crazy* (1943) (Tommy Dorsey), and so on. Or, for Glenn Miller fans, the films featuring the band such as *Sun Valley Serenade* (1941) or *Orchestra Wives* (1941) – whose soundtracks have been made available on LP. Jazz-oriented films that have a wide appeal and are reasonably well known and available are *New Orleans* (1947) (an odd, garbled history with Armstrong and Holiday), *Jivin' in Bop* (1947) (Gillespie, etc); *Jazz Ball* (1957) (a compilation of soundies – see below); and, perhaps best of all, *Jazz on a Summer's Day* (1960) filmed at the 1959 Newport Jazz Festival.

Soundies (mentioned above) were a series of three-minute films, featuring various singers, musicians and bands, made for coin-operated machines in America in the 1930s and 40s; and there were similar Telescriptions made for TV (five-minute duration) in the 1950s. These are not generally available but there is a growing interest in re-issuing them for their valuable documentation and nostalgic interest. A list of films featuring, showing or using as background various eminent jazz musicians is printed in *Encyclopedia of Jazz in the Seventies* [e.g. under Ellington: *Black and Tan* (1929), *A Bundle of Blues* (1933), *Paramount Pictorial* (1934), *Symphony in Black* (1935), *A Date with Duke* (1947) and *Salute to Duke Ellington* (1950)]. This list can be supplemented with the help of the Meeker index, which includes a number of Ellington documentaries; and similar material covering other musicians.

Finger Goes back to normal musical usage, to 'finger' a chord, i.e. to find the chord on the fingerboard (stringed instruments) or 'fingering' – a suggested practical or correct way of playing keyboard music. 'Finger-style' guitar – using the fingers instead of a plectrum. 'Finger popper' – someone who is playing well; a piece of music that lies well under the fingers; a swinging piece of music or musician; hence, 'finger-popping' – snapping the fingers in time to such music.

Five-by-Five A fat person, as in the song *Mr Five-By-Five* (1942) – 'he's five feet tall and five feet wide'. The blues-shouter Jimmy Rushing (1902–1972) who worked for Benny Moten (1929–1935) and Count Basie (1935–1950 and after), and who was roughly that shape anyway, got lumbered with the nickname when he first sang this song at the Golden Gate Theater in San Francisco after Ella Mae Morse had also popularized it.

Five Pennies Name neatly coined by Red Nichols (1905–65), *c.* 1926 for this original five-piece band which remained Five Pennies even when there was a lot more change available. There are records by the Five Pennies with as many as ten men on them. A cent in the USA is commonly called a penny and five pennies equal one nickel.

Fives An obscure title used in connection with early piano music of the 1920–30s period, which some define simply as an early style of piano blues playing of a sad and earthy nature. It then got transferred as a sort of general nickname for all boogie-woogie playing which, it has been claimed, went back to the early 1900s. What seems more likely is that it was simply a name for one particular boogie figure or bass, probably the hallmark of one pianist or area. Several of these terms survive, some of them such as the chimes, the rocks and the chains more explainable than the fives or the trenches, both of which were recorded by Turner Parrish without offering much elucidation.

Flamingo The Flamingo, a venue for modern (largely British) jazz, and lending itself to the derivative title 'Jazz at the Flamingo', occupied several London West End premises during the dozen or so years of its existence. Run by Sam Kruger, it began beneath the Mapleton Restaurant in Leicester Square in 1953, using the Tony Kinsey Trio as resident musicians. For a short time a sort of 'branch' of the Flamingo functioned at the Café Anglais, also in Leicester Square. The club's best years began in the mid-1950s with its move to Wardour Street where the Kinsey group continued and where such newcomers as trumpeter Dizzy Reece and saxophonist Wilton 'Bogey' Gaynair, both from the West Indies, first gained renown. British pianist/vibraphonist Bill Le Sage was a regular there as was baritone-saxophonist Ronnie Ross. The Flamingo and Ronnie Scott's Club (which opened in Gerrard Street in 1959) were little more than 100 yards apart but the following for modern jazz was sufficient to ensure large audiences at the Flamingo until the mid-60s when the inroads made by the younger beat, rock and blues groups devastated the London jazz scene

and removed yet another venue from the map.

Flare A note or chord held at the end of a chorus, usually with a crescendo, to lead the band into a final all-in section. A favourite device of New Orleans players like Louis Armstrong, but also used elsewhere. Also Flare-up.

Flip (1) To become excited by something, turned on by, overwhelmed by a performance. Shortened version of the phrase 'to flip one's lid', i.e. 'to blow one's top'.
(2) In full, 'flip side'; the reverse or other side of a gramophone record, generally referring to the B or commercially less important side, but can simply refer to the reverse. More common in pop than jazz usage. The pop world, having chosen an A side for a single, is capable of putting almost any old rubbish on the B side because it will, in any case, devote its entire promotional effort to the A side and ignore the flip side completely. It often happens, even in the jazz world, that the supposed B or flip side turns up trumps and becomes the best-seller.

Flugelhorn An instrument that might loosely be described as a keyed bugle, developing from the old military bugle *c.* 1828 and a widely used instrument in European military bands by *c.* 1840. It has a wide flared bell, a simpler mechanism than the cornet and uses a deeper mouthpiece than the trumpet and of even greater depth than the cornet's. Its bugle-like sound is distinctive and considered by most writers to have a 'noble' quality to it. 'Why', said one admirer, writing in 1910, 'use sparrows and chaffinches (cornets and trumpets) when you can have a nightingale (flugel) for the same money?' It has been widely, if not predominantly, used in jazz, a great many trumpeters liking to try it on occasions, e.g. Kenny Wheeler who turns to it frequently, as does Clark Terry. Art Farmer switched to it as his permanent instrument in the 1960s, finding there a

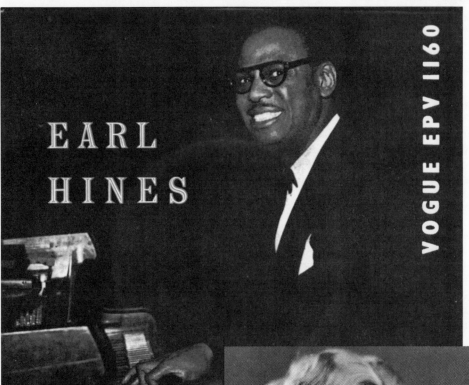

EARL
HINES

VOGUE EPV 1160

Earl 'Fatha' Hines during
a long recording career.
(Vogue Records)

With all Best Wishes to
all British musicians &
rhythm fiends from
"Red" Nichols

Loring 'Red' Nichols in the
1920s. (*Melody Maker*,
Dec. 1929)

The Fox-Trot when it was a jazz novelty dance *c.* 1918. (Star Music Publishing)

rich tone that is unequalled in modern jazz.

Flute Not commonly used in jazz perhaps because it did not have a naturally hot tone at its command, nor was it endowed with sufficient volume. Its breathy tone could, however, be used to good effect, one of its earliest successful practitioners being Wayman Carver, reedman in the Chick Webb band from 1934–40 (latterly under Ella Fitzgerald) and heard on such Webb items as *Hallelujah; I want to be happy*, etc *c*. 1937; also on Spike Hughes 1933 sessions: *Sweet Sue* and *How come you do me*, and in the other 'American Orchestra' recordings of that time. Later, in modern jazz, and with the advantage of microphoning, the flute became further exploited as a new, bright solo tone by such performers as Frank Wess, Bud Shank, Buddy Collette, Herbie Mann, Harold McNair. With the coming of the next generation, and the exploitation of vocal devices whereby a growling or buzzing in the player's throat added other qualities to the flute's natural sound, the flute stepped almost into the avant-garde. Roland Kirk and Eric Dolphy in particular increased the instrument's emotional range and musical versatility, while much later players, relying on acoustic phenomena difficult for the layman to grasp, actually create the impression of three, even four, strands of sound at once. James Newton is an outstanding exponent.

Four Brothers Title of a composition by Jimmy Giuffre to feature Woody Herman's saxophone section of three tenors and a baritone, then (1944) played by Stan Getz, Zoot Sims, Herbie Steward, and Serge Chaloff. That particular reed section, notwithstanding some bad blood between Zoot Sims and Chaloff, quickly became known as *The Four Brothers*, and that edition of the band as a whole is sometimes referred to as *The Four Brothers Band* as an alternative to *Second Herd*.

Foxtrot W. C. Handy in *Father of the*

Blues (1941) said: 'jazz grew up around the fox trot and is still mainly supported by it'. Probably using foxtrot as a dance typifying all modern walking jazz dances, it bears out the contention that jazz was a music designed for dancing. The foxtrot was introduced to the ballroom in the USA *c*. 1914. Said to have got its name from comedian Harry Fox[1] who introduced a few trotting steps into his routine at the *Ziegfeld Follies* in 1913 to a ragtime accompaniment. The early foxtrot actually included trotting steps but these soon disappeared in favour of the smoother gliding steps which led to its popularity. It came in on the heels of similar dances like the horse trot and the fish walk. Also partly derives from the Bunny Hug.

There could be an alternative derivation from the slang word 'fox' – a beautiful (and usually clever) girl; from the earlier 'foxy'.

Frankie and Johnny A ballad claimed to be based on the true story of the shooting of her lover, the 16-year-old Albert Britt, by Frankie Baker (both black) on 15 October 1899 in a lodging-house at 212 Targee Street, St. Louis, Missouri. That is the St. Louis version. The story, from whatever source, has slipped into American folklore as well as into jazz. In its original form, as *Frankie and Albert*, it has given rise (according to John Lomax) to some 300 variant versions. The ones he prints in *American Ballads and Folksongs* (1934) came from Texas *c*. 1909 and a composite effort from Connecticut, North Carolina, Mississippi, Illinois, Tennessee and Texas as sung by Leadbelly. Some authorities put it even further back in time; one suggestion for the origin being the shooting of Charles Selver by his wife Frankie at Toe River

---

[1] According to black actor Tom Fletcher (in *100 years of the Negro in Show Business*) bandleader Hughie Woolford told him that, during an engagement at the Trouville Restaurant, Long Beach, Long Island, he had written a melody (which he called the *Trouville canter*) to which Harry Fox, a patron of the place, added some dance steps. It was, according to Woolford, *his* idea to call the dance the Fox trot, and he was indignant to find later that Fox was using the dance in his act without any acknowledgement to Woolford.

in North Carolina in 1831 (Townley). Lomax seems to support the more modern source and reported that Frankie Baker was still alive and well at the time of his writing (1934).

Generally assumed to be of annonymous authorship, it did, however, first appear in print in 1904 under the title of *He done me wrong* with both words and music credited to Hughie Cannon. It was published as *Frankie and Johnny* (a publisher's title) in 1912 and was then popularized by the Leighton Brothers. It has had numerous jazz recordings, notably by Ethel Waters (1938), Duke Ellington (1945) and Erroll Garner, as *Frankie and Garni* (1947). Charley Patton recorded it as *Frankie and Albert*. The same melody (with a different lyric) is used in *Stack o' Lee blues* recorded by Ma Rainey in 1925.

Franklin Street Street in the old Storyville district of New Orleans which ran parallel to Rampart Street. Renamed Crozat Street.

Freak Something technically or aurally unusual, an unorthodox style; freak sounds as exploited in New Orleans brass playing, later in the Ellington band. Probably the intended usage in Morton's *Freakish* (1929) or King Oliver's *Call of the freaks* (1929). The word, as with many jazz terms, also has a possible sexual connotation, in this case queer or sexually freakish, thus used in George Hannah's *Freakish blues*.

Also a fanatic for anything, a compulsive collector and follower, a jazz freak – one with an overriding passion for jazz.

Free jazz An attempt to put a label on to a form of post-Parker and avant-garde jazz in which all the old disciplines and restrictions had been relinquished. The musicians are free to play as they wish, entering into a form of instant collaboration with each other. The first appearance of the expression 'free jazz' is thought (by German jazz writer Joachim Berendt) to have been as the title of an album by the Ornette Coleman Double Quintet in 1960.

Sometimes referred to as 'free form' jazz.

French Quarter The older, creole section of the city of New Orleans. See under **New Orleans** for a fuller description.
Book: *The French Quarter* by Herbert Asbury. New York: Knopf, 1936.

Friars' Inn, Friars' Society Orchestra Popular Chicago nightspot; a favourite haunt of the Chicago underworld. The famous Friars' Society Orchestra that played there in the 1920s was a pioneering white group which included Paul Mares – cornet; Leon Roppolo – clarinet; and George Brunis (from New Orleans) – trombone. They later renamed themselves the New Orleans Rhythm Kings. Title confusions arise over such as *Friars' Point Shuffle*, a Red McKenzie piece recorded by the Jungle Band and the Louisiana Rhythm Kings in 1928, and by Eddie Condon's Chicagoans in 1939 and possibly having some connection with the above. There are other titles which could refer to the small town of Friars Point, Mississippi, but there is no known connection between this and Red McKenzie (Townley).

Front Common musical parlance for leading a band, i.e. standing in front of it, and looking good. Often has the added connotation of a star soloist being the leading attraction of a band that was not necessarily his own, e.g. Louis Armstrong in the 1930s fronted the bands of Carroll Dickerson, Luis Russell, Les Hite, Charlie Gaines and Chick Webb, among others, with recordings issued as by Louis Armstrong and his Orchestra.

Front line The melody instruments of the band: trumpet, trombone, clarinet, etc., who generally stand or sit in front of the rhythm section.

Fulton County Jail Prison in Atlanta, Georgia, which had poignant associations for many itinerant blues singers and musicians. Situated at 208 Hunter Street, it was built in 1888, replacing an older establishment, and was considered a model prison – nicknamed the 'Big Rock'. It was not used after 1961 and was demolished in 1969.

Funky Funk is a word that has had many meanings in its time, deriving from various sources; for example, a state of fear or panic (noun), commonly used in the phrase 'blue funk', probably Flemish in origin *c*. 1700; or (verb) to back out of anything, to fight shy, to be afraid. Another stream of meaning, and the one that seems to have got into the jazz language, derives from an older English usage, *c*. 1600, meaning a strong smell or stink, later (*c*. 1700) (verb) to cause a strong smell or stink. This became transferred to the noxious habit of smoking *c*. 1700, to blow smoke on a person, to polute the air with smoking. In this sense the word slipped into the American language and we find it being used in New Orleans in the late 1800s as a description of the lowest of dives, presumably evil, unpleasant, odorous places, the cause of the stink being in one well-known instance candidly attributed to 'funky butts', that is smelly buttocks or bottoms. (See also entry following.) At this stage it does not seem to have been applied directly as a description of the actual music. This happened later, probably in the 1950s, when it came into usage among black musicians to describe an uncomplicated, heavy, rhythmic music full of feeling, reflecting the heritage of the blues and gospel song and the African background. It seems never to have been used in a derogatory sense, but simply as a plain but strong assertion of the gutter side of jazz and hence an important word.

Some cool, totally intellectual jazz could thus be described as not being funky. The best and most lasting of modern jazz was that which retained its funkiness and at least some elements of what has been described as 'the melancholy, pensive, or bittersweet mood associated with the blues' (W & F), jazz with sadness, depth, feeling; earthy, blues-tinged; but not necessarily archaic. In this sense generally used adjectively, that is, funky. More loosely employed by persons not sensing its true import, it is sometimes used to mean merely groovy or swinging but this is less common as groovy itself suffices here. What the jazz addict really looks for in his music, the thing that differentiates it from the classical stream, is its funkiness, the spirited passion that was born in the 'funky' atmosphere of the New Orleans jazz haunts and which is the important undying element even in an age of much more intellectual jazz-making.

Funky Butt Hall Its familiar name deriving as explained above, the Funky Butt Hall was a dance-hall and dive in New Orleans at 1319 Perdido Street between Library and Franklin Streets, known as the place where the Buddy Bolden Band frequently played and where they were heard by many of the subsequent trail-blazers of jazz such as Louis Armstrong. It was not, at that time or any time, its correct and official name, which was then Kinney's Hall, but it was almost always referred to as the Funky Butt. Earlier still it had been more respectably known as Union Sons Hall (or Masonic Hall) and, by the 1930s, it had lived down its intermediate past and become a church, now gone and the site of the Louisiana State offices.

Fusion A name coined for the coming together of any two or more distinct styles of music (not necessarily involving jazz) producing a separately identifiable and often new form. The distinction of having used it first in a jazz context might belong to record producer Denis Preston, who in the mid-60s put together a jazz quintet led by alto saxophonist Joe Harriott and a quintet of Indian musicians led by Calcutta-born violinist John Mayer. He called the resultant music 'Indo-Jazz Fusions'.

Gallion Name for the slaves' quarters on the old plantations, and subsequently, after the abolition of slavery, used more widely for any section of a city or town where the black people lived a segregated life. Used in such titles as: *Down in the gallion*; *Out of the gallion*.

Galveston A name which frequently crops up in blues history, a place often passed through by itinerant musicians. The terminus of six railroads and an important port of entry on the Gulf of Mexico. City on Galveston Island, Texas, to the south of Houston, population *c*. 67 000, and named after Bernado de Galvez, a Spanish governor of Louisiana, in 1780.

Gas Originally suggesting a degree of emptiness, flatulence, even untruth; the interpretation has gradually become perverted to mean (from *c*. 1945) in common Harlem parlance, anything considered exceptional, successful; a 'real gas', applied to other things and people outside jazz. By the 1950s it was especially used in jazz, verbally, to gas or be gassed; as a noun, gasser. A word that came in with the modern jazz era, it also carries the implication of being really cool and far-out, specifically applied to the more progressive element of jazz and other things from *c*. 1935. Also used of something that is very funny; occasionally still retains the old meaning, from *c*. 1850, of boastful talk.

Gate (1) From *c*. 1935 a term used to express admiration of an exceptional musician, especially in the swing era. Possibly a shortened form of alligator, particularly when applied to a devotee of jazz, but could have some connection with the neatly coined phrase 'to swing like a gate', the natural attribute of a hep, with-it musician of genuine ability.
(2) A musicial engagement or date, in this case presumably deriving from gate, meaning the money collected at the door, or the number of spectators contributing to the amount, gate-money; a term in use from *c*. 1890 (F & W). Could be, as has been suggested, a portmanteau of 'engagement' and 'date' or, more directly, referring to the gate as the means of entry. Rarely encountered.
(3) Used in a more general, friendly way as simply a greeting to a fellow musician or jazz enthusiast, to any hep person, generally male. Said to have been originated by Louis Armstrong and later popularized in this way by comedian Jerry Colonna leading to the salutation 'greetings, Gate'. By 1953 gate had clearly extended its range to mean a desirable male companion, a date in the broader slang sense of the person one is due to meet. In a song of that year, by Burton Lane and Dorothy Fields, *Have feet, will dance* occur the lines: 'Have dress/will press/have shoes/will shine/have date/with a gate/at nine'.

Gatemouth (1) A gossip; one who knows and talks about everyone else's business, and
(2) from an associated line of thought, one with a big mouth, like a gate; or a large 'swinging' lower lip; a name affectionately applied to Louis Armstrong in his early days; an alternative to Dippermouth, superseded by Satchelmouth which eventually became Satch. Title: *Gatemouth* (New Orleans Wanderers) (1926).

Geechie An American nickname which is duly given to those who come from Georgia, specifically black people from the Ogeechie River area, likewise the most southerly part of South Carolina and its islands; just as all Geordies come from Tyneside and all Scouses from Liverpool. Also used in a rather condescending way by urban blacks when referring to their country cousins from the rural South in general. The best-known bearer of the name was one Julius 'Geechie' Fields (b. 1903) who is remembered for his mutinously growling trombone work on some of the Morton Red Hot Peppers recordings.

Georgia Southern state of the USA, north of Florida on the eastern seaboard, bordered on the west by Alabama, on the north-east by South Carolina. A part of the Deep South, sentimentally alluded to in various songs such as *Georgia on my mind* by Hoagy Carmichael (1930).

Georgia grind see **Ballin' the Jack**

Georgians Name of a group prominent in the British jazz-cum-dance-band scene of the 1930s. Originally formed in 1934 on the band-within-a-band principal by Lew Stone in order to feature the solo talents of his trumpeter Nat Gonella. Gonella was known as 'The Georgia Boy' owing to his success with the song *Georgia*, which he performed in an imitation Armstrong style; hence the Georgians. The idea just pre-dated similar small band efforts by Goodman, Shaw and Dorsey. The group, mainly performing as a variety act playing the Archer Street style with rather more genuine jazz than most (thanks to Gonella's presence), largely consisted of members of the Stone band. It continued thus until 1935, when Nat Gonella and his Georgians began an entirely separate existence. There was an earlier group of this name in America, an offshoot of the Paul Specht band, in the 1920s, directed by trumpeter Frank Guarente.

Ghost bands Faintly pejorative term for those bands which operate under a deceased leader's name. The most famous of all ghost bands was the one which toured for many years, using a succession of leaders, as the Glenn Miller (d. 1944) Orchestra, under the rigorous control of the Glenn Miller Estate. Other posthumous bands have been those using the names of Jimmy Dorsey (d. 1957) (for a long time led by the extremely competent trumpeter Lee Castle – real name, incidentally, Castaldo), Tommy Dorsey (d. 1956), and Ted Heath (d. 1969). In general terms, what they do is to play the original band's arrangements for a large proportion of their programmes, alongside other material arranged 'in the style of'. They also attempt, where possible, to include musicians who worked, no matter how briefly, under the leaders concerned. Ghost bands rely strongly on nostalgia, an element not to be under-rated in popular entertainment.

A better-than-average ghost band was fielded in 1985 – The Count Basie (d. 1984) Orchestra, led by one-time Basie trumpeter Thad Jones. Thad Jones (brother of Hank, pianist; and Elvin, drummer) is a considerable musical and physical personality in his own right, with long experience of leading a big band, in particular the excellent orchestra for which he and drummer Mel Lewis were jointly responsible.

Ghost notes Explained by Fred Elizalde (in 'Ghost Notes' – *Melody Maker*, July 1927) as: 'notes which are fingered but not played – or played with varying degrees of softness – so that their presence is felt or implied more than actually heard.' Applied to the piano, these quietly played notes, in the prevailing harmony, have a rhythmic · function, imparting an additional element of swing. Used by ragtime composers like Joplin as a quietly-heard inner harmony and a favourite device of Morton's. Also known as shadow notes.

Gig (1) Has come to mean (in jazz and other musical fields) most specifically an engagement, particularly a one-night engagement, a one-night stand for a musician. Earlier it had been the name for a good time or party at which music, generally of a jazz kind, would have been used; then of a jam session, jazz party or simply a gathering of musicians and fans; the one-off character of these leading to its professional meaning. Used in these senses, either as a noun or a verb; a gig or to gig.

In recent years the meaning tends to have spread beyond the single engagement to include a residency or a season in one particular location. It has also spilled out from music to be used of any job, any piece of gainful employment.
(2) Used in the swing era (less frequently) to describe a jazz arrangement or performance that met with strong approval.

Gin mill Loosely used in general American slang for any kind of speakeasy – an establishment in which bootleg and home-made liquor were sold during Prohibition (1920–1933). More strictly originally applied to such places where the 'gin' (or other alcoholic drink) was actually made on the premises. Became part of the jazz vocabulary with the recording of *Gin mill blues* by Joe Sullivan in 1933. Widened in application to mean any cheap sort of bar or nightclub – or any drinking place, especially one of low repute or standards.

Gitbox Occasional slang for a guitar, used amongst musicians.

Go To be in full swing; really going, really swinging. First used in this sense *c.* 1919 and became common again *c.* 1946 in bop circles. (See also **Gone**.)

Golden leaf The best quality marijuana.

Gone Probably deriving from the alcoholic or narcotic imputation of being 'real gone', that is, under the influence; and from **Go** (as above), it suggested a performer or performance where involvement in an intense and satisfying creation was the only thing in mind. From this, in modern jazz performance,

it has the wider meaning of being generally cool, hip, exciting, satisfying.

One of its peculiar uses is well illustrated in a famous joke: A hip musician presents himself at the lunch counter and says: 'Gimme a piece of apple pie'. The girl replies: 'The apple pie's gone'. 'Crazy' says the musician, 'gimme *two* pieces.'

Goof (1) A stupid or ineffectual person.
(2) To make a mistake, blunder.
(3) A narcotics addict. To be in a dream world under the influence of narcotics. Goofy-butt – a marijuana cigarette.

Goofus A novelty instrument available in the USA in the 1920s, a part of the prevailing campaign to make learning and playing an instrument as painless as possible and within reach of the unmusical. In 1927, the British firm of Keith Prowse were retailing a goofus at £2.12.6 (£2.63p or *c.*$3.65). Shaped like a saxophone, it was mechanically a cross between an accordion and a mouthorgan. The player blew through a tube to supply air for two rows of chromatic brass reeds, of the harmonica type, one to each note. It covered two octaves with a key for each reed, arranged in the same position as a piano keyboard.

A distinguished exponent of this undistinguished instrument was the bass-saxophonist Adrian Rollini and the sound of the goofus can clearly be heard on some of the 1927 recordings he made with Red Nichols; for example *Feelin' no pain* (15 August, 1927). Rollini featured the instrument in a group known as the Goofus Five (a small unit from the California Ramblers) which made a number of recordings between 1924 and 1927. It was a weak-sounding instrument, somewhat like a leaking accordion, with no obvious future in jazz and it only had a short novelty vogue. A goofus in good condition would probably have considerable rarity value today.

The name goofus, presumably applied in a spirit of friendly mockery, was not the real or original name of the instrument, but it is the one that has stuck with

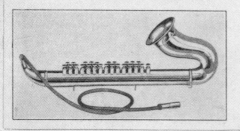

This rare and short-lived instrument as advertised and popularized *c.* 1928. (*Melody Maker*, Dec. 1928)

The promises of the developing Phonograph of the 1890s. (*Melody Maker*, April 1928)

THE NEW YORK TIMES, SEPTEMBER 26, 19...

Jazz: The Herman Herd

'Real Shouting Band' at Basin Street East

By JOHN S. WILSON

The 16 men in Woody Herman's current orchestra, whose past appearances in New York have been at the Metropole, where circumstances require that they play while standing stretched out in a long line behind the bar, are now working on the more normally organized bandstand at Basin Street East.

Chairs are provided but the band continues to play standing up because Mr. Herman believes that this is one of the factors that has contributed to making the present Herman Herd the most provocative big jazz band to appear in many years.

This is, as Mr. Herman accurately describes it, "a real shouting band," a band that sets feet tapping and heads bobbing. Spurred by a brilliant rhythm section (Nat Pierce, piano; Chuck Andrus, bass; Jake Hanna, drums), it generates an electric excitement and a sense of overwhelming power that can be compared only with the band of the mid-nineteen-forties with which Mr. Herman rose to the top ranks of jazz.

Roars Through Passages

It is, for the most part, a young band and it roars through passages with ...

the line and the trombonists at the other could not hear each other and had to sense what was happening at the other end.

The subsequent success of the band — it is booked through September, 1964, and is already set for 12 weeks in Las Vegas in 1965 — does not mean, Mr. Herman said, that there is any revival of interest in big bands. "This is not something that's ...ning with the band busi...

Woody Herman

The Herman Herd arrive in England (detail from the 1964 programme).

it. Originally manufactured by the French firm of Couesnon et Cie, the makers called it the Couesnophone – which no-one outside France could pronounce with certainty.

See: 'The Goofus and How to Play It' by Adrian Rollini in *Melody Maker* (March, 1928).

Gospel, gospel music, gospel song A fringe activity in terms of actual jazz *performance*, but a factor of immense importance in the history and development of jazz. As far as we can tell, the first instrumental jazz, and in particular its close cousin ragtime, was richer in European elements than obviously African ones. From the very beginning (whenever that was), however, the vocal spirituals of the slave and ex-slave black population of the southern United States seem to have been steeped in Africanisms. This is in spite of the fact that deep in the background of American black religious song is a collection of hymns – which began circulating in the colonies in the 1730s – by English non-conformist minister Dr Isaac Watts (1674–1748). Clearly, the untutored but harmonically adventurous singing, together with – to European ears – an unorthodox approach to rhythm, and a level of vocally expressed emotion unheard in any English church, set it apart immediately from any other kind of music then known. It began to impinge upon the outside world in the 1870s when the Fisk Jubilee Singers, of the black Fisk University, started what turned out to be a very long series of national and then international tours. They deliberately diluted their style, but it was still strong enough to be both exotic and moving to those who were experiencing black music for the first time.

It is tempting to assume that somewhere along the way both the exultant and the lamenting elements in black spiritual music must have become woven into the fabric of what developed into jazz itself. Certainly early and classic ragtime, as they have come down to us, expressed nothing beyond a restrained gaiety in one

direction and a wistful melancholy in the other. Also, the first records (1917) by the Original Dixieland Jazz Band – which are all we have to go on – are at most 'jolly', hinting at no emotional expression whatever. Yet by the mid-20s, by which time King Oliver and Louis Armstrong were safely on record, overt emotionalism was an essential ingredient of a worthwhile jazz performance, and that element must have come from somewhere. The sanctified side seems a likely source.

No matter how alike some jazz and some gospel music might sound to the jazz enthusiast, their functions, their performance and (in all but the rarest cases) their performers, have maintained a rigid segregation. That does not mean, however, that spiritual music has been exclusively other-worldly. During the early 19th century, when there was a considerable movement of fugitive blacks from the slave-owning South to the relatively liberal North, along the so-called 'Underground railroad', many spirituals contained encoded references and messages. *Crossing the Jordan* and *Going to the Promised Land* could be taken either way; those involved could be counted upon to understand.

Gospel music first began to impinge upon the ordinary jazz *aficionado* in the late 30s when records by Sister Rosetta Tharpe (1921–73) started to circulate. Powerfully backed by the rocking piano of Sammy Price, these were to all intents and purposes jazz performances. Sister Rosetta Tharpe (Rosetta Nubin) was a remarkable woman who nearly got away with working on both sides of the dividing line. She somehow contrived to have a career in sanctified music and to be a popular vocalist with such bands as Cab Calloway's and Lucky Millinder's, and only fell foul of her religious supporters during the 50s after a blues recording session. Only Aretha Franklin, in the pop music world, has bettered Sister Rosetta's ability to appeal to two audiences. In that context it is interesting to note that the *Georgia Tom*, of secular and often scurrilous blues fame during the 1920s, is the same man as Thomas A. Dorsey who, after a final religious conversion in 1929 (he had experienced twinges on previous occasions), composed a body of black spiritual music as influential in its way as the work of Dr Isaac Watts over 200 years earlier. *Precious Lord* is probably the most famous, most often performed, of his religious songs.

A gospel ingredient of a very deliberate, powerful kind came into jazz during the 1950s, when musicians like Horace Silver, Junior Mance, Les McCann, Bobby Timmons (all pianists) and Cannonball Adderley began to incorporate recognizably 'churchy' or 'Amen corner' elements into their playing.

Gospel performers who have appealed to jazz listeners include Mahalia Jackson; Marian Williams; Professor Alex Bradford; Sister Rosetta Tharpe; Marie Knight; Brother John Sellers. There is of course, an immense, commercially rich, separate gospel world alongside, and sometimes spilling over into pop music, but that lies beyond the scope of this book.

Gotham Popular name for New York. (See **Apple**, **Big Apple**.)

Gramercy Square Residential area of Manhattan, New York on Lexington Avenue between 20th and 21st Streets. Gramercy was also the name of a Manhattan telephone exchange, before all-figure, forgettable numbers superseded memorable names. Perpetuated into the digital era by fond memories of (and several records by) the Gramercy Five, the small band which Artie Shaw led intermittently during the 40s.

Gramophone (1), Phonograph It was a happy coincidence that the gramophone came to maturity just as ragtime and jazz were emerging. The commercial availability of this immutably recorded documentation did much to speed up the spread of jazz throughout the world, and offered a permanent chronicle of much

that would otherwise have been lost for ever. The only regret is that jazz and ragtime did not avail themselves of the cylinder or disc even earlier than they did.

Thomas Alva Edison (1847–1931) patented his cylinder phonograph in 1877 and put it into production in 1878. The cylinder was not easy to duplicate and, although Edison stubbornly ensured its survival until *c.* 1929, it was soon rivalled and gradually ousted by the flat disc patented by Emile Berliner (1851–1929) in 1888. The wax disc was firmly established by *c.* 1899, revolving at speeds from around 70 to 83 rpm (78 rpm was standardized *c.* 1918) with the 10-inch record coming in about 1901 and the 12-inch in 1903. In theory, therefore, jazz, in its formative stages, could have been reasonably audibly documented nearly 20 years earlier than it was. Certainly the work of the ragtime pioneers could have been captured.

From 1878 to *c.* 1924/5 recordings were acoustic, relying on the power of soundwaves themselves to move a cutter, a diaphragm and a needle. By 1925 electrical recording via a microphone was established and the degree of realism was substantially increased. The quality of recording was, in fact, better than the means of reproducing it. Old recordings from these early years, transferred to LP, are often of surprising quality. Recent 'stereo' transfers, done by new digital techniques and presented on the BBC by Australian sound engineer Robert Parker, have been incredibly revealing, allowing us to hear, for example, Bessie Smith almost as if just recorded. The long-playing record began to supersede the 78 rpm disc in the early 1950s; the stereo record came in the late 1950s; and digital recording in the 1980s.

The honour of having the first true jazz recording issued is generally accorded to the Original Dixieland Jazz Band with *Livery stable blues/Original Dixieland one-step*, recorded by RCA Victor in February 1917. Columbia had actually recorded them a few weeks earlier but had rejected the results, which were issued much later. Jazz, in its purest form, had been kept off record partly because it was still not widely accepted, partly because it was a black music. The first issued recording of a black jazz group is generally considered to be Ory's Sunshine Orchestra – *Ory's Creole trombone/Society blues* issued on the Sunshine label in 1921. The first known vocal blues record was *Crazy blues* sung by Mamie Smith who recorded it on 10 August 1920, accompanied by a small group of black musicians. She became the first black artist to have anything resembling a hit record. The cautious General Phonograph Corporation, having changed the song title from its original *Harlem blues*, was taken by surprise when the record sold over 100 000 copies in its first month. The whole industry was suddenly made aware of a new source of talent and an equally new market. Jazz got into its stride with the recording made in Chicago of the King Oliver Jazz Band, with Louis Armstrong, in March 1923. The recording of New Orleans jazz in New Orleans itself seems not to have started until March 1924, when several groups, including Johnny De Droit's New Orleans Jazz Orchestra, were recorded by the Okeh Company.

However, recordings had been issued before 1917 that at least bore some relation to jazz or were the progenitors of it in ragtime or cakewalk shape. The instrument that best impinged itself on the primitive equipment was the banjo with its sharp, incisive tones. A great number of banjo solos and ensembles were recorded from the beginning of the century onward. They help us to establish that much of the nature of ragtime derived from the natural syncopations of the banjo.

The piano, on the other hand, remained a difficult instrument to record right up to the electrical era, owing to its many overtones; so satisfactory piano recordings came at a somewhat later date, thus missing the classic ragtime era.

The voice was always feasible, though often made unrecognizable, on record and the gramophone was invaluable in capturing the sounds of early singers, including many stars of British music-hall and American vaudeville. There was not a great call for blues singers amongst the white record-buying public, but recordings by black artists issued as 'race' records became a viable proposition, creating their own black market in the 1920s and became the forerunners of the later rhythm and blues boom.

Books: (general) *The Fabulous Phonograph* by Roland Gelatt (1956, rev. 1977); *From Tin-Foil to Stereo* by Oliver Read and Walter L. Welch (1959, rev. 1976). (See also **Recording** and **Discography**.)

***Gramophone, The* (2)** British monthly magazine, devoted mainly to record reviews, founded in 1923 by Compton Mackenzie (with an editorial office in Herm) and controlled by him and his brother-in-law Christopher Stone until 1950. It is predominantly interested in classical music but has maintained a section of jazz record reviews noted, in later years since *c*. 1957, for their unhysterical reliability and objectivity. For many years in the quirkish hands of Edgar Jackson (1895–1967); later reviewers have included Brian Rust, Charles Fox, Alun Morgan and John Postgate.

Book: *The Gramophone Jubilee Book 1923–1973* edited by Roger Wimbush. 310p. London: Gramophone Publications, 1973.

Gramophone Record, The, Gramophone Record Review Monthly British magazine founded by Leonard Hibbs (a pioneer jazz enthusiast and erstwhile editor of *Swing Music*) in October 1933. Later it became *Gramophone Record Review* and was published from Cornwall by the St. Anthony Press in St. Austell. Like *The Gramophone* it was predominantly of classical leanings but always had good popular and jazz coverage, Hibbs' policy in this respect being enthusiastically continued by Peter Gammond who edited the magazine from 1966 to 70, after it had been taken over by the Hanover Press and became *Audio Record Review*. In 1970 it was amalgamated with *Hi-Fi News*. Jazz and blues were covered at various times by such authorities as Jeff Adam, Ernest Borneman, Peter Clayton, Arthur Jackson, Albert McCarthy, Paul Oliver, and Stan Britt, Mike Butcher, Burnett James, and latterly Ken Hyder.

Grand Terrace Café, ballroom, nightclub at 3955 South Parkway in Chicago, opened on 28 December 1928. It was managed by one Edward Fox but was reputedly controlled by Joe Fosco of the Al Capone gang and was much used by the underworld. In its early days it was for whites only, though the entertainment was black. The first band to be booked there was led by Earl Hines who remained in residence until the old club closed in 1937 and moved to new premises at 317 East 35th Street, where the old Sunset Café had been.

Greasy spoon A low-class, cheap, unsavoury restaurant. Often colloquially shortened to spoon with the 'greasy' implied. Likewise the term greasy vest is also used, hence vest – a dirty establishment. Grease – a general slang expression for food.

Great Adjective used as liberally and as indiscriminately in jazz as elsewhere in the musical and sporting fields. What constitutes a 'jazz great' is clearly a matter of opinion. In some cases, for example Armstrong, Ellington, and Parker, there is little argument. Over-liberal use does, however, diminish the accolade. Likewise, when applied to a performance. Not of any particular significance. More regular form in the modern jazz field since *c.* 1950 is 'the greatest', but that has also spread into other areas of endeavour. The use of the word great, to mean excellent, superb, wonderful, goes back to *c.* 1839 in the USA.

Greystone Ballroom see **Detroit**

Groovy see **In the groove**

Growl A technique applied to the playing of wind instruments, particularly cornet, trumpet or trombone (occasionally saxophone and clarinet), whereby a growl in the throat of the player is transmitted through the lips and mouthpiece and into the tone of the note being produced, which then itself takes on a growling, dirty, slightly menacing quality. It was a trick much favoured in the early Jungle Band, Cotton Club days of the Ellington orchestra and much used, even over-used, by such players as Bubber Miley and Joe 'Tricky Sam' Nanton. Employed with restraint, it can add a tremendous effect, particularly if the growling frequencies are accurately timed with the pulse of the music. There are particularly good examples in recordings of early Ellington pieces like *Black and tan fantasy* (1927) and *Creole love call* (1927). The technique has been applied to the saxophone by players like Coleman Hawkins and Ben Webster.

Guitar There is a tendency to look upon the guitar as a 'modern' interloper into jazz, the instrument that replaced the banjo. At a certain stage of jazz history it did but there was much interplay of the two instruments before that. The banjo has a historic place in the plantation-style black music, its percussive sound and lively rhythms very much a part of the jig, folk-dancing tradition, right up to the cakewalk era. While the banjo might be said to be the ragtime rhythm instrument of the two, the guitar was very much the instrumental partner to the early blues singers. It was an integral part of that stream of music that came in from Latin America and the West Indies; and it had a far stronger and longer history in European music than the banjo, which only came in as a sort of novelty item from the boom period of black-faced minstrelsy.

The guitar was probably used in more early emergent jazz groups than is commonly imagined, particularly when those bands favoured a violin lead and a wider use of stringed instruments. In the well-known early photograph of the Bolden Band the guitar is prominently there.

In the early days of recognizable jazz the banjo tended to be in more frequent use because it stood up better to the competition of the lead trumpet, trombone, clarinet format and because it came out better via early recording techniques. Indeed, both within and without the jazz field the banjo was probably the most popular recording instrument of the turn of the century period, its sharp tones coming through the murky technical qualities of the recordings with maximum effect. It was therefore the dominant rhythm instrument in the early days of jazz and was deemed by revivalists to be the only genuine sound. In fact, many of those who played the banjo during this period may well have moved to it from the guitar. As recording techniques and guitars themselves became better, the banjo was quickly pushed out again during the 1927–30 period in favour of the much more flexible and less assertive guitar which fitted in better with the woodwind/saxophone leadership of the 1930s.

The changeover time is pretty coincidental throughout jazz. Fred Guy in the Ellington band was playing banjo in the late 1920s recordings and occasionally even as late as 1936, but by 1930 was mainly using guitar. This was repeated throughout the jazz world.

At this point the banjo, then guitar, was mainly supplying a steady strummed accompaniment with an occasional brief break or even more occasionally something imaginative written in by somebody like Ellington or Morton. Gradually a new race of guitarists asserted themselves and started to provide a more mobile and varied background. Prominent names include: Eddie Lang (1902–33), Teddy Bunn (b. 1909–78), the Belgian-born gypsy Django Reinhardt (1910–53), Lonnie Johnson (1899–1970).

The really enormous change in the guitar's fortunes came with the arrival of electrical amplification. By as early as the mid-1920s experimenters were working on ways of giving the guitar a louder voice by electro-magnetic means, but it was not until the early 1930s that any real

progress was made. Eddie Durham (b. 1908), guitarist, trombonist, and arranger, seems to have evolved a set-up whereby he had a separate microphone, placed as close as possible to the sound-hole of the guitar, connected to a separate amplifier and individual speaker operating outside the public address system of whatever venue the band – Bennie Moten's – was working in. This enabled him to play what were probably the first fully audible guitar solos in a big band setting in public. By the mid-1930s the external, detached microphone had been replaced by the electric pick-up on the guitar itself, and the instrument was ready for its final liberation. As far as jazz is concerned, liberation was personified by Charlie Christian (1919–42) whose brilliant inventiveness, unparalleled technique and instinctive understanding of the amplified guitar not only made it a virtually new instrument, but laid some of the foundations of what soon became modern jazz, or bebop. He achieved national and international prominence with Benny Goodman, and had already made an incalculable contribution to jazz history by the time of his death from tuberculosis in 1942.

From Christian onwards, the amplified guitar has been a front line instrument in jazz. Among its greatest practitioners are or have been Wes Montgomery (1925–68), Jim Hall (b. 1930), Barney Kessel (b. 1923), Grant Green (b. 1931), George Barnes (1921–77), George Benson (b. 1943), Kenny Burrell (b. 1931) and Herb Ellis (b. 1921). Les Paul (b. 1916) (real name Lester Polfus), while a fine guitarist in his own right, has been responsible for many technical improvements to the amplified instrument. The potentially biggest advancement in actual playing technique has taken place only in the mid-1980s, with the emergence of the young guitarist Stanley Jordan (b. 1960). Thanks to the extreme sensitivity of modern pick-ups, Jordan is able to play the guitar more like a piano, getting the notes with the fingertips of both hands, which strike the strings as well as merely stopping them.

Gut bucket A bucket used in barrel-houses and cheap drinking dives to catch the drippings or 'gutterings' from leaky barrels. The term gutbucket, like barrel-house, became synonymous with the sort of lowdown, gully-low (as low as possible), gutty or gutsy jazz played on such premises.

Half-valve A technical device, sometimes known as cocked-valve, favoured by (mainly) cornet players whereby one of the pistons is depressed to a point about halfway through its travel, partly restricting the passage of air and resulting not in a change of pitch but an alteration in timbre. The effect is a somewhat choked sound, quite unlike that produced by any kind of mute. Rex Stewart was its chief exponent, while Ruby Braff, Digby Fairweather and others have made occasional use of it. Valve-trombonists find it an agreeable addition to their armoury and Bob Brookmeyer employs it with exceptional skill.

Halfway House Roadhouse on City Park Avenue at Pontchartrain Boulevard, New Orleans, flourishing from 1914 to 30. Abbie Brunies, after fronting Papa Laine 'Reliance' units at Bucktown and Milneburg, led the famous Halfway House Orchestra there from 1919 to 26. Clarinettist Leon Roppolo played in its ranks.

Hamfat A somewhat derogartory term, deriving from the theatrical 'ham'; a performer of inferior, over-obvious, corny, abilities; 'hamfat bands' – lacking in skill or subtlety. More jocularly used in minstrel circles and probably in that spirit by the Harlem Hamfats, a pleasantly lively but uncomplicated group led by trumpeter Herb Morand from *c.* 1935, recorded extensively 1936–8.

Hard bop The kind of bop music strongly associated with black performers in New York, Chicago and Detroit and seen as more virile and forceful than the slightly more detached and laid-back West Coast and predominantly white schools. Bop, particularly as played by black musicians, that is funky, has soul and, to some degree, reinstates the hot element of earlier jazz. Has been described as 'extrovert modern' and was consciously played and written about from *c.* 1954/5. Aggressive music, not shy of hinting at gospel music and rock, played by such musicians as Art Blakey. Sonny Rollins and Freddie Hubbard. Much of the Blue Note label's late-50s, 1960s output was hard bop.

From 'hard' – intense, aggressive as in hard swinging, hard driving.

Harlem A predominantly black district of New York. The southern limit was Central Park at 110th Street, the northern the Harlem River and 158th Street, the eastern the East River and the western Amsterdam Avenue, but the area is spreading. For a time, in the 1920s and 1930s, the cultural capital of black America and very much the centre of New York jazz activities from the 1920s.

Harlem started to turn into a black district in the early years of the 20th century when black real-estate men, notably Philip A. Payton, were able to persuade white property owners to rent their apartment houses to black tenants. This became possible because of over-ambitious speculating and building in the locality. Whites had not spread up Seventh Avenue in anything like the numbers that had been anticipated, and many of these expensive buildings were under-tenanted. This happened at precisely the moment when the black population of New York was outgrowing its old location on the West Side. Given the chance, thousands of black families migrated up to Harlem, a movement augmented in the First World War when many Negroes came up from the South and the West Indies to work in factories and shipyards. The segregation seems to have arisen spontaneously as the result of the bitter rivalry between the newcomers and already well-established work forces such as the Irish and Italians. Harlem, around 1918 (according to Ethel Waters – *His Eye is on The Sparrow*) was not then an exclusively black area except in a narrow region from 130th to 140th Streets between Fifth and Seventh Avenues. 125th Street, later to be Harlem's main thoroughfare, was still a white boulevard in 1918 and blacks were not welcome there except as the occupiers of the 'Peanut Gallery' at the Alhambra Theater where many black artistes appeared.

135th Street, subject of an early Gershwin one-act opera – originally *Blue Monday* (1922); renamed *135th Street* (1925) – was the site of a black club called Leroy's where such pianists as Willie 'The Lion' Smith built their reputations from 1918 onward.

The first all-coloured theatre in Harlem was The Crescent, opened in 1909. It was small, holding only about 200 people. It later became a cheap movie house. The more famous Lincoln Theater, which held nearly 1000, opened a few doors away on 135th Street in 1915 and became the main Negro venue.

The Lafayette Theater at 2227 Seventh Avenue between 131st and 132nd Streets, built in 1912, had a more controversial history and at first was dominated by white entertainers and segregated its audience. The city council issued a decree against this and eventually the theatre was taken over by black entertainers. In 1913, a black orchestra first played in the pit.

By 1919, Harlem was a well-established and defined Negro quarter with numerous clubs featuring the newly formed 'jazz' groups. The top entertainment spot became the famous Apollo Theatre at 253 West 125th Street. Clubs that flourished into recent times and the present included Count Basie's at 2245 Seventh Avenue at 132nd Street; Well's next door to Basie's; The Prelude at 3219 Broadway at 129th Street; and Small's Paradise at 135th Street and Seventh Avenue. (See also **The Cotton Club**.)

Harlem jazz is a name given to the kind of jazz that Harlem developed commercially, a straightforward, swinging style; generally excitable, sometimes merely showy. In its better aspects the sort that has slotted into the mainstream category.

The Harlem Renaissance, which lasted for much of the 1920s and continued for a while into the 30s, lies beyond the scope of this book. Suffice it to say here that black exponents of all the arts – poetry, drama, the novel, painting, music and ballet – flourished briefly but gloriously for a few years giving rise to an optimism among liberal black Americans which was sadly to prove unfounded.

The lasting contribution of Harlem to the nomenclature of jazz was the powerful, swinging, two-fisted yet articulate piano style often referred to as Harlem stride piano, whose practitioners were many but whose undisputed masters were James P. Johnson, Willie 'The Lion' Smith and Fats Waller.

Harlem Hamfats see **Hamfat**

Harney One of the originators of commercial ragtime, popularizing it onstage in New York *c*. 1896, and author of an early ragtime instructor was Benjamin (Ben) Harney (1871–1938). Although not highly rated as a performer or composer (in spite of having written the popular *Mister Johnson* and *You've been a good old wagon*) he remains important as a controversial name in the early black v. white contest. Most early ragtime historians, sometimes biased in their desire to prove that white could be as good as black, generally referred to him as a white performer and bracketed him with William H. Krell, composer of the first published rag, and later Joseph Lamb, as a leading white protagonist of the art; cf. Blesh: '1896 was the year when a twenty-five-year-old white player, Ben Harney, from Middleboro, Kentucky, made the first public New York hit with piano ragtime'. It had become accepted that Harney was white and he was thus portrayed, as a white Keystone Cop, on the cover of *Mister Johnson (turn me loose)* holding the collar of his small black vaudeville partner Tom Mack.

The white claim is, however, strongly contested in several places, notably in Alec Wilder's *American Popular Song* where he quotes Eubie Blake in support: 'In discussing Harney's life and work with me, Eubie Blake observed, "He's dead, and all of his people must be", before adding: "Do you know that Ben Harney was a Negro?" I hadn't known, of course. Mr Blake then provided a clue to Harney's great success as a performer. "Ben Harney played ragtime like white people played it".' Willie 'The Lion' Smith also baldly refers to him as 'a great Negro ragtime originator'.

It is probably now correct, on this evidence, to accept Harney as black. Photographs show him to be of the definitely light-skinned type (one who is often referred to as a creole), who could easily pass as a white. If you could do this in those difficult times it could only be a help to a stage career, and therefore you would take advantage of it.

Harp In jazz, any reference to the harp rarely means the heavenly or seven-pedalled concert variety, but the blues musician's mouth harp, or harmonica (curiously enough, the name 'mouth organ', insisted on by Larry Adler for the chromatic instrument he uses, is seldom encountered). That said, however, there is one very famous jazz record on which the conventional harp is played extremely effectively by Casper Reardon – *Junk man*, made under Jack Teagarden's name in 1934. Other performers on the orthodox harp who have produced acceptable results in a jazz setting include

David Snell, Dorothy Ashby, Corky Hale and Adele Girard (wife of clarinettist Joe Marsala).

Hawthorne Occurs in the title *Hawthorne nights*, a tune written by saxophonist/composer/arranger Bill Holman for Zoot Sims. Zoot spent much of his adolescence in Hawthorne, on the outskirts of Los Angeles.

Hayfoot, strawfoot Hayfoot – the left foot; strawfoot – the right foot. Old mnemonic for helping illiterate army recruits remember which was which; cf. Townley, an old English expression dating back to around 1757, but used in the USA certainly as far back as Civil War times. During the Second World War Duke Ellington recorded a monumentally dull song of this title.

Head arrangements Ensembles, riffs, etc, worked out at rehearsal but not written down. The Ellington band was famed for working by this method, hence the lack of written scores. Head riffs, etc.

Hear Me Talkin' To Ya Essential jazz book, sub-titled 'The Story of Jazz by the men who made it', edited by Nat Shapiro (b. 1922) and Nat Hentoff (b. 1925). It is an anthology of quotes from and interviews with jazz musicians and provides an unmatched source of horse's mouth material for all subsequent jazz researchers and enthusiasts. Published New York: Rinehart, 1955; London: Peter Davies, 1955.

Heebie jeebies Dance of the 1920s period made famous by the dancer known as Butterbeans – of the duo Butterbeans and Susie (Mr & Mrs Jodie Edwards). It was of the 'eccentric' variety, a fidgety step during which Butterbeans scratched himself in time to the music. Louis Armstrong, who had worked with Butterbeans, recorded a piece of this name in 1926 but, although the lyrics (which Armstrong is said to have improvised) mention a dance, it is more likely it was the older meaning of the word –

The famous Quintette of the Hot Club de France (l to r) Stephane Grapelly, Joseph Reinhardt, Louis Vola, Django Reinhardt & Roger Chaput (or Pierre Ferret) c. 1934. (Photo: Will Collins & Lew Grade Ltd)

Irving Mills

WILFRID VAN WYCK *present*

HUMPHREY LYTTELTON
AND HIS BAND

**Sunday
June 26th**

**Royal
Festival Hall**

General Manager : T. E. BEAN

SOUVENIR PROGRAMME   PRICE ONE SHILLING

'I've got the heebie jeebies', i.e. feeling 'nervous, frightened or worried' (W & F) – that inspired it. The dance lent something to such post-twist dances as the Bug and the Monkey (Stearns).

Hep, hip There was hardly a modicum of difference in the use of these near-synonyms, one of which tended to supplant the other. Hep, which is the older, in wide use from *c.* 1915 but coming into musical use in jazz *c.* 1925 particularly in the swing and jive areas. In the broadest sense to 'get hep' simply meant to be aware of what was going on, particularly of the latest fashions and developments. Armstrong, in 1924, talks of 'beginning to get hep' by mingling with the older musicians. The hep person, whether performer or enthusiast (more especially the latter) who is completely *au fait* with, immersed in, aware of, jazz and its latest goings-on. By 1938 or so the more synthetic hepcat was in use for a devotee of jazz and swing. As W & F say, it is usually used by people who didn't really know what hep meant; or used in a derogatory way by those who did.

By *c.* 1945 hep had been almost entirely replaced by hip which initially meant very much the same thing – in the know, with-it, used widely in connection with all kinds of modish things like dress, drink and drugs, but also specifically applied to the jazz *aficionado* who was aware of the latest developments, not a square; one who, to use another slang phrase, 'collared the jive'. Thus hipster became the modern equivalent of the hepcat: 'When it was hip to be hep, I was hep', from *I'm hip* (a song by Dave Frishberg).

But hip gradually took on more political and sociological undertones; hipster or hippie was a member of the beat generation, cool and protesting. Probably through mis-applied newspaper usage, 'hippie' in particular came to mean 'dropout'; a dropout is often the very reverse of hip.

Hep to the jive In common terms, aware,

worldy-wise. In jazz, occasionally but now archaic, having an appreciation of jazz – particularly swing era period *c.* 1935–42.

Herd Collective name given to various bands led by clarinettist Woody Herman (1913–87). Herman joined the Isham Jones band in 1934 and when Jones retired in 1936 some of the band, with the addition of another half-dozen or so, formed the first Herman band. There seems to be some confusion as to whether this was ever officially billed as a Herd. The nickname seems to have first been given in a review in *Metronome* in 1939. At this time they were generally billed as 'The band that plays the blues'. The band's great hit *Woodchoppers Ball* came in 1939, a number that promoted the fast 12-bar blues and sowed a seed of rock 'n' roll. The band broke up during the war and the official First Herd gradually emerged in the early 1940s, deserting the old Dixieland style for a modern sound, with Neal Hefti and Ralph Burns arrangements, Dave Tough as foundation on drums and, by 1943, a five-piece trumpet section. The First Herd's hits were *Apple honey* and *Caldonia*, but it broke up, through internal stresses in the band, in December 1946. The Second Herd, with an even more modern sound, known as 'the Four Brothers Band', was formed in 1947 and broke up at the end of 1949, Herman having lost $175 000 on the venture. The Third Herd was formed in 1953, touring Europe in 1954. Its fortunes are difficult to follow as the name was applied to various scratch bands during the 1950s. In 1959 the Herman Band had a British tour, with a nucleus of American musicians supplemented by nine British, the group being billed as the Anglo-American Herd. A 'Fourth' Herd was formed in 1962 and operated under such names as the Stampeding Herd. Herman emerges every now and then with a new 'herd', the numbering system having been long discarded.

Hickory House An establishment in

Manhattan, at 144 West 52nd Street, famous from the 1930s and through the 50s for its steaks and its jazz. Its bandstand was completely surrounded by its circular bar. The house band in the period around 1937 usually consisted of clarinettist Joe Marsala, normally with his brother Marty Marsala on trumpet, and often with his wife, Adele Girard, on harp (how the harp was heard over the din of an active bar is hard to imagine). Buddy Rich played drums there before he was out of his teens, and in the late 30s the Hickory House held informal Sunday afternoon jam sessions, with members of whatever bands were in town sitting in.

Another celebrated long-term residency occurred when Marian McPartland was booked to play the Hickory House for a few weeks with her trio in 1952, and stayed, almost without a break, until 1960. Billy Taylor was resident there in the 1960s.

Hides Another musicians' name for drums, particularly the drum sets (or traps) used in jazz and dance bands. (See also **Skins**, **Traps**.)

High-hat, hi-hat Percussion device in which two cymbals mounted one above the other on a music stand-like contraption can be made to clash together by the top one being lifted and released by a foot pedal, thus giving the drummer another rhythm option. Used mainly in dance-type music for a steady sock rhythm.

Hip see **Hep**

Hip chick A with-it young lady, especially one who is into jazz, particularly modern jazz.

Histories of jazz In the early days of jazz emergence (as discussed under **Bibliography**) a number of books appeared that (quite excusably) missed the mark by not understanding the nature of the new phenomenon. It was quite a while before any sustained histories of jazz

appeared (not until it had a history, in fact) and a worthy early attempt was made by Robert Goffin – *Aux Frontières du jazz* (1932), though this might be classified, like the Ramsey & Smith *Jazzmen* (1939) as an 'appraisal' rather than an organized history. It was Goffin's 1948 *Nouvelle histoire du jazz, du Congo au bebop* (translated in USA as *Jazz from the Congo to the Metropolitan* and in UK as *Jazz from Congo to Swing*) that provided many young enthusiasts in the 1940s with their first textbook. After this there was an eager demand for the enthusiastic but restricted *Shining Trumpets: a History of Jazz* by Rudi Blesh (1899–1900) published in 1946 but not available in London until 1949 and frantically imported by fact-starved British jazz fans. Its limited view of the traditional jazz world was greatly enlarged by the Barry Ulanov (b. 1918) *History of Jazz in America* (1952) which took a wider and more up-to-date look at things, dealing with the bebop areas as fully and romantically as it dealt with earlier material. This was well complemented by the Keepnews & Grauer *Pictorial History of Jazz* (1955) which came as a literal eye-opener to many jazz fans.

A welcome paperback from Penguin – *Jazz* by Rex Harris (1904–85) – was well organized but also suffered from a narrowness of view. The first really scholarly and unbiased study came in the shape of the Marshall Stearns (1908–67) *The Story of Jazz* (1956, various reprints). Gunther Schuller's (b. 1925) *Early Jazz* appeared in 1968 as Vol. 1 of a proposed history. The next volumes have been keenly awaited to offer further analytical insight. There is news from OUP of possible activity from the American guru in the near future.

At the moment the best all-round practical history is probably the latest: *The Making of Jazz* (1978) by James Lincoln Collier, offering the objective sense and fairness that a standard book on any subject should possess. Books that deal with smaller sections of specialized jazz history will be found listed under the appropriate subject.

Hitch's Happy Harmonists Mainly known to jazz collectors as the group in which a youthful Hoagy Carmichael made his first appearance on record in his own *Washboard blues* (1925). The Happy Harmonists were a group that hailed from Evansville, Indiana, originally organized by Curt Hitch (dates unknown) in 1922, when they played in a ragtime-cum-dixieland style in local spots. Their reputation spread through Southern Indiana, and they were asked to make two sides for Gennett in September 1923 and again in 1924. It was after a date at Indiana University that they were joined by Carmichael who was then running his own band there, the Collegians. By then they were playing in an early swing or sock style, a result of local contacts with the Wolverines. Group disbanded in 1930.
See: 'Hitch's Happy Harmonists' by George W. Kay in *Jazz Journal*, Volume 9, Number 4 – April, 1956.

Hitchy koo Traditionally said to be the phrase uttered in America while admiring and caressing an infant, the American equivalent of 'diddums den', etc. With the word 'baby' coyly transferred to any young girl, sweetheart, lover and general object of affection, it became used as a term of endearment in the Tin Pan Alley ragtime song days as in the popular 1912 song by Muir, Abrahams and Gilbert *Hitchy Koo* – 'Oh! ev'ry ev'ning hear him sing, It's the cutest little thing . . . got the cutest little swing, Hitchy Koo, Hitchy Koo, Hitchy Koo.' It became, like 'It's a bear', one of the post-war catch phrases. Title aptly appropriated by producer Raymond Hitchcock for a series of *Hitchy Koo* revues 1917–20.

Hokum Anything done in music, or other fields of entertainment, purely to please the lowest tastes; hackneyed, trite, insincere tricks or phrases. From the more general American slang usage for flattery, insincerity, empty nonsense.

Holler A song of a folky, bluesey nature delivered in a declamatory way. A less sophisticated forerunner of the blues-shouting of the Kansas City school. Earlier, a way of singing developed by the untutored blacks as worksongs: each occupation – cotton picking, bale toting or harvesting – having its own distinctive kind of holler. The jazz equivalent of the city street-criers art. The early hollers are full of the slides and elisions that became the common language of the blues. Sometimes the holler was a means of giving orders to the slave workers which they then repeated in chorus. Hollers were frequently solitary field shouts to break the monotony of lonely work, but almost certainly they also carried coded messages about secret meetings, escapes and other items of black information.

Honky-tonk, tonk A low class sporting-house, of the kind to be found in early jazz days in New Orleans and Chicago (e.g. the Red Onion) supplying crude drink and unsophisticated food. The main purpose of its existence, however, was usually the gambling room at the back, which also acted as a bookmaker's establishment. Most honky-tonks (as described by Jelly Roll Morton and others) were filthy places. Many of the clients were lousy and the women available (another part of the service) were of the lowest possible character. The entertainment was usually provided by a pianist, generally one must assume on a very inferior class of piano, and there was plenty of money to be made in tips. Morton recalls that he considered it a bad night if he didn't take $100, but we are not obliged to believe him. Such places attracted struggling musicians to New Orleans from all over the South and beyond. The general noise in the honky-tonks, led, so legend tells, to a fairly rumbustuous and insensitive mode of playing, with a good rhythm and heavy bass, otherwise known as barrelhouse and a first cousin to the boogie-woogie style. Even Morton discarded his delicate left hand in such circumstances and pounded it out with the rest. (See also **Barrelhouse**.)

Hoof, hoofer Humorous synonym for foot; hence to dance, to hoof it used of either professional or social dancing. But a hoofer is more specifically a professional dancer, a term originally applied in clog-dancing, later jazz and tap-dancing days, later to any stage dancer.

Hooked To be addicted to something, especially narcotics, but also used in a wider sense. Hooker – one who gets others hooked. Also a prostitute, from hookshop – a brothel.

Hoosier One who comes from the state of Indiana, and thus, snidely, a hick. There was a novelty group, with jazz overtones, in the 1940s called The Hoosier Hotshots.

Hopes Hall Name given to two dance halls in New Orleans, one at the corner of Burgundy and Spain Streets which was much used by jazz bands from *c.* 1900 (also called, at times, Esperance Hall or Jackson Hall); and one at 922 North Liberty Street, HQ of the Society of Friends of Hope (also known as Jackson Hall and Co-operators Hall).

Hop-head An opium addict. Hop meaning opium, term used since *c.* 1887. Also used since *c.* 1898 for any narcotic drug as well as opium. Abbreviated to hop, also used for an addict; also hop-fiend (scarcer). Hopjoint – an opium den or (from hops rather than hop) cheap saloon. Hopped-up – under the influence. Hop Alley – a street in the Chinese quarter of some towns where opium dens would probably be located.

Horn By no means the simple, straightforward word it seems as, to begin with, it seldom refers to any member of the legitimate horn family as understood by classical musicians since these are relatively uncommon in a jazz context. It used to be applied to brass instruments generally; then it came to include more or less any wind instrument. Finally, it is now quite possible to hear of a piano being a particular musician's horn. One cannot help feeling, however, that at least some of these have crept in through the medium of print rather than as direct speech. Horn seems to be more frequently encountered on the backs of record sleeves and in magazine articles than in conversation.

Horsecollar Fairly common nickname amongst early black musicians, but the only bearer at all widely known was one William Roscoe 'Horsecollar' Draper, who is to be found in some of the Morton Red Hot Peppers line-ups. Presumably, name usually given to one who was an enthusiastic drinker from the American slang use of 'horse-collar' meaning the head on a glass of beer.

Hot An adjective in early use to describe jazz-based music of an exciting, emotionally-charged and often fast kind. We find the word associated with black music making, which even then presumably had a hint of jazz flavouring in it, as early as 1842, the year when, in a dancehall frequented by black people, George Foster heard a band consisting of a fiddler, a trumpeter and a drummer. In *New York By Gaslight* (1850) he describes the trumpeter as producing 'red-hot needles of sound' (significantly, he also found music of a similar nature being played in Philadelphia). Hot continued to be associated with early jazz by its pioneer promoters and publicists: 'the hottest band in town', the word implying something novel and exciting, with, perhaps, just a remote suggestion of the sexual connotations that the word also carried. From initially merely conveying the physical excitement of jazz it began, at an early stage, to have more explicit meaning for the jazz enthusiast. A hot tone was achieved, pre-eminently on the trumpet, by a fast vibrato, biting attack, rhythmic propulsion and a generally fullblooded approach. To its early devotees, the best jazz, the true jazz, was hot, and the word came to be synonymous with jazz without further reference to the music. In France it may have been 'le jazz hot' in full, but on the formation of the Hot Club de France in 1932, jazz was amply implied without specific mention. Likewise, numerous organizations in the US, which gathered under the banner of the United Hot Clubs of America in 1935. No doubt the impetus for this usage had been given in the previous decade by such recording bands as Louis Armstrong's Hot 5s and 7s, and Jelly Roll Morton's Red Hot Peppers. The use of 'hot' declined as the fashion for using the word 'swing' gained ground; the vernacular cannot support too big a vocabulary at any one time, and not only did hot become old fashioned, but its users revealed themselves to be old fashioned as well.

Nowadays it is a useful critical device for pointing up the contrast with cool – part of the eternal problem of trying to describe sound in words. It is also used, with a kind of defiance, by die-hard adherents of the original hot music (that of the 1920s and early 1930s, and music played today in imitation thereof) as a public avowal of where their allegiance lies.

Hot Club de France An association of enthusiasts formed in Paris in 1932 with the object of promoting 'real jazz'. A leading light was the critic Hugues Panassié (1912–1974) who maintained strict and prescribed ideas as to what 'real jazz' was, and edited its magazine *Jazz Hot*, published from 1935–9 in French and English. The honorary President was Louis Armstrong.

This loosely-knit society acquired a musical focal point in the extraordinary all-string quintet which came into being in 1934. The unique band consisted of Stephane Grappelly (as his name was then spelled) on violin; the Belgian-born gipsy guitarist Django Reinhardt, two rhythm guitarists – Joseph Reinhardt (Django's brother) and Roger Chaput – and the bass player Louis Vola. Nothing remotely like the Quintette Of The Hot Club Of France had ever existed in jazz before, and Reinhardt's virtuoso style in particular was quickly recognized almost everywhere as the first contribution to jazz which owed nothing whatever to

American and Afro-American culture. Django, in other words, was the first European to bring something of his own to the music.

Hot Lips A publicity man's creation, one would guess, not imaginative enough to be natural jazz slang. Inevitably applied to trumpeters, the best-known bearer of the name was Oran 'Hot Lips' Page (1908–54), a performer whose style was undoubtedly hot. The American-based British trumpeter Henry 'Hot Lips' Levine (b. 1907) was a degree or two cooler.

Hot man A short-lived term applied, in the early days when jazz was an emergent novelty, to one who played jazz or hot music as opposed to the straighter, sweeter variety.

Hot News One of the earliest British magazines to deal with jazz and the first to devote its pages entirely to the subject in a serious manner; it first appeared in April 1935 (sub-titled 'Rhythm Record Review') just a month after the rival *Swing Music*. The founder and editor was Eric Ballard (founder of No. 1 Rhythm Club in 1933) who published it from Wakehurst Road, London, SW11. It managed, for its time, to print some informative articles by such contributors as Hugues Panassié and trombonist Preston Jackson and to report on the rather confused jazz-cum-dance band scene of the times. Sadly, it did not manage to raise much circulation, lost money in its rivalry with *Swing Music*, and only lasted until October.

Hotsie-totsie, hotsy-totsy Slang expression of *c.* 1925 meaning that everything was satisfactory and pleasing, in other words, hunky-dory. Not of special jazz significance except that it was taken up by a group of white New York jazzmen with an opportunist manager, *c.* 1927–30, who worked under the name of Irving Mills and his Hotsy-Totsy Gang.

House rent see **Rent party**

Humph Straightforward abbreviation of Humphrey Lyttelton (b. 1921), British trumpeter and bandleader (also cartoonist, broadcaster, author). Lyttelton had the unique distinction of coming into traditional jazz from a background of Eton (his father was a Master and he a scholar) and the commissioned ranks of the Guards. He was also, at the time of his musical emergence, a recent ex-art student (Camberwell) which was all too much for members of the British press, who wrote about him not because he was a good trumpet player – a matter to which they were quite indifferent – but because he was good copy. This was, in fact, of some benefit to the British jazz scene, giving it wider public coverage than it might otherwise have had. His early playing days were spent in George Webb's Dixielanders, which he quickly came to dominate and then to take over. He began leading his own band in 1948 and can claim an unbroken career as leader ever since.

Books: *I Play as I Please* by Humphrey Lyttelton. 200p. London: MacGibbon & Kee, 1954; Jazz Book Club, 1957; Pan Books, 1959. *Second Chorus* by Humphrey Lyttelton. 198p. London: MacGibbon & Kee, 1958; Jazz Book Club, 1960. *Take It From the Top* by Humphrey Lyttelton. 164p. London: Robson, 1975: and various books on jazz.

Ibrahim, Abdullah The adopted Islamic name of South-African born pianist and composer Dollar Brand (b. 1934). It somehow remains necessary to point this out since, in spite of his having used the newer name ever since his conversion to Islam in 1968, he is almost invariably billed, getting on for 20 years later, as 'Abdullah Ibrahim – Dollar Brand'.

Icky An inbred nonsense language used by and only comprehensible to members of the Ben Pollack band. It was the invention of the banjoist Dick Morgan whose nickname was Icky. Also one who played in a sweet, corny manner; a dance band musician.

Imperial Orchestra Early New Orleans dance orchestra led by the clarinettist Manuel Perez from 1901–8.

Improvisation Long considered to be one of the key elements of jazz. Most early reference-book definitions laid emphasis on jazz being an 'improvised' music. Taking the word in its literal sense of 'something made up on the spur of the moment' there is logically only a small amount of jazz that is wholly improvised and what there is (in jam session form, etc) often ends up by sounding rather chaotic. True improvisation only succeeds generally by having simple foundations. The nature of jazz-making, as with any other music, implies a constant repetition of ideas, phrases and tricks so that most jazz performances have some stable basis; and, as jazz progressed, it became less improvised and more arranged. Duke Ellington wrote of his disbelief in unadulterated improvisation: 'it is my firm belief that there has never been anybody who has blown even two bars worth listening to who didn't have some idea about what he was going to play, before he started.' This is not to say that jazz should not have a spontaneous improvisatory nature. Jazz improvisation is the style of playing rather than the substance; the feeling of freedom that comes through not being tied to the written note or strict time units even in arranged jazz.

In spite of the foregoing, there is now much music being played of a totally improvised nature. A great deal of it is performed by musicians who are or have been known in a jazz context, and there is therefore a tendency to consider this extreme manifestation of free-form playing as yet one more extension of jazz. The freer it becomes, however, the more it resembles the completely improvised sounds coming from some artists whose roots are in academic, 'straight' or classical music. Some promoters, writers and commentators prefer the single category 'improvised music' to cover both these phenomena.

In Dahomey First all-black show to be seen in London (1903) in which Bert Williams and George Walker introduced the cakewalk and ragtime strains to England.

In the barrel A phrase, used as a song title, meaning 'stoney broke'; literally having no clothes and wearing a barrel.

In the groove Phrase introduced in the swing era of the 1930s and 1940s, meaning to play in a settled, swinging, gratifying way that comes over infectiously to the audience. Presumably derived from the gramophone world. Phrase extended beyond purely jazz meaning nowadays. Hence groovy (1) being in the mood and spirit to play 'in the groove', or simply feeling in a blithe state generally; (2) in sympathy with the music; (3) another form of 'in the groove'. 'Musically, groovy is real good' (Quoted from Longstreet: *The Real Jazz* (1956)).

Ivories An early term, perhaps more current in Tin Pan Alley but around in some jazz titles. Literally – the piano keys (once made of ivory), hence the piano. 'To tickle the ivories' – play the piano. A tickler – a pianist.

Jack the Bear Early black pianist, real name John Wilson, who came from Pennsylvania. Regular rent-party operator, also a dope addict and gambler, who was latterly active in Harlem. His own party piece, entitled *The dream*, was actually written by Jess Pickett. Immortalized in Duke Ellington's *Jack the Bear* (1940).

Jam, jam-session George Frazier elaborately defined a jam-session as 'an informal gathering of temperamentally congenial jazz musicians who play unrehearsed and unscored music for their own enjoyment' – and who could say better than that, taking or leaving the 'temperamentally congenial' bit? That's the ideal and what has come over on one or two occasions on record. Most jazz musicians enjoy the freedom that jamming allows, the essential rhythmic drive, the lack of inhibition. Frequently it was a highly

competitive activity and something of a gladiatorial atmosphere could be generated when two or more exponents of the same instrument were involved. The commonest examples were the 'tenor battles' which took place in Kansas City in the 30s and 40s between local heroes and visiting challengers. Any musician who, in the opinion of the onlookers, trounced another, was said to have carved or cut him. Earlier 'jam' had occasionally been used as a synonym for jazz.

Jazz (1) Distinctive musical style, deriving from an Afro-American background, that took shape around the beginning of the 20th century in the USA; and, by the 1920s, had become effectively influential in most of the Western world and subsequently the dominating voice of popular music.

Jazz has no melodic or harmonic

features that could not be found in other musical spheres. Its distinguishing trait is a propulsive and flexible rhythmical movement, the result of melodic phrasing that falls around the normal main beats of the bar; frequently anticipating them and giving the music an exaggerated sense of impetus and a dominating rhythmic exhilaration, regardless of tempo. In the pioneering jazz styles the beat was relentlessly emphasized and though later jazz styles have been self-consciously inclined to diminish the rhythmic dominance, underlying inflexible rhythms under variously syncopated phrasing is still the distinguishing mark of jazz. There is no exclusive jazz 'rhythm' but it tends to favour a steady 2/4 or 4/4.

Jazz grew in an organic, unorganized way in America as the accidental juxtaposition of several musical strains. Its beginnings must be found in the folk-music of various nationalities that was taken to America by various early settlers: much of it from the British Isles, notably Scotland; from European countries like Hungary where there was a strongly individual gipsy folk tradition; with the syncopated rhythms of the Spanish cultures getting there by the roundabout route of the West Indies and South America. The intensely rhythmical dance-music played on the fiddle (an instrument common to all European cultures) soon found a typically American form. Styles developed in strongly musical areas like the Appalachian Mountains running down through Virginia and North Carolina spread through the cotton country of the South, where black musicians took up the strains and added their own musical traditions.

America evolved its own distinctive folk styles during the 19th century, these emerging strongly in the composed works of the early 1800s through the jig strains of *Arkansas traveller* and *Turkey in the straw* and the more commercial songs like *I wish I was in Dixie's land* and the works of Stephen Foster and others. The most distinctive elements in these were the major-keyed and frequently syncopated

melodic lines; much of the character surely arising from what historians have called banjo rhythms, by now an established instrument.

These were the kind of dances and songs that were now re-imported to Europe in the minstrel shows of the 1860s and later commercialised by the bands led by Sousa and others, conditioning the world for the appearance of jazz. The first emergence of music that strongly emphasized the syncopated elements effectively was in the shape of ragtime, one of the offshoots of jazz growth in a form that could be composed and written in the traditional way.

These points should be made in order to balance the over-strong assertions in much early jazz writing that jazz was simply a music that descended directly from African sources. What becomes apparent, as a more objective view is taken, is that the black slave population of America, amongst whom jazz acquired its richest growth, was now able to sow the seeds of its own traditions in the very rich soil of an already strong American tradition, the two combining to create jazz. It is impossible that jazz could ever have become what it is without the African influence, but it is also arguable that it could not have developed the same way anywhere else but America. Jazz, as a matter of historical fact, did not develop in Africa – as might be expected. Neither were the people who developed it any longer Africans; they were native Americans by this time in history.

There is little point today in prolonging the white versus black arguments that used to rage. It is easy enough to prove that much of the best black jazz – Morton, Bechet, Armstrong, Bessie Smith – has a more natural freedom of expression than some carefully chosen white examples. But jazz was equally developed by both white and black musicians, the best white musicians proving in no way inferior, even if their work is differently flavoured.

To put any accurate date to the actual creation of jazz is impossible. Its early history is completely obscured by the lack

Programme of the first British Tour in 1958 which included Ella Fitzgerald, Oscar Peterson, Dizzy Gillespie, Roy Eldridge, Stan Getz, Coleman Hawkins, Sonny Stitt and others.

YOUNG MAN

WITH

A HORN

BAKER

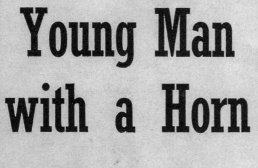

Young Man
with a Horn

by Dorothy Baker

A JAZZ BOOK CLUB PRODUCTION

5

JAZZ
BOOK CLUB

reinganum

of documentation and informed interest. Africans were coming into America from 1609 onward and must, as is human nature, have been creating their own music from early times. The simmering cauldron of jazz could only be savoured when the Civil War and the emancipation of the blacks allowed jazz to be publicly and commercially promoted, providing, at the same time, a natural audience for it.

Jazz (2) Adoption of the name 'Jazz' has centred in the histories around the story of the Original Dixieland Jazz Band. It is substantially reported that it was during their engagement at Schiller's Café in Chicago in 1916 (then billed as Johnny Stein's Band) that the word 'jass' was first applied to the music when an inebriated 'retired vaudeville entertainer' leapt to his feet in excitement and yelled out: 'Jass it up, boys!'. 'Jass' up to then had been a Negro word brought from the South and fashionably current in the Chicago underworld, with the specific connections with sexual intercourse and its enjoyment. Nobody up to then had thought to apply it to the newly-emerging music; but it was logical enough that they should. It is reported that this useful customer was hired every night to be there and cry out 'Jass it up, boys!'; and thus the band quickly became known as Stein's Dixie Jass Band. Later at Reisenweber's in New York, it was billed as the Original Dixieland Jass Band; then, perhaps as the result of a printer's error (a key influence in many etymological innovations) as the Original Dixieland Jasz Band (thus printed in an advert of the times), then as 'jaz' and finally 'jazz' – an eye-catching combination of letters.

The strong evidence of the word being used in its sexual connotation and generally to engender excitement and action suggests that it might have been applied to musical entertainment at an obscure earlier time. But it was probably not until after its adjectival initiation in connection with the ODJB that it was widely used as a noun. W & F give jazz as meaning

'copulation; the vagina; sex; a woman considered solely as a sexual object', thus used by Negroes in the South 'since long before 1900'. Lafcadio Hearn had come across the verb in creole patois c. 1875 used in its derivative sense of to excite, titillate, speed things up. Its early usage might have been a pejorative one, the speaker indicating that it was no more than degraded, brothel music. Jelly Roll Morton said that he had actually used it specifically in connection with his music from c. 1902.

A theory that the word derived from the name of a singer, one Jazzbo Brown, seems to be apocryphal and not supported by any authority beyond certain early fairy-tale histories. While the word jazz-bo, a sharply dressed person, goes well back to pre-jazz times.

The word 'jazz' came into wide use in the 1920s – as in 'jazz it up', 'jazz that thing' and so on; but it was not immediately accepted as a noun. It was also applied to such things as dress, people in the sense of colourful, in an exaggerated way 'jazzy'; some of this going back to the 'jazz-bo' origin.

Jazz (3) Short-lived, influential American publication sub-titled 'a quarterly of American Music', published 1958–61. It was concerned with the definition and function of jazz and was a much quoted source as in Robert S. Gold's *A Jazz Lexicon* (1964).

Jazz at the Philharmonic (JATP) Jazz promotions which were the brainchild of Norman Granz (b. 1918). He was originally a film editor at the MGM studios and, just before Army service 1941–4, started organizing 'all-star' jam sessions in Los Angeles in 1940, involving such names as Nat 'King' Cole, Oscar Moore, Willie Smith, Lester Young, Lee Young and Don Byas. As a sideline to film editing he decided to continue these ventures and organized a jazz concert at the Philharmonic Auditorium in Los Angeles on 2 July 1944 from whence the name *Jazz at the Philharmonic* was culled.

Granz said that he 'wanted to prove

that there was money to be made in good jazz' not only for himself but for the people who played it. Those who helped him to prove his theory on that occasion were Illinois Jacquet, Nat 'King' Cole, Joe Sullivan, Barney Bigard, Meade Lux Lewis, Les Paul, J. J. Johnson, Joe Thomas and others. His success as a producer later had him described as the 'Sol Hurok of Jazz'. He firmly pursued a non-racial policy and in several cities refused to present a JATP concert before a segregated audience. In 1949 he received the Russwurm Award for his contribution to race relations. Following the success of the original concert he took his 'show' on a tour of the Western states and Canada in 1945 but it was a financial failure until some of the records made by the unit began to have success and JATP got out of the red. He supervised a film of the musicians called *Jammin' the Blues* which got an Academy Award nomination. Supervising his own records, he released them on the Philo and Asch labels, then from 1948–51 on Mercury. In 1951 he recovered all the rights and issued his own Clef label, adding the Norgran logo in 1954. In 1957 these were all combined on the Verve marque. The JATP unit began to tour in Europe in the late 50s, the first British tour being 2–18 May 1958, with Oscar Peterson, Ella Fitzgerald, Dizzy Gillespie, Roy Eldridge, Stan Getz, Coleman Hawkins, Sonny Stitt and others. Later there were tours in Japan and Australia, Granz also organizing concerts by such artists as Peterson and Duke Ellington. Granz returned to record-production in the early 70s with the Pablo label.

Jazz band No firm claims can be made as to which was the first musical ensemble that had the right to call itself a jazz band. Probably there were many such groups (early bands-within-bands) playing in the brass bands of the 1880/90s. One of the first organized bands (of jazz shape) known to the authors of *New Orleans Jazz* (1967, rev. 1984) was led by guitarist Charlie Galloway (*c.* 1860–1916), who frequently played with Buddy Bolden from *c.* 1889. 'Papa' Jack Laine's *Reliance Bands* from 1892 were among the first to become known as genuine jazz-playing groups. Thereafter, jazz-styled bands proliferated, though the actual term Jazz was not in common use until after *c.* 1917.

Jazzbo, jazzbow Makeshift instrument that was made up of a kazoo inserted into an old saxophone or trombone body to give it amplification and a fuller tone. It was used in the spasm or early blues bands. Brownie McGhee (b. 1915) used the device and there is a photograph of him with jazzbo in operation – see *Black, Whites and Blues* by Tony Russell. London: Studio Vista, 1970.

Jazz Book Club Valuable enterprise started in 1956 by the British publishers Sidgwick & Jackson under the editorship of Herbert Jones, aided by a distinguished panel of selectors. The first issue (No. 1) was *Mister Jelly Roll* by Alan Lomax and it continued to put out some six to seven titles a year until 1967, 66 issues in all plus various optional extras, building up, for those who took advantage, a valuable reference library of jazz books.

The regular issues (1–66) were:
1956
1. *Mister Jelly Roll* by Alan Lomax (1950)[1]
2. *American Jazz Music* by Wilder Hobson (1939)
3. *We Called it Music* by Eddie Condon & Thomas Sugrue (1947)
4. *I Play As I Please* by Humphrey Lyttelton (1954)
1957
5. *Young Man With a Horn* by Dorothy Baker (1935)
6. *King Joe Oliver* by Brian Rust & Walter C. Allen (1955)
7. *Satchmo* by Louis Armstrong (1953)
8. *Jazz in Perspective* by Iain Lang (1947)
9. *Big Bill Blues* by William Broonzy & Yannick Bruynoghe (1955)

---

[1] Date of first publication.

LONDON

1. Archer Street
2. Asman's (New Row)
3. Club 11 *
4. Conway Hall
5. Denmark Street (Tin Pan Alley)
6. Dobell's (old) *
7. Flamingo *
8. 100 Oxford Street
9. Ray's
10. Ronnie Scott's (Old Place) *
11. Savoy
12. Roundhouse p.h.
13. Kettner's, Romilly Street
14. Pizza On The Park (Knightsbridge)
15. Pizza Express, Dean Street
16. Ronnie Scott's (Frith Street)
17. Dobell's (present)

* No longer in existence

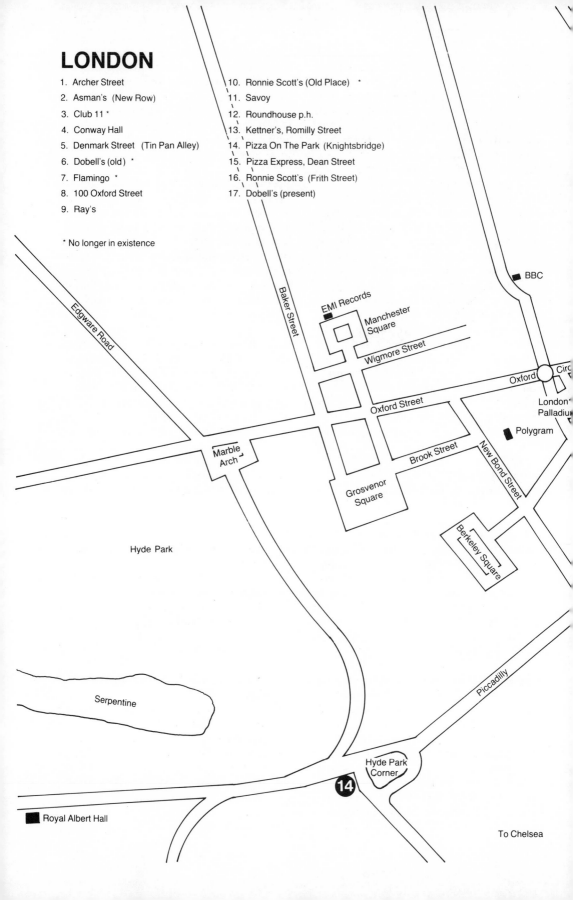

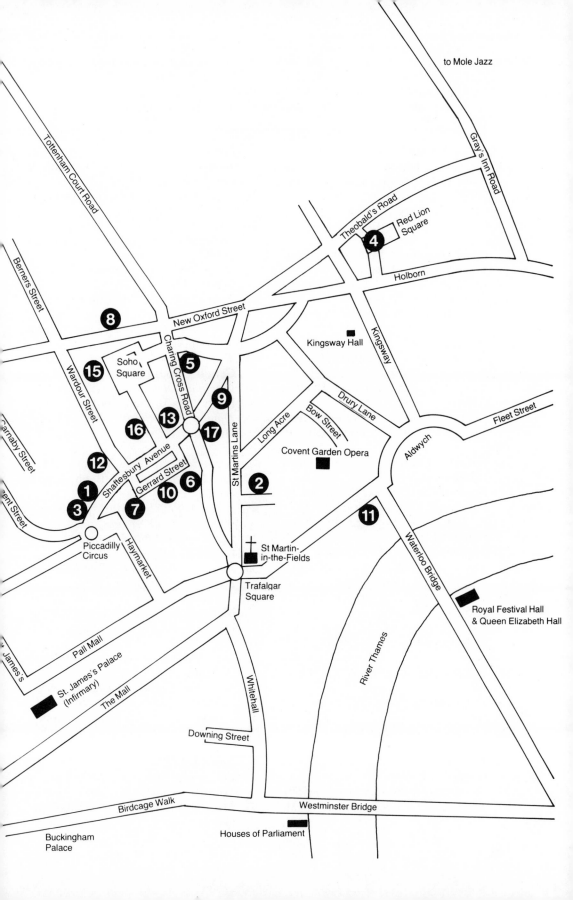

1958

10. *Play That Music* edited by Sinclair Traill & Gerald Lascelles (1957)
11. *His Eye is on the Sparrow* by Ethel Waters (1951)
12. *Jazz: its Evolution and Essence* by André Hodeir (1954)
13. *Jazzmen* edited by Frederic Ramsey & Charles Edward Smith (1939)
14. *Count Basie* by Raymond Horricks (1957)

1959

15. *Concerning Jazz* edited by Sinclair Traill & Gerald Lascelles (1957)
16. *Really the Blues* by Mezz Mezzrow & Bernard Wolfe (1946)
17. *Jazz Hot and Hybrid* by Winthrop Sargeant (1946)
18. *Dictionary of Jazz* by Hugues Panassié & Madeleine Gautier (1956)
19. *Jazz in Britain* by David Boulton (1958)
20. *Duke Ellington: his Life and Music* edited by Peter Gammond (1958)

1960

21. *Second Chorus* by Humphrey Lyttelton (1959)
22. *Bugles for Beiderbecke* by Charles H. Wareing & George Garlick (1958)
23. *A Handbook of Jazz* by Barry Ulanov (1957)
24. *World in a Jug* by Roland Gant
25. *They All Played Ragtime* by Harriet Janis & Rudi Blesh (1950)
26. *The Jazz Scene* by Francis Newton (1959)
27. *These Jazzmen of Our Time* edited by Raymond Horricks (1959)

1961

28. *Father of the Blues* by W. C. Handy (1941)
29. *The Horn* by John Clellon Holmes (1958)
30. *Jam Session* edited by Ralph Gleason (1958)
31. *The Book of Jazz* by Leonard Feather (1957)
32. *Enjoying Jazz* by Rex Harris (1960)
33. *The Country Blues* by Samuel Charters (1959)

34. *The Sound of Surprise* by Whitney Balliet (1959)

1962

35. *The Art of Jazz* edited by Martin Williams (1959)
36. *Treat it Gentle* by Sidney Bechet (1960)
37. *Jack Teagarden* by Jay D. Smith & Len Guttridge (1960)
38. *Jazz Era: the Forties* edited by Stanley Dance (1961)

1963

39. *Death of a Music* by Henry Pleasants (1961)
40. *Blues Fell This Morning* by Paul Oliver (1960)
41. *Essays on Jazz* by Burnett James (1961)
42. *Call Him George* by Jay Allison Stuart (1961)
43. *The Jazz Word* edited by Dom Cerulli (1960)
44. *Original Dixieland Jazz Band* by Harry Otis Brunn (1960)
45. *Django Reinhardt* by Charles Delauney (1954)

1964

46. *Night Song* by John Williams (1961)
47. *The Reluctant Art* by Benny Green (1962)
48. *Jazz: a People's Music* by Sidney Finkelstein (1948)
49. *Jazz and the White Americans* by Neil Leonard (1962)
50. *Man Walking on Eggshells* by Herbert A. Simmons (1962)
51. *Trumpet on the Wing* by Wingy Manone & Paul Vandervoort II (1948)

1965

52. *Jazz Panorama* edited by Martin Williams (1962)
53. *Bird: the Legend of Charlie Parker* by Robert George Reisner (1962)
54. *Toward Jazz* by André Hodeir (1962)
55. *The New Jazz Book* by Joachim Berendt (1959)
56. *Dinosaurs in the Morning* by Whitney Balliett (1962)
57. *My Life in Jazz* by Max Kaminsky (1963)

1966
58. *Frontiers of Jazz* edited by Ralph de Toledano (1947)
59. *Blues People* by Le Roi Jones (1963)
60. *Music on My Mind* by Willie 'The Lion' Smith & George Hoefer (1964)
61. *Giants of Jazz* by Studs Terkel (1957)
62. *Negro Folk Music* by Harold Courlander (1963)
1967
63. *The Real Jazz* by Hugues Panassié (1942)
64. *Conversation with the Blues* by Paul Oliver (1965)
65. *14 Miles on a Clear Night* by Peter Gammond & Peter Clayton (1966)
66. *Ain't Misbehavin: the Story of Fats Waller* by W. T. Ed. Kirkeby (1966)
Extras included:
Jazz edited by Albert McCarthy & Nat Hentoff (1959); *This is Jazz* edited by Ken Williamson (1960); *The Sound* by Ross Russell (1900); *The Book of Bilk* by Peter Leslie (1961); *A History of Popular Music in America* by Sigmund Spaeth (1948); *The Decca Book of Jazz* edited by Peter Gammond (1958); *Esquire's World of Jazz* (1962); *Just Jazz – 4* edited by Gerald Lascelles & Sinclair Traill (1960); *The Encyclopedia of Jazz* by Leonard Feather (1955); *Lady Sings the Blues* by Billie Holiday (1956).

Jazz Directory Well-intentioned and well-worked discography that has remained a constant source of frustration to jazz record collectors because it only goes up to Fred Longshaw. Volume 1, A–B, compiled by Dave Carey, Albert J. McCarthy and Ralph G. V. Venables first appeared in July, 1949 published by The Delphic Press, Fordingbridge, Hampshire. Volumes 2–4 appeared from the same source in 1950, 51 and 52. Volumes 5–6, encouragingly taken over by Cassell & Co., appeared in 1955 and 57. Then, alas, no more.

Jazz Forum Historic jazz periodical, a 'Quarterly Review of Jazz and Literature', of irregular habits, edited by Albert McCarthy (b. 1920) and issued by the Delphic Press from 1946, surviving for five issues until 1947. Decidedly on the arty side, it offered some good features by distinguished contributors and was a pioneer in the linking of jazz and poetry; also had useful discographies of then 'under-rated' musicians.

Jazz Hot The magazine of the Hot Club de France edited by Hugues Panassié (1912–74) under that title from 1935 to 1939 and published in French and English. Began publication again after the Second World War as *Bulletin du Hot Club de France*, still edited by Panassié, but now published in French only.

Jazz in Britain Since the early 1800s the mutual exchange of musical and theatrical products between Britain and the USA has been continual and almost automatic. Before that time it was mainly a matter of the New World taking and copying from the Old. By 1800 or so the British became increasingly aware of worthwhile happenings in American music and felt its influences, although, until the turn of the next century the cultural movement was still preponderantly in a western direction. Most of the British musical shows, for example, went to America but, until the 1890s, very few came the other way.

America itself suppressed what was to be its most valuable and influential spring of musical creativity by preventing for three centuries, for social and racial reasons, the emergence of black music and entertainment, the basis of jazz; so naturally the impact was even more delayed in Britain. The first substantial taste of black musical flavours, though in a strangely disguised form, was experienced through the 'nigger' minstrel shows of the mid-1860s in which blacked-up white artistes introduced the British to the lively nature of indigenous American music – much of it, though, of white origin. A little more of the true flavour was experienced when the Fisk Jubilee Singers, a black choral group from an American Negro university, toured England in 1873 and introduced the Negro spiritual.

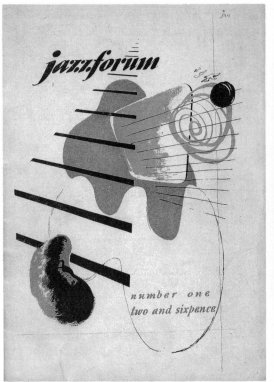

Short-lived arty jazz magazine of the 50s.

One of the longest lasting British jazz magazines founded in 1948.

First issue of a respected jazz periodical featuring Benny Carter.

Special number of *Jazz News* published in 1962.

JAZZ MUSIC

Volume 3 Number 6.   Price: One and S

An excellent British jazz magazine in mid-career, 1947. Brad Gowans on the cover.

I should like you to know how delighted I was with the work of the orchestra which played with me on my first English records for the "Vocalion Swing Series." It was really a pleasure to play with these musicians.

In particular, I want you to listen to the clarinet playing of Andy McDevitt, and the trumpet solos by Duncan Whyte and Tommy McQuater.

I hope you will like my solo work and will be as happy as I was myself about the general results.

Sincerely yours,

Benny Carter.

Letter from Benny Carter regarding the Decca sessions of 1936, offering considerable encouragement to British jazz.

It was still a great novelty when the first all-black show arrived at the Shaftesbury Theatre in London in 1903 – *In Dahomey* with a score by Will Marion Cook and the famous dancer Bert Williams in the cast. It started a craze for ragtime songs and dances of the cakewalk kind.

In 1912 a visiting American vaudeville group, the American Ragtime Octette (with Melville Gideon at the piano) appeared at the London Palladium, and England caught the flavour of the second wave of ragtime fervour in the phoney strains of the Irving Berlin kind. By 1917, various American variety artists brought in jazz-flavoured songs and in that year there were copies of sheet music around with titles like *When I hear that jazz band play*. Without actually hearing the real thing, Britain was getting increasingly jazz conscious by the end of the First World War. Harry and Burton Lester's Jazz Boys were billed at the Metropolitan Music Hall in 1918 and the first British band to be so-named, Harry Pilcer and his Jazz Band, had recorded; but neither of these actually played true jazz. The music was talked of and written about in a completely uninformed way.

It was timely and relevant that the publisher Darewski issued in 1919 a number called *At the jazz band ball* because the introducers of that number in America, the Original Dixieland Jazz Band, were on their way across the Atlantic to join the cast of the revue *Joy Bells* at the Hippodrome, where they opened on 7 April 1919. They were sacked after one appearance, at the behest of the star George Robey who refused to appear on the same bill. Apparently he resented their popularity. The ODJB went instead to the London Palladium, and later the Hammersmith Palais, where they captivated and excited all who heard them.

The Dixieland Jazz Band caused a tremendous stir amongst British musicians who, having heard the real thing for the first time, were now eager to embark in imitation. No one had heard a clarinet played in that way before nor heard such an exciting cacophony of counterpoint. Oddly enough, very little attention was paid to the first black band to arrive, Will Marion Cook's Southern Syncopated Orchestra, also in 1919; apart, that is, from a Swiss conductor, Ernest Ansermet, who made particular note of the playing of a clarinettist in their ranks called Sidney Bechet. The band actually recorded for Columbia but the records were never issued. Thus was the scene set for British jazz to make its first imitative steps.

Much of the early development and diffusion of jazz in Britain happened in the dance band field. The first commercial band to show a strong jazz influence was perhaps Jack Hylton's (1894–1965) c. 1922. In Cambridge a young Spanish musician, Fred Elizalde (1907–79), in stylistic imitation of the California Ramblers, formed a group first known as the Varsity Band and around 1926/7 Elizalde was a leading voice in commercial jazz developments. He was followed by 'Spike' Hughes (1908–87) and his Decca Dents. All these activities gained another burst of inspiration in 1930 when the Ted Lewis band came to England with such players as Muggsy Spanier, George Brunis and Jimmy Dorsey. In 1933 Lew Stone (1898–1969), hitherto the pianist in the Roy Fox (1901–82) band, took over and, with the Casa Loma Orchestra as model, and a young trumpeter called Nat Gonella in the lineup, recorded some inspired big band jazz. The jazz strain became stronger in the 1930s in the bands led by Bert Ambrose (1897–1971) and Henry Hall (b. 1898) particularly when the American arranger, bandleader, saxophonist Benny Carter came over to work in England as Hall's arranger in 1936. The visits, in the 1930s, of such jazzmen as Armstrong, Ellington, Hawkins and Waller encouraged the upsurge of genuine small-group jazz pioneered by such people as George Scott-Wood and Freddy Gardner and capped by the emergence of a true British jazz great in the shape of trombonist George Chisholm who recorded *Rosetta* with his Jive Five in 1938.

A new boost came in 1940 when the BBC asked Harry Parry to organize a Sextet for a pioneering programme called Radio Rhythm Club, which introduced such people as George Shearing. This was closely followed by excellent (if Archer Street-type) bands led by Sid Phillips, Joe Daniels and Harry Gold. By 1942 the Vic Lewis/Jack Parnell Jazzmen were in action as a sort of bridging link between the old and the new.

Around 1945 the traditional boom was in full force closely matched by the rise of modern jazz in Britain. The history of British jazz thereafter is beyond the scope of this present volume but is dealt with sectionally under various headings and aspects.

Books: *Jazz in Britain* by David Boulton. 206p. London: W. H. Allen, 1958. *The Decca Book of Jazz* edited by Peter Gammond. 431p. London: Muller, 1958 (chapters by Mark White & Tony Hall on British jazz). *A History of Jazz in Britain 1919–50* by Jim Godbolt. 306p. London: Quartet Books, 1984.

Jazz Journal British jazz monthly founded by Sinclair Traill (1904–1981) in 1948, a specialist magazine that avoided some of the excesses of its more serious contemporaries and took a middle-of-the-road approach to jazz. Taken over in quick succession by Novellos, the music publishers, and Pitman's; then in 1983 was acquired by its editor, Eddie Cooke, who continued to bring it out, independently, as *Jazz Journal International*.

Jazzmen A journalistic jazz book, edited by Frederic Ramsey Jr and Charles Edward Smith in 1939, which went for much of its information, with the best of intentions, to some of the surviving older jazz musicians. Either through fading memory or, in one case, purposeful distortion, some inaccuracies were perpetrated which were then unquestioningly copied by subsequent writers. In spite of this, with a distinguished panel of contributors including William Russell, Wilder Hobson, Otis Ferguson and Roger Pryor Dodge as well as the editors, it was a sensitive book for its period and offered a deeper insight into

jazz and than most books on the subject up to then. It was the inspiration for many a budding enthusiasm for jazz.

Jazz Messengers A group formed in 1954 by drummer Art Blakey and pianist Horace Silver. Their music was described as hard bop and laid great emphasis on percussive rhythm, riffs and instrumental inter-reaction. When Silver left the group in 1956 to form his own quintet, many famous pianists such as Thelonious Monk and Bobby Timmons filled the piano bench. As time passed, Art Blakey became established not only as leader but as a kind of 'schoolmaster' to several generations of saxophone and trumpet players. On tenor these included Hank Mobley, Johnny Griffin and Branford Marsalis. The trumpeters ran from Freddie Hubbard, through Johnny Hardman to the phenomenal Wynton Marsalis and Terence Blanchard.

Jazz Monthly British jazz magazine founded in March 1955 by the critic and discographer Albert J. McCarthy (1920–87) who was its editor until 1972. Described itself as 'The Magazine of Intelligent Jazz Appreciation' and lived up to its claims with literate articles and making a fetish of accuracy, but occasionally got a little too serious. Excellent record reviews with detailed discographies reflected its founder's concerns.

With the April 1971 issue, in spite of anguished protests from most of its contributors, it became *Jazz & Blues Monthly* (it cost 20p). In December 1972, Albert McCarthy ceased to be editor and was replaced by Max Harrison. To some extent the fall in circulation was arrested, but by then it was too late for its publishers, Hanover Press, and the periodical folded with the December 1973 issue.

Jazz Music British bi-monthly magazine, edited by Max Jones (b. 1917) from Primrose Hill, London, first published in 1942 and lasting until 1960. An influential publication during the war years, when jazz material was scarce and knowledge sketchy; it included authoritative articles, reviews and useful discographies. Jazz Music Books also issued a dozen or so booklets in the years 1944–6 which included such titles as *Piano Jazz*; *A Tribute to Huddie Ledbetter*; *Clarence Williams Discography; This is Jazz* (Blesh); *A Critic Looks at Jazz* (Borneman); *Junkshoppers' Discography*; *Bob Crosby Band* and *Cream of the White Clarinets* retailing (in then current terms) at between 1/- and 2/6.

Jazz News This London-based magazine began in 1956, a time when the British jazz scene was truly busy. Trad was just coming into its boom period, modern jazz concerts played to capacity houses in large venues, and the so-called exchange scheme was just starting, ensuring a steady if not yet very generous supply of visiting American musicians. Before the end of the decade *Jazz News* decided to chance its arm and go weekly, and was perhaps the only jazz magazine to do so. It was of necessity produced quite cheaply, its typesetting standards slipped occasionally, and it was cherished by its regular readers for its misprints almost as much as for its jazz coverage. Early in the 1960s it found itself struggling. Rock and roll had proved to be more than a passing fad and was evolving, in Britain at any rate, into what was generally called The Beat Scene. Although *Jazz News* never tried to cover the activities of the Beat Scene, in 1964 it nonetheless renamed itself *Jazz Beat*, under which half-hearted guise it soldiered on until 1966.

Jazz parties These are latterday examples of the sort of arts patronage that used to be fairly common in the 17th century. Put in an over-simplified way, a jazz party comes into being when a successful American businessman, who happens also to be a jazz enthusiast, decides to organize what really amounts to a private jazz festival. Entrance is by no means free, but by restricting the sale of tickets to those known or personally

recommended to the host, the 'party' nature of the occasion is easily maintained. The musicians are carefully selected – naturally enough according to the preferences of the host – adequately paid and well looked after. Among the first was the series of jazz parties organized by Dick Gibson (a Denver businessman) from 1963 onwards and usually known as the Colorado Jazz Party.

A similar series of jazz parties was later inaugurated by Don Miller, using Paradise Valley, Scotsdale, Arizona as the venue. Miller's parties honour an individual musician each year; the March 1985 guest of honour was trombonist Al Grey.

Jazz Review Still spoken of as probably the best jazz periodical ever to be produced in the USA, in spite of its brief existence from 1958 to 1961. It published articles on jazz, under the editorship of Nat Hentoff and Martin T. Williams, that were always authoritative and meaningful, sometimes a little over-academic, but amongst them were many pieces that have found a permanent place in jazz literature, constantly referred to by the jazz researcher. A selection of these was reprinted in *Jazz Panorama* edited by Martin T. Williams (New York: Cowell-Collier, 1962 and 1964; London: Jazz Book Club, 1965); and a few were in *The Art of Jazz*, edited by Williams (New York: Oxford University Press, 1959; London: Jazz Book Club, 1962, etc.).

Jazz roll A dance which was based on the tango and devised about 1918 in the wake of the newly burgeoning jazz craze. One of its leading exponents was named Morgan and it was also known as the Morgan Roll. It had a short life but exercised some influence on the shaping of the all-conquering foxtrot.

Jazz Singer, The Name of the historic film of 1927 that launched the talkies on their way. It was not actually the first to use the newly-invented Vitaphone system of synchronizing sound and film; background noises had been introduced in a few films and newsreels, but it was in *The Jazz Singer* that somebody actually talked. After recording the Vitaphone backing for his singing scene *Dirty Hands, Dirty Face*, Jolson, carried away, cried: 'Wait a minute! Wait a minute! You ain't heard nothing yet!' and caused a sensation. The talkies were here to stay. The film had nothing whatever to do with jazz (nor did the 1953 remake, nor yet again the completely different story involving Neil Diamond and Laurence Olivier in the late 1970s).

Jazzways Holds a claim as one of the shortest-lived of all jazz 'periodicals' as only Vol. 1, No. 1 was ever issued. A 'Yearbook' of hot music, costing (in 1946) $1, the editor was George S. Rosenthal. The one issue was excellently compiled and contained some valuable material and rare photos. Now a sought-after collectors' item.

Jelly Roll The term has two slang meanings: a sort of baked jam roll, and the sexual act. This ambiguity was gleefully exploited by the writers of songs who perpetrated such masterpieces of *double-entendre* as *I ain't gonna give nobody none of my jelly roll*.

The proudest human bearer of this nickname (said to be founded on the second definition) was Ferdinand Joseph Lamothe, probably born on 20 October 1890 and from an early date in his career always better-known as 'Jelly Roll' Morton. Morton's explanation was that he changed his name to Morton (from Lamothe, as has recently been researched, though he called it Le Menthe, which is the way most subsequent reference books have it) because he didn't like being called 'Frenchy'. Always inclined to be somewhat fanciful, he gave that account to John and Alan Lomax, in the course of those long, rambling, colourful and fascinatingly hypnotic conversations that became the Library of Congress recordings and the basis of Alan Lomax's later romanticized biography of Morton. The

more prosaic reason was that his mother remarried, when Morton was three, to a man called Mouton, which he later changed to Morton (presumably because he didn't like being called 'Sheepsie'). Jelly Roll was christened Ferdinand at the behest of his godmother, Eulalie Echo, after the King of Spain.

The acquisition of the name 'Jelly Roll' has been explained as a tribute to Morton's formidable sexual prowess; but there is very little that can be proved in that direction. As a youth he played the piano in various sporting-houses and there is no reason to disbelieve that he might have been well-endowed in those days. But it could equally well have arisen from one of his chosen sidelines as a pimp – a procurer rather than a practitioner of 'jelly roll'. He was also known as a gambler and pool-shark, a born hustler, but in later life, as a married man, he appears to have become a reformed character and a disciplinarian over work. He would never allow any drinking at recording sessions. His wife is reported as saying that 'he was not what you would call a very high-sexed man' and didn't want it often. A bit of a let-down for someone bearing the title of 'Jelly Roll'.

Apart from the universally acclaimed value of his music-making both as a talented composer and the organizer of the famous recordings made with his Red Hot Peppers, Morton has sadly been remembered as a boaster and exaggerator. This is largely due to the controversial utterances he made in a letter to the magazine *Downbeat* in 1938, which have long annoyed historians. It was in the shape of a heated reply, by this time fanned by years of unjust neglect, to the 'Believe It Or Not' man Robert Ripley's unbalanced estimate as to the part that W. C. Handy had played in the creation of jazz – Ripley having introduced Handy on a radio programme as 'the originator of jazz, stomps and blues'. Morton wrote indignantly: 'New Orleans is the cradle of jazz, and I myself, happened to be the creator in the year 1902'. This remark was ever after widely and deliberately misunderstood, partly (and justifiably) because no one could actually believe that any one man could 'create' something as organic as jazz. However, there has been growing evidence since that some of his music, written in the early 1900s, clearly shows that his ideas were advanced even then beyond the mechanical figurations of ragtime and could only be played with jazz phrasing (see **King Porter**). Morton, one of the most rational of jazz philosophers, clearly knew and thought about what he was doing and probably felt, in all honesty, that he *had* been the prime instigator of the move toward what we would call jazz rather than ragtime. He was certainly a conscious and deliberate innovator.

Morton not only created his own legends but was a confident debunker of others. In his conversations with Lomax he laid about him with great zeal and apparent authority. *Tiger rag*, for example, long accredited to Nick La Rocca and the Original Dixieland Jazz Band, was revealed by Morton to be based on several old and well-known quadrille and dance movements. Morton's points were later confirmed by Sidney Bechet in his autobiography.

Jig In its earliest usage, going back to Elizabethan days and the 15th century in the British Isles, a jig was a country dance, characterized by lively jumping movements, its name probably derived from the old French verb 'giguer' meaning to leap or gambol. The music, provided by pipe and fiddle bands, particularly of the Scottish and Irish variety, was prominent amongst the 'folk-music' taken to America by the various settlers from Britain and became the basis of a great deal of the hill-billy, blue-grass, folk-dance music of that country, much of it in 6/8 or other triple rhythms.

The term got into black music as being almost synonymous with rag; the interplay of jig, jag, rag being fairly explicable, and some even see it as the source of the word rag. There is a hint, however, that what was called jig music was one of the links between the formal classical ragtime as played by Scott Joplin and others and the new jazz idiom – the kind of music that Morton was developing in his early days. The St. Louis pianist Tom Turpin (1873–1922) was said to be an exponent of jig piano, a rather more unschooled sort of ragtime that had its basis in plantation music and minstrelsy, more loosely swinging. The term did not remain in use once ragtime and jazz were well established.

Jim Crow In the evolving days of black-faced minstrelsy in the late 1820s, one of the most famous of the performers who offered somewhat phoney Negro songs and dances on the American stage was Thomas D. Rice (1808–60). In fact, most of the material used was of British origin, as was the rather amorphous tune of *Jim Crow*.

Rice, while on tour in 1828, had watched an old, deformed Negro doing a strange dance with a little jump in it while he sang 'Weel about and turn about and do just so; every time I weel about I jump Jim Crow'. Rice took the song into his act, adapting it to a melody compounded of an Irish folk tune and an English theatre song and achieved enormous popularity with it, dressed in the tattered style of the original singer. He introduced it to New York in 1832 and to London in 1836. Not only did it help spark off nearly 70 years of minstrel show craze, but it put a new phrase into the American language. From its nonsensical nothingness in the song, Jim Crow became, by obscure routes, firstly a popular name for a Negro, particularly a poor one, and thence a somewhat derogatory name for segregated areas, especially on transport, buses and trains, for black travellers. From there it became the term for the doctrines of segregation, discrimination and intolerance as practised against blacks in the USA. Used both as a noun as in 'the manifestations of Jim Crow' and as a verb 'to Jim Crow someone'.

The opposite, Crow Jim or Crow Jimism, is used of anti-white prejudice on the part of Negroes.

Jim-jam To jam, to jazz it up, to jump, to play in a lively manner. The jim-jams also used as another name for the dance known as the heebie-jeebies.

Jimmy Ryan's New York club originally on 52nd Street, then at 154 West 54th Street, near Sixth Avenue, close to **Condon**'s (both now demolished). It was a popular if primitive venue for Dixieland bands.

Jimtown Colloquial name (black and white usage) for the black quarter of an American town. Derives from **Jim Crow**.

Jitterbug, jitterbugging The original use of the term, before it got wider currency in the 1930s, was simply descriptive of a sexual reaction to music (W & F/Gold). As these reactions became, in the words of Ellington 'mere exhibitionism . . . purely physical response that accompanies the worst phases of sensationalism by various players', the term was first applied to those who, though not musicians, had a burning enthusiasm for jazz, particularly of the swing music variety; thence to those who had an uncontrollable desire to dance to such music. The jitterbug 'style' based on various black jive dances (the terms eventually becoming synonymous) was evolved during the swing era, progressing from a demonstration of youthful vigour to a high degree of athleticism. Jitterbugging – dancing to swing music.

Jive Not quite all things to all speakers but a word whose meaning is much affected – even to the extent of sometimes being reversed – according to who is using it and the context in which it is being used.

Its earliest meaning as a verb, was to deceive, to fool, to kid, and in that sense it made one of its first appearances in print as the title of a Louis Armstrong Hot Five record in 1928: *Don't jive me*; 'Don't give me that jive'. It is certain, therefore, to have been around a considerable time before that. It still meant that and nothing else to Mezz

Mezzrow (and his collaborator Bernard Wolfe) in 1946, when *Really The Blues*, with its terse glossary, was published. That is also the first interpretation given in W & F (1960). But some time about 1935 or 1936, when the Swing Era was entering its decade of triumph, 'jive' as a noun also started to mean the music itself, while the verb to jive meant to dance to that music in a particularly uninhibited way; 'jiving' and 'jitterbugging' were almost exactly synonymous. For a while 'jive' also joined the plethora of slang words for marijuana, or a cigarette made from it; it further became the generic term for the jazz musicians' own jargon and slang. In its 'modified jitterbugging' connotation it achieved such extensive currency that in England even Victor Silvester, the arbiter of strict tempo dance music, found it politic (in 1944) to organize a Jive Band.

Perhaps the most memorable occurrence of the word as part of a title is in the startling *The shoes of the fisherman's wife are some jive-ass slippers* by Charles Mingus.

Joe Turner The subject of what some authorities (e.g. Niles) consider to be one of the prototype blues songs, a black folk song of considerable antiquity known long before folk-blues were a recognized art. The traditional tune is a common blues source and, as is the nature of folksong, it has acquired a number of variants in various regions of the USA, probably in use well before the Joe Turner story became attached to it around the turn of the century. The Joe Turner of the now familiar song was, correctly, one Joe Turney (the change probably coming about simply as a mistaken pronunciation) who was the brother of Pete Turney, the governor of Tennessee from 1892–6. Joe was known in Memphis as a 'long chain man' who regularly came to the city to lead batches of convicts to the penitentiary at Nashville. He was thus a figure of awesome unpopularity. Other versions (e.g. the Handy arrangement) portray Joe Turner as a convict himself, while a version recorded by Big Bill

The 'Jelly Roll' blues first written in 1905. As well as recording with his Red Hot Peppers, Jelly Roll Morton accompanied various blues singers on record.

As depicted on the original sheet-music cover.

Decisions to be made on the juke-box, a 1950s model. (Photo: Decca Record Co. Ltd)

Broonzy actually portrays Joe Turner as a kind man. His story and activities were freely adapted to suit other towns and locations.

John Henry Subject of one of the classic worksongs that eventually went into the blues repertoire. Like most folk legends it has many variants, being based on an occurrence in the 1870s when the 'steel drivin' man' John Henry decided that he could outdrive a steam-drill during the work on the Big Bend Tunnel on the C & O Railroad. The usual version has it that he died of exhaustion – 'this old hammer killed John Henry' – but he may actually have died in one of the common railroad work-gang accidents. The song became a popular item in the worksong and chain-gang repertoire sung by both blacks and whites. It has been performed under other titles such as *Spike driver blues*, and the hero is known in some versions as Bill Wilson.

Johnson Park see **Lincoln Park**

Joplin 'A Western gambling and mining town' in the south-west corner of Missouri, USA, a 'hick' town, according to its most famous musical inhabitant, the white ragtime pianist and composer Percy Wenrich (1880–1952). It was not, as some may suppose, named after Scott Joplin or vice versa, though coincidentally he visited it in 1894 with his Texas Medley Quartette just before he first achieved fame as a ragtime composer. Somewhat confusingly, in the circumstances, Percy Wenrich was always known as 'the Joplin Kid'.

Jubilee A religious song in black revivalist circles that tells of the future happiness to come in Heaven when all earthly tribulations have ended. The atmosphere is suggested in Ellington's *Jubilee stomp* (1928) and the song *Alabama jubilee* (1915).

Jug Literally an empty beer or wine jug, or whatever, into which one blew a deep note which ended up giving a sort of tuba-like sound. The same can be achieved by blowing across the top of a narrow-necked jug but the ones usually portrayed in photos of jug bands seem to be of a wide open type.

Jug band Any band with its bass foundation supplied by a jug-blower. In the beginning such bands (sometimes referred to as spasm bands) were the only way the poorer blacks, who could not afford orthodox instruments, could perform. Besides the jug, there might be a washboard and a home-made string bass and a banjo if available; the melody instruments would be mainly kazoos, jews' (or jaws') harps and other cheap items. Like skiffle groups much later on, however, these jug bands had an appeal in their own right; some of them became relatively famous and quite widely recorded, like Gus Cannon's Jug Stompers, active in Memphis in the late 20s to early 30s. Cannon, incidentally, was the begetter of a simple little song called *Walk right in*, a huge record hit for The Rooftop Singers in 1963; Gus Cannon was actually ferreted out from obscurity and given the credit and some unexpected money.

Jughead An alcoholic; also an army name for a mule, hence a stupid person.

Juice Liquor. As a verb – to drink. Juiced – drunk. Juicehead – a drunkard. Juice joint – a drinking establishment.

Juke, juke-box Or juke house – a cheap roadhouse in the USA, hence also a name for the kind of music, an early rather amateurish kind of jazz, that was played in such places. From juke house – a brothel. A night out visiting such haunts was known as juking. In the 1930s, the live music was replaced by the new coin-operated record player on which one could choose from a number of available popular, jazz or race records: these instruments – many of them manufactured by Wurlitzer, of cinema organ fame – became known as juke-boxes or jukes. The juke-box became a valuable source of jazz dissemination, as it was later for rock and pop. Many of Billie Holiday's mid-30s records started life as cheap cover versions, made specifically for the black juke-box market, of white Tin Pan Alley hits. By 1939, it has been estimated that there were about 225 000 in the USA, consuming between them 13 million records; by 1942 the number of instruments had risen to nearer 400 000. Juke has also meant a place, usually in rural areas, and with an exclusively black clientele, where the blues are performed.

Jump A word which came into wide use around 1938 during the swing era, suggesting that bouncy sort of rhythm and playing that the swing bands tried to achieve. 'Jump' appeared in a vast number of swing era and later titles: *Jumpin' at the Woodside*; *Jumpin' punkins*; *Jumpin' with Symphony Sid*; *Jump steady blues*; *Second balcony jump*; *The jumping jive*; *Do you wanna jump, children?* The term 'jump band', more or less self-explanatory, seems to have been not so much a contemporary coining as a handy category called into being a shade later to cover such groups as Louis Jordan's Tympany Five and other small, extrovert and very jumping outfits. The British alto saxophonist and clarinettist Bruce Turner led a small outfit, his Jump Band, in the late 1950s and early 1960s. 'Jumping' can and does also mean lively in a broader sense, as in Fats Waller's *The joint is jumpin'*.

Jump Steady Name of a club in downtown Los Angeles that was a jazz haunt in the early 1920s. Jelly Roll Morton and Jimmy Rushing coincided there in 1923. Rushing described it as 'a rough place; you had to check your weapons at the door before you could get in.' The name has the usual sexual connotations. (See **Jump**.)

Jungle band/music/style Jazz, mainly of the big band variety, that made exaggerated use of muted brass, the wa-wa in particular, tom-toms, etc, to suggest the sort of noises that were considered to emanate from the black man's presumed natural habitat – the jungle. It was not, at any time, a particularly tactful adjective to use, and has since fallen into some disrepute. Jungle music was part of the means of attracting white customers to the society clubs of the 30s, such as the Cotton Club in Harlem where Duke Ellington relied heavily on the jungle style and adept exponents such as Cootie Williams and 'Tricky Sam' Nanton. It must be said, however, that Ellington's jungle pieces outlived their questionable beginnings and are amongst his most distinctive achievements, e.g. *Echoes of the jungle* and *Jungle nights in Harlem*. He regularly recorded under the name of The Jungle Band, as did many others.

Kansas City, KC, Kaycee A city divided by a state boundary that follows the Kansas and Missouri rivers, which join there, into Kansas City, Kansas (population *c*. 122 000) and Kansas City, Missouri (population *c*. 475 000). It functions, however, as one city, sharing its administration and facilities. Kansas City comes after Chicago as the second biggest livestock centre of the USA, mainly located in the Kansas sector; the Missouri city, while also handling cattle, is the distribution point for the great wheat-producing area of Kansas and the southwest.

Kansas City jazz It is probable that a form of jazz began to develop in Kansas City at the same time as it was developing in New Orleans but its significant growth came after 1917 and the gradual north-ward spread of jazz. While New Orleans, Chicago and New York acted as focal points for jazz in the South and much of the eastern half of the USA, Kansas City was the great clearing house for the jazz talent of the whole of the Middle-West.

A lavish range of nightlife inevitably developed there to serve the big-butter-and-egg men who came in from the prairie lands; ragtime and brass music were flourishing by the early 1900s when ragtime pianist James Scott settled there in 1914. Prototype Kansas City groups were led by Bennie Moten and George E. Lee. What became known as Kansas City style, neither more nor less clearly defined than any other regional or city style that the jazz historians try to deline-ate,[1] might be summed up in the first place as a sort of organized jam session – soloists play against simple riffs. The riff, the repeated musical phrase, became very much a hallmark of Kansas City jazz and as the bands increased in size in the 1920s, with small sections of saxophones or brass replacing the one-of-each-instru-ment set-up, the more organized, pre-arranged sort of jazz became popular in the ten-piece bands that were normal by *c.* 1927.

Written arrangements came in *c.* 1927, pioneered by such musicians as Jesse Stone – a pianist-leader, and the saxophonist, Ben Smith. The restless 2/4 of New Orleans jazz went out of fashion and the more flowing 4/4 took its place. The bands led by bassist Walter Page and the veteran Bennie Moten are now seen as the prototypes of the swing bands of the 1930s, introducing the characteristics of swing in their riffs and chase choruses and concerted breaks.

Kansas City's attractions as a jazz centre were much enhanced during the years of Prohibition (1920–33) when thanks to the corrupt administration of the City by Tom Pendergast, drinking and gambling establishments flourished

without hindrance. In the vocabulary of the day, the place was 'wide open'.

Kazoo Small, cheap musical instrument usually of metal, shaped like a cigar, or even like a crude model of a submarine, the 'conning tower' being a short cylin-drical projection, terminating in a membrane stretched over a wire mesh. This creates a similar effect to comb-and-paper – except that the result is louder – when the player voices a note into one end of the tube (the sound is a vocal one, the kazoo simply modifying it). The playing either of the kazoo or comb-and-paper was a feature of many of the spasm and washboard bands, often in combi-nation with other makeshift instruments such as the jug and suitcase. When Red McKenzie indulged in this form of performance in the 1920s–early 1930s he called it 'blue blowing', hence the band his name is mostly associated with, the Mound City Blue Blowers. Various auth-orities describe his instrument as comb-and-paper, comb-and-tin-can, or kazoo but photographic evidence, and Eddie Condon's testimony (*We Called It Music*) suggest that he was exclusively a comb-and-paper man.

Kelly's Stables Small, first-floor (second storey) night spot in Chicago, operating throughout Prohibition until the law stepped in and closed it in 1930. Famous in jazz history because for its final six years Johnny Dodds, New Orleans clarinet genius, led a small band there. The establishment took its name from the owner, Burt Kelly (according to Chilton – Bert).

Kentucky Club New York downtown basement nightclub on 49th Street and Broadway, mainly a haunt of theatre and show business people and the *nouveau-riche* of the 1920s. When Duke Ellington and his early group became the house band there in September 1923, it was known as the Hollywood Club and was owned and managed by Leo Bernstein. The Ellington band became a fashionable attraction to show business frequenters

[1] See 'Kansas City and the Southwest' by Franklin S. Driggs in *Jazz* edited by Nat Hentoff and Albert McCarthy (1959).

like Jimmy Durante and Al Jolson and brought prosperity. It was renamed the Kentucky Club and survived the Prohibition years without getting into serious trouble. Ellington played residencies at the club, on and off between tours from 1924 to 1928, until he moved to the prestigious Cotton Club.

Kicks Pleasurable experience, a thrill, excitement of a satisfying kind. By no means confined to jazz use, and in the altered form of 'to get a kick' out of something, well known in Cole Porter's *I get a kick out of you*. In a much narrower, jazz sense, however, to play for kicks, to kick it around implies playing for the sheer pleasure of it rather than for financial gain. Also used, generally in the singular, for example Harlem Kick, as the place where one experienced kicks. The verb to kick exists quite separately in the connotation to kick (that is, to conquer) the (drug) habit – to come off narcotics.

Kill To please an audience beyond the point of possible criticism, to induce exhilaration. Hence a killer-diller, now somewhat archaic, an exciting knock-out experience. Benny Goodman was fond of the phrase, often announcing his next number as a killer-diller. Likewise, in black usage, a killout. A person of exciting character or ability might be described as a 'killer'.

King Porter It was in 1906, while playing in Memphis, that Jelly Roll Morton wrote his *King Porter stomp*, naming it after his friend, pianist Porter King, for whom he had a great admiration. It has been suggested (Blesh & Janis: *They All Played Ragtime*) that King may have had a hand in its composition, but this cannot be confirmed. One of Morton's most substantial and inspired compositions, it is in ragtime form though its 'modern' phrasing does not allow it to be played naturally in a ragtime manner. It is therefore a piece of substantial evidence in support of Morton's claims to be thinking in the newer jazz idiom in the early 1900s. It became a favourite of the New Orleans bands and a jazz standard, though not actually copyrighted until 1924. Later it had a new lease of life when orchestrated by Fletcher Henderson and was recorded by his band in 1928 and 1932; later by Benny Goodman and others; sometimes as *New King Porter stomp*. Porter King was said to come from Florida and first met Morton in Mobile.

Lady, Lady Day Name given to singer Billie Holiday (1915–59) who was born Eleanora, but called herself Billie after the actress Billie Dove whom she admired. Her first singing job was at Jerry Preston's Club in New York, alternatively known as 'The Patagonia', after prohibition as 'The Log Cabin' and more familiarly as 'Pod's and Jerry's'. It was here that she was nicknamed Duchess or Lady because she acted that way. It became Lady Day (from Holiday) when she first worked with Lester Young in 1937. Young, credited with the invention of much of the fashionable 'hip' talk and vocabulary of the 40s and 50s, called her Lady Day and she dubbed him The President, shortened to Prez.

Lafayette Theater see **Harlem**

Lake Pontchartrain The large lake on the northern borders of New Orleans, some five miles from the city centre. It is actually an inland bay being connected to the Gulf of Mexico by a narrow passage which

Billie Holiday at the peak of her career *c.* 1935. (Photo: Associated Booking Corps)

Mr. Lightly and Politely (Stanley Dance) himself with Duke Ellington in 1935. (Photo: Stanley F. Dance)

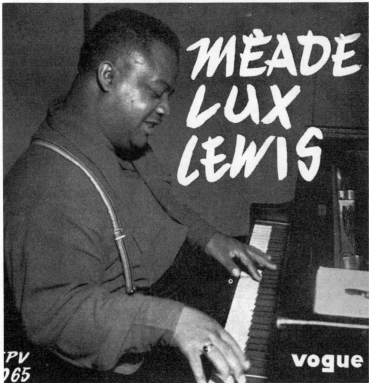

Meade Lux Lewis pulls the piano up to him in the 1940s. (Vogue Records Limited: photo: *Melody Maker*)

is now crossed by a bridge and causeway between Jefferson and Tammany. The popular stretch of shoreline north of New Orleans is known as Lakefront, and Lakeshore Drive runs along some five miles of its length, crowded in the summer and a great tourist attraction. The West End section, some half-a-mile long, with its harbour, is noted for seafood restaurants; and, in the old New Orleans days, was the site of many cafés where jazz musicians found employment – indeed it was there where Morton said that jazz had its main beginnings. Going east there is now the University of New Orleans campus (founded in 1958), the Mardi Gras Fountain (built in 1962) and at the eastern end the New Orleans Lakefront Airport for light aircraft. The lake and its various resorts are mentioned in many jazz titles, including Jelly Roll Mortons' *Pontchartrain blues* (1930). Across the lake lies Mandeville, a popular venue for lake excursions.

Lame Square, but curable.

Lead Take the solo or leading part. Play lead trumpet, etc. Lead man – first chair of a section. Leader – conductor or organizer of a band. Also lead sheet, a simple version or outline of a song on which to improvise. Sometimes the copy of an orchestral score given to the producer or engineer at a recording session, for his guidance.

Legit, legitimate To play in the straight mode, not jazzed. Classical music.

Lenox Avenue Main thoroughfare in Harlem, New York, going north from 110th Street to 145th Street. It was named after a millionaire philanthropist and book-collector, whose collection became part of the founding material of the New York Public Library.

Lenox Club Popular New York nightclub in the 1920s on 135th Street; one of the smaller kind, less pricey and phoney than places like the Cotton Club and Connie's Inn, 'less floor show and more music and

. . . popular with both white and colored musicians' (Charters & Kunstadt). The resident band *c.* 1928 was Cliff Jackson's Krazy Kats which underwent many changes and there was a popular singer known as 'Freckles'. The club was in full swing most nights from about 11 pm to at least 7 am and many musicians, including those from Ellington's band at the Cotton Club would come in to jam with the regulars.

Leroy's Nightclub at 135th Street and Fifth Avenue, one of the oldest cabarets in Harlem, opened by Leroy Wilkins *c.* 1910. According to Willie 'The Lion' Smith, it was 'the place where all the dictys from the Negro show world, the prize fighters, and the sports stopped in for an evening's entertainment'. In spite of later bootlegging and gangster background it was an orderly place, Leroy insisting on decorous behaviour from his girls and tuxedos for staff, musicians and customers alike. The resident band was led for many years by pianist Bob Hawkins. Willie 'The Lion' Smith took over in 1919 and helped to make the club a popular venue for show business people, and singers such as Ethel Waters and the ill-fated Florence Mills would drop in.

Lester Loosely applied to any odd sort of colloquial phrase, privately used by the jazz fraternity. A tribute to Lester Young (1909–59) who, beside being a saxophonist of genius, had a quirky and lively imagination and seems to have been responsible for a large percentage of the jive talk current in his day and after. 'Sounds like a lester to me!' (cf Hines, 1966).

Liberty Inn Nightclub in downtown Chicago standing at the junction of North Clark Street and Erie Street. At one time known as the Breakfast Club.

Lick An alternative term for a break, a short improvised solo or section insertion, usually with the rhythm silent. By *c.* 1938 it was being used more generally to mean any sort of improvisation, particularly a short phrase – hot lick, solid lick, etc.

The original slang meaning of lick was a blow, so its new meaning may have followed the transition of the meaning of the word blow in jazz, i.e. to play. Often used latterly in a faintly derogatory way to describe a musician's personal clichés, the ones he falls back on when invention runs dry.

The Lighthouse Jazz night-club at 30 Pier Avenue, Hermosa Beach, California, opened in 1949 and run by one-time Stan Kenton bass-player Howard Rumsey. He formed his own band there in 1949 and built the reputation of the club as the best-known jazz haunt in California during the years when jazz was very much in vogue on the West Coast. Musicians who worked for him included Shorty Rogers, Shelly Manne, Bob Cooper, Max Roach, Jimmy Giuffre and Victor Feldman, playing and recording under the name of the Lighthouse All Stars. It closed as a jazz venue in 1971 when Rumsey found new premises in Redonda Beach and opened Concerts by the Sea in 1972.

Lightly and politely To play in a smooth, effortless, accomplished sort of way. Name of a column in *Jazz Journal* written for many years by British jazz critic Stanley Dance.

Lincoln Gardens Chicago dance-hall situated at what was the intersection of 31st and Cottage Grove Avenues. A large venue with an impressive canopied entrance, it was originally known as the Royal Garden and was then situated at 459 East 31st Street, only changing the name after moving to the above address. King Oliver led his Creole Jazz Band there from mid-June 1922 and it was where Louis Armstrong subsequently joined him. They played there until February 1924 when they left for a tour of the Eastern States and played on the riverboats. The band returned to Lincoln Gardens with a new and inferior line-up

in June 1924. Business fell off and by November the hall was only open for three nights a week. A grand new revival opening was planned for December 1924 but the premises caught fire and it never materialized.

Lincoln Park Pleasure complex in the south-west area of New Orleans by South Carrollton Avenue, opened in 1902 under the auspices of the Standard Brewing Company. It contained a theatre, a gymnasium and a skating rink in the middle of which was a bandstand. For concerts and picnics the Excelsior Band and John Robichaux's orchestra were used and Buddy Bolden appeared there. Mostly Bolden was at the adjacent Johnson Park the other side of Short Street, a baseball park that had picnic parties. Legend has it that Bolden, playing at Johnson Park, would point his horn toward Lincoln Park were Robichaux was in action and draw the crowds away with the sound of his jazz. Lincoln Park closed in 1930 and was lost in building developments. Johnson Park also opened in 1902 and was closed in 1909. Later, Bolden and Robichaux both appeared at the Lincoln Gardens, still in intense rivalry.

Lincoln Theater see **Harlem**

Lindy Hop The mode of black dancing that developed with the jazz age, later becoming known as the jitterbug or jive and by 1948 (briefly and confusingly) as be-bop. It was a style of dancing that was open to constant improvisation and invention, new steps continually being added by highly competitive dancers out to make a reputation.

The Lindy went back to the early 1900s and was introduced in 1913 in the *Darktown Follies* by Ethel Williams and Johnny Peters. It then had a basic step which was a kick and hop three times on each foot, hence the 'hop' part of the title. It was said to be based on an even earlier Negro dance, known as the Texas Tommy. The Lindy part was probably from the prototype name for a coloured girl, Lindy Lou, which went right back to the minstrel days and the early 1800s. In 1927, when Lindbergh made his historic hop across the Atlantic, promoters cashed in and called it the Lindbergh hop. But that did not last long and it went back to being the Lindy soon after. At this time there was a Lindy marathon at the Manhattan Casino and it was about then that dancers started to move away from the old formalized steps, incorporating movements from other dances such as the Charleston. Inventing new steps, which they called breakaways, they made the Lindy ever more acrobatic and improvisational.

It is not often realized how much dance fashions, notably the Lindy and its variations, affected the course of jazz. At places like the Savoy Ballroom in Harlem the musicians inspired the dancers to new heights but equally the dancers would inspire the musicians to invent new 'licks' and rhythmic patterns. The Lindy was one of the driving forces behind the growth of swing. The riffs got the momentum going and the dancers would cut loose against the solos. Marshall Stearns (cf. *Jazz Dance*) has described the Lindy as 'choreographed swing music'.

The Lindy remained a dance for black circles until around 1936 when, with swing at its height, white society began to get intrigued by this energetic new dance, with the couples joining and separating. White people began to go to the Savoy Ballroom just to watch the dancing. There the moderates did the floor steps at one end of the ballroom while the experts discovered new excesses at the other. Panassié describes the dance as 'the male dancer spinning his partner, whom he holds by the hand and round the waist, first to the right, then to the left, then between his legs, then round his neck, finally bringing her back in front of him through a somersault'. Such steps as the Back Flip, Over the Head and the Snatch were added. At this time it became widely known as the Jitterbug and the craze was further intensified by the exhilarating Lindy Hoppers who appeared in

the Marx Brothers' *A Day at the Races* and the Congeroo Dancers in *Hellzapoppin'*. To the public the jitterbug craze seemed to arrive out of thin air around 1937 when youngsters first 'jitterbugged in the aisles' to the strains of the Benny Goodman Band at the Paramount Theatre, but the Lindy had been building up to that for 40 years or so.

Liner LP record covers in the USA are frequently made in two distinct pieces, a front and a back. The back portion is the liner, on which the information, if any, is printed, which thus becomes the liner-note. In the UK the tendency is to refer to the whole, generally known as a sleeve, and hence sleeve-note is more common in Britain.

Line-up Popular term for the personnel of a jazz group.

Lion, The Nickname of William Henry Joseph Bonaparte Bertholoff Smith (1897–1973), pianist and composer, the subject of Duke Ellington's *Portrait of The Lion* (1940). According to his own story: 'During the first war, I was one of the few to volunteer to go to the front and fire a French seventy-five – and of those who did, few returned. I stayed at the front for fifty-one days without relief. I was known from that time on as Sergeant William H. Smith "The Lion".' He was possibly the only jazz musician to earn his nickname for bravery.

Lip The point of contact between the player and a wind instrument.

A preoccupation of brass players who have a lot of lip trouble owing to the constant pressure of the mouthpiece. Louis Armstrong was a martyr to it all his career. Used as a verb, meaning to play a brass instrument, especially in jazz.

Little Jazz Name given to trumpeter Roy Eldridge (b. 1911), partly for his small stature, partly in admiration for his constant, diligent practice.

Little Rock City and State Capital of Arkansas, population *c.* 110 000. Remembered in Joe Sullivan's *Little Rock Getaway* (1933) written after his marriage to a girl from Little Rock in 1933.

Locked hands Piano style in which the left hand doubles the top note of the right.

Lockjaw Nickname of tenor-saxophonist Eddie Davis (1922–86) often modified among *cognoscenti* to 'Jaws' long before the appearance of a film of that name. A very 'in' nickname, said to have been earned by his immobile, rock-steady embouchure while playing. One of the few musicians to have booking-agency experience in the early 60s; and was later both road-manager and playing member of the Count Basie band for some years.

Long hair Popular and jazz world's adjective for serious or academic music and those who play it. Also applies to other arts.

Loose wig An exceptionally uninhibited performer; a way-out musician. One whose wig has flipped beyond the norm.

Lot Oblique term implying playing well, impressively, of exceptional quality. As in the phrase 'to play a lot of horn'.

Louisiana Five Early dixieland band organized as a recording group in 1919. Never played in New Orleans but included in its ranks Yellow Nunez on clarinet and Anton Lada on drums.

Louisiana Rhythm Kings Jazz recording group of the late 1920s and early 1930s made up of white musicians such as Red Nichols, Miff Mole, Jack Teagarden, Benny Goodman, Glenn Miller, Jimmy Dorsey, Adrian Rollini, Arthur Schutt, Eddie Condon and Dave Tough.

Low down Jazz, especially blues-oriented, of a slow, intense, sad nature. Music full of soul and feeling.

Lux The nickname of Chicago-born boogie-woogie pianist Meade 'Lux' Anderson Lewis (1905–64) was given to him when a child when the family called him 'The Duke of Luxembourg', abbreviated to Lux. After an early career in jazz he became a taxi driver. Discovered by John Hammond in 1935, he was brought back into music and then re-recorded his famous *Honky tonk train blues*. The first time was in 1927.

Lyric Theater Less notorious than Lulu White's Mahogany Hall but more important in mass entertainment terms was Boudiran and Bennett's Lyric Theater on the corner of Burgundy and Iberville Streets in New Orleans. In 1980 this long-vanished black theatre (the only live entertainment auditorium for black audiences in New Orleans) achieved international fame as the setting for the hit musical production *One Mo' Time*. Held together by the slightest of plots, the show gave its New York and London audiences a very convincing idea of what black vaudeville was like in the 1920s, just before the real Lyric burned down. It was the venue at which Bessie Smith appeared and would be important in jazz history on that count alone; but both Ma Rainey and Ethel Waters ('Mama String-bean' in her youth) also performed there. As an interesting by-product, the London production of *One Mo' Time* brought to England two veteran jazz trumpeters – first Bill Dillard, later Wallace Davenport, while the New York production included another veteran, Jabbo Smith.

Mahogany Hall A palatial four-story brothel, built of marble for the famed New Orleans octoroon madam, Miss Lulu White. It was prominently situated near the corner of Bienville and Basin Streets at No. 235 Basin Street, and cost $40 000 to build even in 1897. Outside, it was distinguished by an elegant tower and weathervane; inside, it had five lavishly furnished parlours and 15 bedrooms, each with a bath, hot and cold water and toilet. It had steam-heating and boasted an elevator which accommodated two people. There was an adjoining dance hall-cum-music saloon, known as Anderson's Arlington Annex which occupied the corner site from 1901.

It was considered, certainly by its owner, as a very high-class establishment of its kind, all the prostitutes being (according to the *Blue Book*) 'born and bred Louisiana girls', 'gifted with nature's best charms' ($25 to $50 a go). Lulu White herself, when she first launched her enterprise, was an elegant lady with beautiful black hair and blue eyes who was probably worthy of her title 'Queen of the Demi-Monde', and she was well educated in musical and literary matters.

She liked to provide the best in musical entertainment for her customers and made a point of employing accomplished piano 'professors' including Richard M. Jones and Clarence Williams, and other fine jazz musicians. The regular pianist from 1903–12 was one Kid Ross.

The building, immortalized in *Mahogany Hall stomp* written by Spencer Williams (he was Lulu White's nephew), was put to other uses after Storyville was closed in 1917. By 1945 the mansion had become a warehouse and the one-time dance-hall was a children's club. It was finally pulled down in 1949/50, the last of the Basin Street brothels to be demol-ished, and all that now remains on the site is a modest one-storey structure; most of the area being taken over by Krauss's Department Store.

Mainstream A useful categorical term coined in the 1950s by British-born, American-based jazz writer and critic and historian Stanley Dance, which he defined as: 'a kind of jazz which, while neither "traditional" nor "modern", is better than both.' Generally employed to describe the music of jazz musicians who were by no means past their prime but who had formed their styles and made their reputations before or during the swing era and who found themselves out of fashion and short of work when the jazz audience divided itself into modern and traditional, paying scant attention to what lay in between. Mainstream musicians include Dicky Wells, Buck Clayton, Bill Coleman, Vic Dickenson and to some extent Coleman Hawkins (though he understood bebop) and Earl Hines (who had in fact influenced pianists right up to Bud Powell). It is worth noting, incidentally, that it was Stanley Dance who set Earl Hines off on a whole new career, which lasted from 1964, when Dance persuaded him to do some solo and trio recitals in New York, until his death in 1983.

Other musicians who might justifiably be categorized as mainstream are Ben Webster, Buster Bailey, Buddy Tate and, although of a later generation, Ruby Braff.

Maple Leaf Club A drinking club in Sedalia, Missouri, which was a popular venue for pianists in the burgeoning ragtime era. Scott Joplin was the resident pianist there for some time in the 1890s and he immortalized it in his best-known and most successful composition *Maple Leaf rag* (1899) which he rightly prophesied would make him the 'king of ragtime composers'. After being offered to several publishers who turned it down, the piece was published by John Stark of Sedalia who had heard Joplin playing it in the club and expressed his admiration. It was an immediate sell-out in Sedalia and was the making of both Joplin and Stark who then moved his business to the more affluent town of St. Louis. The Maple Leaf Club proprietors were always very proud of this musical tribute even before its success.

Marable The pianist and bandleader Fate Marable from Paducah, Kentucky (1890–1947) has a special niche in history as a kind of musical director of the bands working on various Mississippi riverboats between 1907 and 1940. At the age of 17 he joined the steamboat 'J.S.' which operated from Little Rock, Arkansas and soon formed his own Kentucky Jazz Band. Working on various Streckfus Line boats he employed many famous jazzmen such as Armstrong, the Dodds brothers, Pops Foster, Zutty Singelton and many more for whom the excursion boats were a regular source of work. The degree to which Marable actually 'employed' the musicians is not clear, and *Jazz New Orleans 1885–1963* by Samuel B. Charters (Oak Publications) suggests that the Streckfus family did the actual hiring. Marable collaborated as leader in the 1930s with the equally famous Charlie Creath (1890–1951). He was also a famed performer on the traditional riverboat instrument, the steam calliope. His ubiquity during the 'exodus' period (just about every other New Orleans jazz musician seems to have worked under him at some time or other) has tended to make him appear, incorrectly, to be the prime organizer of the 'leave New Orleans' movement.

Mardi Gras Mardi Gras is the Tuesday before Ash Wednesday, a traditional day for celebration before the self-denials of Lent. In England people merely eat a few desultory pancakes, but in New Orleans it is the great Carnival of the year, with a culminating four days leading up to Fat Tuesday itself with a whole day of parading headed by Zulu, Rex (King of the Carnival), Comus and numerous others; the whole thing replete with jazz bands; and in the evening the Carnival balls. It has a historic significance in New Orleans as it was on a Shrove Tuesday that the pioneer French founders arrived at this part of the Mississippi on 4 March 1699.

Marquee The Marquee Club opened in Oxford Street, London, in a large basement beneath the Academy Cinema at the corner of Poland Street in 1958. The music it offered was largely traditional to mainstream at first, with regular appearances by the bands of Chris Barber and Humphrey Lyttelton. Chiefly through Chris Barber, however, the Marquee was aware very early on of the infant British blues scene, and by the end of the decade Alexis Korner (1928–84) and Cyril Davies (1932–64) were frequently to be heard there.

In 1964 the Marquee moved to a new location in Wardour Street, among the film company offices and preview theatres, where it remains to this day. Its musical policy steadily changed, however, and although jazz continued to be presented there for several years, the young British blues and rock groups gradually took over, so that by the late 1960s the Marquee and jazz were no longer synonymous. This development was perhaps aided by the conversion of the back part of the premises into what its owner, Harold Pendleton, has described as a 'joke studio', a primitively equipped yet atmospheric little set-up in which The Who were to make their first demos. As the studio's reputation among rock groups spread, so its facilities were enlarged and improved, and there is now an entire generation of fans and musicians unaware of the Marquee's one-time importance to jazz in Britain.

Mason-Dixon Line A term still in popular

The famous dance band magazine as it was in its first years.

Edgar Jackson (1895–1967), the *Melody Maker's* first editor. (Photo: Edgar Jackson)

The Midnite Follies, ragtime revival band of the 1980s. (Photo: ASV Records)

and frequent jazz usage in the USA as a symbolic division between North and South; 'south of the Mason-Dixon line' was a phrase in southward yearning lyrics. It has its basis in the boundary line between Pennsylvania and Maryland which was finally agreed after negotiations that went on from 1763 to 1767.

The line was worked out by two British astronomers, Charles Mason and Jeremiah Dixon, who had been called in to end the prolonged boundary dispute between these two states. It became the symbolic line between the slave states of the South and the free states of the North and a focal point of divergence in the American Civil War of 1861–5. It has long seemed obvious to conclude that the names Dixie and Dixieland were derived from Dixon (but then why not Mason-Dixieland or even Masieland?) but it is now considered by some authorities that this was not the case. (See **Dixie**.)

In crude journalese the line between North and South is sometimes referred to as the Cotton Curtain.

McKinney, McKinney's Cotton Pickers
William McKinney (1895–1969), drummer and bandleader, goes down in history not so much as executant but as one of the first notable name band leaders. After serving in World War I he played in a circus band before settling in Springfield, Ohio where he became leader of the Synco Septet (later Synco Jazz Band). Evolving more into a business manager than musician he organized various residential venues ending up in 1926 at the Greystone Ballroom in Detroit where the band received its first billing as McKinney's Cotton Pickers. The band remained in Detroit until 1930 after which it split up, part of it becoming the Don Redman Band. Benny Carter was a prominent member for many years. Eventually there were several bands working as the Cotton Pickers under McKinney's management until he retired from the music world in 1940. From 1937 he also managed the Cosy Café in Detroit.

Mellophone An instrument developed from the tenor cor, itself an attempt to produce a more easily manageable version of the french horn for military and amateur band use. It was circular like the horn, slightly smaller, pitched in F (or, with the use of a slide, in Eb), had a wide mouthpiece but ended up having a less exciting tone quality than the difficult genuine french horn. The tenor cor was introduced in the 1860s by Besson in Paris and Distin in London and it was occasionally used in early jazz bands.

In the 1920s C. G. Conn brought out an instrument called the mellophone which was basically the same but with the bell point forwards and this had a limited use in jazz, particularly in the hands of its most famed practitioner, the delightfully-named Dudley Fosdick (1902–1957) (and his brother Gene) who employed it in such bands as the Hoosier Hotshots and with various groups led by Red Nichols.

Mellow A jazz performance, thus described, would be just right – skilfully done but groovy, sincere and moving – ripe. Seems to have first come into use in the 1930s and still used of some modern jazz which has a warm, bluesy feeling about it. A favourite word with guitarist/pianist/raconteur/humorist Slim Gaillard. Fine quality – as in mellow pot – the best grade of marijuana. Not jazz but associated – to be moderately and pleasantly drunk or high (W & F). *Mellow little fellow* (Harlem Hamfats).

Melody Maker British journal devoted to dance and popular music in general, with brass band and cinema organ interests in particular in early issues, and a variable interest in jazz throughout its history until recent years. Started in January 1926 as the house-magazine of music-publisher Lawrence Wright; it was then a small 32-page pamphlet costing 3d. By March of that year (now costing 6d and soon to be 1/-) it became an independent and substantial monthly publication styling itself *The Melody Maker and British Metronome* 'the only independent Magazine for all who are directly or indirectly interested in the production of Popular Music'. It was published from 19 Denmark Street and was edited by Edgar Jackson (1895–1967). Its attitude to jazz was ambivalent until *c.* 1930, most of it dictated by the often uninformed and prejudiced views of its editor. It started out by carrying an attack on jazz by Jack Hylton but it gradually had to accept the new styles as a permanent part of the scene. The record reviews, done by Jackson under the pseudonym of 'Needlepoint', showed a strong bias toward white jazz and remained scathing about 'nigger' music for some time. In its 1927 pages (where the adverts were offering a folio of *100 'Hot' Breaks for the Cornet*) such strange and conflicting comments were to be found:

'Probably arising from the negroid origin of these dances, undue indulgence in jazz appears to cause the heel bone to protrude, and the music, when vocalised, induces nasal production'

'Jazz has nearly died out in America'

' "Hot" music, which has taken America by storm, will soon be the rage in London, where it has just been introduced'

Jazz insights improved when Fred Elizalde joined the panel of writers; and even more so when Spike Hughes, under the name of 'Mike' took over the jazz reviews in 1930. Edgar Jackson had left at the end of 1929 to become manager of the Hylton band, and the assistant-editor P. Mathison Brooks took over. *Melody Maker* kept a fair percentage of jazz coverage until *c.* 1982, including a 'Collectors' Corner' originated by Sinclair Traill in 1941 and running, with the help of Max Jones (b. 1917) and others until the late 50s.

The magazine was taken over by Odhams Press in March 1928 and changed to a newspaper format in 1933, becoming a weekly in the same year. (See chapters 2 and 3 in *A History of Jazz in Britain 1919–1950* by Jim Godbolt. London: Quartet Books, 1984.)

Memphis The largest city in Tennessee, population *c.* 500 000 – some 40% of it black, on the Mississippi River. Founded in 1819 and named after Memphis in Egypt 'the place of good abode' (Townley). A centre for the cotton and timber commerce, it was a major blues development area in the 1920s and 30s. W. C. Handy's *Memphis blues* was originally written as a campaign song in 1909 on behalf of one *Mr Crump* (its original title) who was duly elected Mayor.

Memphis Five The personnel of the band that billed themselves as the Original Memphis Five included a number of players who had no particular connection with Memphis: Phil Napoleon (Boston), Miff Mole (New York), Frank Signorelli (New York), etc., but it seems to have been adopted as a suitable general operating name, although the players frequently recorded under various other names for various companies, such as Fosdick's Hoosiers when Fosdick was present on *mellophone*, or Ladd's Black Aces and Lanin's Southern Serenaders. Prolific recorders during the early 1920s.

Mess-around A dance of the 1920s. Defined in *Trumpet On The Wing* by Wingy Manone (Jazz Book Club 1964) as: 'a kind of dance where you just messed around with your feet in one place, letting your body do most of the work, while keeping time by snapping your fingers . . .' There is a reference to it in *Don't forget to mess around*, recorded by Louis Armstrong and his Hot Five in 1926, and in *Pinetop's boogie-woogie* (1928) where, included in Pinetop's spoken instructions is the direction: 'And when I say "hit it!", I want everybody to mess around'.

Metronome American monthly magazine dealing with jazz and popular music. Founded as long ago as 1883 when its main interests were in the brass band field, it moved with the times and covered jazz when appropriate. Latterly run from 114 East 32nd Street, New York, it ceased publication in 1961. During its jazz years its editors included Leonard Feather, Barry Ulanov, George Simon and Dan Morganstern. A *Metronome Yearbook* was issued from 1950 to 1961.

The magazine was a useful source of information as to the movements of bands and musicians and listed important recording dates. Its style was once described as 'debased journalese' and its criteria 'Box-office success'. Albert J. McCarthy once wrote of it: 'no magazine has reviewed records so scandalously unfairly, and the stupid articles are calculated to arouse the hostility of any person having the slightest historical knowledge of jazz. If the editors should happen to like any musician who plays something of artistic merit it is purely coincidental'. Its tastes were reflected in the polls which elected the Metronome All-Star bands of the swing era which made yearly recordings of large ensembles packed with 'star' soloists from the big bands. Some of these have, by now, become of historic interest, overlapping into the modern jazz era.

Mezz One of the most colourful personalities of jazz, Milton Mesirow (1899–1972), better known as 'Mezz' Mezzrow, white clarinettist and saxophonist made it his jazz aim to play and live like the black musicians that he admired. He first took up the saxophone while serving a jail sentence, thenceforth played with many of the pioneering groups including the Wolverines, the Chicago Rhythm Kings and the loosely associated members of the so-called Austin High School Gang. Worked frequently in Europe, particularly Paris, throughout his career; and was brought back to notable prominence in the 1938 recordings with Ladnier, Bechet and others on sessions organized by Hugues Panassié.

He was equally known as a prominent pusher of narcotics. He had the honour of the marijuana cigarette being named a 'mezz' in recognition of his services to the drug cause. His colourful career was meatily and colloquially documented in one of the most revealing and exciting jazz books of its day, *Really the Blues* (1946) which he wrote in collaboration with Bernard Wolfe. There is probably a degree of truth in the notion that he owed his participation in some recording sessions less to his abilities as a clarinettist than to his reliability as a supplier of the best quality marijuana. It has to be said, though, that his quirky, sometimes wayward playing made up in jazz feeling whatever it might have lacked in technical skill.

Mickey Mouse music Any jazz (or offshoot of it, especially dance music) that has recourse to funny or silly trick effects or is generally of the insincere, phonily jolly nature that is regarded by the righteous as unnecessary commercialism. A derogatory term, as defined by Stephen Longstreet (in *The Real Jazz Old and New*, (1956): 'A mickey-mouse band is a real corny outfit that pushes trombone sounds and uses out-of-tune saxes'. Derives, somewhat unfairly we feel, from the Disney character.

Midnite Follies Orchestra British jazz group jointly led by Keith Nichols and Alan Cohen which ably and excitingly recreates the music of the 1930s and around. Has often featured American-born singer Johnny M.

Milneburg Summer resort on Lake Pontchartrain near to New Orleans. Thanks mainly to Jelly Roll Morton's composition *Milneburg Joys* there has always been confusion, outside Milneburg itself, with regard to its spelling. Most recordings have it as 'Milenberg' because the first printer spelled it that way in error. This was deliberately perpetuated in the Melrose *Blues and Stomps*, Vol. 2 (with a note to that effect), and Milenberg persists. It was written by Morton in memory of the outings and picnics he had there in the days of his boyhood and youth. The area was named after Alexander Milne, a Scotsman who was born in Fochabers, Scotland in 1742 and emigrated to New Orleans in 1776. An astute business man, he bought most of the land, mainly swamp, between the city and Lake Pontchartrain. The suburb that gradually grew up on the lakeside was dutifully called Milneburg.

Milne died in 1838, at 96, one of New Orleans' first millionaires, and left all his money to various charities. The Milne Boys Home and the Milne Home School for Girls still flourish in New Orleans as does the Milne Institute (now Milne High School) in Fochabers, built in 1843/4 from money left for that purpose by Milne. The old resort disappeared in the 1930s. The lake front was built up and made into an amusement park called Pontchartrain Beach. Once a summer rendezvous for jazz musicians, the lake resorts of West End, Milneburg, Bucktown (all immortalized in jazz titles) and Spanish Fort have either disappeared or are now mainly amusement arcades full of canned music.

Minstrels, blackface minstrels, minstrel shows While jazz was never part of the minstrel scene, which flourished mainly between *c*. 1840s and the early 1900s, the rise to popularity of the minstrel show was to some extent instrumental in bringing black music to public prominence, and developing the typical plantation type of melody and the musical stream that led to the emergence of ragtime and subsequently jazz. The white American theatre, unavoidably aware that there was a new stream of music of black origin fermenting in its midst, began to exploit this in a way that strikes the modern observer as tasteless and even offensive. Having limited the possibilities for black performers and musicians to practise the trade themselves, whites began blacking-up their faces and dressing in what they considered an appropriate manner and performing songs and dances and speaking in a comic and condescending imitation of the Negro, who was unthinkingly looked upon as a buffoon and born serf.

It is not really easy to explain why the black-face minstrel show became as popular as it did, but the craze assumed vast proportions, firstly in the USA, where such exponents as Edwin P.

Christy (whose name became synonymous with minstrelsy) led well-organized troupes, and later in England. In fact, the minstrel show and its repertoire grew up side by side with the music hall tradition, its politely comic and sentimental Foster-type songs appealing to a middle-class audience while the lower class disported themselves at the music halls. Both shared publishing and promotional outlets, both flourished and declined together, both put the popular music business on its feet. Without question, minstrel shows had opened the way for genuine black entertainment and music to develop in the theatre. On the debit side, the minstrel shows exploited the 'nigger', 'coon', 'darkie' aspect of black American life even to the point of establishing a convention whereby black performers themselves blacked up; on the credit side it helped the nation to an awareness of a new musical culture that was soon to become the world's property.

Minton's Playhouse The revolution of ideas that changed the face of jazz and brought in the 'modern' era was probably happening in many nightspots, in the early 40s. Thoughtful black musicians in several locations would have been trying to find out what it was in the weirdly mongrel music called jazz that they could claim as their own. There must have been many trying to winnow out all the corn and hokum that the white entertainment world had added to it since it began and to get back to the blues and the oblique language of true jazz. But it was Minton's that stood out as the one really important setting for the bop revolution of the 1940s. All the important modern jazzmen played there together at some time and it was there that the new trends took shape. Minton's, as one critic wrote: 'may well be the most important single shrine in the jazz world'.

Minton's Playhouse, at 210 West 118th Street in New York's Harlem, was started by ex-tenor saxophonist Henry Minton in 1938 and became a popular nightspot for a black clientele. The stars from the Apollo Theater used to come and dine

Early sheet-music from the black-faced minstrel period *c.* 1860/70.

Stan Kenton's Band was the first to come to England in 1956 after the lifting of the MU ban.

Below John Coltrane – modern jazz virtuoso. (Photo: EMI Records Ltd)

BRITAIN '56
Souvenir Programme

there, enjoying a Negro cuisine of fried chicken, seasoned vegetables and the like with free whisky. In 1940, the management was taken over by saxophonist and ex-bandleader Teddy Hill. He organized a house-band made up of ex-members of his own band and others including Kenny Clarke whom he'd previously fired (drummer and leader), Joe Guy (trumpet), Nick Fenton (bass) and Thelonious Monk (piano). The bandstand was shared from time to time by groups led by other progressive musicians. Hill in 1941 started a regular Monday Celebrity Night which brought in a mixture of established stars such as Lester Young, Ben Webster, Coleman Hawkins and other mainstreamers to mingle and contest with such newcomers as Dizzy Gillespie, Charlie Christian and Charlie Parker. Minton's became a stewpot of new musical ideas from which evolved the new bop style that was to change the face of jazz.

See: 'Setting for a Revolution: Minton's 1941' in *Esquire's World of Jazz* (1963).

Mississippi The river up which jazz is supposed to have come from New Orleans in order to reach the rest of the USA and, eventually, the world. Allowing for gross oversimplification and the possibility that a music akin to jazz was developing in many cities other than New Orleans, it is to some extent true, for it is one of the great rivers and a vital factor in the commercial and, subsequently, cultural life of the United States. Flowing from Lake Itasca in northern Minnesota it runs for 2300 miles (3701 km) south to the Gulf of Mexico, joined along its course by the major tributary rivers Missouri, Ohio and Arkansas. These rivers between them take water from no fewer than 31 states.

In the days when overland transport was a hazardous business, the river was the ideal way to send agricultural and mineral products down to the sea to be exported to South America, Europe and the rest of the world, and for imported goods to reach the towns and cities of central and southern USA. The Span-iards were the first to explore its possibilities, soon followed by the more business-like French. An expedition led by two French-Canadian brothers, Sieur d'Iberville and Sieur d'Bienville, set out to colonize the land along the river and – having moved a British party on – founded the City of New Orleans, almost 100 miles from the river's mouth, in 1718. After establishing itself as a main commercial route, the river soon became a valuable cultural link between such cities as (reading south to north) New Orleans, Memphis and St. Louis and thence the rest of the country. The spread of popular culture over a vast area was speeded up by the big riverboats – floating, mobile dancehalls and entertainment palaces, aboard which most musicians from places along the river would have worked at one time or another.

Modern jazz As with its equivalent usage in other musical areas and the arts in general, the term 'modern' is infinitely movable and flexible in its interpretation. In jazz history it became most firmly attached to the innovatory jazz happenings of the early 1940s that developed at Minton's and elsewhere when the simple harmonies and four-square rhythms of jazz up to then were replaced by the new, technically more adroit, harmonic and rhythmic approach pioneered by such players as Parker, Gillespie and Monk. These changes had been foreshadowed by earlier musicians of the order of bassist Jimmy Blanton, guitarist Charlie Christian and saxophonist Lester Young in various big and small bands – and 'modern' was justifiably used at this juncture (as in the book *Modern Jazz* by Alun Morgan and Raymond Horricks) since this was clearly the first time that jazz had moved on from many of the characteristics that had made it recognizable as jazz to its earliest followers. It was still a 'hot', indeed sometimes frantic, music, but it needed a cool head and a sophisticated musical intellect in order to play it. It was a deliberate move to modernity and demanded revised sympathies, a widening of loyalties, that some of the more dogmatic critics could not encompass. To over-simplify to a dangerous extent, where a musician – say, Bobby Hackett, on cornet – had been content to extemporize elegant variations on the melody of a tune, often staying quite close to the original and creating his effect by subtle changes of inflection and phrasing, modern jazz – bebop – went more than skin deep. With the moderns the harmonic structure, the chordal scaffolding on which the tune was built became the important thing. With the basic chord sequence in his head, the young modernist roamed as freely as he dared through the possibilities of notes implied by those chords. It was thus feasible to get a long way from the familiar top line of the tune, thereby creating something apparently quite different. It is not immediately obvious, for example, that *Ko Ko*, by Charlie Parker, used as its point of departure *Cherokee* by the Englishman Ray Noble. Much more radical, however, was the rhythmic shift. In the standard 4/4 time of the swing era, the 1st and 3rd beats of the bar were 'strong' and beats 2 and 4 were 'weak'. Bop players tended to push the main stress on to the 2nd and 4th beats, and would begin and end their phrases at points which would throw older musicians off balance. Drummers, especially Kenny Clarke, started using the big ride cymbal to lay down the time, and to keep the bass drum for unexpected accents and 'explosions'. In that way there arose a form of jazz which seemed as different as Impressionism from the painting which had preceded it.

Of course, what was then termed 'modern' jazz has itself become old-hat in the light of further developments; but up to now 'modern' jazz is still used to cover in a very loose way all that has happened since the 1940s. From that point on, jazz has been hung up on its own nomenclature. To start with, 'modern' jazz has existed for forty-odd years – in other words for half the known history of the music. Inevitably, there have been attempts to identify develop-

ments and changes. The word cool crept into the vocabulary to signify the slightly detached, intellectually serene music of people like Gerry Mulligan and, once he had moved on from Parker's immediate circle, Miles Davis. There was the so-called hard bop phenomenon, mainly in New York, in the 1950s and early 1960s.

Avant-garde was used for a while to cover the next phase, when the remaining disciplines of chord structure, chorus length and time signature were felt to be too restricting. The names of Ornette Coleman (alto), Albert Ayler (tenor), Eric Dolphy (alto, flute, bass clarinet), Archie Shepp (tenor, soprano), Pharoah Sanders (tenor), Cecil Taylor (piano), Steve Lacy (soprano) came to be familiar as listeners grappled with the complexities of a form of jazz which was also sometimes called 'free'. John Coltrane (tenor, soprano) starting in hard bop, strode like a giant across the 'free' scene, while Sonny Rollins (tenor) stopped just short of the avant-garde.

Latterday manifestations of jazz have gone in many directions, with the protagonists of the totally extemporized forms drawing ever closer to their counterparts from the 'classical', 'academic', 'serious' (again, vocabulary is the problem) side, making it hard to tell one from the other. To the performers themselves, of course, and to those who claim to understand it, *what* it is is irrelevant.

Some musicians – in particular, Miles Davis – have moved steadily into a fusion of jazz with rock and built up an immense following by so doing.

To sum up: the word 'modern' has been stretched beyond its limit, and we now need some new terms simply in order to be able to communicate. One new label, for a particular manifestation of the desire to be different, might well be 'energy music'.

Books: *Jazz Masters Of The 40s* by Ira Gitler; New York, The Macmillan Co; London, Collier-Macmillan, 1966. *Four Lives In The Bebop Business* by A. B. Spellman; London MacGibbon & Kee 1966. *Mingus: A Critical Biography* by Brian Priestley; London 1982 Quartet Books. *John Coltrane* by Bill Cole; New York, Schirmer Books 1976; London, Collier Macmillan, 1977. *Jazz People* by

Valerie Wilmer; London, Allison & Busby 1970. *Dizzy* by Dizzy Gillespie with Al Fraser; London W. H. Allen, 1980. *Miles Davis* by Ian Carr; London, Quartet Books, 1982; London, Paladin 1984; *Notes And Tones* interviews conducted by Arthur Taylor; London, Quartet Books, 1983. *Jazz Cataclysm* by Barry McRae; London Dent 1967. New York Barnes 1967.

Modern Jazz Quartet Group founded in 1952 by pianist/composer John Lewis (b. 1920) with Milt Jackson (b. 1923) on vibes, Percy Heath (b. 1923) on bass and Kenny Clarke (1914–85) on drums (replaced in 1954 by Connie Kay (b. 1927)). The group, outwardly sombre and serious, played elegant, precise (but, paradoxically, funky) music, formally improvised in a classical manner that some thought put too much restraint on the potentially groovy talents of Jackson and Clarke. The tone was more suited to Connie Kay who played his percussion instruments as if they were made of glass, and latterly the music got even more refined in sound. But, throughout, some beautifully shaped and conceived music resulted. It was mutually decided to wind up the quartet and its official demise was marked by a magnificent *Last Concert* recording. The farewell proved to be impermanent, however, and, starting in 1982, the group has re-formed for specific tours or engagements.

Moldy fig A derisive term used of those whose tastes were outmoded, specifically a person who preferred the older forms of jazz to the bebop innovations of the 40s. More specific than 'square', it was called into being by the strange fact that the eruption of bebop into the public consciousness coincided almost exactly with the revival of interest in early, even archaic, New Orleans jazz, thus splitting the jazz world into two diametrically opposed camps. 'Moldy Fig' was the modernists' name for the purists, and was in use by about 1946. The credit for inventing the term often goes to critic Leonard Feather who rubbed in the point by spelling it 'mouldy figge'.

In a piece called 'The Argot of Jazz' (*New York Sunday Times*, 18 August 1957) Eliott Horne defines a 'fig' as a traditionalist, 'a cat for whom jazz sort of ended with the swing era'; and a 'moldy fig' as a shade worse – 'the swing era was avant-garde for this guy'.

Mole Jazz One of London's leading jazz record shops, owned and run by Graham Griffiths and a group of partners, at 374 Grays Inn Road, London, since 1978. Operates its own sporadically active record label (artists include Art Pepper, Tubby Hayes) from the same address.

Monterey The jazz festival held at Monterey, about 100 miles (160km) south of San Francisco, was started in 1958 by ex-disc jockey-turned-store owner Jimmy Lyons (b. 1918). Among the artists the first year were Dizzy Gillespie, Louis Armstrong, Max Roach, Dave Brubeck, Billie Holiday (she would be dead before the second year's event), The Modern Jazz Quartet. There have been several musical directors, including Dizzy Gillespie, Benny Carter and John Lewis. The current musical director is guitarist, composer, arranger Mundell Lowe.

Montreux, Montreux Festival The Swiss town of Montreux, at the eastern end of Lake Geneva (known to the Swiss as Lac Lemain) in the Vaud canton, population *c*. 20 000, was a fringe ski resort, very much founded on the predominantly British devotion to winter sports in more affluent times. Some of its hotels still have an uncannily British atmosphere about them and the whole town has the genteel aspect of Eastbourne or Cheltenham. The adjacent 15th-century fortress, the Château de Chillon and its famous prisoner were given international notoriety by a poem written by Lord Byron.

Montreux and adjoining Vevey were once favourite resorts of musicians and artists and still many of international affluence reside in the more elevated environs of the town. Montreux had a famous casino as a central attraction. This was burned down and was replaced by a modern monstrosity that sadly lacks the Victorian naughtiness of the original. Losing out to better situated ski-resorts, Montreux has set itself up as a festival centre. Although its facilities are far from ideal, it holds well-established regular festivals devoted to Music, Films and Jazz. The Montreux Jazz Festival has now achieved international standing and many recordings have been made there.

Mooche A dance step included in various social dances of the early 1900s. Also known earlier as *The Congo Grind*, it was basically 'a shuffle forward with both feet, hips first, feet following' and was described in one dance book as 'a hip-grinding ragtime dance'. The step was used in Perry Bradford's *Scratchin' the gravel* dance in 1917.

Perpetuated most memorably in jazz in *The mooche*, a number written by Duke Ellington and Irving Mills in 1928 and long featured by the band. The popular song *Minnie the moocher* might have connections; but then again, 'to mooche' has other meanings. In English, 'mooching' is the disconsolate, apparently aimless trudging of a person pre-occupied with his own, usually depressing thoughts (though it also once meant 'playing truant'). The American language has concentrated on one of the many minor English meanings – 'to get someone else to pay for one's entertainment, drinks, etc.'. 'To scrounge' would be the English equivalent, and since Minnie the moocher in the song, was an opium addict, she may well have had to do plenty of scrounging – mooching – in order to support the habit. It might be no more than coincidence but 'Moose the Mooche' was the code-name, to those in the know, of the pusher who supplied Charlie Parker with his drugs when Bird was in California. He is celebrated in the Charlie Parker tune named after him. His real name was Emry Byrd.

Mound City The popular nickname for the city of St. Louis, Missouri.

Muggsy Chicago-born cornettist Francis Joseph Spanier (1906–67) was nick-named 'Muggsy', not because of his homely countenance which looked like a well-squeezed orange and fully deserved the title but after one 'Muggsy' McGraw, an admired football coach. Spanier was a fine player who did good work throughout his career but is mainly remembered for 16 tracks made with his Ragtime Band in 1939.

MU (Musicians' Union) ban Musicians' Union ban is a somewhat inaccurate shorthand for the rift which existed for over 20 years between the Musicians' Union in Britain and the American Federation of Musicians. The trouble began in 1935, when, at the last moment, the AF of M objected so strongly to the proposal that Jack Hylton should take his British band to America for a series of concerts that the whole tour was called off. The MU in Britain retaliated and from then until 1956 each union excluded the others members from its territory. The ban was not consistent since it applied only to performers in the popular and jazz fields; classical musicians were exempt. It also led to some strange anomalies as during the war American musicians were constant visitors to the UK either as service personnel or sent to entertain them. The ban was modified in 1956 after long negotiations, and as a first result the Stan Kenton band from America was exchanged for the Ted Heath band from England. The man-for-man exchange worked out had obvious disadvantages as America needed visiting jazz musicians like it needed the Black Death, whereas Britain was hungry for American jazz stars. The system began to work better when British music in the shape of the Beatles and other pop groups (included in the reckoning) were wanted in USA; so once again we were able to hear American jazzmen without having to travel to the Continent.

Muskrat The muskrat is a large kind of water rat common in North America, its name derived from its musk-like odour. It was a popular source of income among the rural Creoles and Cajuns of Louisiana who trapped it for its fur. Even such a humble creature has been honoured in jazz – notably in a number *Muskrat ramble* composed by trombonist Kid Ory in 1925, an amalgamation of several traditional marching tunes from 19th-century New Orleans. It became one of the most popular numbers among New Orleans jazz bands.

The occasional tendency to spell it *muskat* may well stem from a confusion with Muscat or Muscat Hill, a local name for a district in Shreveport, Louisiana. It has even been suggested that *Muscat ramble* – another spelling – was an allusion to the unsteady gait of those who had drunk too much muscatel. It seems most likely that Ory had the zoological muskrat in mind. Muskrat has occasionally been used as a slang name for a moustache.

Mute A device used for modifying, softening or altering the tone of an instrument. While most instruments have some such appropriate devices available, the ones of most concern in jazz are those for cornet, trumpet or trombone, the use of which has been part of the growing language and style of jazz-playing. The most primitive muting device for the smaller brass instruments is the player's hand, clenched, fanned out or waved in front of the bell. Purpose-built implements range from the straight mute, which merely softens the sound, and the more elaborate pear-shaped Conn mute, to various contraptions which have derived from the original artefacts which some jazz musicians held in the bells of their instruments to obtain talking or growling effects, such as a glass or bottle, a derby hat or a plumber's rubber plunger. From these came the wa-wa mute (with a movable part to vary the tone), the plunger mute and the manufactured derby. Various musicians have invented their own devices. The main object is to obtain an array of artificial tones that add flexibility and colour to playing. One bandleader who was particularly interested in the tonal possibilities of mutes was Duke Ellington who used such experts as Bubber Miley, Cootie Williams and Joe Nanton in his Kentucky and Cotton Club days (and later) to achieve the famous Jungle Band sound.

Name band A term in general use in the swing era to categorize a band, generally a large one, that was fronted by a prominent leader such as Benny Goodman, Artie Shaw, Harry James and so on. A band which a promoter could sell on its name alone.

National Federation of Jazz Organizations of Great Britain and Northern Ireland (NFJO) Organization founded in June 1948 to protect and promote jazz in Great Britain. Its founders included Rex Harris, Ray Sonin, Joseph Feldman, Bert Wilcox, Ken Lindsay and Sinclair Traill. Organized annual concerts (Hammer-smith Palais and elsewhere) (traditional and modern) and promoted the visits of overseas musicians after the bans (1935–1956) had been lifted. *Jazz News* started as the monthly organ of the Federation.

National Youth Jazz Orchestra (NYJO) A British big band, offering training to young instrumentalists and – to a lesser degree – singers. It was founded in 1966 and is run by Bill Ashton. Prominent British musicians who have passed through its ranks include Steve Arguelles (drums), Jamie Talbot, Chris Biscoe, Tim Whitehead (saxophones), Guy

Barker (trumpet). NYJO has recorded several LPs, latterly on its own NYJO label.

Needle, The Short-lived jazz monthly published from Jackson Heights, New York and edited by Robert Reynolds. Started publication in June 1944 and finished in 1945. From Vol. 2 onward it concentrated on New Orleans jazz and blues and contained some valuable articles and reviews.

Negro, nigger, etc. Throughout the written history of jazz there has been some difficulty in finding an objective, unslanted name for black Americans. The desire to be neither offensive nor frivolous on the part of the white sympathiser, or to be circumspect on the part of the black, arising from the long history of slavery, prejudice and apartheid (which still flourishes in some parts of the world), is hard to satisfy within the existing vocabulary. The word negro, although a genuine and accurate ethnic term, generally used objectively and scientifically for black people of African origin with the characteristic negroid features, is perhaps too much a reminder of past history for people who like to be thought of as Americans. Moreover, it was tainted in the past by the almost entirely derogatory perversion of the word negro into such forms as 'nigger', 'nigga' or 'nigra' by the slave-owning white elements of the southern states. It was taken up, mostly in a genuinely jocular way, by others in the USA and abroad simply as a descriptive term and used in song-titles and elsewhere in the burgeoning period of black music and jazz *c.* 1850–1920. Thereafter, any such use began to smack once again of condescension and bias. As late as 1927/8 such publications as the *Melody Maker* in England were still writing about 'nigger' music; and in 1927 the Spanish-born jazz musician and composer Fred Elizalde wrote a suite called *The Heart of a Nigger* which was presented at the London Palladium by Bert Ambrose's Mayfair Orchestra. The *Melody Maker*, praising

it as 'a marvellous piece of work' noticed with amusement that on the posters it had been altered (and they clearly wondered why) to *The Heart of a Coon*.

The alternative use of the word 'coon' (deriving from raccoon which the southern Negroes were said to enjoy hunting and eating), was in use by the early 1800s; the song *Zip coon* was published in 1829. 'Coon' was probably thought less offensive in a racial (racist) sense but was nonetheless rather slanted to suggest simplicity and clownishness, even idiocy, and was so used in the USA (maybe as a mistake for goon) for portraying the black races, as many whites liked to do, in the golliwog image. It comes as something of a shock, therefore, to discover that the writer (Ernest Hogan) of a song called *All coons look alike to me* was in fact black. The girl in the song is so besotted with her particular boyfriend that she cannot distinguish him from the rest of the black males. It is difficult to decide at this range whether the word 'coon' was being used in irony, resignation, or as straightforward matter of course. Whatever the answer, it became an unacceptable word concurrently with nigger, and the colloquial 'darkie'.

In recent times a conscious avoidance of the word Negro has been deemed correct (some American editions of British books undergoing amendment as a result) in accordance with the thoughts behind the Black Movement in America, black power, etc. Black Music became the accepted classification of all music of Afro-American origin. But already there seems to have been a slight adjustment back to Negro as being less conscious of the colour aspect (also simply as a way of reducing repetition of 'black'). It is still a fraught and difficult subject. Whatever word is used, it will, until the world's moronic and unthinking racial and colour prejudices are finally eradicated, still leave those who would most like to be unconcerned with such prejudices uneasy at whatever form they use. The ideal will have arrived when there is no longer need to differentiate.

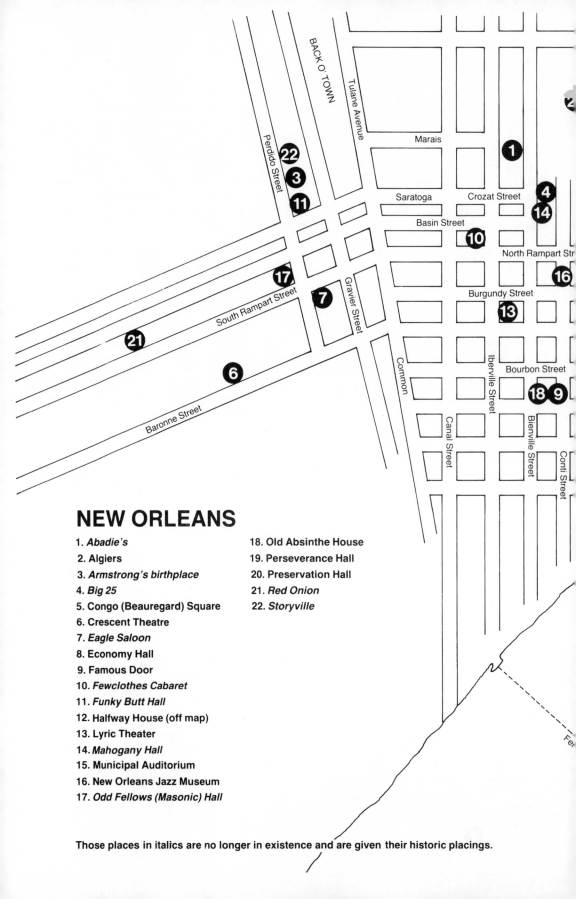

NEW ORLEANS

1. *Abadie's*
2. Algiers
3. *Armstrong's birthplace*
4. *Big 25*
5. Congo (Beauregard) Square
6. Crescent Theatre
7. *Eagle Saloon*
8. Economy Hall
9. Famous Door
10. *Fewclothes Cabaret*
11. *Funky Butt Hall*
12. Halfway House (off map)
13. Lyric Theater
14. *Mahogany Hall*
15. Municipal Auditorium
16. New Orleans Jazz Museum
17. *Odd Fellows (Masonic) Hall*
18. Old Absinthe House
19. Perseverance Hall
20. Preservation Hall
21. *Red Onion*
22. *Storyville*

Those places in italics are no longer in existence and are given their historic placings.

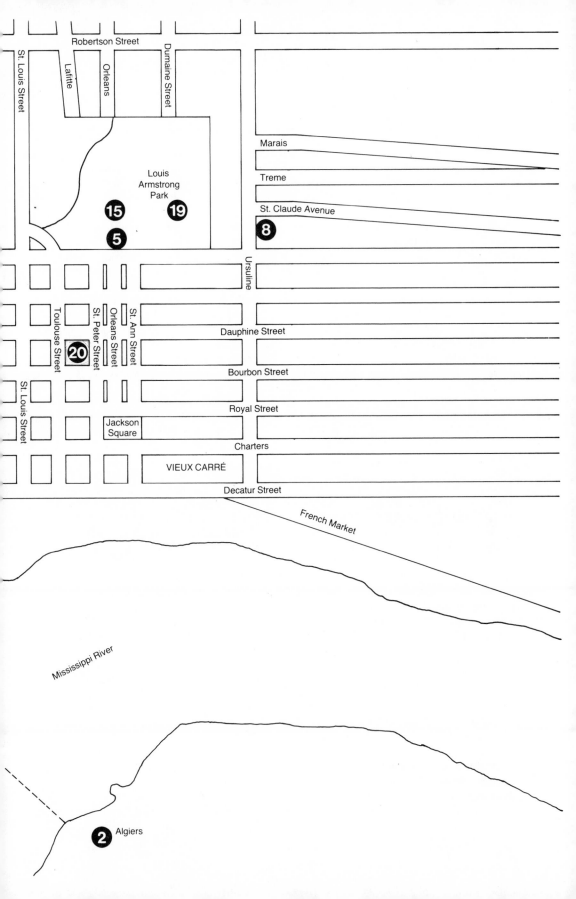

Robertson Street

Lafitte

Orleans

Dumaine Street

St. Louis Street

Marais

Treme

St. Claude Avenue

Louis Armstrong Park

15   **19**

5

8

Ursuline

Toulouse Street

St. Peter Street

Orleans Street

St. Ann Street

Dauphine Street

20

Bourbon Street

St. Louis Street

Royal Street

Jackson Square

Charters

VIEUX CARRÉ

Decatur Street

French Market

Mississippi River

2 Algiers

New Orleans Largest city and seaport of Louisiana (capital Baton Rouge) in southern USA, lying on the Mississippi River some 90 miles (145 km) from its final exit into the Gulf of Mexico through the Mississippi River Delta area, which extends north to Vicksburg. It has become the most famous place-name in the annals of jazz and is generally credited as being the 'birthplace' of the music, though many careful historians would now rather consider it as the 'incubator' – a fine distinction. Geographically it makes sense that a hybrid popular folk art like jazz should be developed in what was then the major southern port of the USA, the outlet for multifarious trade that came down the vast lengths of the Mississippi and the towns and cities thereon and along the burgeoning railroad system; a melting-pot for the peripatetic humanity that attracts and feeds the 'entertainment' business in its widest possible sense; thriving off the after-hours labourer with money to spend.

New Orleans was founded in 1718 by the brothers D'Iberville and D'Bienville who led the expeditionary force to explore and exploit the Mississippi from 1698 on. Their choice for the site of New Orleans was not exactly a wise one, though the access to Lake Pontchartrain to the north was considered a useful asset. Almost exactly at, and sometimes below, sea-level, the city was constantly in danger from floods and hurricanes, most of it being built on reclaimed swamp and marshland; which still has a disastrous effect on housing whose foundations never settle. It is said that a cellar is more or less unknown in New Orleans. The city had to be protected by raised levees with pumping stations constantly at work. By 1721, much of the old original French Quarter (Vieux Carré) was established and there were nearly 500 inhabitants. In 1722 it was made the State capital, a privilege it held for nearly 100 years; but that same year a hurricane almost obliterated the city. It was now rebuilt in the typical American way with wide, straight streets intersecting at right-angles, though the housing style remained predominantly French. The considerable dominance of French culture is still reflected in the majority of the street names, as well as in the name of the city itself.

There were many contenders for the possession of this valuable port, the British included, but it was the Spanish who took possession in 1762. It was eventually regained by the French in 1800, then sold to the Americans as part of the Louisiana Purchase in 1803. By 1775 there were 5000 inhabitants with the boom period that followed shooting this figure to 24 000 by 1810. War against the British in 1812 and many epidemics of yellow fever reduced the growth for a while; but soon the introduction of the steamboat opened up the profitable commerce with the upper reaches of the Mississippi and by 1820 the population was back to 25 000. By 1840 it was 102 000. Further prosperity came with the opening of the railroads and by 1850 some 25 000 Irish had swelled the numbers. In the developing jazz years, around 1900, the population hovered around a quarter of a million.

New Orleans, in spite of extensive travelling facilities, remained culturally isolated from the rest of the USA. It has been described as 'the most Northern Caribbean city'. To add to the original French Creole founders came a mixture of people and cultures from the West Indies and South America, from the rest of North America and Europe, the latter predominantly French and Spanish. It was also described as 'the Marseilles of the USA'. Like most seaport cities, it became a place of wild contrasts; the beautiful, elegant tree-lined avenues where 'the rich merchants did dwell' contrasting with the crowded ghettoes of the poorer areas, the squalor of the commercial districts. As a main outlet for the cotton trade it naturally had a large black population. By 1810 New Orleans was the fifth largest city in the USA. For some years it remained prosperous, certainly through the two World War periods, but it began to decline thereafter. In 1950 it was still the South's largest city with 570 000 inhabitants but by 1970 it had dropped again to fifth place.

New Orleans, because of its geographical alignment in a southward bend of the Mississippi and with the less acute bend of Lake Pontchartrain to the north, has long been nicknamed the Crescent City. A more recent nickname is the Big Easy. The natives pronounce the name something like Noo-Orlins or Noo-Orlyins. As the Mississippi actually flows north for a short distance through the city, Uptown, i.e. up-river, is in the south of the city, and Downtown is north.

Like most seaports and cities New Orleans is divided into various cultural and national areas. In the broadest terms Canal Street, running from the river almost to the shores of Lake Pontchartrain, separates the newer American section from the old French city. The French Quarter, the Vieux Carré, was the original city and is still full of 18th- and early 19th-century buildings and still very much the cultural centre. Its borders are Esplanade Avenue, the Mississippi, Canal Street and North Rampart Street. The famous French Market is on the river front by Jackson Square. Although predominantly Creole, the area is less so than it once was and a large Sicilian contingent, amongst others, also lives in the area.

It is often written that the area known as Storyville, 38 blocks set aside as an area of licensed prostitution from 1897 to 1917, and a fertile area of jazz development, lay within the French Quarter. In fact, it was just beyond its bounds to the north-west of Canal Street. Storyville has frequently been pinpointed as the birthplace of New Orleans jazz but some historians, like Al Rose, have modified this statement: 'though Storyville may have been the forge in which some of the pure gold jazz was smelted, it was really born in the dance halls and saloons of the New Orleans lakefront areas like Milneburg, Bucktown and along South Rampart and Bourbon Streets'. The fact that jazz moved up-river to Memphis, St. Louis, Kansas City, Chicago and thence

to New York and the world around 1917, the year Storyville closed, is probably coincidental rather than precisely linked. It was perhaps more simply that the richest pickings in New Orleans were now exhausted anyway so that jazz, as the new blood of entertainment and popular music, quite naturally flowed out to the other cities of rich promise. 1917 was about the right time and it would have happened anyway.

Within New Orleans there are various other areas of cultural significance: German, Latin-American, Chinese and so on – as in any industrial city. The other well-defined areas are Uptown – including the Central Business District (just up-river from the French Quarter and the equivalent of London's City – bustling on weekdays, deserted during the weekend); the Garden District, the Irish Channel and the University area. The Garden District and Lower Garden District are the best residential areas full of fine Victorian mansions dating from the days of the cotton boom; the Irish Channel is the working-class area. Algiers, over the river from the French Quartet, is populated by the older New Orleans families, partly seedy, partly *nouveau riche* – a sort of Islington in London terms. Lakefront is the city's entertainment area, lined with good seafood restaurants.

The jazz-oriented view of New Orleans is, perhaps, a slightly exaggerated one. In a book called *Music in New Orleans* (1966) by Henry A. Kmen (1915–78), which many ardent jazz seekers may have perused with disappointment, there is an excellent documentation of the city's thriving musical life, mainly centred on the French opera and the famous operahouses, the balls, concerts and brass bands; with a mere chapter at the end taking a cursory but informed glance at the beginnings of Negro music in the city. There is quite a lot of jazz in New Orleans but it is still only a small part of the city's musical life.

It has long been assumed, the assumptions backed by definite claims by early musicians such as Armstrong, Morton

7.30 - 8.0 p.m. **Joe Daniels** and his Dixieland Jazz Band

8.0 - 8.30 p.m. **Humphrey Lyttelton** and his Band

8.30 - 9.0 p.m. **Harry Gold** and his Pieces of Eight

9.0 - 9.30 p.m. **Freddy Randall** and his Band

9.30 p.m. **Lou Preager** *introduces*

"JAZZ PARADE"

featuring

9.30 - 9.45 The **Crane River** Jazz Band

9.45 - 10.0 **Chris Barber** and his New Orleans
Dance Band

10.0 - 10.15 **Mick Mulligan** and his Magnolia
Jazz Band

10.15 - 10.30 **Mike Daniels** and his Delta Band

Compered by
JAMES ASMAN

10.30 - 10.45 p.m. **Joe Daniels** and his Dixieland Jazz Band

10.45 - 11.0 p.m. **Freddy Randall** and his Band

11.0 - 11.15 p.m. **Harry Gold** and his Pieces of Eight

11.15 - 11.30 p.m. **Humphrey Lyttelton** and his Band

THE KING

General Compere: **MARK WHITE**
(By permission of the Directors of Empress Hall)

LUDO PRESS LTD., S.W.18

~The Palais~
Dancing News

No. 5 Vol. 1   March 19th, 1951   Price 6d

HAMMERSMITH PALAIS LTD.
(Managing Director: Claude Langdon)

in conjunction with

THE NATIONAL
FEDERATION OF JAZZ ORGANISATIONS
(President: The Marquess of Donegall)

present

The Second Annual
"JAZZ BAND BALL"

A CAVALCADE OF JAZZ from 1901 to 1951

Comperes:
The Marquess of Donegall
James Asman   Lou Preager
Sinclair Traill   Mark White

7.30 - 8.0 p.m.   **The Crane River Jazz Band**

8.0 - 8.30 p.m.   **Humphrey Lyttelton and his Band**

8.30 - 9.0 p.m.   **The Christie Brothers Stompers**
(with Denny Coffey)

9.0 - 9.30 p.m.   **Freddy Randall and his Band**

9.30 - 10.0 p.m.   **King Oliver Memorial**
Compere : Rex Harris
Guest Artist : Nigel Carter (Trumpet)

10.0 - 10.30 p.m.   **The Crane River Jazz Band**

10.30 - 11.0 p.m.   **Freddy Randall and his Band**

11.0 - 11.30 p.m.   **The Christie Brothers Stompers**
(with Denny Coffey)

11.30 - 12 midnt.   **Humphrey Lyttelton and his Band**

THE QUEEN

Our Guest Singer this evening is
Neva Raphaello

You can hear Neva between 9.0 and 9.30
with Freddy Randall's Band and again
between 11.30 and midnight with
Humphrey Lyttelton's Band

Ludo Press, Ltd., S.W.18

EMPRESS HALL
LONDON, S.W.6.   PHONE: FULHAM 1212

By arrangement with Claude Langdon

THE NATIONAL FEDERATION
OF JAZZ ORGANISATIONS
(President : The Marquess of Donegall)

— *present* —

The Third Annual
"JAZZ BAND BALL"

including

A KING OLIVER MEMORIAL

(Born : 1885   Died : 1938)

Wednesday, April 30th, 1952   Programme : Price 6d.

NFJO Jazz Band Balls of the 1950s.

The Old Absinthe House, portrayed on the sleeve of a New Orleans-based recording. (Tempo Records, 1959).

THE LONDON
JAZZ CLUB

MACK'S RESTAU'RANT
100 OXFORD STREET, W.I.

PRESENTS YOUR . . . . . .

"SATURDAY NIGHT JAZZ"

SATURDAY, MARCH 25th, 1950.

SPECIAL TWO-BAND SESSION.

HUMPHREY LYTTELTON AND HIS BAND
with
NEVA RAPHAELLO

MIC'. MULLIGAN'S MAGNOLIA JAZZ BAND
with
GEORGE MELLEY.

Economical programmes were the order of the day in 1950.

Right Catalogue of a valuable series issued by Decca in 1957. (The Decca Record Co. Ltd)

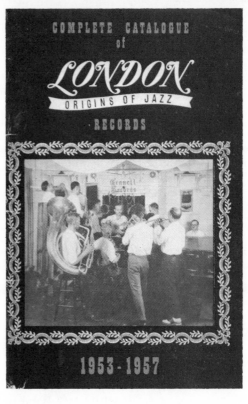

COMPLETE CATALOGUE
of
LONDON
ORIGINS OF JAZZ
RECORDS

1953 - 1957

and others, that jazz began in New Orleans. In the light of our still vague but gradually increasing knowledge of the ways of popular music-making, the statement might be modified to say that jazz first emerged in a discernible way and began its commercial growth in New Orleans, finding there a fertile and profitable centre for its early development and exploitation.

But who actually first played a musical phrase with the new jazz intonation is never going to be discovered and the arguments will rage and the theories be propounded for as long as anyone is interested in discussing jazz.

New Orleans jazz Was there, in fact, a definitive New Orleans style; or was it simply the early experimental form that jazz would have taken on wherever it happened to develop? By New Orleans style we generally understand a small group, usually one of each instrument involved (though departures from this came early), with cornet or trumpet leading the ensemble and making the initial statement of the theme – a tenor role; the trombone playing an underlying counterpoint – a bass role; the clarinet playing a decorative ad lib high register part. Each of the solo instruments takes it in turn to assume the lead, the others generally continuing to play in improvised counterpoint or riffs. The front line instruments are backed by a rhythm section – a drummer with an elementary kit keeping a steady beat going; a banjo or guitar chording in a matchingly relentless way; and a wind-bass, tuba or bass-saxophone, later a string-bass.

It is said that the typical line-up, as above, arose because of the availability from *c.* 1865 onward of discarded Civil War military band instruments. The cornet, perhaps, but the standard Civil War band, apart from four or five big units (Schwarz: *Bands of America*) was *c.* 17 players, comprising four cornets, three altos, three baritones, three basses (horns not saxes), three snare drums and a bass drum. Most of the typical brass

instruments never got into jazz beyond the flexible trumpet and trombone.

Although parading was a large part of New Orleans band activities, this was done mainly by specialized brass bands, the jazz units functioning mostly in dance halls. Presumably most of these places would have a piano of sorts and this would have been an early part of the grouping.

Books: *Jazz: New Orleans 1885–1963: an Index to the Negro Musicians of New Orleans* by Samuel B. Charters. 173p. rev. ed. New York: Oak Publications, 1963; *New Orleans Jazz: a Family Album* by Al Rose & Edmond Souchon. 362p. 3rd rev. ed. Baton Rouge: Louisiana State University Press, 1984; *New Orleans, the Revival: a Tape and Discography of Negro Traditional Jazz Recorded in New Orleans or by New Orleans Bands, 1937–1972* by Tom Stagg & Charlie Crump. 332p. New Orleans: Bashall Eaves, 1973; *Preservation Hall Portraits* by Larry Borenstein & Bill Russell. np. Baton Rouge: Louisiana State University Press, 1968.

New Orleans Jazz Archive More fully the William Ransom Hogan Jazz Archive, it was founded in 1958 with the help of a $75 000 grant from the Ford Foundation at Tulane University. Its work included most notably an encouragement to study jazz seriously and comprehensively and the making of many archival recordings of surviving pioneer jazzmen. The museum's first curator was William Russell, succeeded by Richard B. Allen in 1969 and Curt Jerde in 1980. The archive (which will gradually be made public) contains over 1500 reels of interviews, over 25 000 records, 15 000 pieces of sheet music, including rare early rags and blues, photographs, posters, a comprehensive collection of jazz books and periodicals, all of which are being catalogued for the use of researchers. The collection is part of the Howard-Tilton Memorial Library at Tulane.

New Orleans Jazz Band Dixieland co-op group operating 1918–22 in New Orleans of which Jimmy Durante (1893–1980), later famous on stage and screen, was the pianist.

New Orleans Jazz Club Founded in an

informal way in 1949 by Johnny Wiggs (1899–1977) as a place to play, preserve and appreciate the legacy of New Orleans jazz, it organized monthly meetings at a New Orleans hotel which attracted large audiences. It did much to revive interest in surviving pioneer musicians and in the general study of jazz. Also presents 'Jazz on Sunday Afternoon' concerts, a weekly radio show 'Jazz from Congo Square', runs a magazine *Second Line* and launched the New Orleans Jazz Museum.

New Orleans Jazz Museum Housed at 333 Conti Street (previously at 1017 Dumaine Street and Economy Hall) the Museum was founded in 1959 by Edmond 'Doc' Souchon (1897–1968), obstetrician and jazz musician (guitar, banjo and vocalist) and originally run by the New Orleans Jazz Club. Its other co-founders included Myra Menville and Helen Arlt. The costs becoming too much of a burden, the collection was handed over to the Louisiana State Museum in 1972. Its curator since 1979 has been Don Marquis, and guitarist Danny Barker was an assistant curator for some years. The collection includes many instruments used by jazz musicians, such as Louis Armstrong's first cornet, Larry Shields' clarinet, Tom Brown's trombone, posters, banners, contracts, music, recordings, films, photographs and a library.

New Orleans Ragtime Orchestra Group formed in 1967 to play and record music of the 'Red Book' classic ragtime kind, cakewalks and early jazz numbers of *c.* 1890–1915 period in particular. Travelled throughout USA and came to Europe under the leadership of pianist Lars Ivar Edegran.

New Orleans rhythm and blues In the years when New Orleans jazz was purely a matter of moldy fig revival, New Orleans came into its own again in the rock and roll era of the 1950s with a special 'happy-go-lucky' sound that had something of the old jazz spirit in its roots. Its flavour has been described as 'strong drums, heavy bass, light piano, heavy guitar, light horn sound, and strong lead vocals', and many recordings in this vein were made in Cosimo Matassa's studios in the French Quarter of New Orleans. The larger record companies latched on to this new New Orleans music and hits in the vein were produced by such artists as Roy Brown (b. 1925), Fats Domino (b. 1928), Ray Charles, (b. 1932), Little Richard (b. 1932) and many others. The success spawned new local record companies such as Johnny Vincent's Ace label founded in 1955. The boom in this style and the new classic New Orleans vintage more or less came to an end *c.* 1962.

New Orleans Rhythm Kings Famous white band formed in 1922 and led by the trumpeter Paul Mares. In its early days, playing at the Friar's Inn in Chicago, it was known as the Friar's Inn Orchestra and included in its ranks such historic names as Leon Ropollo (clarinet), George Brunies (trombone) and Elmer Schoebel (piano). Their name and early position in jazz history have tended to give them a legendary aura. They made some immortal records; Ropollo was an inspired player on occasions and Brunies a fine natural exponent of tailgate trombone, but, in the words of Barry Ulanov: 'the ensemble sounds weak and the inspiration lags'. They made their first recordings as the Friars Society Orchestra in September 1922 at the Gennett studios in Richmond by which time Ben Pollack had taken over on drums, but the original drummer, Frank Snyder, was back for the next session in March 1923. Trumpeter Emmett Hardy played with them for a while. A recording session in August 1923 saw the unusual innovation of a black musician, Jelly Roll Morton, sitting in with the band for four sides. For a time they played at the Cascades Ballroom in Chicago. Mares and Ropollo went to New York in 1924 and the group disbanded but was reorganized by Mares for a short time in 1925. A recording band under the same name operated in

NEW YORK Place names past and present

1. Apollo Theater
2. Arcadia Ballroom
3. Band Box
4. Beefsteak Charlie's
5. Bellevue Hospital
6. Big John's
7. Birdland
8. Bop City
9. Brittwood Bar
10. Café Society (2)
11. Capitol Palace
12. Carnegie Hall
13. Condon's
14. Connie's Inn
15. Cotton Club
16. Count Basie's
17. Crescent Theater
18. Famous Door
19. Hickory House
20. Jimmy Ryan's
21. Kentucky Club
22. Lafayette Theater
23. Lenox Club
24. Leroy's
25. Minton's
26. New York Jazz Museum
27. Nick's (off map)
28. Reisenweber's
29. Rhythm Club
30. Roseland Ballroom
31. Royal Roost
32. Savoy Ballroom
33. Small's Paradise
34. Spotlite Club
35. Sugar Hill
36. Three Deuces
37. Village Gate
38. Village Vanguard
39. Wall Street

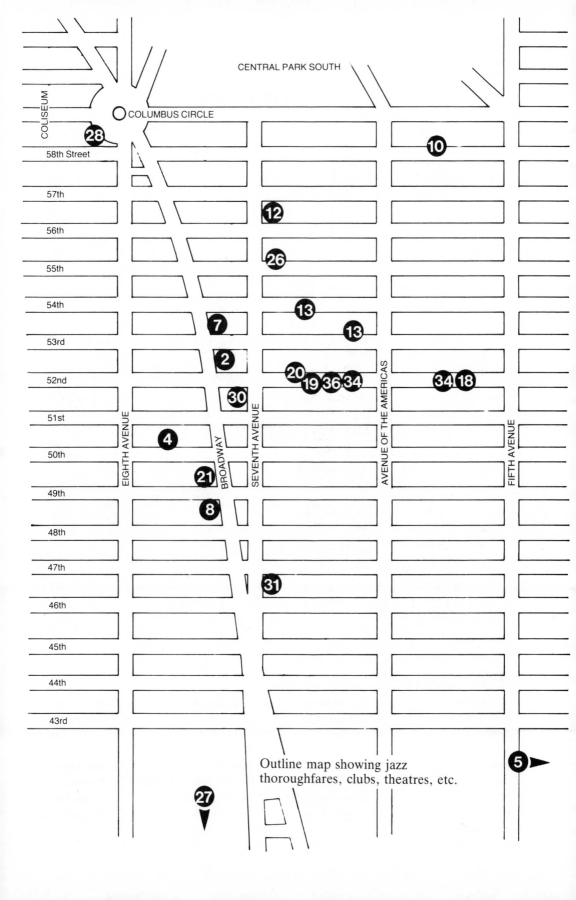

CENTRAL PARK SOUTH

COLISEUM

COLUMBUS CIRCLE

28

58th Street

57th

12

56th

10

26

55th

54th

13

7

53rd

13

2

20

19 36 34

34 18

52nd

30

51st

EIGHTH AVENUE

BROADWAY

SEVENTH AVENUE

AVENUE OF THE AMERICAS

FIFTH AVENUE

4

50th

21

49th

8

48th

47th

31

46th

45th

44th

43rd

5

Outline map showing jazz
thoroughfares, clubs, theatres, etc.

27

the 1930s, led by Muggsy Spanier with only Brunies of the originals left.

Newport Jazz Festival Jazz Festival founded and produced from 1954 by pianist/singer/club owner George Wein (b. 1925) at Newport, Rhode Island. Apart from 1961 there was a festival at Newport each year until vandals curtailed the 1971 event; thereafter, it was moved to New York City, expanding at the same time from a three to four-day event to ten days. Similar festivals have been produced under the Newport banner in other locations in the USA and since 1964 a touring version has visited various places in Europe. George Wein, a jazz performer in his early days, started his own club, the Storyville, in Boston in 1950. Beside the Newport Festival he has also produced the New Orleans Jazz Festival since 1970 and in 1974 inaugurated La Grande Parade du Jazz at Nice in France. In 1974 he founded the New York Jazz Repertory Company. Various live recordings have been made at the Newport Festivals; and a notable film, *Jazz on a Summer's Day* (1959).

For a while after its move away from Newport the festival was known as Newport in New York. With the coming of commercial sponsors, however, the Newport connections have been completely severed, so that the event's recent manifestations have been as the Kool Festival, after the cigarette company which underwrote it. In 1986 the Japanese-based audio engineering film of JUC took over sponsorship.

New York The commercial and cultural, if not the administrative capital of America, and thus the great magnet – for immigrants from other lands, for tourists, and for every known form of entertainment, including jazz. There was an embryo black population – mostly slaves – in New York by the early 18th century. Conceivably, therefore, New York didn't have to wait for jazz 'to come up the river' (courtesy of Fate Marable) via Chicago, but already had something vaguely resembling primitive jazz right

from the beginning. If that was the case, there was proportionally less of it than in New Orleans and it was not remarked upon. What is clear is that by the second and third decades of the 20th century, New York was the place to come to for any jazz musician who hankered for fame and, in moments of giddy optimism, fortune. Ragtime was certainly in New York by the early 1900s, for it was at that period already a national craze; failing other evidence, it seems that New York's only actual contribution to jazz, therefore, was the loosening up of ragtime, making possible its evolution into New York, or Harlem, stride piano, a category no one seems to question.

If we seek a moment when jazz made a *chronicled* impact on New York, then we have to accept that it was when the Original Dixieland Jazz Band, billed as the 'first' 'jazz' band, opened at Reisenweber's '400' room in 1917. From that point on, New York began to attract exponents of each successive kind of jazz, so that – except for the lightweight and jolly music played by the bands which gathered around Red Nichols, with the convenient label of 'New York jazz' (see below) – there has never been a clearly definable New York style. That said, however, when a more detached, tidier manifestation of bebop began to be apparent on the West Coast in the early 1950s, New York seemed to respond almost deliberately with the more raw, overtly emotional jazz which a little later would be referred to as 'hard bop'. But the fact remains that New York is the place that jazz musicians from everywhere else try to get to sooner or later, so that the city and its environs harbour, somewhere within an area housing well over seven million people, examples of jazz of almost every style.

New York jazz At one point in jazz history writing there was a tendency to give the label New York jazz to the kind of precise, lightly swinging sort of jazz that was, roughly speaking, played by the kind of white groups that were led by Red Nichols, Phil Napoleon and Miff

Mole from whose ranks such key figures of the swing era as Benny Goodman and Glenn Miller emerged. Only in that this sort of music had its centre in New York on the fringes of the entertainment world, was it a valid label. But it didn't take into account the fact that in Harlem many of the important developments in black jazz were taking place. It seems wiser, in the face of the multifarious melting-pot activities that took place in New York from the time of the ODJB's initial impact there *c*. 1917, to accept the edicts of Coleman Hawkins and others that there was no such thing, really, as typical New York jazz. An opinion that the fascinating detail to be found in *Jazz: a History of the New York Scene* by Samuel B. Charters and Leonard Kunstadt (New York: Doubleday, 1962; repr. Da Capo, 1981), and other books on the subject, will substantiate.

New York currently has about 50 jazz venues which may be checked by telephoning Jazzline on [0101] [212] 423 0488.

NFJO see **National Federation of Jazz Organizations**

Nice Jazz Festival Annual jazz festival held in the ancient Roman amphitheatre, the Arènes des Cimiez, in the French resort of Nice, probably now the most prestigious in Europe. The festival (properly La Grande Parade du Jazz) was founded by promoter George Wein (b. 1925) in 1974 and has thrived ever since.

Nicknames The word 'nickname' itself means simply an extra name, the original form being an 'eke-name' – eke meaning 'also', as in *John Gilpin* – 'a train band captain eke was he of famous London Town'. The word went back to Chaucerian days. By means of those inexplicable contortions that language goes through (either as a result of some misprint in a latterday British newspaper or simply through too much alcohol) the word became 'nekename' and, finally, nickname. Nicknames tend to be used either in a derisory way when at a

distance from the subject or as familiar pleasantries by intimate associates. Most of the ones in jazz fall into the latter category. It is interesting to note that the word nickname has also been applied to a name erroneously given, a perpetuated error, as when Wesleyans became known as Methodists.

Jazz is replete with them, some wildly obscure. We deal with a few for which we have been able to find reasonably valid explanation. We omit those which are obvious corruptions or abbreviations of true names, e.g. 'Eubie' for James Hubert Blake, 'Klook' a portmanteau version of Kenny and Clarke, or such shortenings as 'Tadd', 'Natty' or 'Tal' (short for Talmadge); or others, like 'Cutty' Cutshall, used simply for their onomatopoeic euphony. In most cases, here, a reference to the real name will be sufficiently revealing.

Those nicknames which refer to such personal traits as obesity are also fairly obvious – e.g. 'Fats' (Domino, Pichon, Waller), 'Tubby' (Hall, Hayes), 'Chubby' (Jackson) or 'Ham'; likewise stature as in 'Big' (Sid Catlett) or 'Big T' (Teagarden). There are a great variety of names affectionately relating to smallness. An interesting one is 'Stump' Evans – often referred to as 'Stomp' in early listings as perhaps seeming more appropriate to a jazz musician. There were many named 'Shorty' (cut off my legs and call me . . .) (Baker, Rogers, Sherrock) while various small animals have been a popular source of reference, as with Johnny 'Rabbit' Hodges, 'Bunny' Berigan and 'Chick' Webb. There was also 'Half-Pint' Jaxon who was reported to be 5′ 2″ (1.57 m) tall. Perversely (and jazz and Cockney slang take a delight in paradoxical naming), 'Tiny' is also often applied to those of considerable stature (Bradshaw, Grimes, Parham). Neither is 'Slim' always used in its correct physical sense, being more of a friendly pleasantry like 'Buster'.

Physical defects, as in 'Cripple' Clarence Lofton, are generally referred to in a kindly humorous and roundabout way. Those unfortunate enough to find themselves at some point in their career deprived of an arm are generally known as 'Wingy' (Carpenter, Manone), or a leg 'Pegleg'. There are numerous musicians simply referred to as 'Blind' or 'Blind Boy' but often the less direct approach was sought as in 'Big Eye' (Nelson). 'King' Oliver (referred to elsewhere) was earlier known as 'Bad Eye' or 'Monocles' owing to an early injury to his left eye. The Olympia Orchestra in which he played was sometimes known as the 'Monocles' Orchestra.

The more personal nicknames are infinite in number and some are often difficult to explain in a logical manner. For individual nicknames see entries under: BABY, BEAN, BEARCAT, BIFFLY, BIG CHIEF, BIG FOOT, BIG T, BIRD, BIX (see comments), BOJANGLES, BRICKTOP, BUNK, BUNNY, BUSTER, CANNONBALL, CAT, CHICK, CHIPPIE, CHU, CLEANHEAD, COUNT, COW-COW, DIPPERMOUTH, DOC, DUKE, FACE, FATHA, FIVE-BY-FIVE, GATEMOUTH, GEECHIE, HORSECOLLAR, HOT LIPS, JACK THE BEAR, JELLY ROLL, THE LION, LOCKJAW, LUX, MEZZ, MUGGSY, PINETOP, POPS, PREZ, RABBIT, RED, SATCHMO, SKIP, SLOW DRAG, SMACK, SPIKE, STALEBREAD, SWEE'PEA, SYMPHONY SID, TRICKY SAM, TURK, WINGY, YARDBIRD, YAS YAS GIRL, ZOOT and ZUTTY.

It is interesting to note that the American preoccupation with strip cartoons is reflected in the use of many popular cartoon names as nicknames, e.g. 'Peanuts'.

Nick's Dixieland haunt opened in New York's Greenwich Village by Nick Rongetti in 1936 on Seventh Avenue and 10th Street. For many years it vied as a traditionalists' mecca with Eddie Condon's club, but when Condon moved to the upper East Side, Nick's was left to carry the Greenwich Village banner alone. Among those who purveyed their art there, were Pee Wee Russell, Jack Teagarden, Muggsy Spanier, Bobby Hackett, Wild Bill Davison, Max Kaminsky, Miff Mole, Bud Freeman, Sidney Bechet, Phil Napoloen, Joe Marsala and George Brunies. During its last years the club was run by Nick's widow. It closed in August 1963 when its lease ended, leaving Greenwich village with only isolated Dixieland bashes in a largely cool jazz environment.

Nigger see **Negro**

NORK see **New Orleans Rhythm Kings**

Notes Quarterly 'Magazine devoted to Music and its Literature' published by the Music Library Association of Amerca since 1943.[1] Mainly bibliographical and mainly classical but includes the majority of books on popular music and jazz amongst its reviews and a valuable source of reference.

Number Widely-used term in jazz, and elsewhere in popular music, for an item, composition, song, etc – a jazz number. Probably derives from early dancing days when the various dances were numbered in a programme so that partners could be booked ahead; likewise in the music-hall/vaudeville world, where the items in the programme were also numbered; these numbers were often displayed at the side of the stage.

No. 1 Rhythm Club The first of many jazz appreciation societies founded in June 1933. It met at The Mecca Café, Chancery Lane, London WC2, 8–11 pm every Monday to be regaled by the latest jazz releases put on by such members as Jeff Aldam, Bill Elliott, Leonard Feather, Edwin Hinchcliffe, Reg Southon and George Penniket.

NYJO see **National Youth Jazz Orchestra**

---

[1] Earlier title, 'Notes for Members' (1934–43).

ODJB see **Original Dixieland Jazz Band**

Ofay A black and mainly derogatory term for a white person, possibly a pig latin perversion of the closely approximate 'foe'; an early manifestation of racial tensions in the USA. Also possibly a contraction of 'old fay'. Often used in the shortened form of 'fay'.

Off-beat See afterbeat. Off-beat used especially in connection with a cymbal played on the afterbeat – off-beat cymbal. Now has the additional meaning of something unusual, weird, unconventional; and is thus particularly applicable to many manifestations in the music and arts world.

Old Absinthe House Historical building in New Orleans at 238 Bourbon Street at the corner of Bienville Street, dating back to 1801. There has been an absinthe bar there since 1861; absinthe was a once popular drink made illegal in its original form in 1905 because it contained wormwood which was said to cause insanity. The modern version is without this ingredient and mainly enjoyed in such drinks as Absinthe frappé. During the 1920s and 30s it was a regular engagement venue for New Orleans pianists.

Olympia Orchestra Jazz dance orchestra, operating in New Orleans in 1900–14 and led by cornettist Freddie Keppard which included some famous pioneer names in its ranks: such as King Oliver, Alphonse Picou, Sidney Bechet, Clarence Williams.

100 Oxford Street Shrine of British jazz since 1942, when it became the home of the Feldman Swing Club. Subsequently used as the London Jazz Club premises, then the Humphrey Lyttelton Club and

eventually becoming known as the 100 Club run, in 1985, by Roger Horton and Ted Morton. The premises had originally opened in 1930s as a dance hall.

One-step A popular dance of *c.* 1910 which was one of the first (after the Boston) to popularize the simple walking step that was to become the staple diet of the ballrooms, after the era of the more hectic polkas, etc., was over. A tune especially composed for its introduction was *Bogey walk* by James M. Gallatly. Various versions then appeared under such names as the Judy Walk, the Bunny Hug, the Turkey Trot, all using the steps of the Castle Walk as introduced by Mr & Mrs Vernon Castle. The one-step, reaching a peak of popularity in 1914, gradually became assimilated in the dances of the ragtime era and the later quickstep and foxtrot. Bearing in mind the affiliation of jazz with the dance, early bands would have had to provide music that was suited to the one-step at this time. A sample that has survived is the *Original Dixieland One-Step* recorded by the Original Dixieland Jazz Band in 1917.

Onyx Club Manhattan speakeasy which opened in 1927 at 35 West 52nd Street. After the end of Prohibition in 1933 it became an authorized club and moved to 72 West 52nd. Popular entertainers there were the Spirits of Rhythm, and Art Tatum was the regular intermission pianist. Burned down in 1935 and reopened with Stuff Smith, Jonah Jones, John Kirby and Maxine Sullivan amongst the artists engaged. Moved to No. 62 in 1937 and closed in 1939. In 1942 a new Onyx Club, unconnected with the management of the older one, opened at 57 West 52nd Street, which also proved a lively venue for jazz; those appearing included Henry Allen, Cozy Cole, Roy Eldridge, Ben Webster and vocalists Billy Holiday and Sarah Vaughan. Became a strip club in 1949.

Orchestra see **Band**

Orchestra USA A chamber-sized orchestra of 40 players, formed, late 1961, on a co-operative basis by pianist/composer/MJQ member John Lewis. The intention was that it should be capable of playing every kind of music, jazz and non-jazz, from early classical to late 20th century. It was also expected to play any music which attempted to blend the European and Afro-American disciplines: the music which its first conductor, Gunther Schuller, called 'Third Stream'.

Organ The organ had no significant place in the development of jazz, being an instrument mainly inaccessible to the pioneer groups and only becoming available in a few modern dance halls and theatres with the advent of the cinema organ era in the 1920s. There were thus few early keyboard exponents who took to the organ and no specialists on the instrument until the 1940s.

One pianist who loved to play the organ was Fats Waller. After a few informal lessons during the intervals at a local Harlem cinema, he became, for a time, the resident organist at the Lincoln Theater, New York. He was one of the few who managed to compensate for the Wurlitzer or church organ's comparative slowness to speak, and contrived to swing even though the sound would be half a beat or more behind his fingers. Waller recorded several organ solos. Latterly Dick Hyman has appeared in the role of jazz organist, playing as a duo with cornettist Ruby Braff for Wurlitzer organ preservation societies and the like. They have a record, on Concord, in this format. Michael Garrick is an extremely impressive jazz organist.

With the invention of the electronic organ (notably the Hammond) in the mid-1930s, an almost entirely new instrument was put at the disposal of jazz keyboard players, a quite early, if only occasional, exponent being Count Basie, others have since built their reputations entirely as jazz organists, though most have also played piano. They include Jimmy Smith, Milt Buckner, Wild Bill Davis, Mike Carr, Eddie Louiss, Hazel Scott and Bill Doggett.

We must point out that there are those who contend that it is not possible to play jazz on the organ at all. You enter discussions on this entirely at your own risk.

Organ chords Sustained chords used as a background to a solo played by the brass and/or saxophones which give the effect of an organ. In early jazz it was a simple means of laying down the harmonic background to each bar, giving the soloist firm guidance; cf. Panassié: 'During a jam session a player beginning a solo can often be heard to say: "gimme an organ".'

Original Creole Orchestra Band led by cornettist Freddie Keppard from *c.* 1913–17, which included George Baquet, Jimmie Noone, 'Big Eye' Louis Nelson and Dink Johnson.

Original Dixieland Jazz Band Familiarly known amongst the jazz *aficionados* as ODJB, it resides in history as being the first band to record a genuine jazz session (although this, like all such claims, is considered open and prone to question).

The eventual nucleus of the ODJB had all played together or separately in various New Orleans bands from *c.* 1905 onward. A visiting Chicago café owner, one Harry James, had heard the new and raucous ragtime music that these white musicians played in imitation of the emerging black music and eventually brought a group of them to Chicago, under the name of Stein's Dixie Jass Band which played at a popular 31st Street café called Schiller's. Following a disagreement over salaries, and the growing popularity of the band, they moved to various Chicago and New York venues, finally arriving at the '400 Room' at the new Reisenweber Building, 'New York's newest, largest and best-equipped restaurant'. Their fame increased and the band's title adjectivally passed in evolution from 'jass' to 'jasz' to 'jaz', and finally became, on 2 February 1917, 'The Famous Original Dixieland *Jazz* Band', thus reported and advertised in the *New York Times*, whether by accident or intent, is not quite certain. (See **Jazz**.)

By this time this celebrated white band, led by cornettist Nick La Rocca, had acquired its basic line-up of Larry Shields (clarinet), Eddie Edwards (trombone), (replaced 1918–20 by Emile Christian), Henry Ragas (piano) and Tony Sbarbaro (he later called himself Spargo) (drums). On 26 February 1917, after an unsuccessful flirtation with Columbia Records, the ODJB was recorded by the Victor Talking Machine Company. Their repertoire numbers *Livery Stable Blues* and *Dixieland Jass Band One-Step* (later called *Original Dixieland One-Step*) became the 'first' jazz phonograph record to be issued. The inferior Columbia titles, recorded in January 1917, were eventually issued.

The ODJB also had the task of helping to introduce jazz to Great Britain. Leaving Reisenweber's in January 1919, they sailed to England, the personnel now La Rocca, Emile Christian (trombone), Shields, J. Russel Robinson (piano) and Sbarbaro. They first appeared on 7 April at the Hippodrome in a revue *Joy Bells* whose star was George Robey. They lasted for one night, as Robey, furious at their riotous success, said that either the band went or he did. Now a highly popular attraction, they reappeared at the Palladium, and also in Glasgow, had a command performance before George V, and ended their tour at the Hammersmith Palais de Danse. It was at this stage that J. Russel Robinson (a successful composer who wrote *Margie* among many) felt that the band was getting too commercial and walked out. He was replaced by a British pianist Billy Jones

who thus became a jazz legend sought out and gazed at by those in the know when he spent his later working years as the landlord of a pub in Chelsea. British musicians were particularly interested in hearing Larry Shields' clarinet, this being the first time the instrument had been heard in this sort of context in England.

The ODJB disbanded in 1925, although later they reassembled for a Dallas exhibition in 1936 and at the time cut a new series of recordings of their old numbers with the advantage of electrical sound.
Book: *The Story of the Original Dixieland Jazzband* by H. O. Brunn. Baton Rouge: Louisiana State University Press, 1960; London: Sidgwick & Jackson 1961; Jazz Book Club, 1963.

Origins of Jazz Series A momentous series of jazz re-issues (for that time), consisting of 65 10″ LPs of early jazz material drawn from the Gennett, Paramount and other pioneering labels. The material was first collected in the USA by Riverside, edited by Bill Grauer and Orrin Keepnews, as 'Jazz Archives', a series title used by London (a Decca subsidiary) in England for the first issues in December 1953 and early 1954 but changed to 'Origins of Jazz' for copyright reasons thereafter. The British sleeves were redesigned and reannotated, and the issues continued until April 1957.

Out of this world A term of superlative praise, ungrudging admiration, implying that something is heavenly, extraordinary, inspired, perfect. Not confined to jazz and in general usage from about 1920.

The metaphor is carried further by the use of the word 'cloud' – as in 'on Cloud Seven', 'Cloud Nine' or any preferred number.

Outside Not often encountered, but used occasionally to indicate that an improvising musician has either abandoned the concept of restricting his thinking to a particular key, or has begun to think in two or more keys simultaneously. A specific reference to this occurs in the sleeve-notes to *Mack The Knife/The*

Sextet of Orchestra USA – an album of treatments, arranged by Mike Zwerin, of some of the music written by Kurt Weill for various Bertold Brecht stage works. At one point, Zwerin is quoted: 'In the last chorus (of *Alabama song*) the piano and bass parts are actual extracts from the original score, but the harmonic changes in Eric's (Eric Dolphy's) part are a variation. By keeping to these changes, Eric automatically played what musicians call "outside" – that is, polytonally.'

Eric Dolphy was the brilliantly inventive alto saxophone and flute player who explored the hitherto largely ignored possibilities of the bass clarinet as a jazz instrument.

Pad A term originally derived from the world of narcotics, where it was the bed or couch on which one reclined while taking opium, and by extension the room where such activities went on. Later it was used generally of any temporary room, lodging, hotel apartment, etc, and – particularly among jazz musicians – a place where short-term accommodation could be found during a tour. Later expanded again to cover more permanent rooming arrangements or even a house. 'Let's meet at my pad'. There was once a jazz haunt in New York City which called itself The Pad. The word 'crib' is similarly used; and also 'roost'.

Then there is the literal meaning – the felt, leather (or other material) pads that are used on the keys of various wind instruments to close selected holes or lengths of tubing to the passage of air (the equivalent of 'stopping' a string). One further use borrows yet another everyday connotation in the notepad or pad of paper sense, so that it becomes a word for a band's collection or 'book' of arrangements. A tune is said to be 'in the band's pad'.

Outside all of that was one early specific use of 'pad' as the room used for business by a prostitute.

Palomar The Palomar Ballroom in Hollywood was *the* Major public dancing venue on the West Coast in the 1930s, and would have earned a small place in jazz history on the strength of that alone.

Of greater moment, however, is that it was the scene of one specific and significant event, on 21 August 1935, which helps us to date the actual beginning of the Swing Era with some exactitude. That was the moment when the still-new Benny Goodman Orchestra, at the end of a near-disastrous coast-to-coast tour during which most of the older customers had made it fairly plain, night after night, that they hated the band, suddenly found itself successful in a way that no band had ever been up to that point. The explanation is a social historian's dream. Just before the tour started, Goodman and his musicians had occupied the last segment of a three-band coast-to-coast radio programme, emanating from New York, called *Let's Dance*. Most respectable East Coast listeners were safely in their beds by the time the brash young Goodmanites hit the airwaves. It was otherwise in California, where, with its four-hour time difference from New York, the 'kids' (the term 'teenagers' had not yet emerged) and young adults caught the band in mid-evening. It was this young audience, already Goodman fans thanks to radio, who filled the Palomar that night in 1935. Goodman still had a battle or two to win, and it was not until the eruption of something akin to Beatlemania in 1937 at the Paramount Theater, New York, that the world at large finally realized that this new phenomenon, swing, was on the loose. Nonetheless, to the Palomar belongs the distinction of being the place where those immediately involved became aware of what was happening. It was no freak incident, either, for the Goodman band were kept at the Palomar for a highly successful two months.

Panama Café A Chicago nightclub at 307 East 58th Street. The original *Panama* or *Panama Rag*, written by William H. Tyers in 1920, one of the most played of all early jazz numbers – NORK, Ory, Noone, Armstrong, etc. – a piece of three strains, the third now not much used, seems to have had no connection with this establishment. It is said to have been written for the use of a vaudeville act known as Aida Overton Walker and her Panama Girls.

Paramount Theatre If the Benny Goodman Orchestra's engagement at the Palomar Ballroom in California in 1935 launched the Swing Era as a patchily local phenomenon, the band's appearance at the Paramount Theatre in New York in March 1937 confirmed it as a national craze. In 1937 the Paramount was offering what the trade knew as 'cine-variety' – feature films on the screen alternating with live acts on stage – in continuous performance from mid-morning to late evening. At 35 cents the price was just within the reach of what the press would refer to as 'the kids' (they were in fact late teens and early twenties) who turned up at the Paramount in the sort of numbers and in the state of anticipatory excitement which were then new to popular entertainment, but which would be repeated in turn at other venues for Frank Sinatra, Elvis Presley and The Beatles. The Claudette Colbert/Fred MacMurray film *Maid of Salem* was politely endured; it was the band the mainly young customers were waiting for, and they showed their appreciation noisily and energetically, causing some quite unnecessary alarm by crowding the front of the stage and attempting to dance in the aisles. The music happened to be magnificent, since the Goodman band was at its peak, but it was the *reaction* to the music which was news and which was picked up eagerly by editors and newscasters all over the US. In this way both Goodman's fame and the impact of the swing era assumed national proportions at the same moment; the style was set for nearly a decade of popular music, a decade in which jazz and pop overlapped to a greater extent than they had done before, or would do again.

Party piano A jovial kind of eight-to-the-bar boogie-woogie or barrelhouse piano. The sort that would be played at rent parties. Blues-based piano style prevalent in the 1930s.

Pasamala A dance with associated music that has been declared by one authority to be the precursor of ragtime. Originally known as the *Pas Ma La* (patois version of the French *pas mêlé* – a mixed step) it was a dance song that combined folk dance movements with the ragtime type music of the time. Published in 1895, it now became known as the *Pasamala*: 'Hand upon yo' head, let your mind roll far/Back, back, back and look at the stars', says the lyric; the basic movement being a forward walk and then three hops backwards with the knees bent. It would appear to be an off-shoot of ragtime rather than its derivation.

Patois A provincial form of any language, a dialect, the language spoken in a limited area. In jazz, the patois of particular interest is the kind of pidgin French first spoken in Louisiana, especially New Orleans, by French families' black servants who could not master the language completely. It became widely used among the French Creoles themselves, and is the basis of a large literature of songs from Louisiana and the other Southern states. It is also sometimes used to describe the specialist language attached to any particular sphere of activity, e.g. jazz patois, in

'The Jazz Pianist'. (Drawing: Richard Cole)

Right Another excellent but short-lived magazine of the 1940s.

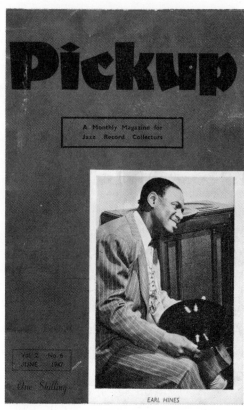

EARL HINES

Player pianos: upright and grand models dating from 1920 and *c.* 1926. Steinway Welte & Duo Art. (The British Piano Museum)

Commercialized ragtime offerings *c*. 1910. (Music: Francis, Day & Hunter)

Sophie Tucker advertised in the 1920s. (*Melody Maker*, June 1928)

which case it is not so much true patois as jargon.

Pendley Manor The location, near Tring, in Hertfordshire, to which the Bracknell Festival migrated when it was announced that South Hill Park, Bracknell, would not accommodate a jazz festival after 1984. The 1985 'Jazz At The Manor' continued the policy established during the preceding ten years at Bracknell, and the bill included Art Blakey (b. 1919) & the Jazz Messengers, the Liberation Music Orchestra, featuring bass player Charlie Haden (b. 1937), tenor saxophonist Dewey Redman (b. 1931) and drummer Paul Motian (b. 1931), and a group led by British tenor saxophonist Alan Skidmore (b. 1942) called Tenor Tonic. Pendley was fated to be a one-off affair, as negotiations were put in hand early in 1986 for the festival to return to its old home in Bracknell.

Perdido Street Famous street of New Orleans, historically full of jazz activity, in what is known as the Front of Town district. It runs more or less S to N to the west of, and nearly parallel to, Canal Street and Gravier Street (see map). Immortalized in *Perdido Street blues* by the New Orleans Wanderers (1926) and others. It was in Jane Alley, off Perdido Street, that Louis Armstrong was born, and he wrote the tune in memory of it, making a definitive recording in 1940. The Juan Tizol composition of 1942, *Perdido*, has no connection; the title is a Spanish word meaning 'lost'.

Perseverance Hall There have been several Masonic Halls of this name in New Orleans, the best known of which, at 907 St. Claude Avenue and Dumaine Street, stands in the Louis Armstrong Park as a memorial to Kid Rena (1898–1949) who regularly played for dances there.

Piano From the beginning, certainly from ragtime days, jazz has always involved the piano even in street parades if suitable transport could be found. As a band

instrument the piano has always had an important implementary role, its chordal fullness nicely filling up the gaps, being both a rich addition to the rhythm section and a solo instrument on an equal footing with the other front-line players. The piano was there from the recorded beginnings of jazz; J. Russell Robinson in the ODJB, Lil Hardin (Armstrong) in the Oliver band. It was only a few revival bands that decided to do without it in a zealous urge for the imaginary purity of early days. It is not possible to pinpoint its first appearance in a jazz band, as presumably most dance-halls, honky-tonks, etc. would have had one.

By the Swing Era of the 1930s, with the bigger band no longer needing the piano as a body-builder, the piano takes on a more concerto-like role, a popular pulpit for bandleaders such as Henderson, Basie, Hines and Waller. The most integrated and imaginative use of the piano was probably in the hands of Duke Ellington who used it as a tone-colour as never before, the blue-print for his orchestral conceptions.

Most important to jazz history is the role of the piano as a soloist; virtually the only instrument in jazz that can perform effectively on its own for sustained periods. Various aspects of piano-playing are dealt with under: **Barrelhouse**, **Boogie-woogie**, **Honky-tonk**, **Jig**, **Ragtime**, **Stride**, etc.

Pianola, player-piano, piano rolls Before the gramophone was sufficiently advanced to be of any true service to jazz, or any other music, the mechanical piano with its punched rolls was there to give a much better service – at least to the piano repertoire. The Pianola, invented by an American, Edwin S. Votey, was put on the market in the USA by the Aeolian Company in 1897. The original pianola was a separate unit which was pushed up to the normal piano and depressed the piano keys with protruding felt-covered wooden levers.

By 1901, the mechanism had been built into specially constructed pianos, more correctly known as player-pianos as the name pianola was really a copyright name by Aeolian for the earlier device. The instruments now incorporated controls for speed and volume and a fine degree of touch variation could be achieved through these in conjunction with the pedals which supplied air to the mechanism. By following the instructions printed on the roll, a fair approximation of the original performance could be obtained. Later, some very sophisticated instruments (some in grand piano form) became available, including Welte's 'Mignon' (German), Aeolian's 'Duo-Art' and the American Piano Company's 'Ampico' copyright systems which, manufacturing the rolls by an electrical system, gave the means of a very exact reproduction of gradations of touch and speed in the playing of the original pianist. To hear, for example, a Fats Waller roll played on a good instrument is like being in the presence of a ghost as the keys reproduce his style with uncanny accuracy.

The only snag with piano rolls is that there was always the temptation to edit. An extra hole or two punched in the roll could easily add a few extra notes or make improvements. The temptation was always there to 'compose' music for piano rolls that did more then ten ordinary fingers could possibly do. Some did this without compunction and included chords with 30 notes on occasions. On the whole, most of the ragtime and early jazz rolls, notably produced by the QRS company, did not succumb overmuch to this temptation and the roll remains a useful way of getting a glimpse of some of the old ragtime and jig pianists who were around too early to record, e.g. Scott Joplin. There was also a special breed of pianists who worked mainly for piano roll companies. Though nothing can be taken as reliable by way of speeds and the degree of editing, the rolls do provide something more realistic than the phonographs of the early days could. Several archival record companies like Biograph, Edison, Riverside, Swaggie and so on, have liberally transferred a lot of the pianola repertore to LP disc.

Pick To play banjo, mandolin or guitar with a plectrum – pick style – as opposed to finger style.

Pickup An introductory phrase or notes, one or two bars, that lead into a chorus or performance. Much liked by boogie players. Used to help a band to come in together.

Pickup A now historical monthly jazz magazine of the small ($5\frac{1}{2} \times 8\frac{1}{2}$ in/14 $\times$ 20 cm) variety which was edited by Sinclair Traill (1904–1981) and T. B. Denby and had a short span of life in the postwar years, 1946/7. It was full of the self-righteous bickerings and puritanism of the period, but contained some valuable research and discographical material; also an extensive 'wanted' and 'disposals' record section.

Pickup band, group A group made up of musicians, many from the ranks of more permanent bands, brought together for the purpose of a one-off performance, a recording or broadcast. Sometimes, in the latter cases, referred to as a 'studio' band. Derives from the US 'pick-up', to give a lift in an automobile, *c.* 1925.

Piece Widely used jazz slang for an instrument. Particularly collectively as in 'ten-piece band'.

Pine Top Name given to boogie-woogie pianist and vocalist Clarence Smith (born in Birmingham, Alabama) (1904–29), reputedly because he had a rather pointed head. Worked as an entertainer mainly in Pittsburgh and for a time was accompanist to Ma Rainey. Settled in Chicago and there recorded his most famous piece *Pine Top's boogie-woogie* (1928) whose fruits he did not live to enjoy as he was accidentally shot in a dance-hall fracas in 1929.

Pipe Musician's slang for the saxophone – generally implying the tenor instruments; the alto being referred to as 'small pipe' and the baritone as 'big pipe'. Not current for some time.

Plantation Café Chicago night spot on 35th Street, between Prairie and Calumet Streets and opposite the Sunset Café. King Oliver joined the Dave Peyton Symphonic Syncopators there in December 1924, after the closure of the Lincoln Gardens. By February, he had taken over the engagement with his own Dixie Syncopators with Tommy Ladnier on second cornet, Albert Nicholas and Barney Bigard (reeds), and Luis Russell (pianist/arranger). The band played at the Plantation until March 1927 with various changes of personnel. There was also a floorshow which, during this period, was advertised as 'The Hottest Show in Any Chicago Café'. Eventually, gang warfare, then rife in Chicago, and subsequent police raids, forced the club to close intermittently during early 1927 and it was finally destroyed by fire in March. Rebuilt in June it reopened with a band again led by Dave Peyton. Immortalized in Luis Russell's *Plantation Joys* (1926). There was also a less-famed Plantation Café in Los Angeles.

Plantation Orchestra Early jazz orchestra formed by Will Vodery that was an important spreader of the jazz gospel. Featuring trumpeter Johnny Dunn with his pioneering wa-wa effects, it toured Europe in 1923 and came to England in 1926 as the pit orchestra for the famous *Blackbirds* revue, the first notable black revue to impress London with its star Florence Mills.

'Play that thing' Exhortation first popularized as a spoken coda to *Dippermouth blues.*

Pop Now used specifically to identify the teenage music that has developed from rhythm-and-blues and rock which has taken over the popular music scene since the late 1950s now, in itself, a specialized area of popular music-making; the pop scene, pop music, *Top of the Pops*, etc. During the 1930s one specialized use of pops – in the plural – was by the Boston Philharmonic Orchestra, a slightly smaller form of which, under the name

'Boston Pops Orchestra' would perform gala concerts of relatively light music. For the British market, records by this orchestra were labelled 'Boston Promenade Orchestra'.

Pops Term of once friendly endearment generally applied to an older person in the American vernacular, particularly liked amongst black jazz musicians. Louis Armstrong was a liberal user of the word and was often thus dubbed in return. Paul Whiteman was also known as Pops by the musicians who worked for him and liked him (which most of them did). Latterly one suspects that the name has sometimes taken on a more derogatory flavour, suggesting that the recipient is a trifle square, if not actually geriatric. But also used, in the right quarters, still as a complimentary address for anyone considered, on the other hand, hip.

Popular music, popular song Just as 'classical' has always been an unsatisfactory term for the 'serious' or 'academic' side of music-making, even to the extent of being wrongly used in view of its more specific meaning, so has 'popular' remained an inadequate adjective to describe all that lies outside the boundaries of the 'serious' or 'classical' areas. Nevertheless, we mainly know what we mean when we use it, and attempts to provide a more precise title have not been able to oust a now established usage. Jazz itself, of course, belongs partly to the popular music scene though much of it, in commercial terms, is not widely popular. This is further complicated by the fact that implicit in the be-bop revolution in the mid-1940s, and in most of the developments since, is the jazz musician's growing awareness of jazz not as a branch of showbiz, but as an art.

It remains true, however, that popular music began to be slightly affected by jazz with the coming of ragtime in the early 1900s, and then more and more heavily and directly influenced by jazz phrasing and syncopation, from the early 1920s onwards; so that it is true to say that by the late 20th century no part of western popular music is completely untouched by jazz. Some forms of pop music, especially that with a strong blues feel, derive almost exclusively from jazz. The vigour of jazz underlies the now complete Americanization of our popular music in the verbal sense also, since the words are today sung in American, no matter what the origins of the singer.

Pot Earlier 'pot' generally meant a cheap sort of home-made whisky, common in the Prohibition era, made in a pot or bucket instead of in the proper way. Later the name was given to marijuana, especially in cigarette form. Smoking pot.

Preservation Hall By the early 1940s jazz had almost ceased to be a viable activity in New Orleans until art-dealer Larry Borenstein took steps to revive it and keep it alive by asking what surviving musicians he could find to play jazz in his gallery. Here the reputations of such as George Lewis (1900–68), Punch Miller (1894–1971), Jim Robinson (1890–1976) and Johnny Wiggs (1899–1977) were reinstated. The momentum was maintained from 1961 by the promotion of these activities at Preservation Hall, 726 St. Peter Street, under the guidance of Allen Jaffe. It become a sort of Clef Club for New Orleans musicians, organising concerts and tours and helping the dependants of impoverished ex-musicians. A valuable archive of photos, records and other documents was also kept on the premises. The resident band there has been led for some years by George 'Kid Sheik' Colar (b. 1908).

The original history of Preservation Hall goes back to 1861 when it was built, becoming, during the golden age of New Orleans jazz, a workaday dance hall where most of the famous names played at one time. Carefully preserved in an appropriate state of decrepitude, with dirty windows and paint peeling, Preservation Hall perpetuates the ambience of the old New Orleans jazz days for posterity, and is now a focal point for tourists looking for the commodity for which the city is famous.

Book: *Preservation Hall Portraits* by Larry Borenstein & Bill Russell. np. Baton Rouge: Louisiana State University Press, 1968. Reproductions of the archive's portraits together with biographical sketches.

Prez Sometimes **Pres**. Short for 'President', an admiring nickname conferred upon tenor saxophonist Lester Young (1909–59) by Billie Holiday. Tradition has it that a president was the most important kind of person she could think of, and she named Lester accordingly. It is perhaps worth noting that pianist Jimmy Rowles claimed in a BBC radio interview that in the period when he first knew Lester Young, in the early 1940s, nobody around him seemed to use the presidential title, but called him 'Bubber' instead.

On the American West Coast in the 1970s a band called Prez Conference was formed to play some of Lester's solos transcribed for a full saxophone section, after the manner of Supersax and its transcriptions of Charlie Parker solos.

Progressive jazz A term much favoured by followers of Stan Kenton (1912–79) to describe a form of jazz – especially big band jazz – which rather self-consciously set out to be up-to-date. To a certain extent it was a latterday manifestation of the urge which had motivated Paul Whiteman (1890–1967) three decades earlier, though in all other respects Kenton, a competent jazz pianist and a fine arranger, and Whiteman were utterly dissimilar. 'Progressive' was part of the vocabulary of the early and mid-1950s, alongside and occasionally overlapping the area covered by the word 'cool'. It was essentialy a white phenomenon with an almost exclusively white following, partly accounted for by its fondness for devices borrowed from modern European music.

Prohibition While such a matter is hardly a part of musical history, the years of Prohibition (when intoxicating liquors were banned in the USA) were very much a part of the practical, economic and historical background of jazz. This coincided, as the gramophone did, with its most important years of growth and dictated the circumstances under which it developed. A linked history of jazz and Prohibition would make a fascinating study, not least because jazzmen, as a race, seem so reliant on alcohol – sometimes for their inspiration, and nearly always for the premises on which they perform.

Considering the insane repercussions that Prohibition, as instigated by the Eighteenth Amendment in 1919, had upon American life, the ease with which the proposals went through was remarkable. There was undoubtedly much, even a majority, opposition to Prohibition, but the 'dry' leaders took advantage of the war, in which America had become totally involved, to push their ideals. Clean living had become accepted to help the war effort and the act was put through with very little thought of what its results might be. To start its course, Congress hurriedly passed Minnesota Congressman Andrew Joseph Volstead's National Prohibition Enforcement Act on 8 and 10 October 1919. President Wilson attempted a veto but it was finally pushed through. The Eighteenth Amendment (liquor prohibition) was ratified on 16 January 1919 and proclaimed on 29 January to take effect on 16 January 1920.

From the beginning its enforcement was almost an impossibility. In 1920, in a huge country like America with 18 700 miles (30 094 km) of coastline, there were just 1520 enforcement agents; and by 1920 the wartime fervour had gone and the majority of the public were anti-Prohibition and dying for a drink. The conditions that ensued have been described as 'rum-ships rolling in the sea outside the twelve-mile limit and transferring their cargoes of whisky by night to fast cabin cruisers, beer-running trucks being hijacked on the interurban boulevards by bandits with Thompson sub-machine guns, illicit stills turning out alcohol by the carload, the fashionable dinner party beginning with contraband cocktails as a matter of course, ladies and gentlemen undergoing scrutiny from behind the curtained grill of the speakeasy, and Alphonse Capone, multi-millionaire master of the Chicago bootleggers, driving through the streets in an armor-plated car with bullet-proof windows'.

It was against this background that jazz went through its vital developing years. Most jazzmen in that period would have been directly or indirectly employed by one of the gangster syndicates that split the cities between them and which settled their boundary disputes by bloody gun battles. Most of the musicians kept on good terms with their employers and were treated well. But even a prominent figure like Armstrong had at one time to go around with bodyguards as he was under threat from a gang trying to get him to move to their territory. Many of the musicians themselves carried guns.

The Amendment, generously referred to as the 'noble experiment', was finally repealed on 5 December 1933 by the 21st Amendment; and America went back to normal, less-hysterical drinking habits; quite probably consuming less liquor than they had, in defiance, during the years of prohibition. (See also **Alcohol**.)

Put-on In fairly general use by the mid-1980s in the sense of 'to deceive', 'to kid', 'to fool' and, by a slight extension, 'to mock', 'to take the mickey'. Trombonist Mike Zwerin, to whom belongs the honour of being the last entry in Leonard Feather's *Encyclopedia of Jazz*, says that 'put on' was originally jazz slang. It is at the root of the irony of jazz humour. 'We would laugh at what was not supposed to be funny. Being put on was passing a test. We'd tell "sick" cancer, multiple-sclerosis and elephantitis jokes just because they were not supposed to be funny. This expressed our anarchistic life-view' (*Close Enough For Jazz* – Quartet Books, 1983). The inference to be drawn is that if the hearer of these sick jokes showed no discomfiture, then he or she had successfully come through the ordeal implicit in the putting-on by the teller.

Quadroon, octoroon Words encountered frequently in accounts of New Orleans in the early days of jazz. Used correctly, they denoted a person of one quarter and one eighth Negro blood respectively. In practice, they were probably applied willy-nilly to anyone of obviously mixed ancestry and of relatively light skin.

Rabbit A nickname given to those of small stature and nocturnal habits. The best-known jazz rabbit was probably Johnny (real name Cornelius) Hodges (1907–70) who spent most of his life burrowing around in the Ellington band. He was also known as Squaty (or Squatty) Roo, and as Jeep.

Race records, music Between the date of Thomas Edison's invention of the phonograph in 1877, the beginnings of commercial exploitation of records a decade or so later and the 1920s, a great deal had happened and a great deal had been recorded. Yet in the land of ragtime and jazz, indeed of the birth of recording, there was, as in other spheres, very little promotion of the art of black musicians, singers and actors. The *Chicago Defender*, a weekly newspaper which was aimed at the black population, with a circulation of some 250 000, had forcibly commented on this situation at the beginning of 1916, pointing out that it was now up to black people to demand black artistes. In the autumn of the same year they continued their campaign by saying that 'records of the Race's great artists will be placed on the market' once it was ascertained 'how many Victrolas are owned by members of our race'. Their efforts fizzled out through lack of support but at least the word and the idea of 'race' records had been put into the industry's consciousness.

A few black artistes, mainly in minstrel vein and performing with a white audience in mind, could be found in the lists; but the real beginnings came in 1920 when the General Phonograph Company, issued, on Okeh 4113, in July 1920 a recording of two songs by the black composer Perry Bradford – *That thing called love* and *You can't keep a good man down* sung by Mamie Smith. In fact, they had wanted to use Sophie Tucker but Bradford persuaded the company to use a black singer, Mamie Smith. The sales were good and Mamie Smith made some more recordings in the summer. It was one side from the session held on 10 August 1920 which acted almost like a detonator for the whole 'race' record phenomenon. *Crazy blues*, backed with *It's right here for you* sold in unprecedented quantities, largely to a black audience which had not been taken seriously before as a potential market. Other labels heard the tills ringing and almost every prominent company had its recording by a coloured artist by the beginning of 1922. In 1921, Harry Pace had left the Pace and Handy Music Company in New York, set up on his own and started to issue a label called

193

Black Swan. At last there was a company with a deliberate policy in this direction. Pace said: 'Black Swan records are made to meet what we consider a legitimate and growing demand' and he advertised his wares as 'The only Genuine Colored Record'. At the same time Okeh, the first in the field, now also went into the market seriously and in January 1922 were advertising what they called their 'colored catalog'. Almost without thinking about it they reiterated their old slogan and in a *Chicago Defender* advert stated: 'All the greatest Race phonograph stars can be heard on Okeh records. Ask for our complete list of Okeh race records'. The term did not fully catch on until early 1923; thereafter it became the accepted one. Most of the big companies and many smaller ones continued to issue separate 'race series' records until well into the 1940s. By that time the kind of rhythm and blues music that they contained was about to become the common language of pop music, both black and white, and there was no need for further phonographic segregation.

Rag A composition, generally for piano but also in band and other instrumental forms, which is generally in several contrasting sections, based on older dance and march forms, with a regularly syncopated melody over a strict and usually stately 2/4 vamp accompaniment. The form developed gradually from earlier minstrel music and grew alongside the cakewalk. The first piece of music to use rag in its title is generally credited as being William H. Krell's *Mississippi rag*, published in 1897 but this piece by a white bandmaster, as in the case of several others published almost simultaneously, was more a cakewalk in nature. Ann Charters points to earlier pieces with more ragtime character, though not actually bearing the name (for further discussion see under **Ragtime**) such as Charles Gimble's *Paraphrase de Concert on Old Black Joe* (1877).

Ragtime, ragtime dance, ragtime song
There have been many fanciful and semi-

logical explanations of the source of the word 'rag' and, hence, ragtime The most fanciful finds a link between it and the Indian raga. The least interesting but the most likely is that some unknown listener to an early band requested an encore of what he could only describe as the 'ragged' item he had heard. The name was taken up by the band who referred to their 'raggy' numbers, soon shortened to rags. The name gained wider circulation in the Upper Mississippi area, around St. Louis where the music was developing and ragtime became its official name. There was perhaps some aural relationship with jig. A music that was a rather looser form of ragtime was for a time known as jig-time, and the terms might have been interchangeable.[1]

It seems probable that music in the ragtime idiom was being played for some time before it became known as such. The first published ragtime title (see **Rag**) was probably *Mississippi rag* (1897) which was written by a white bandleader William H. Krell; thus historically pre-empting the first jazz record which came from a white band: a coincidental quirk of jazz history. The name immediately caught on and in the same year such items as *Rag Medley*, *Ragtime march*, *Bundle of rags*, *Louisiana rag* and Harney's *Ragtime Instructor* all appeared. Some of these could more accurately have been described as cakewalks. The first black rag was *Harlem rag* by Tom Turpin (1873–1922). Scott Joplin's first ragtime piece, *Original rags*, was published in 1899.

It is accurate enough to speak of the ragtime element in jazz, particularly in the white Dixieland strain, but it is not perhaps quite right to see ragtime as the true ancestor or first manifestation of jazz. It was more of a complementary activity which became absorbed into jazz as both emerged. The real black jazz came from a source of folksongs and blues. Ragtime, sharing only some syncopated elements, is probably a more

---

[1] Interesting to note that the French, having no exact equivalent, called ragtime 'le temps du chiffon'.

contrived development of strains of American music – not entirely black, e.g. the band march as typified by the Sousa repertoire (with its several sections not following the normal song pattern); the undeniably American characteristics that were emerging in such songs as *Dixie* and the similar compositions of such writers as Henry Clay Work (1832–84), Stephen Foster (1826–64) and the black composer James Bland (1854–1911); the rhythmic elements from the Caribbean that had been exploited by the creole composer Louis Moreau Gottschalk (1829–69); the banjo characteristics that were exploited in such diverse areas as folk-dance, country-music and the minstrel shows. Ragtime was an imitation and amalgamation of most of these. It developed, as jazz did, as an accompaniment to the dance, the nature of ragtime to a large extent being shaped by the demands of the current dances of the cakewalk variety – and, to some extent, vice versa. Ragtime is not particularly black in character, its forms, harmonies and rhythms being predominantly Euro-American. The 'different' nature of jazz expression and the deep melancholy of the blues are not to be found in ragtime.

Ragtime is mainly thought of as a piano music; coming at a time when the parlour-piano was a popular feature in any reasonably affluent household and printed music in great demand. But it was also widely exploited as a band music, cakewalk and rag being freely interchangeable titles. In date of appearance, many 'ragtime' songs actually pre-date piano ragtime. Such titles as *You've been a good ole wagon; Mr. Johnson turn me loose* and *There'll be a hot time in the old town tonight*, were in the normal song shape, rather than ragtime form; and it is upon these that the later ragtime songs of such composers as Irving Berlin (b. 1888) are based rather than piano rags, as is often wrongly assumed in their malignment.

What is now categorized as classic ragtime is the formal rag written by composers, both black and white, who contributed to the ragtime repertoire in the relatively short period *c.* 1897–1912, after which ragtime was diffused into other piano styles and into the main jazz stream. Prominent among the composers were Scott Joplin (1868–1917) who even ventured to write a ragtime opera, (with little success at the time but since resurrected) *Treemonisha* (1911); Tom Turpin (1873–1922); James Scott (1886–1938); Joseph Lamb (white) (1887–1960); and many others. Some Tin Pan Alley composers like Percy Wenrich (1880–1952) tried their hands at rags with varying success.

While jazz was incubating in New Orleans and Chicago, ragtime had its main area of growth in the St. Louis area before moving on, like jazz, to New York, then out to the wide world. It is not easy to explain these localized divisions of labour; perhaps because they were never quite as localized as the written histories have since made out in their obsession with categories. What we are really plotting is the commercialized outlet that allowed the music to find its public. Jazz became a national craze in America by the turn of the century and reached Britain and Europe, mainly by way of stage acts (for few of the ragtime pianists ever got abroad) by the early 1900s.[1]

After the initial impact of the early ragtime manifestations there was a renewed craze for the ragtime song and dance around 1912, which led toward the Charleston era and ran into the beginnings of commercial jazz. Ragtime was revived again in the 1940s but mainly in Dixieland jazz band versions and done in a manner, on tinny honky-tonk pianos, that emphasized its comedy elements. A proper reappraisal of ragtime did not come until the 1970s when it was demonstrated by pianists such as Joshua Rifkin (b. 1944) that ragtime, played straight from its forgotten sheet-music, was a surprisingly lyrical and charming music.

---

[1] Ragtime of a kind was heard in England during the reign of Queen Victoria. American banjoists Harry Clark and Burt Earle came in 1899 playing such thing's as *Hot foot Sue* which they recorded that year. Banjoist Voss L. Osman came in 1900 with *A ragtime skedaddle*, etc.

After this discovery it was utilized in several ballets and a scholarly reappraisal of the music took place, including the reissue of many classic rags, notably the complete works of Scott Joplin and his opera *Treemonisha*, now staged over 60 years after its creation.

Books: *They All Played Ragtime* by Rudi Blesh & Harriet Janis. 338p. New York: Knopf, 1950; repr. 1966 & 1971; *The Art of Ragtime* by William J. Schafer & Johannes Riedel. 249p. Baton Rouge: Louisiana State University Press, 1973; *Scott Joplin and the Ragtime Era* by Peter Gammond. 223p. London: Sphere Books, 1975; *This is Ragtime* by Terry Waldo. 244p. New York: Hawthorn Books, 1976: New York: St. Martin's Press, 1975; *Rags and Ragtime* by David Jasen & Trebor Jay Tichenor. New York: Seabury Press, 1978; *Ragtime* by Edward A. Berlin. 248p. Berkeley: University of California Press, 1980.

Railroads The vastness of the USA has always made railway travel of great significance and importance. The opening up of the West depended on the laying of railroad tracks as quickly as possible, as overland travel was slow and dangerous and transport by river either uncertain or impossible. The itinerant musician, like the hobo, relied on the railroads for his mobility and it was not surprising that they became so much a part of the folklore of America and the subject of so many folksongs and blues. The legends start with the actual building of the railroads, the hardship and danger that the workers were subjected to, the hundreds of lives that were lost, the bitter battles that were fought for and against the encroachment into the agricultural lands. Stories surrounding various characters and events soon circulated; the best-known example being the ballad that tells the story of John Henry, said to be a steel-driller who worked on the Big Bend Tunnel section of the Chesapeake and Ohio (C & O) Railroad. He set out to prove that a man could outdo a mechanical steel-drill and died in the attempt.

Once the railroads were there they were the source of many tales of courage, foolhardiness and daring. The lines and the locomotives remained hazardous until well into modern times and, as the stagecoach drivers had before, the engin-eers (drivers), firemen and brakemen ran many risks trying to get their trains there on time, or simply prove that they could do it faster than ever before. On the same Chesapeake and Ohio Railroad that John Henry helped to build, engineer George Alley was killed in 1890 near Hinton, West Virginia and his story is told in *Engine One-Forty-Three*. The classic tale of *Casey Jones* is probably one of the best-known. He worked in the 1890s on the Mississippi section of the Illinois Central Railroad (IC). His real name was John Luther Jones but he was nicknamed Casey because he came from Cayce in Kentucky. He stuck to the controls of his runaway train and was killed near Vaughan in Mississippi on 30 April 1900. The disaster that befell a Southern Railway mail express at Danville, Virginia on 27 September 1903 is remembered in *The wreck of the Old 97*. Two Virginian Railway trains crashed at Ingleside, West Virginia on 24 May 1927 and the engineer and fireman of one of them were scalded to death, the other crew escaping. This was immortalized in *The wreck of the Virginian*.

The notorious attacks on stagecoaches that were a part of Western lore were continued on pioneering mail trains in the days of the roaring West and right into modern times. The Autremont Brothers robbed a Southern Pacific train at the Siskiyou Pass in Oregon on 11 October 1923, murdering all four of the train's crew.

But it was not all tragedy, even though a lot of hardship and heartburn are connected with railroad travel, the most popular theme of all probably being that of the train taking a loved one away – as in *Yellow Dog blues* which spotlighted the point where the Yellow Dog (the Yazoo Delta Railroad) crossed the Southern Railroad at Moorhead in Mississippi – both now a part of the Illinois Central Railroad.

One of the earliest operating lines in the USA was the Pontchartrain Railroad that ran between New Orleans and Milneburg and, opening in 1831, was in use until 1932. But it was the big long-distance railways that opened up America and dictated its geography. Most of the commercial centres naturally grew at points where two or more railroads crossed or joined. Dallas was on the Missouri–Dallas–Texas route where it crossed the Texas & Pacific Line. Kansas City was at the meeting point of the Atchison, Topeka & Santa Fe Railroad, the Missouri–Dallas–Texas, the Chicago Great Western and the Wabash Railroads. Many of these railroads are better-known in jazz by their initials, which have to be deciphered in most cases (see Townley), e.g. the A & V – the Alabam & Vicksburg Railroad running from Meridian, Mississippi to Vicksburg. In its early days it was connected by ferry (and from 1930 by a bridge) over the Mississippi to the Vicksburg, Shreveport and Pacific Railroad on the Louisiana side. Both of these are now part of the Southern Railroad system. The C & A was the Chicago & Alton Railroad linking Kansas City with Chicago by way of St. Louis. The CP was the Central Pacific Line.

Many trains earned their own popular names. The Wabash Cannonball seems to have cropped up on more than one railroad, but the two authenticated ones in the 1880s were the expresses that ran from Chicago to Kansas City and from St. Louis to Omaha. Cannonball was a general name for almost any express train. There was the Peanut Special, which ran from Columbia to Chester, South Carolina; the Orange Blossom Special, which was a Seaboard Railway express; the Sunshine Special, which operated on the Missouri–Pacific Railroad between St. Louis and New Orleans and then on to Los Angeles and Mexico City via Houston. One of the great luxury trains of Hollywood peak days was the Super Chief which was a sort of Orient Express of America, running from Chicago to Los Angeles on the Atchison, Topeka & Santa Fe Railroad, covering the 2200 mile (3540 km) trip in around 40 hours. It had private rooms and provided food to the highest hotel standards, catering for Hollywood stars and million-aires who could afford its fares from 1936 onward. The Chicago Flyer ran on the same famous line. The Royal Palm Special was another prestige express which ran from Chicago to Miami by way of three railroads – the Cleveland, Chicago, Cincinnatti and St. Louis, the Southern and the Florida East Coast Railroad. Of lesser ilk, presumably, was the 219 that ran to the West out of New Orleans, its actual destination not now remembered but it seems of romantic import to many.

The explanation of the famous 'A' train was given by Billy Strayhorn in the 13 February 1967 issue of *Down Beat*. When the Sixth Avenue Subway was being built in New York, new trains were given alphabetical numbers. Many travellers to Harlem mistakenly got on the 'D' train and ended up where they didn't want to be because they ought to have been on the 'A' train. It was the equivalent of getting on the Circle Line and ending up in Paddington when you wanted to be on the District Line for Hammersmith.

Some trains that have got into jazz titles were purely imaginary, or perhaps based on some hazily remembered line, like the *Daybreak Express* and the *Happy-go-lucky local* that exercised Duke Ellington's imagination, the first as background music to a film about a commuter train into New York. Likewise the famous *Honky-tonk train blues*, one of many that translated railroad sounds into musical terms.

By comparison, British jazz has not shown any deep affection or regard for its railroad system, otherwise we might have had an *LNER* or *LMS blues*, or even a *British Railway blues*. In America the Great Train Robbery would have been certain meat for a ballad or two and the Piccadilly Line would have provided good swing era material. Those that have dwelt on the subject include *Blue for Waterloo* (Lyttelton) – reminding travellers of the direction indicators in the underground for those seeking main line stations and *Bakerloo non-stop* (Kenny Baker).

Ramble The general import of the use of this word in a title is not the common English one of rambling as in the lines 'he rambled and he rambled until the butchers had to cut him down' – either to walk or to wander, physically and mentally. But used more in the sense of 'fast-moving', thus used by hoboes and others as a description of an express train – a rambler. Hence *Muskrat ramble* is a brisk number.

Rampart Street Street of New Orleans, famous for its parades, which runs through the Downtown area, roughly parallel to the Mississippi River and north of Burgundy Street. Divided during its length into South Rampart, Rampart and North Rampart. (See map of New Orleans.)

Rapollo A widely perpetuated misspelling of the name of Leon J. Ropollo (1902–43), famed clarinettist of the Friar's Society Orchestra (later New Orleans Rhythm Kings). After a brief period of inspired activity he became a victim of drugs, was confined to a mental asylum *c*. 1925 and remained there until his death.

Ray's Jazz Shop One of the best specialist shops at 180 Shaftesbury Avenue in London, taking its name from its proprietor, Ray Smith, enthusiast, sometime bass player and ardent cricketer. Although trading under its present name only since 1983, the shop has a long history, starting in the late 1940s as an adjunct of the International Book Shop, later better known as Collet's. Having occupied several addresses in Charing Cross Road, it settled in 1956 into premises in New Oxford Street which it shared with Collet's Folk Record Shop ('mostly Russian 78s, that was', recalls Ray Smith). In 1976 the jazz and folk shops moved into back-to-back locations whereby the jazz shop acquired its present-day Shaftesbury Avenue frontage, while the folk shop, now defunct, faced Monmouth Street. This arrangement lasted until mid-1983, when Collet's relinquished the jazz record side of their business, selling it to Ray Smith, who had worked in the jazz shop ever since its move to New Oxford Street in 1956.

Razzy Dazzy Spasm Band see **Stalebread**

Read Simply, the ability to read music. But from this it has acquired a wider sense of understanding, comprehending and even to dig – often used as a synonym for this last term. In jazz, it has usually implied a rather more educated sort of musician, used with praiseworthy or derogatory inflection according to the standpoint.[1] The reader was generally one who went on to higher things.

Really the Blues When this book was published – a frank and racy autobiography of jazz clarinettist and drug-pusher Milton 'Mezz' Mezzrow (1899–1972), written in collaboration with Bernard Wolfe (New York: Random House, 1946) – it had considerable impact on most readers. It portrayed the jazz life with a frank honesty and knowledgeable insight that went way beyond the normal textbook world of styles and trends. It was dedicated, amongst others, to 'all the junkies and lushheads in two-bit scratch-pads and the flophouse grads in morgue iceboxes' as well as to the musicians he admired. It remains one of the classics of jazz literature.

Re-bop Kind of jivey, sort of swing that was current *c*. 1946, just before modern jazz took over, playing with advanced chords. Typified in Hampton's 1940 *Hey-baba-re-bop* (recorded in 1946). Soon absorbed into bebop and bop.

Record Changer A magazine that

---

[1] For instance: it was kept a closely-guarded secret that Eddie Edwards, trombonist of the Original Dixieland Jazz Band, could read music well. The publicity men assured everyone that the band couldn't read a note between them and Edwards (in the words of H. O. Brunn) 'might well be considered a dangerous reactionary and a threat to the sublime musical virginity of the organisation'.

provided a special service for the jazz collector and buyer, published in the USA (1942–55).

Record Research A 'magazine of record statistics and information' published in the USA since 1955. Devoted mainly to discographical material (some non-jazz) with occasional articles and a record 'auction' section. Also publishes *Blues Research* (1959).

Red Familiar nickname in jazz and elsewhere, the American equivalent of the British 'Ginger'. Well-known white bearers of this distinction included Red Norvo (b. 1908), also an assumed name as he was really Kenneth Norville. He was musically unusual, in that he was originally a xylophone player and only made the change to vibraphone relatively late and with reluctance. Ernest Loring Nichols, cornet player and bandleader (1905–65), was another distinguished Red. (See **Five Pennies**.) There was also blue-blower William 'Red' McKenzie (1899–1948); Charles Richards (b. 1912), pianist and vocalist. Red Rodney (r.n. Robert Chudnick; b. 1927, Philadelphia) has described how he, as a white trumpet player, went on tour in the South with Charlie Parker by being billed as 'Albino Red'. Bass player Red (Keith) Mitchel has made Scandinavia his home after doing work with most of the big post-Parker names, including Gerry Mulligan and Dizzy Gillespie.

There were also several gingery black musicians such as trumpeter Henry 'Red' Allen (1908–67); bassist George Sylvester Callender (b. 1918); and trumpeter Reuben Reeves (1905–75) who was also known as 'River'.

Among pianists, Red (William) Garland (1923–84) is among the most important bearers of the name, partly due to his key role in Miles Davis groups in the late 1950s. Two blues pianists are worth mentioning here also, partly to dispel the confusion which exists between them. Speckled Red was really Rufus Perryman; Piano Red was Willie Perryman. They were related, some sources referring to them as half-brothers, others as cousins.

Red Barn Romantic name of the unromantic suburban public house at Bexleyheath on the borders of south-east London and north-west Kent, in which George Webb's Dixielanders made most of their early appearances in 1944. It is thus an authentic shrine of the British traditionalist movement, though George Webb's band actually began its audible existence in the canteen of the Vickers Armstrong war-equipment factory at nearby Crayford, where pianist George Webb and trombonist Eddie Harvey, another founder-member, were workers. George Webb now runs a pub in Essex and Eddie Harvey teaches music at Haileybury School. On 4 July 1985 a plaque, bearing the names of the original members of the band and a brief explanation of the historical significance of the location, was unveiled by singer/author George Melly.

Red hot mamma A short-lived title for a female singer of the large, bosomy, earthy type; generally a popularized version of the classic blues singer with a style nearer to blues-shouting rather than the urban blues. The sort of singer that you would expect to hear performing a song like *There'll be a hot time in the old town tonight* – which many classic blues singers did, thus adopting the red hot mamma role occasionally. Colour was immaterial. The white performer Sophie Tucker (1884–1966), built on the above plan and often strident, famous for her song *Some of these days you're going to miss me, honey*, billed herself as 'The Last of the Red Hot Mammas'.

Red Hot Peppers The name Jelly Roll Morton (1890–1941) chose for his touring and recording band from *c.* 1925. The band travelled round in a bus with a large sign on the side blazoning the name; while Morton and his wife followed round in a Lincoln automobile. The first recordings under this name were made

Useful catalogue. issued by the
Parlophone label, 1946 edition.
(Parlophone Company Ltd)

NFJO Festival in its Richmond
days.

Tin Pan Alley publicity display in the 1930s. (Photo: Sydney W. Newbery, B. Feldman & Co)

in September 1926 and the best of them remain some of the great classics of jazz.

Red Onion A honky-tonk in New Orleans situated at the junction of South Rampart Street and Julia Street. The resident musicians in the jazz heyday were, according to Morton, Buddy Carter and Game Kid. But Louis Armstrong and Johnny Dodds also played there and a Louis Armstrong-led group, called the Red Onion Jazz Babies, recorded eight sides in 1924. *Red Onion blues*, written by Clarence Williams, and which presumably had at least a verbal connection, was not recorded until 1940, by Johnny Dodds and his orchestra. There was also a *Red Onion rag* written by Abe Olman in 1887 and published in 1912.

Reisenweber's The former Reisenweber Restaurant in New York is remembered as the place where the Original Dixieland Jazz Band did much to spread the new gospel of jazz, opening there in the '400' Club Room on 27 January 1917. They commemorated the association in *Reisenweber rag* recorded that year. The restaurant was owned and run by one Max Hart and was situated at 58th Street and Eighth Avenue on Columbus Circle, Manhattan.

Release Another musicians' term for the 'middle eight' or middle part of the standard 32-bar song form A-A-B-A; the B section. Also known as the bridge or bridge passage, or 'channel'.

Reliance Band The Reliance Band was a dance orchestra led and organized by 'Papa' Jack Laine (1873–1966) from *c.* 1890, probably under this name from *c.* 1892 when it drew some personnel from the Reliance Brass Band. Has claims to be the first band that might have played in the authentic jazz idiom that would be recognizable as such today. Being a great success, Papa Laine organized several units bearing the same name which spread the jazz gospel through the Gulf Coast states in the early 1900s until *c.* 1913. They included such players as

Henry Ragas, Stalebread Lacoume, Anton Lada and Tony Sbarbaro.

Reliance Brass Band Parade and concert band run by 'Papa' Jack Laine from *c.* 1892 to 1913. Many of its players also performed in the pioneering Reliance Band (above).

Reno Club This nightspot in Kansas City must hold some sort of record for the difference between the squalor of the premises and the brilliance of the music which came out of them. Here the Count Basie band, with Lester Young in it, hit its first great peak in 1935. Yet an anonymous article at that time described the place as 'one of the most unsavoury holes' in Kansas City. The band was performing 'some of the country's finest arrangements under the noses of pimps, bags and shipping clerks who may or may not appreciate them fully'.

Rent party An activity akin to the parlor socials put on by churches or schools to help pay their expenses. A small admission fee was charged, food and drink was sold and there would be an entertainment. Similar functions were also used as electioneering aids by local politicians. They became highly organized functions during the Prohibition years when drinking had to go underground. Coming to and during the subsequent Depression years, the idea caught on of having similar affairs at private houses simply to help pay the rent. After the genuine rent parties came the arranged money-making events put on by professional organizers and often highly priced. The professional house rent party might be arranged and advertised months ahead and provided a regular source of income for freelancing musicians, particularly pianists, with players like James P. Johnson, Willie 'The Lion' Smith and Fats Waller foremost in demand. They were also referred to by musicians as jumps or shouts.

Rhythm Within all spheres of music-making there is often a mistaken use of the word 'rhythm'; frequently confusing it, as in 'fast rhythm' or 'slow rhythm', with 'tempo' – the speed at which a piece is played. Within jazz, where so much uninformed emphasis is put on 'rhythm', as in such songs as *I got rhythm*, there is an added tendency to use the word rhythm when something else is intended, not only tempo, but other elements of jazz altogether which should more correctly be referred to as swing, for example. Rhythm, strictly, is the regular beat that underlies all music, however inconspicuously. In jazz, rhythm is particularly emphasized, especially in the traditional forms, though still essential to all jazz if it is to remain recognizable as such. Rhythm is a pulse that is identifiable in mathematical terms, in jazz generally 2/4 or 4/4, a regular number of beats to the bar.

Some of the confusion arises from speaking of jazz rhythm (which must be accepted as now common parlance) as if it was something special. To keep to the strict definition, the rhythms of jazz are the same as the rhythms of other music and do not in themselves give jazz its characteristic propulsive nature. What is meant, rightly or wrongly, by jazz or ragtime rhythm, and what their natures arise from, is the placing of the melodic notes, their lengths, values and emphasis, in relation to the steady pulse of the underlying rhythm, i.e. syncopation. In jazz, the melodic stresses tend to anticipate the rhythm, giving it its characteristic pulse, beat or swing, a loose yet propulsive feeling to the music, which is so often referred to as jazz rhythm.

Panassié puts it that 'it is principally by its rhythmic strength that jazz is distinguished from other types of music'. More analytically, the rhythmic impulse of jazz, one of its dominant elements, arises from a constant awareness that a metronomic beat is holding together a very flexible counterpoint. In general what is referred to as jazz rhythm should be classified as swing.

Rhythm and blues, R&B Name adopted for the kind of music that typified many of the later race recordings. The race label becoming unpopular, the term rhythm and blues gradually superseded it. The style by then was basically that of the urban blues-cum-blues-shouting style of Joe Turner or Jimmy Rushing, the blues with a strong rhythmic impulse. Rhythm and blues then reached a wider market and, with rock and roll, was one of the basic ingredients of the new pop music era of the 1950s. No longer a black music for a black audience but a term that is used to define the deeper more jazz-oriented strains of pop.

Rhythm Club The original Rhythm Club was in Harlem, New York in the basement of a building next to the Lafayette Theater at 168 West 132nd Street. In the burgeoning years of 1924/5 it became very much a centre for jazz musicians, with cheap food and a continuous jam session going on instead of the usual floorshow. It was a recognized place for bandleaders to go to recruit their sidemen, and all the prominent jazz musicians in New York would play there after their regular engagements. In 1925, Sidney Bechet led the house band there, to be succeeded by Willie 'The Lion' Smith with Johnny Hodges in his band. As the club became too popular with the general public the jazz musicians moved the Rhythm Club to the Nest Club on 133rd Street and the old club became the Hoofers Club, a centre for the dancing fraternity.

Rhythm section The group of instruments that provides the rhythmic basis of a jazz ensemble. The dividing line between what is a melody or front-line instrument is not always easy to define. In the older traditional bands the rhythm section could clearly be said to include drums, double-bass or tuba, guitar or banjo and often the piano. But in later groups the piano, guitar and bass might be functioning as solo instruments. Generally speaking, the rhythm section is that which lays down the beat and the harmonic background. Some rhythm sections have added considerably to the character of the band, e.g. the Green/

Page/Jones basis of the early Basie band or the Guy/Braud/Greer group in the Ellington orchestra.

Rhythm Style Series of booklets issued by Parlophone, 1940, 42, 44, 46 and 48 listing all their specialist jazz releases with personnels compiled by Edgar Jackson.

Richmond Town in Indiana, population *c*. 45 000 which is remembered in jazz annals as the location of the early Gennett recording studios, whose closeness to the railroad tracks is said to have caused many a session to be halted while a train went by.

Richmond Richmond in Surrey was the location of the National Jazz Festival from 1961 to 1965. Inevitably, it became known by its venue rather than by its official title, and the Richmond Jazz Festival has an affectionate place in the memories of British jazz enthusiasts of that time.

An entirely British bill was able to fill the Richmond Athletic Association ground for the first two-day event, with names like Chris Barber, John Dankworth, Joe Harriott, Tubby Hayes, Ken Colyer and Alex Welsh. The third and fourth years at Richmond coincided with the emergence of the blues-based pop/rock groups like the Rolling Stones, and gradually that aspect of the British music scene began to assert itself. This not only altered the flavour of the occasion but enlarged the attendance, with the result that it outgrew the Richmond site. In 1966 it moved to Windsor, by which time it had already altered its billing to 'Jazz & Blues Festival'. The event then led a nomadic existence, using venues at Sunbury (Kempton Park Racecourse) and Plumpton (in Sussex) before settling for the rest of its existence into a large site in Reading. All this time the jazz content had been dwindling in the face of the rising tide of rock, and from 1970 to 1983, when the series came to an end, it was no longer part of the jazz calendar.

Ride Jazz musicians' slang for an improvised jazz solo; a phrase taken over from the dance world, where to ride was to dance well and freely in an inspired manner. Also to swing freely and propulsively in performance. A physical sort of tempo sometimes reinforced by ride cymbal playing. A ride cymbal is a smaller, sharper sounding cymbal than the one usually used in the classical orchestra.

Ride-out The final, flowing, abandoned and musically excited chorus of a jazz performance. A swinging sort of free-for-all.

Riff Originally a repeated, brief and distinctive phrase used as an accompanying motif, generally played by the other lead instruments in harmony as backing to the soloist. Morton described riffs as 'figures' – saying 'no jazz piano player can really play good jazz unless they try to give an imitation of a band, that is, by providing a basis of riffs'. This repetitive figure was gradually seen as an end in itself; given prominence and rhythmic insistence, it became a significant ingredient of big band arrangements in the swing era of the 1930s, whole section riffs now providing the required propulsion and excitement demanded by the swing idiom. Finally, the riff assumed prime importance and many numbers were written in which the riff was the dominant feature, with brief solos only a decorative addition. Such passages were found in quite early pieces such as Morton's *King Porter stomp* and *The Pearls*. In many jazz numbers, the common chords of the 12-bar blues are utilized in a passage later formalized as the popular *In the mood*, so effectively used as a riff number by the Glenn Miller Band.

That is one sense of the word. Confusingly, it is also used by some as meaning an improvised phrase or passage by a soloist or section playing in harmony, almost synonymous with the word lick – which suggests an isolated short phrase which is not necessarily repeated immediately but which will recur as a distinctive feature of the number.

As Panassié points out (*Dictionary of Jazz*): some critics have thought the riff to be a demonstration of a lack of imagination, but in fact the riff is something that goes right back in the history of jazz to the ring shouts and hollers, the blues and spirituals, worksongs and the like, where repetition had a very dramatic effect, building in intensity and excitement. This same excitement, when properly achieved, is one of the most exhilarating phenomena of the swing era.

Righteous Described by W & F as 'the most superlative jive word' – righteous jazz is no less than perfect, terrific, wonderful, beautiful and together. The righteous sound is jazz played as it should be played. Well past its vogue by the 1980s, but still encountered.

Rip A short, rapid glissando up to a note used as an occasional exciting attack with the subsequent note played hard and cut off quickly.

Riverboats The paddle-wheel steam riverboats that plied the Mississippi and elsewhere deserve a history to themselves as an important part of the background lore of jazz history. They were a much used means of transport in the 19th century, carrying cotton and other goods, as well as passengers, up and down the rivers and across the lakes. In the more luxurious boats entertainment was provided, to alleviate the boredom of a trip that might take several days, by calliopes and bands for dancing; a regular source of employment for many early jazzmen. A famous name in this area was bandleader Fate Marable (1890–1947) who organized many of the bands that played on the prominent Streckfus Line boats. Some of the boats (many not self-propelled ones) became purely entertainment centres, floating theatres or gambling saloons, travelling from town to town, the famous showboats (as portrayed in the Kern musical) competing fiercely for patronage.

Some of the more famous stern-wheelers that played such a prominent part in New Orleans jazz life included the pre-World War I SS *Camelia*, the celebrated SS *Capitol* (scrapped in 1942), SS *Dixie* which ran the sea route to New York in the 1920s and 30s, SS *Greater New Orleans*, SS *Island Queen* (1920s – 30s), SS *J.S.* with one of the Fate Marable bands always aboard, SS *Madison* on Lake Pontchartrain, SS *Mandeville* (1915–28) – lake run from West End to Mandeville, SS *New Camelia* – lake excursion, SS *President* – a modern successor to the SS *Capitol* built in 1942 and still running, SS *St. Paul* – another early Marable venue, and SS *Susquehanna* 1923–5 on Lake Pontchartrain. Details from *New Orleans Jazz* by Al Rose & Edmond Souchon. Baton Rouge: Louisiana State University Press, rev. 1984.

Rock, rocking A word that came into jazz *c.* 1935, earlier descriptive of dancing or sexual activities – 'my man rocks me with a steady roll'. Suggests powerful, driving jazz which 'rocks the joint', to jump or to swing. Used thus in an Ellington title *Rockin' in rhythm* (1930). Later, as a diminutive of 'rock and roll' and taking on a wider category of pop music it was entirely taken out of jazz hands.

Like the word jazz itself, 'rock' seems to have been part of a whole thesaurus of synonyms for sex. 'Rock me baby, rock me just one more time' was surely – in the first place – a demand for an encore which had nothing to do with music. The fact that rock and rocking also had a perfectly legitimate meaning which could be applied to an obvious aspect of some jazz rhythms was extremely convenient. In that context there can be little doubt that the 1930 Duke Ellington number, *Rockin' in rhythm*, helped to put the word into general currency. That didn't save Alan Freed, the American disc jockey, from a certain amount of puritan stick when he openly began to refer to the music he was broadcasting in the 1950s as 'rock & roll'.

Rock and rocking, in their purely

rhythmic connotations, have never left the jazz vocabulary, and a band or a venue can still be said to be rocking. But when pop music went through its dramatic metamorphosis in the 1960s, 'Rock' as a noun attached itself not only to the new, heavy, loud, iconoclastic music, but to the stratum of society which supported and played it. By 'rock culture' is implied an entire philosophy – one which in its early days looked benignly upon total freedom of behaviour, including experimenting with drugs. Meanwhile, in the musical sense, it was only a matter of time before jazz and rock – which at first seemed natural enemies – should start to draw closer to each other. The key figure in this was Miles Davis (b. 1926), and his move in the direction of rock starts to become unmistakable with the 1968 album *Filles de Kilimanjaro*. That trend has continued ever since, and there are many one-time Miles Davis enthusiasts who could not follow him into the new territory, and who have a 'cut-off point', where Miles is concerned, in the late 1960s.

It was inevitable that other bands fusing jazz with some aspects of rock should emerge from the Miles Davis group itself. Joe Zawinul (b. 1932) and Wayne Shorter (b. 1933), members of the band during this period, formed Weather Report. Chick Corea (b. 1941) became a founder member of Return To Forever. John McLaughlin (b. 1942) started the rock-band-with-eastern-overtones, The Mahavishnu Orchestra. Herbie Hancock had a huge popular hit with an album called *Headhunters*. All this had happened by 1973. The British trumpeter Ian Carr (b. 1933), heavily influenced by Miles Davis (and author of a splendid biography of him), formed Nucleus in 1970, and in the 1980s has been a member of the ten-piece European band which simply calls itself The United Jazz And Rock Ensemble. Practically every gradation between pure jazz and pure rock is now represented somewhere, and the subject has outgrown the scope of this book.

Rock Island Town in Rock Island County, Illinois, population *c.* 50 000; situated on the opposite side of the river to Davenport where the Rock and Mississippi rivers join. It was connected to Chicago by the Chicago & Rock Island Line railroad. Later the line was extended as far as Kansas City and St. Louis and became known as the Chicago, Rock Island and Pacific Railroad (CRIP). Made familiar worldwide by the Leadbelly number *Rock Island Line* (which is generally assumed to refer to the Texas section of the railroad) which he recorded in 1944. It became widely popular as the song of the skiffle craze in England when recorded by Lonnie Donegan in 1955.

Ronnie Scott's Club Jazz club founded in 1959 by saxophonists Ronnie Scott and Pete King, at 39 Gerrard Street, London, a short street roughly parallel with Shaftesbury Avenue. In 1967 Ronnie's moved to 47 Frith Street, London. Still flourishing after 27 years of activity, presenting both British and visiting overseas jazz musicians. The first American jazz musician to appear (at the old club) was tenor saxophonist Zoot Sims (1925–85).

Issues its own news sheet, *Jazz at Ronnie Scott's*, bi-monthly, edited by Jim Godbolt.

Book: *Let's Join Hands and Contact the Living: Ronnie Scott and his Club* by John Fordham, 224p. London: 1986.

Rosebud Café Saloon and club in St. Louis where, in the 1890s, the pioneer ragtime pianists met to swap ideas and play, it becoming their unofficial headquarters *c.* 1895. It was owned and run by pianist Tom Turpin, destined to be the first black ragtime composer to appear in print – with his *Harlem Rag* (1897). Prior to Thomas Million Turpin's reign as resident landlord to the ragtimers at the Rosebud, his father 'Honest' John Turpin had run a similar establishment, well-liked and frequented by pianists, which he called the Silver Dollar Saloon.

Roseland Ballroom A large ballroom in

New York's midtown district which was situated at 1658 Broadway, near 51st Street, which opened at the beginning of 1919. Although the dancing clientele were white, the ballroom pioneered the use of black orchestras as well as white in the early 1920s and 1930s, many of them, of course, commercial dance orchestras, but bands such as Fletcher Henderson's were among the earliest occupants of the bandstand. It was at the Roseland that Louis Armstrong joined the Henderson band in 1924. McKinney's Cotton Pickers were there in 1928. Much later, Count Basie's orchestra was another regular. They recorded *Roseland Shuffle* as a tribute. The hall was closed at the end of December, 1956, and later demolished.

Royal Garden Café Famous jazz haunt in Chicago which opened in 1918 at 31st Street and Cottage Grove Avenue. When a regular band was thought necessary, bassist Bill Johnson was asked to form one and he at first sent for Buddy Petit who refused to leave New Orleans. King Joe Oliver came instead with clarinettist Jimmie Noone. Later, Sidney Bechet joined them and Freddie Keppard was second cornet for a while. The establishment then moved to 459 East 31st Street and was renamed Lincoln Gardens where Oliver, after a short stint on the West Coast, returned to organise his famous Creole Jazz Band, later adding Louis Armstrong as second cornet. The original café was commemorated in Spencer and Clarence Williams' *Royal Garden blues* (1920). Jimmie Noone later claimed that he and Oliver wrote the original *Royal Garden blues* for the band to play and then sold the title to Clarence Williams who published it as his own.

Royal Roost Renowned nightclub on Broadway near 47th Street and Times Square, New York, its name reflecting its origins as a chicken-in-the-basket restaurant. It added the attraction of a band from 1946 on, and Basie, Gillespie and Charlie Parker were among the famous names who led groups there (recently re-issued on LP). Another attraction was a nightly disc-jockey show run by Symphony Sid Torin, a popular broadcaster on various New York radio stations during the 1940s, in Boston in the 50s, and a promoter of jazz concerts.

Gave its name to an extremely influential, if short-lived, nine-piece band which appeared there for two weeks in 1948 under the leadership of Miles Davis. This recorded 1949/50 and had an immense effect on what was to become 'cool' jazz.

Rub-board In some cajun and zydeco bands the washboard has evolved into a corrugated metal sheet, hung from the player's shoulders, rather like the front half of a medieval tabard. The wearer performs by running metal objects, usually spoon handles, over the ridges.

Rug-cutter To rug-cut originally and specifically meant to get into a dance-hall for nothing or to dance free as one would at a party – thus used in Harlem *c*. 1930–35. A rug-cutter was one who went to the type of rent-party where jive music was played in the 1930s; cutting up the rugs of the host with their antics; rather disdainful suggestion of someone too poor to pay for admission to a ballroom. Hence, for a time, *c*. 1935 period, it was commonly used of one who danced in the vigorous and athletic style of the day to swing music, especially one who was expert in the jitterbug style of dancing. Now obsolete. There was a similar phrase rug-shaking (rug-shaker) used in the 1920s of those who danced the shimmy.

Running wild Playing in an exciting, uninhibited manner. The song *Running wild* was written by A. Harrington Gibbs in 1922, about the time the phrase was in limited, publicity use.

Rural blues see **Country blues**

S

Sack A dress of a loose fitting kind over the bust, waist and hips but slightly gathered in at the hem. A common style in the 1920s. Armstrong's invitation to a lady to *Drop that sack* speaks for itself.

St. James' Infirmary Now well-known as a minor-keyed blues number in the jazz repetoire. Its history goes right back to Norman times when St. James' Hospital for female lepers was founded in London. Henry VIII grabbed the site when he came to the throne and turned it into St. James' Palace in 1533. The original institution was the foundation of a number of variant folksongs such as *The unfortunate rake* and *The young trooper cut down in his prime*, which appeared in print in the 18th century. These were taken to America in due course and took on such guises as *The dying cowboy* and *The streets of Laredo*; finally getting into the blues repertoire as *Gambler's blues* and, once again, *St. James's Infirmary*.

St. Louis City of Missouri, USA, population *c*. 750 000, lying on the Mississippi some 17 miles (27 km) south of the confluence of the Mississippi and Missouri rivers. First settled in 1764 by the French and named after Louis XV. St. Louis (pronounced by the inhabitants as Lewis) was to the development of ragtime what New Orleans was to jazz: the centre of its growth and exploitation. By *c*. 1885 St. Louis had taken on that free-and-easy character that was common to ports of call all over the world. It was not exactly a seaport, but it had something of that nature as the northerly outlet to the Mississippi for cotton, agricultural and mining products being sent to the port of New Orleans; with the usual itinerant population with money to spend and in need of entertainment. It was to St. Louis in 1885 that Scott Joplin (1868–1917), like so many others of his kind, went and found kindred spirits in the ragtime world at places like 'Honest John' Turpin's Silver Dollar Saloon and later, by around 1895, at the Rosebud Café run by John's son Tom in Market Street. The St. Louis Exposition State Fair of 1904 (celebrating the Louisiana Purchase) brought a great influx of trade and cultural life to the city. St. Louis was immortalized in W. C. Handy's most famous composition, the *St. Louis blues*, written in 1914. In 1927 the city was devastated by a cyclone which killed 84 people and caused 100 million dollars worth of damage.

St. Louis was not the source of any definable overall jazz style as Chicago and Kansas City had been, but it was yet another melting pot of jazz, with its strategic geographical position, right from the beginning. A notable musician and influential organizing figure there from *c*. 1918 was trumpeter Charlie Creath (1890–1915) who led several bands in the 1920s before working with Fate Marable (1890–1947) on the riverboat SS *Capitol*. If no general St. Louis style emerged there have been strong claims made for a St. Louis school of trumpet-players, with common ground to be found between such people as: Joe Thomas (1909–84), Harold 'Shorty' Baker (1913–66), Clark Terry (b. 1920) and Miles Davis (b. 1926), as well as lesser figures (all born or brought up in St. Louis).
See: 'The St. Louis Sound' by John Postgate in *Jazz Monthly* (April 1968).

Salty Seems to have had various meanings at various times, including: daring, unbelievable, obscene, violent, horrible, unpalatable and angry. It is in this last sense that it is taken in the blues phrase 'my man jumped salty on me', 'salty mama', etc. By the 1950s, however, in jive parlance, it had somehow come to mean smart, lively, hep.

Salty dog In its own right, on the other hand, means either a sexy, teasing sort of girl or a sexy but rather untrustworthy sort of man.

San Francisco Large port and commercial city of California on the West Coast of USA, population *c.* 750 000. Founded by the Spanish in 1776, it became a boom town at the time of the great Gold Rush *c.* 1850. American jazzmen had played in cities on the Pacific seaboard as far back as the heyday of ragtime, but the West Coast was not considered a natural breeding ground for jazz until the 1940s. Then there was a sudden upsurge of both traditional revivalist jazz, led by Lu Watters (b. 1911), and the Yerba Buena Jazz Band and a new school of modern jazz headed by local musicians (see **West Coast jazz**). The revival was almost entirely a San Francisco phenomenon, while the modernist activities mainly centred on Los Angeles where the film, TV and recording studios abound, calling for high 'academic' professional standards.

Satchmo Eventually the most popular and well-established of Louis Armstrong's various nicknames. How the final form came about is still a bit of a mystery. Armstrong had long been referred to as Satchelmouth and thus referred to himself (and/or his trumpet) in a 1930 recording of *You're driving me crazy*. With their usual penchant for abbreviation, some musicians referred to him as Satchmo but Armstrong was not aware of this himself until he came to England and was greeted as Satchmo (firstly, according to him, by the then editor of *Melody Maker*, Percy Mathison Brooks). In England some advertising copy had appeared in which first the Selmer trumpet he used had been nick-named Satch-Mo. But it seems clear that Armstrong did not get around to using this abbreviated form until he came to England in July 1932, and that its creation came about in a somewhat haphazard rather than deliberate way.

Savannah Syncopators Name used by the King Oliver band in the mid-1920s to early 30s in Chicago and New York and on record. Also briefly by a group led by Jimmie Noone in 1929.

Also used as a generic name for the kind of country blues music that has a close affinity with its African ancestry and is still played there.

See: *Savannah Syncopators* by Paul Oliver. London: Studio Vista, 1970.

Savoy Ballroom on South Parkway Street in Chicago opened in 1927. The following year the resident band was Carroll Dickerson's Orchestra in which Louis Armstrong played for a time. The *Savoy blues* that Armstrong recorded with his Hot Five in 1927 (one of the most effectively simple sides he ever made) immortalizes this venue.

Savoy Ballroom (New York) The Savoy Ballroom at 596 Lenox Avenue, between 140th and 141st Streets, in the Harlem district of New York was the better-known venue; probably the most famous ballroom in the history of jazz dancing. It opened on 12 March 1926. From a spacious lobby a marble staircase led up to the vast ballroom itself, a block's length, with a double bandstand on which two bands alternated. It was kept in tip-top condition with a new floor installed every three years. In 1936 it was redecorated at a cost of $50 000. Admission originally was 30 cents before 6pm, 60 cents before 8pm and 85 cents after. The keen dancers, however poor, would do their best to save up for a weekly visit there. The popular night out was Saturday, known as Square's Night because it was so crowded that there was no room for any high-class dancing and anybody could shuffle around. Monday was Ladies' Night, Tuesday was a special

'Dancers Only' night at reduced prices giving the experts room to practise steps, Wednesday and Friday were reserved for club functions, Thursday was 'Kitchen Mechanics' Night' frequented by those mainly in domestic service. The great night was Sunday when it was the custom for celebrities to visit, many by special invitation of the management, and there was an 'Opportunity Contest' with a first prize of $10.

The ballroom advertised itself in the 1930s as 'The Home of Happy Feet' but it was of greater sociological importance to the black community than that might suggest. The regulars called it 'The Track' and, in American parlance, the actual name was usually pronounced 'sav-voy' with the accent on the first syllable. The real dancing fraternity competed there in earnest in the north-east corner, known as 'Cats' Corner' and strictly reserved for the professionals. The steps of a master were watched with great attention but it was a law that nobody's innovations were ever stolen. One of the most famous Savoy dancers was one Shorty Snowden. The Lindy Hop was introduced there in 1936.

The first two bands to be engaged were Fess Williams and his Royal Flush Orchestra and the Charleston Bearcats (with Fletcher Henderson's Roseland Orchestra guesting on the opening night). Nearly all the best orchestras played there at some time, especially the Chick Webb band, long in residence in the 1930s and it was there that he introduced his new vocalist, Ella Fitzgerald. The Savoy Sultans, led by Al Cooper, was the house band from 1937 for many years. Battles of the bands were a popular arranged attraction involving the orchestras of such notable leaders as Fletcher Henderson, Duke Ellington and Cab Calloway. One of the most famous was that between Chick Webb and Benny Goodman in 1937 when over 20 000 people had to be turned away at the door. The Savoy was immortalized in *Stompin' at the Savoy* recorded by Webb in 1934, by Goodman in 1935 and *Savoy stampede* recorded by Benny Carter. A booklet *The Savoy Story* was issued in 1951 to mark the ballroom's 25th anniversary.

Savoy Hotel (London) Famous hotel in London, occupying a site between the Embankment and the Strand. Rupert D'Oyly Carte had built and opened the Savoy Theatre in 1881 as a home for the Gilbert and Sullivan operettas, and having a site for the asking alongside the theatre decided to build a 'grand' hotel there to emulate those he had visited in the USA. Building started in 1884 and the startling new steel-framed building, the first in London to use concrete, was opened in 1889. Never a jazz centre, it catered for a high-class clientele but its orchestras, usually under the title of the Savoy Orpheans in dance-band days, were excellent of their kind, particularly the unit led by the Canadian pianist Carrol Gibbons in the 1930s. Because of its proximity to the BBC's first studios in Savoy Hill, the bands at the hotel were frequently heard on the air in the early days of broadcasting.

The nearest the London Savoy came to establishing a jazz reputation was when, at the end of 1927, a band under Fred Elizalde (1907–79), son of a Philippines industrialist, and recently down from Cambridge, opened there opposite the Orpheans. The music it played was both hot – in the parlance of the day – and revolutionary in an almost Ellingtonian sense. It was too much for most of the Savoy regulars but the band lasted until 1929, making some unusual and still interesting records during that period. Elizalde, a pianist, evolved into a mainly 'serious' composer.

Savoy Orpheans Title used by the dance bands of the Savoy Hotel, London from 1923 to 1927. The Orpheans became synonymous with the best of British dance music in the 1920s, although only officially in existence for four years, managed until 1927 by Wilfred de Mornys and originally directed by Debroy Somers. While still the Orpheans, the band had several American musicians in its ranks and during this time recorded regularly for HMV from 1924. The Canadian pianist in the band, Carroll Gibbons, became its director from 1927. The band's contracts with the Savoy Hotel were terminated in 1927 and a new group under violinist Reggie Batten took over at the beginning of 1928. In 1931 Carroll Gibbons formed a new band for the hotel which was known as the Savoy Hotel Orpheans. Not to be confused with the Smaller Savoy Havana Band which had played in the ballroom of the hotel from 1921 under the direction of Bert Ralton and in 1926–7 (when it was disbanded) under Cyril Ramon. The hotel adopted a two-band policy in 1923 when the Orpheans were first formed. By 1928 there were no less than four bands in simultaneous operation: the New Savoy Orpheans directed by Batten, Fred Elizalde and his Savoy Music, the Andre Pesenti Tango Band, and Moschetto and his Monte Carlo Orchestra.

Savoy Sultans Band led by Al Cooper at the Savoy Ballroom, New York during the late 1930s. The name was reactivated in the 1970s by drummer Panama Francis (b. 1918) who toured with a splendid nine-piece band, playing some of the original group's repertoire and fielding one or two of the original players.

Saxophone, Sax Of all the instruments, the saxophone is the one most associated, in the public and journalistic mind, with jazz. This is in spite of the negligible part it played in the music's early development; it is due instead to the curious notoriety it attained during the 1920s. Having ousted the violin in dancebands, it appeared to lay listeners as a bizarre novelty and, inevitably, a threat to civilization as they knew it. A selection of quotes from various issues of *Punch* from 1924 will give some idea of reaction to it in conservative circles:

'Saxophone players are born, not made', declares a musical critic. Those who bewail our declining birth-rate should find consolation in this great thought.

A man who stole sixteen saxophones from a shop in the West End and melted them down was sentenced to a month's imprisonment. His conduct was, of course, reprehensible. Yet he might have done worse.

An American super-sousaphone is described as the largest brass band instrument ever made. The idea, we fancy, is to use it for asphyxiating saxophones.

At the time when those waggish remarks were printed, the saxophone was a little under 80 years old; it had been invented in the 1840s by a Belgian in Paris, Adolphe Sax (1814–94), whose actual patent for it was taken out in 1846. Sax appears to have been a brilliant, arrogant, imaginative, bombastic man who so enraged rival French instrument-makers that there were three attempts on his life. He already had the invention of the saxhorn to his credit by the time he created the saxophone family, which came into being as the result, in part, of a search for a suitable instrument to fill out the sound of military bands; he was aiming at something with the power of brass and the tonal range of strings. In this he was highly successful, and both the French and Belgian armies swiftly adopted the saxophone. It did less well in the classical field, partly due to academic prejudice against Sax himself, partly because of the fact that – except for Berlioz – 19th-century composers simply seemed not to like it. It is appropriate that it was a mongrel music – jazz – which finally liberated this mongrel instrument.

The saxophone has a clarinet-style single reed and mouthpiece. Yet it is commonly made of brass or some other metal, and the bore of the tube is conical, as in the bugle and the French horn. It has padded keys (like the woodwinds) operated by a complicated system of rods and levers.

The main members of the family working downwards, are: The soprano in Bb, the alto in Eb, the tenor (Bb), the baritone (Eb). Above the soprano is the tiny sopranino (regularly used by Art Themen (b. 1939) but very few others), while at the bottom end comes the bass saxophone, rarer now than in the 1920s, but still encountered occasionally, and played regularly by Harry Gold (b. 1907). The bass saxophone's most famous exponent was Adrian Rollini (1904–56). Right in the middle of the range is the now almost vanished C-melody saxophone, pitched between alto and tenor. Frankie Trumbauer (1901–56) was a multi-instrumentalist, but it was on this saxophone that he concentrated, influencing, with his light, floating tone, the way Lester Young (1909–59) later played tenor. To the ear, the C-melody is close to the alto; visually it resembles the tenor, having that characteristic curve between mouthpiece and crook.

Some of the extra-musical attention which the saxophone has attracted to itself must be due to its shape. The sopranino is straight; the soprano more often straight than curved. Thereafter comes the curly tubing which so inspired cartoonists (usually inaccurately) and aroused irrational and exaggerated responses among writers; in the public prints the most direct possible shorthand for 'jazz' is the deformed 'S' or 'J' shape of the tenor saxophone.

The saxophone got off to a slow start in jazz, mainly because the three-part counterpoint of trumpet, trombone and clarinet, the Holy Trinity of New Orleans music, was so comfortably formalized that there was no very obvious path through that already dense traffic for a fourth and moreover softer voice. Saxes were occasionally used, to be sure, to beef up the ensemble sound, but – as far as we know – no improvising soloist emerged until Sidney Bechet (1897–1959) began to impress audiences with his soprano saxophone playing as a featured member of Will Marion Cook's Southern Syncopated Orchestra in Europe around 1920. Not even that was typical, since the Southern Syncopators were by no means a New Orleans jazz band, and Bechet himself played the soprano with trumpet-like force.

It is not until the late 1920s that we find saxophones speaking with recognizable jazz voices. Bud Freeman (b. 1906) developed a hard, dusty sound on tenor with a flapping shirt-tail of a vibrato and managed, furthermore, to plot a course for it through the busy ensemble sound of the so-called Chicago school. Johnny Hodges (1907–70), himself influenced originally by Bechet, created a creamy, floating, yet at the same time lithely muscular tone on the alto. But the first major step towards the ultimate supremacy of the saxophones was the fashioning by Coleman Hawkins (1901–69) of a burgundy-rich voice on the tenor coupled with an almost architectural sense of construction when it came to solo building. For a time Hawkins' way was *the* way to play the instrument, so that when, in the middle 1930s, Lester Young arrived with his light, graceful, elegant but intensely rhythmic style, he was felt by some to be blaspheming against holy writ. It was Lester's oblique musical thinking and slightly cooler approach, however, which helped prepare the ground for later developments.

The most influential single jazz musician after Louis Armstrong was an alto player – Charlie Parker (1920–55); with him the saxophones, as a family, seem finally to have taken over as the chief agents of innovation. John Coltrane (1926–67) and Ornette Coleman (b. 1930), on tenor and alto respectively, have between them influenced much of the saxophone playing (and a good deal of the jazz) since their emergence in the 1950s (Coleman somewhat later than Coltrane).

Scat A way of jazz singing, which uses wordless phrases or sounds instead of lyrics, in an improvised imitation of instrumental performance. The credit for first putting a scat vocal on record is generally accorded to Louis Armstrong (*the* master of the art) with *Heebie jeebies* in 1926, but there have been many claimants to the actual invention of a vocal device which probably goes well back into jazz history. Jelly Roll Morton asserted that he had heard, and given, scat performances as far back as 1906/7 but credited its origins to one Joe Sims, a comedian from Vicksburg. Whenever it was, it is usually assumed to have originated when someone forgot the words. It became a popular art, practised to the point of over-indulgence by Cab Calloway (b. 1907) in his Cotton Club days and thereafter by many others. The name presumably derives from 'scatty', though W & F say it is from 'scat' the syllable traditionally used (they claim) to scare cats, or – more generally – a sharp invitation to go away, colloquially used from about 1869 and itself derived from the verb to scatter. It all seems a bit unlikely.

Most singers in a jazz context resort to scatting to a greater or lesser extent; those famous for it include Ella Fitzgerald (b. 1918), Anita O'Day (b. 1919), Louis Armstrong (*c.* 1900–71), Mel Tormé (b. 1925), Sarah Vaughan (b. 1924).

Scatting is not to be confused with vocalese, which is the fitting of words to what were originally recorded instrumental solos. A famous example is *Twisted* by Annie Ross (b. 1930), sung to a Wardell Gray solo; another is the setting of words to James Moody's solo on *I'm in the mood for love* by Eddie Jefferson (1918–79). Slightly to confuse the issue, another major vocalese exponent, King Pleasure (R. N. Clarence Beeks, 1922–79) did his own version of the James Moody solo, recorded as *Moody's mood for love*. The ultimate in vocalese ambition was probably realized with the formation in 1958 of Lambert, Hendricks & Ross. In addition to Annie Ross, mentioned above, they were Dave Lambert (1917–66) and Jon Hendricks (b. 1921). They did the whole thing in triplicate, even, at one stage, multitracking their voices (using words written by Hendricks) to duplicate the sound of the entire Count Basie Orchestra.

Scene Slightly 'in' and occasionally irritating, but for some time it has usefully filled a gap taken care of by no other single word. Its ultimate ancestry must surely be the Latin and Greek words respectively for a stage, a tent or booth.

It is an easy progression from theatrical use to general employment to indicate presence in, or arrival at, some sphere of activity, as: 'the motor car arrived upon the scene in the late 19th century'.

The word seems first to have been used in specific connection with what was then modern jazz in the 1950s, and in the beginning tended to mean the actual location of a jazz performance, the place where people gathered to hear jazz played. Gradually it was widened to encompass, in figurative as well as physical terms, the whole ambience in which such an art as jazz thrived. The highly respected left-wing critic Francis Newton entitled his book, published in 1959, *The Jazz Scene*, which probably helped to confirm its new function. In October 1962, BBC radio inaugurated a magazine-format programme, also called *The Jazz Scene*. People wishing to seem hip, especially those given to wearing sunglasses ('shades') indoors, would often talk in the 60s of 'making the scene' – simply being around, and noticed, in places where jazz activities were pursued and where other hip elements foregathered.

Scream To play high and loud, especially on the trumpet; sometimes a long held version of the rip. Screaming solos. Screamer – a trumpeter who makes a habit of such effects. Screamers: high notes generally.

Second line (1) The procession of marchers and dancers which tended to assemble behind and alongside a New Orleans street band. Quotation from Harry Souchon's sleevenote to the Olympia Brass Band of New Orleans (Audiophile AP108): 'As they march along with the band, forming a "second line", the crowd moves sedately and solemnly as the funeral dirges are played. As soon as the band switches to lively jazz marching tunes, the group following them pick up their marching tempo – strutting, shuffling and prancing in perfect time to the music', sometimes

Before deciding on the purchase of a new Saxophone study the merits of

Boosey's New "REGENT" SAXOPHONE

Patent No. 261482

See and test the new "REGENT"! You will be amazed at the wonderful simplicity of manipulation of the new system for the keywork. You will be pleasurably surprised with its first class workmanship and finish and inimitable tone quality. No extra keys are fitted. The instrument has the same vents and keys as the ordinary model, but there are no ugly protruding keys and the vents of the top notes are in a straight line with the finger plates giving the instrument a truer acoustic system.

The "REGENT" has drawn cups and body, and the mechanism is built for strength and long wear.

The instrument is so designed that the ordinary fingering is not altered in any way; you can take the "REGENT" and play it at once with the orthodox fingering.

If you are already a Saxophonist the "REGENT" will improve your tecl...
a t...

On...
to...
pul...
not...
mar...
emb...
ary...
tion...

But...
is...
can...

To...
only...

To...
only...

To...
only...

'R...
fa...

Ran...
mou...
tips...
gilt...
driv...
silk...
rexi...

Some Saxophone History

Its Origin and Early Use

'REGENT' E♭ ALTO

Do not delay
Write NOW for
FREE BOOKLET

Ple...
OU...
an...

N...
A...

BOOSEY & Co. Ltd., 29...

Plenty of encouragement
to buy in the 1930s.

As used in the title of the
famous show – featuring one of
its most famous songs.
(B. Feldman & Co)

Famous jazz number of 1917.
(Roger Graham, Chicago)

playing their own makeshift instruments.

(2) Hence, *Second line*, appropriate title of magazine issued by the New Orleans Jazz Club.

(3) Title of a street band type march by Paul Barbarin (1899–1969); and also of a riff tune originally known as *Holler blues* and later as *Joe Avery's tune* (after Joe 'Kid' Avery (1892–1952) who regularly played it) now played by brass bands as *Second line*.

Section A group of like instruments within a band, for example, a trumpet section, reed section. The rhythm section groups together all the accompanying instruments, for example, drums, guitar, bass and sometimes piano.

Sedalia Town in Missouri, USA, mainly known for its association with the ragtime composer Scott Joplin who was born in Texarkana (a town which bestraddles the border between Texas and Arkansas) in 1868. Originally known as Sedville, it was founded by General George R. Smith in 1859 and named after his daughter, Sarah, who was nicknamed Sed. The site was about 189 miles (304 km) west of St. Louis and 96 miles (154 km) east of Kansas City. There was a railroad through Sedalia by 1861 and thenceforth it prospered; by the 1890s it had a population of some 15 000. Eventually it became the junction of seven different railroads and the terminal of four. Joplin settled there *c*. 1895 and became part of its thriving musical community. He joined various organizations and found regular musical employment in a number of saloons, being resident pianist for some time at the Maple Leaf Club which he immortalized in his most famous rag. An outlet for his works was offered by the Sedalia music publisher John Stark who printed most of his best works and, thriving, moved to St. Louis where Joplin followed.

Send, sent To move, excite. To be sent is to be transported with delight, exhilarated by such things as jazz, to be inspired to play. A 'sender' is one who sends – often referred to as a 'solid sender'. Now very dated, and, when encountered in the 1930s and 40s cuttings, decidedly quaint.

Session Usually used in connection with activities in the recording studio, that is, a recording session – the time allotted to or used for the making of a recording, or part of a recording. In commercial studio terms, a session is usually of three hours' duration and musicians are paid by the session. Also used, less often, as any time in which jazz musicians simply play, as in 'jam session', a period of jamming, or, more widely, 'jazz session'.

Set The time on stage or playing, the band's turn, a set number of items played in one session. A band's act. In use from the 1950s. A band is usually booked to play a number of sets, with rests 'between sets', thence between sets is a regularly-used phrase for the 20–30 minute interval where perhaps a soloist takes over.

Set of threads Bebop era musicians' parlance for a suit of clothes, particularly if stylish or new, in use in the 1950s; sometimes previously (in the 1940s) set of drapes. During the same period, 'threads' might refer to clothing generally.

Shag A dance, somewhat akin to the shake which, as the name suggests, had some suggestion of sexual intercourse in it.

Shake (1) A note played (usually brass or saxophones) with a very emphatic vibrato, often moving between the note and an adjacent semitone – what might, on the piano, be described as a trill (for which shake was the early English name), executed on brass by the fingering rather than the lips.

(2) A dance popular *c*. 1900–30. Originally of highly sexual character, often danced in the nude in the shadier haunts. Became one of the movements in such dances as the shimmy. It was a black American version of the Egyptian belly-dance, done to music of a slow, oriental nature. Such music was sometimes referred to as 'race music' (before the record companies took up this name), 'jungle music' or simply 'shake music'. The shakes and shimmies became an integral part of the black dance scene of the 20s and 30s.

The exhortation to 'shake that thing' therefore has the mixed implication of sexual activity, to dance in an uninhibited way, or to play in a titillating manner. The dance was popularized at the Chicago World Fair in 1890 and later became nationally known as the Hootchy-Kootchy. Originally a woman's sexually suggestive dance, it was later performed by men and led directly to the pelvic movements that accompanied early rock and roll. With slight variants it appeared under such names as the Mooche (performed by Bert Williams in 1903), the grind or quiver (1923) and the Snake Hips (1929).

(3) A party, such as a rent party, to which each guest contributes something toward the paying of the domestic dues. To have a shake, hold a shake.

Shimmy A black American dance. Originally a basic dance movement, that became formulated in the Southern States *c.* 1900; though its origins were undoubtedly to be found in earlier black folk-dance and it may have been imported from Africa. Essentially it is a 'stationary' movement, the feet remaining still while the dancer, with hands on hips, 'shakes' the body. In Atlanta it was also long known as 'the shake' (cf. Perry Bradford) and was danced to Bradford's *Bull frog hop*. By 1910 the dance had become familiarly known as the 'shimmy-sha-wobble' (an entirely descriptive title) and Spencer Williams immortalised this variant when he wrote his *Shim-me-sha-wabble* in 1917 – 'I can't play no piano, can't sing no blues, but I can shim-me-sha-wabble from my head to my shoes' (cf. Stearns: *Jazz Dance*) and it soon became a popular jazz standard. It was Ethel Waters in particular who took up the song and made it famous.

The white entertainers Mae West and Gilda Gray[1] both claimed to be the introducers of the shimmy in 1919; but their credit was only as introducers of the dance to the Broadway stage. Mae West later admitted to seeing the crude black version in Chicago some years before. The shimmy became a basic dance step and used as part of many later novelty dances of the *Ballin' the jack* type.

Also immortalized in Armond Piron and Pete Bocage's *I wish I could shimmy like my sister Kate* ('she shakes like a jelly on a plate') in 1919; and *Shake it and break it* (1921).

Shout A style of blues singing that came in with the big-band era, performing with a forceful shouting tone, more generally referred to as 'blues-shouting'. Very much a part of the Kansas City scene and indulged in by such as Joe Turner, Jimmy Rushing, Wynonie Harris (with Lucky Millinder's band) and Sonny Parker (with Hampton). Latterly, there have been more female blues-shouters with the same approach.

The word is also used of instrumental performances where the tone is deliberately powerful and attacking; particularly associated with a driving sort of piano playing prevalent among the Harlem school, e.g. James P. Johnson who wrote and performed a piece called *Carolina shout*. Similar big band items with the same intent are *Harlem shout* and *Saratoga shout*.

Shreveport City and port on the Red River in Louisiana, population *c.* 165 000. Founded in 1834 and named after an engineer and inventor Henry Shreve who was a pioneer in steamboat construction. Was once the capital of

---

[1] Gilda Gray (real name: Maryanna Mickalski) first made a hit at a nightspot called (after the French original) the Folies Bergère over the Winter Garden Theater on Broadway, between 50th and 51st Street. Billed as 'The Sweetheart of the Shimmy', she was accompanied there by the Original Dixieland Jazz Band. The Band was a big enough attraction on its own (and its leader Nick La Rocca a worthy exponent of the shimmy himself) so Gilda Gray departed to become a rage in the Ziegfeld Follies. The band went on to make *Sister Kate* a popular hit.

Louisiana before Baton Rouge claimed the honour. Like most ports it had a thriving entertainment industry and was a popular stopping place for jazzmen. Celebrated in *Shreveport* (Clarence Williams) and *Shreveport stomp* (Morton).

Shuffle (1) A dance step of the tap variety that dates well back into the 18th century; originally it was a tap step done with both feet so that the sounds were simultaneous and prolonged. Later it became, as the name suggests, a flat-footed dragging step that produces the effect of brushes on a side-drum. The soft-shoe shuffle was a feature of the minstrel stage dance. A well-known exponent in England was Eugene Stratton who performed to the music of Leslie Stuart. There were many variants such as the double-shuffle, back-shuffle, side-shuffle, heel-and-toe-shuffle and so on. Mainly developed in the Southern States of America. Lent its name to many songs of the 1920s and to the famous *Shuffle Along* at the 63rd Street Theater in 1921. With music by Eubie Blake, it was the first really successful black revue on Broadway, running for 504 performances and paving the way for various similar successors.
(2) Shuffle rhythm was an instrumental imitation of the dance step, a doubling up of the beats to give a continuous busy rhythmic effect. It was a favourite device in Chicago jazz, often used in the release passage before the final flare-up or explosion, usually quietly done to create a controlled moment of suspension. In the swing era a shuffle rhythm was popular amongst drummers who liked to use the brushes. Duke Ellington was much addicted to it, and it was handled to perfection by his drummer Sam Woodyard.

Side Referred originally to the perform-ance that was contained on one side of an old 78 rpm record, for example, 'six sides were cut during the 10 April session'. Sometimes carried on into the LP era but now each item is usually referred to as a track.

Sidedoor Pullman see **Box car**

Sideman Any member of a band or orchestra other than the leader.

Sinclair Stories that grew up around the jazz-enthusiast editor of *Jazz Journal*, Sinclair Traill (1904–1981) were many, most of them concerned with his enforced parsimony – jazz journalism not being a lucrative living for someone like Sinclair who liked to deport himself in style. He was an unlikely-looking jazzman, tweedily dressed, long balding, slightly pop-eyed, of the English public-school type, a sort of halfway stage between a bookie and an upper-class punter. The gambit that one ought to have been warned of on a first meeting, but never was, was Sinclair's apparent eagerness to buy the drinks. He would quickly order a half-pint of bitter and the would-be contributor to *Jazz Journal* would, in modesty and deference, ask for the same. However, when the turn for the next round came Sinclair would say: 'Gassy stuff beer, not good for the tum. I'll have a double brandy if you don't mind.' He was very adept at passing the bill in expensive restaurants but many famous jazzmen, including Earl Hines, have been credited with outwitting him on various occasions. The Danish jazz enthusiast, Baron Timme Rosencrantz, is said to have pre-empted one of these financial ploys of Sinclair's by excusing himself towards the close of the meal to go to the toilet, and simply not coming back.

Another odd characteristic was that whenever a living jazz musician's name cropped up in conversation, Sinclair would tap his pocket – the one other men keep their wallets in – and say: 'Ah, so-and-so. Had a letter from him only yesterday'. He died in 1981 and is greatly missed by all his admirers. Immortalized in the number *Truckin' down the Sinclair Traill*.

Single Since the advent of the LP in the 1950s with its several tracks, the old-fashioned record with one item to each side, originally 78 rpm later 45 rpm, has been referred to in the popular music world as a single.

Sit in Generally implies the permitted joining of some band or unit, of which the musician is not a regular member, to enjoy an improvisational blow, or to sit-in at a jam session.

Six Bells Public house in London that was conveniently situated near to the Chenil Galleries in Kings Road, Chelsea, which Decca used to use as a recording studio in the youthful days of British jazz. The rapid exit to the pub at the end of a recording session was the subject of *Six Bells stampede* by Spike Hughes, bass-player, composer and band-leader, later a respectable critic and the official historian of the Glyndebourne Opera House.

Skiffle A skiffle was originally a colloquial name for a rent party. 'Shake' was another. The type of music played, certainly at those held in the poorer parts of New Orleans, Chicago and other jazz centres, was often of an improvisational nature, the improvisation extending to the instruments themselves which might include such things as a jug, a washboard or a packing-case bass. These *ad hoc* ensembles might also be referred to as washboard bands, jug bands or spasm bands, and occasionally skiffle bands. The term was brought back into prominence in the late 1940s and 1950s when revivalist groups performed occasional numbers in the hill-billy style of these spasm bands, with guitar and washboard generally prominent. Some credit for re-establishing the name is given to amateur pianist and journalist Dan Burley (b. 1907) who recorded as Dan Burley and his Skiffle Boys for Circle Records in 1946. One of the most successful British skiffle groups was that led by Lonnie Donegan, originally an offshoot of the Chris Barber Band. It is generally agreed that the British Skiffle Group, as a separate entity, originated in the interval attraction provided by Ken Colyer's band, with Ken playing guitar and Chris Barber playing bass.

Skins A fairly artificial colloquialism for drums. Not much used in jazz circles, where 'hides' is preferred. A drummer would sometimes be referred to as a 'skin-beater'.

Skip Nickname of blues singer/guitarist/pianist Nehemia James (1902–69). He gave two explanations for his nickname – one, that his skill at dancing as a young man was responsible for it; the other – only rarely referred to – was that he earned the name by not staying in any one place or doing any one thing for too long. His high, almost falsetto voice was unlike any other blues singer's. He died in 1969, having enjoyed belated recognition (and royalties) as composer of *I'm so glad*, which was recorded by the rock group, Cream.

Slap An effect applied to various instruments which can be forceful and effective at times but is mainly used for a somewhat comic effect. On the double-bass it is a matter of an exaggerated plucking of the strings so that they slap against the fingerboard with a percussive sound; an effect used by early bass-players like 'Pops' Foster and Wellman Braud. On the saxophone it is a matter of blowing hard so that the reed lifts from its seating and slaps back on it to, producing the humorous effect over-indulged in during the 20s and 30s but out of fashion now; also referred to as 'slap-tongue'.

Slavery The historical fact which lies behind the fusion of African and American musical cultures, and which eventually produced jazz. Slavery in the USA goes back to 1619, the year before the Pilgrim Fathers arrived, when a Dutch ship landed and sold 20 Africans. This trade continued to flourish for more than 200 years, mainly bringing its cargoes from the West Coast of Africa. It is presumed in jazz history that the slaves brought their own African musical heritage with them and jazz grew out of the meeting of that heritage with the various European musical traditions of the colonists. It was not until the end of the 18th century that any attempts at suppressing this slave trade were made and it was not until 1865, after the Civil War was ostensibly fought on the issue, that slavery was finally abolished. By that time the black population of America had grown to nearly five million of whom only about 500 000 were free citizens.

Slide-whistle Also known as the 'swanee' or 'frisco' whistle. A small novelty instrument, blown in penny-whistle style but with a small slide, on the trombone principle, instead of the usual finger-holes, for obtaining the notes. Occasionally used in early jazz, spasm band, instrumental blues groups. Used and recorded by Louis Armstrong and Baby Dodds in the Oliver Creole Jazz Band.

Slip-horn Name for the trombone mainly used by peripheral publicists and radio phonies, rather than musicians. Slush pump is similarly used in the synthetic style of the 1930s.

Slopstick A simple rhythm device, a board with a handle with a hinged beater, used in early New Orleans bands as an adjunct to its rhythm section. (Photograph in *Jazz Journal*, Volume 8, Number 12, December 1955, Page 35.)

Slow drag The phrase is perhaps best known as part of the title of the Scott Joplin/Scott Hayden *Sunflower slow drag* written in 1910. Sub-titled 'a rag-time two step' it had, however, no special characteristics that linked it with the other uses of the term 'drag'. Willie 'The Lion' Smith, introducing a number called *Spanish Venus* by Luckey Roberts (on the LP *Pork and Beans*)[1] says that the black musicians used 'drag' as a synonym for latin-American styled music – 'this is something like what we call rumbas or tangos now. But the coloured people called 'em 'sashay'. It means sway to the left and sway to the right. We call them 'slow drags' and 'sashays'.' Blesh & Janis (in *They All Played Ragtime*) define a

---

[1] Black Lion BLB 0123, recorded 8 November 1966.

'slow drag' as 'rocking music of a medium tempo of the blues kind with 'dragging' rhythms'. The black creole musician Alcide Pavageau (1888–1969) who was nicknamed 'Slow Drag' was first a guitarist and then a bass-player. Even before that he was a dancer in New Orleans, taking up the bass in 1920. The possible association with the latin-styled, Spanish-tinged music, seems likely here.

Slush pump see **Slip-horn**

Smack Nickname of Fletcher Hamilton Henderson (1897–1952), pianist, composer, arranger and bandleader. Smack, as a slang term, has been used of both money and drugs (especially heroin), but neither seems to be applicable here. The name apparently dated back to Henderson's schooldays when he was a good baseball player. It was the sound of bat on ball and a habit he had of smacking his lips that amalgamated into this obscure nickname. It was much disliked by his wife Leora.

A secondary story has it that he smacked his lips when kissing; an improbable tale to account for an equally improbable nickname. His importance, by any name, to jazz is that it was partly due to his arranging skills, his organization of the sounds of which a big band was capable, which set the pattern for the fundamental feel of the swing era. It was with a large proportion of Fletcher Henderson arrangements in its book that Benny Goodman's band reached its position at the top of the heap in 1937.

Small's Paradise Large basement nightclub at 2294 Seventh Avenue, near 135th Street, in New York's Harlem district, opened on 22 October 1925. It could seat nearly 1500 people and was one of the 'black and tans' where white people, downtown socialites, used to go to dance, dine, and watch the black floorshow. The regular band was led by Charlie Johnson, resident leader there for over a decade. It was one of the three main clubs of the day, vying with the Cotton Club and Connie's Inn which also featured large bands and staged revues. Visiting bands included those led by Willie Gant, 'Hot Lips' Page and Elmer Snowden. The owner, Edwin Small, sold out in the 1960s to the famous basketball player Wilt 'the Stilt' Chamberlain. The establishment still survives.

Small pipe Name for the alto-saxophone.

Smear Jazz term for a glissando, particularly applicable to the trombone which used the effect liberally in early jazz; but also achievable on other wind instruments by over-riding the valves.

Smoke Yet another derogatory white term for a Negro. Hence Smoketown – the Negro quarter of a town, particularly in southern USA. Taken further – a smokey moke (moke being a slang word for any brown-skinned person), dark-brown to black. Mainly used in early days and particularly in the minstrel era.

Snag it Deriving from a nautical term 'to snag', to catch on to something. Or, simply, to get with it, to get hold of something good; hence to produce an inspired improvisation. Used as a title by King Oliver in 1926.

Snake Hips Jazz dance of *c.* 1915–30, probably originated in Baltimore, common in New York halls; one of many animal dances, done with a loose movement of the hips.

Society band General name given to the sort of bands that, while they may have had a fair sprinkling of jazz in their playing, were more of the dance-band, string-dominated kind, mainly playing for polite white society dances. A term mainly used in the USA, it would have applied in England to bands like the Savoy Orpheans.

Sock Literally a blow, a hard-hitting action; consequently applied to a sort of hard-hitting, driving big-band jazz in the swing era which became known as sock or sock style. This was emphasized (in the manner of Chick Webb or Gene Krupa, for instance) with heavy off-beat cymbal playing which became known as sock cymbal. Often done with a high-hat cymbal known likewise. Socks has occasionally been used as a term for improvisation, but not common.

Solid Description of those times when everything is fine, exciting, perfect, swinging, a subject for unwavering enthusiasm. Became current in the swing era and was much favoured by Louis Armstrong who put it into regular use – as he said: 'Life can be a drag one minute and a solid sender the next'. Hence it became a description of jazz that had everything right about it. A little old-fashioned now. A solid sender might describe a musician who was on the ball, swinging, lowdown – in fact, solid; or performances in a like state of okayness.

Soul The inner quality of feeling, sincerity, warmth. Became a vogue word in modern jazz, rather than in traditional where soul was assumed; a reaction to the over-cool and mechanical schools – really just playing with a rooted jazz feeling. To play with a blues feeling, in a funky way. Became a term of approval in East Coast jazz and crept into many titles like *Soul brothers*. Soul music specified a kind of music that had something of the old hot gospel fervour and rhythms in it. The term went over into pop music at first more or less as a synonym for gospel song, but quickly losing any religious connotation.

Sound Loosely used word for the style, fashion, manner of a performance, of a player or group, the distinguishing characteristics – e.g., the soul sound, Chicago sound, Ben Webster's sound.

South The South, with reference to the USA, is generally considered to be those States which lie south of the Mason-Dixon line between Maryland and Pennsylvania. The true Southern States of the deep South being such cotton-belt areas as Mississippi, Alabama, Georgia and South Carolina.

South Side The main coloured district of Chicago, the equivalent of New York's Harlem and one of the great nurseries of jazz; particularly of the urban blues, immediate precursor of much of rhythm and blues.

South Street Thoroughfare in the red-light district of Philadelphia, running parallel to Kater Street; immortalized in several jazz numbers.

Southern Syncopated Orchestra Pioneer all-Negro orchestra led by Will Marion Cook (1869–1944) which was the second 'jazz' group to arrive in England after the Original Dixieland Jazz Band in 1919. They did not make as much of an impression on the public but the 36-piece orchestra which included Sidney Bechet in its ranks, made an impact on the more critical, amongst them the Swiss conductor Ernest Ansermet who prophesied that the path that Bechet forged would be the one the world would soon follow. Formed in 1919 and disbanded in 1923, the orchestra was not basically a jazz outfit but included some jazz arrangements in its repertoire in response to the new fashions in music.

Spade A white and mainly derogatory term for a Negro, especially someone with a very dark skin, deriving from the phrase 'as black as the ace of spades'. In use from *c*. 1930.

Spanish tinge The latin-American, mainly habanera based, influence on early jazz that came into New Orleans and elsewhere by way of the West Indies, South America and Mexico. Jelly Roll Morton considered that the Spanish tinge was an essential ingredient of good jazz and, while there is no need to go that far, it was certainly part of the ragtime heritage and helped in the shaping of subsequent jazz phrasing. A fair sprinkling of early jazz numbers, particularly in black creole hands, used this habanera basis. It was a favourite device of the blues pianist Jimmy Yancey. The tinge came back very noticeably in the 1940s vogue for Afro-Cuban jazz.

Spasm band Name, of obscure derivation, categorizing certain amateur groups, formed by hard-up black musicians, and mainly playing for their own amusement (though some gained commercial status) using a variety of cheap, makeshift instruments such as suitcase or packing-case in lieu of drums, washboards for rhythm, jugs instead of tubas, home-made washtub basses, cigar-box fiddles, penny and swanee whistles, paper-and-comb or kazoo as front-line instruments; with a guitar or banjo often the only legitimate member. One such band was active and became well known in New Orleans *c*. 1895, a group of teenage blacks; but there were certainly many more before and around that time. The style and dash and light-hearted spirit, as well as the approximate format, survived in the later semi-professional washboard and jug bands that were good examples of spontaneous music-making.

Speakeasy Name for a bar or club, selling alcohol without a licence or after hours, common since *c*. 1900, but coming into wider use during the Prohibition years in America particularly referring to a joint that sold bootleg whisky. A natural haunt and working-place for jazz and jazzmen.

Spike When musician/critic Patrick Cairns Hughes (1908–87) had the nickname 'Spike' bestowed upon him in his early days he says, in his autobiography, that he assumed it was because he played the double-bass, an instrument dependent on its spike for support. He later discovered, rather disappointingly, that most Irishmen without an O' to their name (and many Hughes) were nicknamed 'Spike' for no clear reason. On the other hand, some bass players are called Spike, e.g. Spike Heatley.

Spirits of Rhythm, The Obscure but interesting group formed in 1929, originally working under such varied titles as Ben Bernie's Nephews, The Nephews and The Five Cousins before becoming The (Five) Spirits of Rhythm in 1934. By the end of 1933 the line-up was Leo Watson (vocal and tipple – a steel-strung ukele), Wilbur & Douglas Daniels (tipples), Teddy Bunn (guitar) and Virgil Scroggins (suitcase). The notable features of this ensemble were the imaginative guitar-playing of Teddy Bunn and the freakish scat singing of Leo Watson, one of the great unappreciated talents of jazz. Although the Spirits made many fine recordings, the best known and most often available are the sides made with Red McKenzie (1899–1948) (who organized the sessions) as straight singer, made in September/October 1934. The Spirits continued to play and record until *c.* 1946 with Bunn and Watson (who also recorded with the Washboard Rhythm Kings and Slim Gaillard) still members.

Spiritual American name for a religious song of uplift and faith, the kind that would be sung by a congregation at a camp-meeting or service of the revivalist sort. The white spiritual developed early in America to provide a species of hymn that was more in keeping with the American musical spirit than those imported from Europe. The black or Negro spiritual developed on similar lines but took on the more fervent aspect of black music that fascinated composers such as Dvořák and Delius. They rightly saw it as the new music of America, and as such it also turned out to be one of the many forerunners of the jazz style. The spiritual was introduced to England and Europe *c.* 1875 by the Fisk Jubilee Singers, a highly successful choir from one of America's early black universities. The spiritual became popular in the minstrel era and in the hands of later soloists like Paul Robeson (1898–1976), almost an art-song from *c.* 1925.

Spook A derogatory name used by a white American for a Negro; and, conversely and with rather more justification and frequency, for a white person

by a Negro. In such use from *c.* 1947. The word came into popular use through its perpetuation in black jazz circles, but it was probably in more restricted use before the jazz era.

Spotlite Club A short-lived club in Manhattan, New York, at 56 West 52nd Street (1944–6) which is remembered as a venue where such artistes as Parker, Gillespie, Hawkins and Billie Holiday appeared.

Square A person not in the know, out-of-fashion, behind the times, not with-it. Not hip. Hence, in jazz, a derogatory term applied to those not able or willing to appreciate the finer points of cool, modern or far-out music; showing a deplorable preference for older modes. Having a conservative or over-conventional outlook. The term is an abbreviation of less widely used, early expressions such as 'squarehead' or 'square John'. Its derogatory implications are 20th century. Earlier 'square' had merely meant, from *c.* 1830, honest, uncomplicated, straightforward, upright, one free from subterfuge or dishonesty; therefore, implicitly, one not clever enough to be involved in such things. A 'squarehead' was an honest man. To 'square' was to settle a matter honourably; but even the verb has lately taken on a more underhand meaning.

Stack o'Lee (or **Stagolee, a Staggerlee** or **Stagger Lee**) A Negro in folk legend who killed a man named Billy Lyons who had cheated him. The story, which crops up in many recorded versions, from out-and-out blues renderings like Ma Rainey's, to modern pop treatments like Neil Diamond's, is predictably confused, Billy Lyons (or Lyon) meeting his death variously for cheating at cards or stealing a stetson hat or both. Possibly based on a real incident that took place in Memphis *c.* 1900.

Stalebread Popular name given to Emile Lacoume (1885–1946), blind New Orleans guitarist/banjoist/pianist who is

The 'basis' of every musician's library. (Francis, Day & Hunter)

Interesting details of Musicians' Union rates from 1938.

Words by I. CAESAR   Music by GEORGE GERSHWIN

SUNG BY

LADDIE CLIFF

IN

ALBERT DE COURVILLE'S

10th LONDON HIPPODROME REVUE

Copyright.   Price 2/- net.

FRANCIS, DAY & HUNTER,
PUBLISHERS OF SMALLWOOD'S PIANO TUTOR.
138-140, CHARING CROSS ROAD, LONDON, W.C. 2.
NEW YORK: T. B. HARMS & FRANCIS, DAY & HUNTER, INC., 62-64, WEST 45TH STREET.
SYDNEY: J. ALBERT & SON, 137-139, KING STREET.

Original British publication of the famous Gershwin number (1919). (Francis, Day & Hunter)

credited, on his New Orleans tombstone, as being 'the originator of jazz music' – a claim more than open to contradiction. However, as leader of the Razzy Dazzy Spasm Band which played on home-made instruments in the streets of Storyville as early as 1897 (honoured as being the first true jazz band – though, again, there are rival claims) he was certainly in at the beginnings. Played at the Lake Pontchartrain resorts in the early 1900s and was a member of the Halfway House Orchestra.

Standard A song or piece that has been accepted as a basic part of any repertoire; widely known and frequently used as a basis of improvisation, a good old standby. A perfect example of a jazz standard (trad) would be *When the Saints go marching in*; of a later known vintage some of the songs by such writers as Gershwin became standards in the swing era, particularly *I got rhythm*; a bebop era equivalent would be *How high the moon*.

State Street Famous street through the Chicago downtown and South Side districts, the location of numerous sporting houses, bars and nightclubs during the jazz era of the 1920s. Immortalized in Jimmy Yancey's *State Street special*; and, where it crosses Madison Street, in Morton's *State and Madison*.

Steamboat Popular name for the riverboat which was steam driven from wood-fired boilers.

Stock Conventional. Especially used of 'stock arrangements', i.e. those done in a standardized, conventional style for general use, therefore those in 'stock' at a music-publisher's and obtained from there. A somewhat contemptuous term.

Stomp A fast, exciting number with a heavy beat, often accentuated with the foot beating on the floor. Hence to 'stomp off' – the beat indicated by several rhythmical taps of the foot. *Stomp off, let's go!* was a number introduced by

Erskine Tate's Vendome Theater Orchestra. A stomp rhythm was popular with the bands of the swing era, for example, *Stompin' at the Savoy* and elsewhere, but also used in earlier titles. *Stomp Off, Lets Go!* is also the title of John Chilton's detailed history of the Bob Crosby Orchestra and Bob Cats (London Jazz Book Service; 1983).

Stoned Apart from its usual meaning of drunk, sloshed, blotto, etc., occasionally used of one who is knocked out by, made ecstatic by a superlative bit of jazz, generally of the cool or far-out kind. In use from *c*. 1956.

Stoptime, stop chorus An effective device where the band or rhythm section playing behind a soloist merely fills in with chords, generally on the first beat of every other bar.

Storyville The tenderloin district of New Orleans designated by the authorities in 1897 as an area for licensed prostitution. Named after Councillor Sidney Story who was responsible for its establishment. It was an attempt to control and confine vice in the city but, in fact, it made it such a flourishing business that the district was closed in 1917 and later most of it was demolished and the area covered by the Iberville housing project. Its area (or areas, as two parts appear to be defined) as laid down in the original edict was: 'From the South side of Custom Street to the North side of St. Louis Street and from the lower or wood side of North Basin Street to the lower or wood side of Robertson Street. And from the upper side of Perdido Street to the lower side of Gravier Street, and from the river side of Franklin Street to the lower, or wood side of Locust Street'. Within this area (just outside the French Quarter) there was intensive employment for pianists, singers and small bands in the various sporting-houses and associated cafés, halls and clubs though the main entertainment areas lay on its fringes in what was known as the Tango Belt. Storyville was generally obliquely referred to by jazzmen as 'The District'. The closing of Storyville is seen historically as the time that jazz was forced out of New Orleans but it may have been more coincidental than casual as it is likely that the new music would have spread anyway to other cities; but certainly many of the New Orleans musicians went to Chicago and elsewhere round about that time.

Storyville A British jazz magazine, first issued in 1965, concerning itself with discography, general articles and a record trading section.

Storyville Club Jazz club in Boston, Massachusetts, founded by promoter George Wein (b. 1925) in 1950. Wein, one-time jazz pianist, went on to start the Newport Jazz Festival in 1954, the New Orleans Festival in 1970, the Grande Parade du Jazz in Nice and the New York Jazz Repertory Company in 1974.

Straight Music in a legitimate, classical manner without jazz inflection. Obviously taken from the more general usage of the term meaning normal or undiluted. Also, in musical and theatrical parlance, a name used for an engagement that runs for a whole week or more in the same place, as opposed to a one-night stand or gig.

Strain Popular music equivalent of section, theme or chorus.

Street, The When encountered on its own in jazz literature, 'The Street' usually refers to 52nd Street, New York, and especially that section of it between Fifth and Sixth Avenues (Sixth Avenue is now officially 'Avenue of the Americas' but nobody ever calls it that). That relatively short stretch contained, from the late 30s until the early 60s, a remarkable concentration of jazz night spots, among them Jimmy Ryan's, the Famous Door, the Three Deuces and The Onyx.

As the 40s gave way to the 50s, bebop gained much ground on 52nd Street, but until then it was also referred to, with some justification, as 'Swing Street'.

Street parade Almost any excuse in New Orleans and other southern cities sufficed as the pretext for a street parade – weddings, funerals, birthdays, special holidays. New Orleans jazz partly developed in the way it did, with its strict marching counterpoint, because of its frequent open-air use on these occasions; hence the terms Parade Bands or Marching Bands. The Second Line was an irregular secondary group of marchers – often youngsters – who would strut along beside or behind the band.

Strictly union Phrase used in the swing era as a synonym for corny, unswinging music, the only qualification needed for the playing of which was membership of a musicians' union. Or, likewise, to make the minimum effort in performance.

Stride piano A style of piano playing, popular in Harlem (and elsewhere – though it became generically known as Harlem stride piano, or just the Harlem style) developing in the 1920s as an extension of earlier styles such as ragtime and jig piano. It got its name from the striding left hand which played what was popularly known then as a vamp bass, alternating between strong notes on the downbeat, usually octaves or upward or downward delayed tenths (or other intervals), and chords on the up or afterbeat. The name came from the rapid steps of the left hand; the effect was of enormous propulsion and an emphasis on beat and swing which was in accord with the general trends of the swing era of the 1930s. Most of its best exponents like James P. Johnson, Art Tatum, Luckey Roberts and Fats Waller put a lot of variety into these basses so that there was no monotony. Some, like Earl Hines or Duke Ellington, would use the stride style more sparingly as an occasional tension builder and most pianists in the traditional mould used it at some time or other. It also came into popular piano music in a diluted form through such players as Carroll Gibbons, Charlie Kunz and Billy Mayerl. With the shying away from the obvious rhythms of traditional jazz that came in the 1940s, stride tended to go out of fashion but continuity was maintained by pianists like Ralph Sutton; while Thelonious Monk, in so many ways the archetypal modernist, frequently indulged in a wonderful, even humorously quirky manifestation of it which is best described as 'stride with a limp'.

Struggle A dance of the slow, shuffling kind that was popular in downtown Chicago in the 1920s in the club area around Armour Avenue.

Strut A high-stepping marching sort of dance movement, in imitation of a cock or hen. The basis of many early dances such as the cakewalk. Hence any piece of music used to accompany such as a dance might be termed a strut. From this evolved the use of the word as a verb meaning to dance well, as in the phrase of *c.* 1915 'to strut one's stuff'; later extended to doing almost anything in one's field of endeavour particularly well, almost an early equivalent of 'to do one's thing'. Inevitably used also as a sexually descriptive word or phrase.

Sugar foot Literally sweet-footed; a name given to one who was a good dancer.

Sugar Hill Sugar is a popular American slang word for money, particularly easy money, easily got and easily spent, and a lot of it. Used in such phrases as 'sugar daddy' or 'sugar man'. This is the basis of Sugar Hill, which has acquired two sharply contrasting connotations. In widespread usage it is a district of Negro brothels or a particular Negro brothel – a place where money is easily made. In New York, Sugar Hill was the name acquired by one of the two well-to-do sections of Harlem when in its heyday from the 20s to the end of the 40s. It was the sloping terrain between 145th and 155th Streets, with Amsterdam Avenue on its western side and Edgecombe Avenue on the east. The other wealthy

segment of Harlem was 'Strivers' Row' – mainly 138th and 139th Streets between Seventh and Eighth Avenues. The poorer parts of central Harlem were sometimes called 'The Valley'.

Suitcase The common or garden suitcase, usually to hand in itinerant musical life, has often come in as a cheap or ready substitute for a drum and has occasionally found its place in discographies. From this 'suitcase' was occasionally used in the 1930s swing era as a slang name for a drum.

Sunset Café Night club in Chicago at 313/7 East 35th Street opposite the Plantation Café where King Oliver once played. It first opened on 3 August 1921 and was a regular venue for jazz orchestras. After playing with Erskine Tate at the Vendome Theatre, Louis Armstrong joined Carroll Dickerson's Orchestra there in 1926, the first time he was to receive star billing as 'Louis Armstrong, World's Greatest Trumpet Player'. The establishment was owned and run by Joe Glaser who would later become Armstrong's manager and remain so for over 30 years. It was also during this time, from 1925 onward, that Armstrong was making his famous Hot Five and Hot Seven recordings; one of them was *Sunset Café stomp* (1926).

Susie Q, Suzie Q or Suzy-Q A dance with a shuffling and sliding step that was introduced at the Cotton Club in 1936, becoming one of the many steps that were used in the era of the Lindy, jive and jitterbug, popularized at the Savoy Ballroom in Harlem.

Swanee Customary misspelling, for the sake of consonance, of Suwannee, a river that flows from the Okefenokee Swamp in Georgia to an outlet in Florida on the Gulf of Mexico. First widely celebrated in Stephen Foster's *Old folks at home* or *Way down upon the Swanee River* in 1851; later in *Swanee* which George Gershwin and Irving Caesar wrote in 15 minutes in 1919. Ethel Waters also sang a charming song called *Shadows on the Swanee* (recorded in 1933).

Swee' Pea This was one of Duke Ellington's nicknames for Billy Strayhorn, and it was used either on its own or not at all (that is, never Swee' Pea Strayhorn). It derives from the Popeye strip cartoon, being the name of the smallest character, a knowing baby at the high-speed crawling stage. (The importance of the Popeye strip to modern mythology is often overlooked; the fast-food chain of Wimpy Bars owes its name to the fondness of another character, J. Wellington Wimpy, for the hamburger. That same portly character is responsible for the fact that the wartime bomber aircraft, the Vickers-Armstrong Wellington, was known as the Wimpy. Yet another character, a bounding animal of no recognizable species, was called the Jeep, and gave its name probably to the US military vehicle and certainly, as one of several nicknames, to Johnny Hodges.)

Billy Strayhorn (1915–1967) submitted work to Duke Ellington in late 1938, hoping to become a lyric writer. Duke recognized his overall musical potential and took him on as a kind of assistant composer/arranger. The scheme worked so well that it soon became impossible to detect where the work of one finished and the other began. Strayhorn composed many pieces for the band, the best-known of which is *Take the 'A' train*, which became Ellington's signature tune. Strayhorn was also known to his intimates as Weely.

Sweet As used by jazz writers and jazz speakers, particularly between the late 20s and perhaps the mid-40s, 'Sweet' was the undesirable opposite of 'hot' – although the word 'hot' itself was not current much beyond the late 30s. 'Sweet' therefore tended to imply 'commercial', 'syrupy', 'uncreative'. As with most other jargon words, however, it carried other implications. In *It don't mean a thing if it ain't got that swing* (1932) for instance, Duke Ellington and/or Irving Mills wrote the line: 'Makes no difference if it's sweet or hot/give that rhythm everything you've got'; 'sweet', in that context, hardly sounds derogatory. 'Sweetie', of course, is a totally different matter. In one form or another it persists in song as a term of endearment; two titles will suffice: *Sweetie dear* (recorded in a tumultuous performance by Sidney Bechet in 1932) and *Blues my naughty sweetie gives to me*, recorded by nearly every one from Ted Lewis – sweet, or at least corny – to Jimmie Noone (pretty hot).

Swing As a verb it describes the act of creating the essential rhythmic propulsion and flowing beat that is the distinguishing mark of an exciting jazz performance. Panassié: 'To play easily and with complete suppleness; there is no true jazz music which does not swing' (*Dictionary of Jazz*). Jelly Roll Morton was one of the first to use it (as a noun) in a title – *Georgia swing*, though his claim to have written it in 1906 (when, according to recent research, he was aged 16) should be taken with more than a pinch of salt. He had certainly recorded it by 1927, but in spite of such relatively early usage, swing is not in evidence as a generally employed word to convey this now accepted sense until *c.* 1930. Such words as syncopation or simply rhythm were used. With his number *It don't mean a thing if it ain't got that swing*, Duke Ellington brought the word into common currency in 1931: and soon after this, jazz began to be referred to as swing music and such exhortations as 'swing it' and comments like 'really swinging' came into regular use. It is difficult to pinpoint the exact moment at which 'swing or swinging' began to have a special jazz meaning because it was in use in its more general sense long before this, and indeed was often applied to music. For example, we find in 1919 the phrase 'a jazz-band in full swing'.

In 1935, Benny Goodman's advertising agents, looking for a good title for their man, borrowed the word and called him 'The King of Swing'. Thereafter, the public, and eventually even the jazz

Arranger pianist Billy Strayhorn with the Master in the 1950s. (Photo: Capitol Records)

Catalogue of HMV's jazz output in the 1940s. (His Master's Voice Records)

Below Syncopation was the craze of the 1920s and was purveyed in some unusual forms. Pickard's Chinese Syncopators in the 1920s. (Photo: Perfect Photo Reproduction)

chroniclers, accepted that swing was now the particular big band music that Goodman and others played, and the word had taken on the special meaning of arranged jazz for larger groups, music in 'swing style'. The Swing Era, during which big-band jazz flourished, is generally defined as being *c.* 1935–46, though a good deal of swing survived after this.

Confusion was rife as many writers and jazz promoters, for example the record companies, fell into the habit of using 'swing' to mean all kinds of jazz, so that the discographical catalogues issued by His Master's Voice from 1940 onward (compiled by Edgar Jackson) were entitled *Swing Music* and included details of the 'Swing Music' Series of issues.

The equivalent Parlophone compilations, by the same compiler, were categorized as *Rhythm Style*. Another example of this indiscriminate employment of 'swing' where 'jazz' would have been more appropriate, is preserved on recordings of the BBC broadcasts direct from the St. Regis Roof, in New York in 1937, in which the compère, Alistair Cooke, refers throughout to what was in effect a jam session, as 'swing' and 'swing music'.

It is now the generally accepted convention to use the noun swing to mean either the inherent impetus of good jazz or the kind of big-band jazz that flourished in the 1935–46 period.

Swing Music The first British magazine to deal mainly with jazz, it was founded by Leonard Hibbs in March 1935, soon becoming the official organ of the Federation of British Rhythm Clubs. It campaigned vigorously for the proper recognition of jazz and its contributors included Spike Hughes and Edgar Jackson. By the end of the first year the magazine, like *Hot News*, was losing money steadily, but Hibbs managed to keep it going through 1936, making a last defiant gesture with a double issue on glossy paper; but it folded in the autumn. He had turned his attention to higher things and founded *Gramophone Record* (in 1933). This became *Gramophone Record Review*, then *Audio Record Review*, before its absorption into *Hi-Fi News* in 1970.

Swing Music Series of booklets compiled by Edgar Jackson and issued by HMV, 1940, 42, 44, 46 and 48, listing all their specialist jazz releases with personnels.

Swing Street Publicity man's name for Fifty-Second Street in the 1930s when it was established as the jazz centre of New York.

Symphonic jazz Grandiose title given to the regular efforts to write jazz music in the larger forms associated with classical music. Much pioneering work in these efforts came from Paul Whiteman (1890–1967) who encouraged professional composers like George Gershwin (1898–1937) and Ferde Grofé (1892–1972) to write such works in the 1920s. These were partly successful because at least the writers came from the world of popular music and were partway in sympathy with the new developments. It was assumed, in the early days, that there would eventually be a fusion of jazz and classical music; but the many subsequent attempts must be counted a total failure since no real masterpiece ever materialized that could satisfy both sides.

At best we end up with watered-down jazz, jazz that lacks both the drive and earthiness of the music created by jazzmen; lacks the improvisatory element. Perhaps, too, the early efforts might have been guided toward success if there had been more symphony orchestra musicians able to play in the idiom, a facility taken for granted today.

The worst failures have come where a classical composer has striven hard to write in a jazz idiom without having a natural sympathy for the music. The best results have come where the composer has kept to his own style but allowed some of the trimmings of jazz to creep in, treating them as part of the equipment natural to a 20th-century composer. Gershwin's *Piano Concerto in F* (1925), Ravel's *Piano Concerto in G* (1932),

Milhaud's *Le Boeuf sur le Toit* (1920), etc, are examples of this.

Symphony Sid Affectionate nickname of Sid Torin, New York jazz disc jockey and compère. Was actually running an R & B show on a New York radio station when he helped to advertise a Dizzy Gillespie concert in 1945 by plugging early bebop records on the air. Quickly became heavily involved in jazz and compèred jazz broadcasts from the Royal Roost for some years. Lester Young wrote a tune dedicated to him: *Jumpin' with Symphony Sid.*

Syncopation Generally written of in early analysis and reference books as a basic requirement of jazz, being the main element that distinguishes jazz from straight music. Jazz is perpetually syncopated, the melodic line always finding points of emphasis away from the main beats of the bar. In ragtime, syncopation was of a mathematical kind that could be notated; in blues-based jazz it was more instinctive and occurred in a way that could never be accurately put down on paper. The early definitions of jazz as a syncopated music are, therefore, still valid.

Early jazz publicists were obsessed with syncopation as the main novelty attraction of jazz, particularly while the flavour was still predominantly ragtime. The 'syncopated orchestra', usually an ensemble that played most of its repertoire in a straightish manner but was prepared to add ragtime and jazz novelties in step with the times, was an important part of the blossoming jazz scene and helped to make the public jazz conscious. Some of the earliest black orchestras involved in these fringe activities were those led by Will Marion Cook (1869–1944), Ford Dabney (1883–1958), Tim Brym (1881–1946), James Reese Europe (1881–1919) (see **Clef Club**), W. C. Handy (1873–1958), Wilbur Sweatman (1882–1961) and Noble Sissle (1889–1975). The bands and orchestras led by the great march composer John Philip Sousa (1854–1932) also did quite a bit of pioneer work in the ragtime and early jazz field.

See: 'Early Syncopated Bands' in *Big Band Jazz* by Albert J. McCarthy (1974); *Jazz – a History of the New York Scene* by Samuel B. Charters & Leonard Kunstadt (1962, repr. 1981).

Tag A two- (or more) bar phrase added on to the end of a chorus or the total performance; a brief coda to round off the piece. A popular device in early New Orleans or Chicago jazz days.

Tailgate Applied to jazz trombone: an uninhibited, rudimentary style of playing involving vigorous use of the slide, common in New Orleans and Dixieland jazz. From the American name for the rear let-down ramp of a cart or truck. Said to have derived from the early days of jazz when bands would travel round in the back of a cart to advertise some coming event like a dance. The trombonist, needing room to manoeuvre his slide, would be put at the back with the tailgate lowered. Hence tailgate trombone, tailgate bands and tailgate style, afterwards a categorical term for that style of playing. It can best be appreciated in numbers like *Ory's Creole trombone*, in the work of George Brunies with the Spanier Ragtimers, Jim Robinson with the Bunk Johnson band or later New Orleans stylists like Santo Pecora, e.g. *Magnolia blues*. Manone recorded a *Tailgate ramble* in 1944.

It is interesting to note that, in the

early years of the 20th century in England, a fairly common Cockney slang word for a trombone was 'push-me-off', short for 'push-me-off-the-pavement'.

Take (1) In recording terms, as in filming, an attempt to get something on wax, tape, etc. Discographers are obsessively concerned as to whether the take used is 1, 1a, 2 or whatever. Very often, in more scholarly compilations, all available takes will be reissued side by side, thus giving an interesting insight into what went on in the studio and some of the creative processes of jazz. Good examples of this are to be found in the Savoy collections of Charlie Parker material, which includes some minute fragments, and which are frequently reissued.
(2) 'Take' can also mean to handle a piece of music, as in to 'take' a chorus or a 'lead' – hence the exhortation to 'take it' or, in the more phoney sort of lingo, to 'take it away'.

Take five Not take No. 5, though it might be, but to take a five-minute break from playing or recording. It might even have the suggested connotation that, after four takes (see above), take five ought to be a breathing space. Title of a famous composition in 5/4 by Paul Desmond.

Talk To play with depth and meaning, literally to make the instrument speak. 'Talk to me', 'now you're talking', 'that's what I'm talking about' are derived phrases; and there is a possible *double entendre* in the title of that essential jazz book *Hear Me Talkin' to Ya*. To 'tell' is similarly used; 'tell me'.

Tango Belt Popular name for the area of New Orleans that surrounded the notorious Storyville district, almost dominated by cabarets, dance halls, cafés and honky-tonks, and given over entirely to amusement and entertainment.

Tea Widely used name for marijuana, one among many. A marijuana cigarette or 'ace' was known as a stick of tea or tea stick. The word is occasionally also applied to other drugs. Tead up – to be under the influence of marijuana. Tea pad – a place where marijuana was taken. Tea party – a gathering to indulge in communal smoking. The best quality tea came from Texas and was consequently known as Texas tea, hence the jazz tune *Texas tea-party*.

Tell Your Story The book *Tell Your Story* by Eric Townley (Chigwell: Storyville Publications, 1976) takes *c.* 2700 jazz and blues titles recorded between 1917–50 and explains their origins, background and meaning. It makes fascinating reading and one is constantly discovering surprising information, e.g. that *Piggly wiggly*, which many must have thought to be a purely nonsensical title (Beale Street Washboard Band, 1929), was derived from the name of a chain of grocery supermarket stores, operating mainly in the Southern States, one of the first in America to offer self-service.

The authors did not come across this book till well after starting the present volume, when it was usefully able to confirm some of their own findings and to offer a lot of new information – which is gratefully acknowledged herewith.

Tenderloin Area of a town or city given over to the vices and pleasures of night life, particularly that part of it associated with prostitution and gambling. Probably first applied to the New York area from 23rd to 42nd Street, west of Broadway, where *c.* 1895 someone (said to be a police officer) said, in a politely evasive way, that it was a good area in which to get a good fillet steak. The name was soon applied to similar areas in Chicago, New Orleans and other pleasure-seeking cities. In full – the tenderloin district. Outside jazz, but within music, *Tenderloin* occurs as the title of an excellent musical by Jerry Bock and Sheldon Harnick (writers of *Fiddler On The Roof*).

Third stream Term coined by composer, french horn player and musicologist Gunther Schuller (b. 1925) in the late

50s to describe music which attempted to bridge the gap between European disciplines and forms and the attitudes and techniques of jazz. These good intentions have not so far – in the mid-80s – resulted in a really satisfying work, although compositions by jazz trombonist, classical cellist and musical teacher David Baker (b. 1931) have come close to it.

In a broader sense, the concept of third stream is part of a general process of breaking down the barriers between one form of music and another, and to this end Gunther Schuller actually founded a Third Stream Department at the New England Conservatory.

Three Deuces A nightclub in New York, at 72 West 52nd Street, once the site of the Onyx Club. It opened in 1940 and became a venue for such musicians as Charlie Parker, Bud Powell, Fats Navarro and Eroll Garner. Named after a famous Chicago speakeasy which flourished in the 1920s.

Tiger rag Early jazz number that became widely popular through its recorded exploitation by the Original Dixieland Jazz Band which, as in the case of several other numbers they used, was copyrighted as the creation of the band and its leader Nick La Rocca. This claim was rather indignantly refuted by Jelly Roll Morton, Sidney Bechet and others who have pointed out that its various contrasted sections derived from earlier well-known quadrille movements and other dances.

Tight like that (this) Phrase with clear sexual connotations; used in a wider sense to imply something supremely good and satisfying. Inspiration for an excellent old jazz number and song recorded by many, including Louis Armstrong and Jimmie Noone.

Tijuana Town on the borders of Mexico and California, population *c.* 225 000, a racing, gambling and entertainment centre for the area. From it came a style of playing that was an amalgam of the latin-American styled Mexican rhythms and Dixieland jazz, dominated by powerful brass over tipica rhythms. It had a period of great commercial popularity in the mid-1960s, with trumpeter Herb Alpert making his reputation in the idiom.[1] But its musical style, as part of the Spanish tinge that coloured much early ragtime and jazz, had been noted long before by the perceptive Jelly Roll Morton who played in the Kansas City Bar in Tijuana as solo pianist in the 1920s; commemorating the fact in his 1923 recording of *Tia Juana* (which was how it was then styled).

Tin Pan Alley Popular name for New York's 28th Street, between Fifth and Sixth Avenues, where a preponderance of song publishers had their premises by the early 1900s. It was thus christened because of the cacophony that poured from the windows there. The phrase 'Tin Pan Alley' became synonymous with the whole world of popular music. It survived in vestigial form into the 1960s, in the Brill Building, a warren of music publishers offices complete with the cubicles for tame composers and lyric writers to work in. Even at that late date, people – now stars – like Carole King (with Gerry Goffin) and Neil Sedaka would turn out songs to order. 'The Brill Building wasn't so much a place as a state of mind', Carole King remembers.

London's equivalent Tin Pan Alley was Denmark Street, a short thoroughfare on the east side of Charing Cross Road. London music publishing has tended to disperse in recent years.

Tin Roof Café New Orleans café which housed many jazz groups on Washington Street and Claiborne Avenue. It was demolished in 1910 and a vinegar factory appeared on the site. Fondly remembered in the New Orleans Rhythm Kings' *Tin Roof blues* (1923).

Tipple, tiple More fully known as the

---

[1] He was also a co-founder of the A & M record label, which has ventured into the jazz field from time to time.

From French quadrille to modernistic hit of the 30s. (Herman Darewski Music Publishing)

A trad. (Drawing by Peter Gammond from *14 Miles on a Clear Night* (Owen))

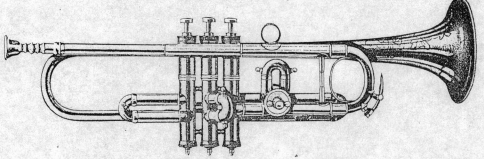
As advertised in the 1920s.

Hawaiian tipple which is defined as 'an oversized ukelele' – a steel-stringed instrument that produces a ringingly percussive sound. Three of these were used to good effect by Leo Watson and friends in The Spirits of Rhythm group in the 1930s. The name goes right back to 19th-century Spain where tiple, tible or timple were treble guitars, smaller than the usual instrument and about the size of a large ukelele. Though how they got to Hawaii is a bit of a mystery.

Tishomingo Small town on the Mississippi Gulf Coast near the Alabama border, population *c.* 500, given a niche in jazz history by the 1917 *Tishomingo blues*, written by Spencer Williams and later recorded by Ellington and many others.

Toddle A slow jazz dance in fashion during the 1920s, a sort of slow foxtrot. Name likewise applied to the music that was played for it. (See under ***East St. Louis toodle-oo***.)

Tom Anderson's A famous New Orleans café at 125 North Rampart Street. On its bandstand many well-known jazzmen used to play, such as Armstrong, Barbarin and Nicholas.

Tom Anderson's Annex Café in Storyville, New Orleans, at Customs House Corner – junction of Basin Street and Iberville Street, a major cutting ground for jazz talent in the early 1900s. Jelly Roll Morton played there and the house band included such names as Manuel Perez, Paul Barbarin, Luis Russell and Albert Nicholas.

Tom Brown's Band from Dixieland Pioneering jazz group led by trombonist Tom Brown (1888–1958), formed in 1915. It took the jazz gospel to Chicago that same year with Ray Lopez (tpt) and Larry Shields (clt), later of the ODJB, in its ranks.

Tonk Abbreviated form of honky-tonk, in use from *c.* 1915.

Too much Term of high praise – his playing was 'too much', similar to 'out of this world', even outclassing 'the most'.

Torch song Name given to a slow ballad whose theme is generally that of unrequited love. Derived from the phrase 'to carry the torch', that is, carrying the memory and sorrow of rejected or unfulfilled love. Songs of regret and revenge. To be torchy is to be the bearer of such unrequited love. Probably the best torch song interpreter in jazz was Billie Holiday.

Tough The greatest and the best. Particularly applied to tenor saxophone players; the pairing of whom has often prompted the billing 'Tough Tenors'.

Touro Hospital, full name the Touro Infirmary, in New Orleans. The cornettist Muggsy Spanier was one of the many admitted there after a physical collapse in 1938, where he was brought back from death's door by the care and skills of Dr Alton Ochsner. Dried out, decoked and back in action, he recorded his thanks in a splendid 1939 jazz classic with his Ragtimers – *Relaxin' at the Touro*; also in other numbers dedicated to the doctor.

Track (1) A single, scrolled item on a long-playing record; likewise on a tape or compact disc.
(2) Negro slang for a dance hall, common in the 1930s but not much used now. The famous Harlem dance hall, the Savoy Ballroom, was familiarly known to its customers as The Track.
(3) Americanism for railway line – railroad track, track 49, etc.

Traditional jazz, trad (1) Jazz in the old two-beat style, diatonic, solidly rhythmic; with those who played it or appreciated it being dubbed traditionalists.

After the 1940s newly created jazz largely ceased to be in traditional modes and became loosely categorized as modern jazz. Thereafter, true traditional jazz was only played by ancient survivors and revivalist bands whose music was also known as traditional jazz. Usually shortened to trad, trad band, etc.

(2) Traditional; a word applied to songs and numbers whose origins and age are difficult to determine, e.g. *When the Saints go marching in* and *Careless love*, and many such items credited to the prolific Anon.

An American equivalent of 'Trad' as applied to a composition, is 'PD' – (In the) Public Domain – i.e. out of copyright.

Traps A collective name for drums and other percussion items, when first brought together in the now traditional drum-kit. The word is a diminutive form of 'trappings'; and is also applied to clothing and other equipment. Today considered archaic. The first such 'drum-kit' assembled in the New Orleans jazz scene was used by Dede 'Dee Dee' Chandler (1866–1925) who is also credited with being the inventor of the bass drum pedal and the first drummer to play true jazz style in a dance band. He is said to have 'played with the grace of a professional juggler' (Rose & Souchon: *New Orleans Jazz*).

Tricky Sam Nickname given to the unique Joe Nanton (1904–1946), the trombonist who rose to fame with the Ellington orchestra from 1926 and remained in the band until his death. The name was given to him by saxophonist Otto Hardwick because 'he could do things with his right hand that most people would have needed to do with three'.

Trombone One of the few instruments in use today that has not changed radically from its original form, going back to medieval times when it was also known as the sackbut, from the French *saquebot*. It came into jazz at the early stage, theoretically as one of those instruments taken over from defunct brass bands of the Civil War era. In early jazz the trombone usually played a contrapuntal bass part to the cornet/trumpet lead and picking up phrases with the unique and typical trombone glissando; a style, known as tailgate trombone, that was played by such early practitioners as Ike Rodgers and Roy Palmer (1892–1963), and given distinction and some soloistic prowess by such as Edward 'Kid' Ory (1886–1973), Honore Dutrey (1894–1935), Jim Robinson (who played in the revived Bunk Johnson Band) (1890–1976), Charlie Green (a fine blues accompanist) (1900–36) and white trombonist George Brunies (1902–74). Their efforts were faithfully reflected by revivalist trombonists such as Turk Murphy (b. 1916) in America and Chris Barber (b. 1930) in England. Within the bigger bands, especially Ellington's, a distinctive growl technique was developed by Charlie Irvis (1899–1939) and notably Joe 'Tricky Sam' Nanton (1904–46), perpetuated by their successors.

The trombone developed its solo potential in the hands of a number of musicians in the 1930s, who generally were to be found in the trombone sections of the big bands as they moved into the swing era: such as Jimmy Harrison (1900–31), Jimmy Archey (1902–67), J. C. Higginbotham (1906–73), Sandy Williams (b. 1906), Vic Dickenson (1906–84), Dicky Wells (1907–85), Benny Morton (1907–86), Albert Wynn (1907–73), Alton Moore (1910–78) and Trummy Young (1912–84). Outstanding white soloists were Floyd O'Brien (1905–68) and Jack Teagarden (1905–64), the latter taking the instrument into grades of solo work that paralleled the efforts of Coleman Hawkins on tenor-saxophone.

Even within classical music the trombone was long looked upon as a brazen sort of instrument mainly used for its blasting qualities. It was the lyrical and often dulcet playing of such as Tommy Dorsey (1905–58) that showed the jazz and classical world alike how sensitive an instrument the trombone could be. Britain's answer to Teagarden was the skilful Scottish trombonist George Chisholm (b. 1915); while many other first-class British musicians were to be found in the dance-band world e.g., Ted Heath (1900–69).

Notable modern jazz trombonists, the instrument now completely emancipated from its trad role, include: Bennie Green (1923–77), J. J. Johnson (b. 1924), Kai Winding (1922–83), Bob Brookmeyer (b. 1929), Grachan Monchur III (b. 1937), Albert Mangelsdorf (b. 1937), Malcolm Griffiths (b. 1941), Gary Valente (b. 1953), Roswell Rudd (b. 1935).

Truck, trucking, truckin' A shuffling, hip-swinging step, usually accompanied by a waggling of the index finger, that was often used as an entrance or exit move by many early black dancers. It was popularized as a speciality dance at the Cotton Club *c*. 1934 and was in vogue during the late 1930s. Ellington recorded an accompanying number *Truckin'* in 1935, with Ivie Anderson as vocalist. A 1943 caption described the steps as conveying 'repressed ecstacy'.

Trumpet Although many early jazz groups were nominally led by violinists, in deference to early dance band and musical custom inherited from Europe, the trumpet (or cornet) soon established itself as the natural tenor lead instrument, supported above and below in the typical New Orleans ensemble by clarinet and trombone. In fact, more early 'trumpeters' tended to play the cheaper and more accessible cornet but, with a few notable exceptions, most cornettists had become trumpeters by the first years of the 1920s, preferring its more biting tone and clear high notes. It remained a dominating instrument in small band jazz and even, sectionized, in big band work of the swing era, but its place as leader would often be usurped later by other instruments in the hands of dominating soloists.

Tub A drum. Tubs – drums.

Tuba This cumbersome bass brass instrument was widely used in early jazz and dance bands with the equivalent function of the string bass. It was particularly useful in the sousaphone version in marching bands where the string bass could not be used. Custom continued its use in the dance hall and elsewhere and because, in the early days, it recorded better, it was still being widely used into the 1920s. The tuba was gradually superseded by the more agile and rounded string bass, most players making the change by *c*. 1930. Those who had been notable as tuba-players included Bill Benford (b. 1903), Pete Briggs (b. 1900), June Cole (1903–1960), John Kirby (1908–1952), Elmer James (1910–1954), Cyrus St. Clair (1890–1955) and Billy Taylor (b. 1906) and most of these made the transfer. It remained in use in revivalist bands and in those where its crisp, humorous tones added fun to the more boisterous sort of Dixieland jazz. Red Callender, a double-bass player still active in all types of jazz in the 80s, and author of an autobiography, *The Unfinished Dream* (1985), is a great enthusiast for the tuba, and plays it whenever he can. Compositions and arrangements by Gil Evans usually find an important role for the tuba.

Turf, The Not so much musicians' slang as the slang used by a whole section of New York's night-life citizens to describe a clearly defined portion of the city. It is best conveyed by quoting from *Jazz Masters of the Thirties* by Rex Stewart (Collier MacMillan, 1972). 'The corner of 135th Street and Lenox Avenue was crowded with the usual throngs of musicians who customarily hung out there, plus a cross section of night-lifers, vaudevillians, race-horse men, and sports who as a rule were never seen on the Turf in broad daylight (the Turf meant the area bounded by the block that extended from Lenox Avenue to Fifth Avenue and ran south to 133rd Street).'

Turk Nickname of Melvin Alton Edward Murphy (b. 1916), San Francisco bandleader and trad trombonist, given to him at high-school, where he earned a reputation as a 'four-letter' (i.e. d-u-m-b) athlete – *vide* Gilbert Millstein in *Jam*

Session (1958) – and was known as The Terrible Turk.

Turkey Trot Dance probably originating in the cakewalk era, but really becoming popular in the 1912–20 period; one of many with animal connotations, e.g. the Bunny Hug, Camel Walk, Grizzly Bear – all finally superseded, like the Charleston and Black Bottom, by the less demanding foxtrot and quickstep.

Tuxedo American name for the dinner-jacket or formal evening-dress with bow tie. Originally derived from the Tuxedo Club in New York in the 1890s, where such dress was obligatory. The musically immortalized Tuxedo Junction was a cross-roads in Birmingham, Alabama, where Ensley Avenue and 20th Street intersected. Situated there was a store which hired out tuxedos where those going out for an evening on the spree would change out of working clothes and appear in their finery (Townley). Through the popularity of the Erskine Hawkins 1930s number *Tuxedo Junction*, later a Glenn Miller hit, the name 'Tuxedo Junction' was widely applied to any dance hall, record shop or café that catered for the fans of the swing craze era.

Tuxedo Orchestra Famous early New Orleans dance band formed *c.* 1910 in which many pioneer jazzmen learned their trade, led by Papa Celestin (1884–1954), operating from the Tuxedo Dance Hall (1909–13) on Franklin Street. From 1913 they called themselves the 'Original' Tuxedo Orchestra, to ward off imitators, e.g. Ridgley's Original Tuxedo Jazz Band, which split off from them in 1925.

Twelfth Street Main street of Kansas City, Missouri, in the middle of the downtown area running between the Kansas and Blue Rivers and crossing the other main thoroughfare, Washington Avenue. Celebrated in Euday Bowman's famous *Twelfth Street rag* (1909).

Two-beat Loosely applied to jazz of the quicker, lively kind; specifically that written in 2/4 time.

Unbooted Unsophisticated, simple, gullible – a country type. Slightly more hip version of 'barefoot'. Lurking in the background is a kinship with 'sans-culottes', a term from French revolutionary times for one of the lower classes. The opposite of 'booted' – to be aware, prepared, with-it.

Uncle Tom A sycophantic Negro; one who accepts the old slave or servant relationship as being the normal one between black and white. One who allows himself to appear inferior to the white people. One who curries favour with whites for gain. Derived from the character in *Uncle Tom's Cabin* by Harriet Beecher Stowe, written in 1852, when such a relationship would have been considered a normal one; the name is now used in an entirely derogatory way. The female equivalent is an Aunt Jane, a recently coined phrase, which has not so far gained general currency.

Upbeat see **Afterbeat**

Uptown Areas of major cities in America so designated in distinction from the downtown area and not necessarily from geographical positioning. Best-known jazz use was in connection with New York's Harlem, generally referred to as Uptown *c.* 1930–45, but not so much since then. Thus became associated with the kind of swinging, stylish, hip music that was bred in Harlem as in *Uptown shuffle* (1939) (Erskine Hawkins) and *Uptown blues* (1940) (Lunceford); also to the kind of person who is hip and in the forefront of things.

Urban blues Blues, like most folksongs, had rural beginnings, particularly emanating from America's Southern States. It was only in the blossoming days of the early 1900s that the blues became urbanized, moving into city areas and beginning to deal with their themes in a more sophisticated way. Deep down there is no real difference between a country and an urban blues, but the urban blues veer toward a more formal shape, leading to the classic jazz-band accompanied blues and blues-shouting of the swing era. See **Country blues**.

Vamp From a verb meaning to patch up in an extempore way, *c.* 1600; hence, in a musical sense, to improvise or extemporize an accompaniment. Generally taken to mean the provision of an elementary accompaniment to a melody, usually with the left hand alternating bass notes on the downbeat with right-hand chords on the afterbeat. It became a popular activity in the do-it-yourself 'anyone can learn to play' craze of the 1920s and 30s, when vamping charts were frequently offered for sale. An elaborated sort of vamp was often used as the introduction to a song, hence the phrase 'vamp till ready', that is, until the soloist is able to effect an entry. The most expected of a rhythm section in early jazz was a steady vamp accompaniment. The popular tune, *Get happy*, by Harold Arlen, is based on a little vamp he used to play at rehearsals.

V-Discs 78 rpm discs made during and for some years after the Second World War for the use of the American Armed Forces. Some of them simply used existing recorded material licensed from recording companies, but there were many original recordings made by jazz musicians who waived all usual royalty payments, and of concerts involving jazz ensembles that did not otherwise get onto disc. They were made on the under-standing that all existing stocks and master recordings were to be destroyed when the V-Disc programme finally came to an end. When the issue of V-Discs ceased in 1948 there was, indeed, much destruction, but inevitably large numbers of the records escaped, and over the years these performances have been released on various labels. Although technically these activities infringe the original agreement, the US authorities have turned a blind eye.

Vendome Theater Silent movie house in Chicago where the band was grandly known as the Little Symphony Orchestra. From 1919 it was led by Erskine Tate, when it became known as Erskine Tate's Vendome Theater Orchestra. Originally a nine-piece band, by the mid-1920s it was up to 15. Louis Armstrong played in the orchestra 1926/7 whilst doubling elsewhere. It was here that he first began to use the trumpet regularly in place of cornet and much improved his reading. In fact, it was because of the Vendome job that Louis made the change from cornet. Collier says that Erskine Tate suggested the move so that the brass sound would be better matched if Louis played trumpet alongside his section mate James Tate, Erskine's brother. Tate left the Vendome in 1928, directing various theatre and dance orchestras until *c.* 1945 when he became a music-teacher.

Verse The verses of popular songs, too often being inferior second thoughts to the chorus added to meet the needs of Tin Pan Alley publishers, seldom feature in jazz performances. Some of them, such as the one Waller appended to *Ain't Misbehavin'*, are indescribably awkward and best left unheard. Some, however, as in such Kern songs as *Ol' Man River* cannot be dispensed with.

Furthermore, many verses, although not musically essential, are very strong, and performances of old tunes like *After you've gone* and *Melancholy baby* gain enormously from the inclusion of their respective verses.

Vibraphone With its more mellow, rounder and more variable tone and dynamics, the vibraphone began to take over from the xylophone in the early 1930s. The big differences between the two instruments are that the xylophone is made of wood, whereas the vibraphone uses metal bars; and that the vibraphone has rotating vanes, driven by an electric motor, in the upper ends of the resonating tubes, beneath the metal bars themselves. The speed of the rotation, and hence of the vibrato effect, is determined by the speed – variable at will – of the electric motor. The word 'vibraharp' will frequently be encountered, particularly in American texts. Originally it differentiated the aluminium version of the instrument (developed by the Deagan company) from the earlier models with heavy steel bars.

In the first place the vibraphone was employed, like the xylophone, for novelty effect by drummers, and acquired its first virtuoso soloist only when Lionel Hampton (b. 1909) took it up from 1930. There happened to be a vibraphone in a studio where he was recording in Los Angeles in that year with Louis Armstrong, and Louis persuaded him to use it. Until that time, Hampton had been a drummer, but he quickly made the vibraphone a front-line instrument in

its own right and gained national and international prominence with it after becoming a member of the Benny Goodman Quartet in 1936. Red Norvo (b. 1908) began on xylophone and moved to vibraphone, with some reluctance, in the early 1940s.

In the post-Charlie Parker jazz world the vibraphone has become a major voice, particularly in the hands of Milt Jackson (b. 1923), Gary Burton (b. 1943), Bobby Hutcherson (b. 1941), Terry Gibbs (b. 1924), Walt Dickerson (considers himself 'ageless', but b. early 1930s), Mike Mainieri (b. 1938). Most of the more recent players have modified the tonal range of the vibraphone by the frequent use of two or more mallets in each hand to produce soft, chordal effects. Gary Burton's particular contribution to its vocabulary was the discovery that, by bearing down on any given tuned bar with a hard mallet, its pitch could be altered slightly, thus making possible the 'bending' of notes.

Victor houseman, The A much-debated discographical mystery that has occupied some of the more searching minds in the critical world from the late 1930s onward.

Discographer and collector Kenneth Hulsizer, was eager to identify an unknown clarinettist listed on the Jelly Roll Morton Red Hot Peppers sessions of March, June and October 1930. In 1938 he had an opportunity to ask Morton himself who said it was a Victor houseman (that is, a staff musician), a white musician named Eddie who, according to Morton, 'tried hard but didn't have it in him'. But this did not satisfy later researchers such as Morton discographer Thomas Cusack who put forward various other names.

The mystery is still without a firm solution. Latest opinions are that Morton was right about the houseman for the 5 March sessions and it was possibly one Eddie Bullock, but that for 19 March it was possibly Lorenzo Tio, but an unknown person on the other sessions. Such is the exciting material of discographical research.

See: 'The Strange Case of the Victor Houseman' by Keith K. Daniels in *Jazz Journal*, Volume 7, Number 5, (May 1954) and various record sleeves.

Village Gate New York jazz venue, founded in the 1950s and still going strong at 160 Bleecker Street and Thompson Street in Greenwich Village. Place for hearing the best in modern jazz ranging from bebop to fusion and salsa. Functions from Tuesday to Saturday 18.00 to 2.00.

Village Vanguard Famous New York cellar jazz club at 178 Seventh Avenue, near 11th Street, which has flourished since the 1930s and remains a strong bastion of mainstream jazz.

Vine Street Well-known street and entertainment area in downtown Kansas City, site of various clubs and nightspots. Hence the name crops up in many jazz titles such as: *Vine Street blues* (Moten) (1924); *Vine Street boogie* (McShann) (1941); *Vine Street breakdown* (Tate); and *Vine Street drag*. There is also a Vine Street in Los Angeles.

Violin Although the violin is not considered to be an integral part of jazz development or a major instrument in the jazz field, its history is far from negligible. It is obvious that a violin would always find itself outplayed in terms of volume by brass and woodwind instruments. This kept it out of most of the bands that made emergent jazz history in the early years of this century. It came back as a solo instrument, in the hands of several virtuoso players when adequate microphone and recording techniques were available.

That the violin, or fiddle, was there right from the start of jazz is, however, beyond question. It would probably have been one of the most widely used instruments in plantation music-making, an important legacy of the folk tradition that was part of American musical history; it was a leading instrument too in all social music-making. Something of European

practice lingered in the residual right of a violinist to be the leader of the orchestra. Many of the early New Orleans bands, wanting to be engaged for the high class 'society' jobs, therefore often felt obliged to have a violin leader; for example, the Olympia Band (in which King Oliver played in his early days) which was led by violinist Armand Piron from *c.* 1912. Piron led his own band from 1918, playing at Tranchina's Restaurant on Lake Pontchartrain, at the New Orleans Country Club, and later in New York. Kid Ory's band at Pete Lala's Club was fronted by Emile Bigard (1890–1935) on violin, the uncle of the clarinettist Barney Bigard (1906–80). Multi-instrumentalist Pete Bocage (1887–1967) played violin in Tom Albert's Band *c.* 1906 and in various society orchestras.

Throughout jazz history the violin has remained a dispensable item. Indeed, to some tastes, the addition of strings to a jazz orchestra was simply a manifestation of commercialization, a sweet touch that inevitably produced an impure end-product.

There did emerge, however, several remarkable jazz violin virtuosi, notable among them Hezekiah Leroy Gordon 'Stuff' Smith (1909–67) who had studied the instrument academically, played in revue bands, then became a jazz practitioner of the first order after playing with Morton in 1928; prominent in the 1930s, leading various small groups. Giuseppe 'Joe' Venuti (1903–78) developed into a jazz player on becoming a schoolfriend of Eddie Lang (1902–33) the guitarist with whom he had a long musical partnership. Joe played and led groups into the 1970s. Within the Ellington band 'Ray' Willis Nance (1913–76), also a trumpeter, vocalist and dancer, provided a special voice until the early 60s.

The European violinist known to all, and still active, is Stephane Grappelly (later Grappelli) (b. 1908) who is primarily remembered as the confrère of Django Reinhardt (1910–53) in the quintet of the Hot Club de France. Later an active soloist and has occasionally even worked in partnership with Yehudi Menuhin. There is a case to be made out for saying that perhaps the greatest jazz fiddle player of all was Eddie South (1904–1962), since he seemed to many listeners to have adapted the instrument to the jazz idiom more completely than anyone else. Unfortunately, he is not well represented on record. Svend Asmussen (b. 1916) from Denmark is another fine jazz violinist who has received less than his due.

It was inevitable that jazz violin should move into the post bebop era, and it did so particularly effectively in the hands of Jean-Luc Ponty (b. 1942) of France, who succeeded in getting a great deal of John Coltrane into his playing. Some of his later work is perhaps too much inclined to a kind of jazz/rock fusion to please hard-core jazz devotees, who have a difficult enough time accepting the instrument anyway. Another, younger, Frenchman, Didier Lockwood is developing along roughly similar lines.

For all the average jazz enthusiasts' lukewarm reception for the violin, the instrument has proved immensely attractive to some of the jazz musicians themselves. As long ago as 1936, Artie Shaw somehow grafted a string quartet onto a rather Dixieland-style band and produced fascinating results. Charlie Parker enjoyed appearing and recording with strings. Stan Getz made some stunning records with string backing, composed and arranged by Eddie Sauter, in 1962.

Viper A marijuana smoker. Much usage in the 1930s and 40s; very dated by the 1980s. But kept in the vocabulary by many early jazz titles such as *If you're a viper* (Rosetta Howard), *Viper's drag* (Fats Waller) and *Sendin' the vipers* (Mezzrow).

Vocalese see **Scat**

Wacky In the widest sense – eccentric, crazy, looney. Similarly used to describe jazz playing of a wild and eccentric kind; e.g. some of the funny-hat sort of Dixieland.

Wail To play or sing with great feeling, to be really in the groove, thus really wailing. A term used in jazz from the 1930s, when it was mainly applied to blues and jazz singing, but by 1950 it had been firmly adopted by the cool element. In Ellington's *Wall Street wail* (1920) it takes on a double meaning.

Walk To play jazz, especially to play jazz well – to really walk. Generally refers to an ensemble rather than an individual. Probably derives from cakewalk where

those who really walked would have taken the cake.

Walking bass Boogie-woogie or barrelhouse bass figure of the kind that ambles up and down the keyboard in leaping octaves or tenths.

Walkin' the Dog One of those animal dances that aped the movements of the animal concerned. Mention of it as a black dance goes back to *c.* 1910, but it only became widely popular in the 1920s, when there was a new vogue for that sort of thing culminating in the foxtrot craze.

Wall Street Famous street in the southern section of Manhattan, the centre of the financial area of New York – as

Threadneedle Street is in the City of London. The notorious Wall Street crash of October 1929 was as disastrous to the jazz world as it was to everyone else. It bankrupted many and started the long Depression years. Such a situation is hinted at in Scott Joplin's *Wall Street rag*, written in 1909, its first strain headed 'Panic in Wall Street, Brokers feeling melancholy'; but the real (1929) thing was the inspiration for Ellington's 1929 *Wall Street wail*.

Washboard A genuine household washboard with its corrugated iron sheet in a wooden frame made a good makeshift rhythm instrument. It was played with a scrubbing motion by means of thimbles, or something similar, worn on the fingers. A good quality washboard was much sought after and certain manufacturer's were much admired: as one blues singer sang – 'a good washboard is hard to find'. Used in many early spasm bands and brought back to popularity in revival jazz of the 1940s as a skiffle instrument. (See also **Rub-board**.)

Washboard band Generic name for the spasm or skiffle type band, originally created out of poverty, but later a stylistic fad. Beside the washboard and guitar, such a band would be likely to utilize a jug-blowing, washtub bass, penny whistle style line-up. The professional bands, like the famous Washboard Rhythm Kings and various groups involving leading washboarder Jimmy Bertrand (1900–60), used the washboard for the hilarious, racy rhythmic effect that was in keeping with the spirit of their music (as did the revival scrubbers) rather than out of economic necessity.

Washtub bass A makeshift instrument making use of an inverted washtub (or similarly-shaped barrel or drum) with a string attached to one side and thence attached to a broom handle which is held against the rim of the tub. When the string is pulled taut and plucked it produces a note that can be varied according to tautness and makes a functional one-string bass. It had an ancestor in the African earth-bow with which a similar effect is achieved by using a hide membrane stretched over a depression in the ground; a contrivance found in the Congo and Central Africa.

Wa-wa, wah-wah A sound resembling the human voice enunciating an exaggerated 'w'; achieved on brass instruments by the use of wa-wa mute, which has a flat end with an aperture over which the hand may be moved to get the effect of vocalized and animal sounds. A wah-wah pedal, activating electronic circuits, is a popular device, producing similar effects on the electric guitar (and some other electronic instruments).

Weather Report One of the most successful modern groups to combine jazz and rock, founded in 1971 with its key figures the stony-toned saxist Wayne Shorter (b. 1933), pianist Joe Zawinul (b. 1932) and Czech bassist Miroslav Vitous (b. 1947). Based on similar experiments in rock/jazz fusion by Miles Davis (b. 1926) (with whom both Shorter and Zawinul had worked), the basic elements were an attacking ensemble and carefully planned instrumental textures producing a group sound that precluded most solo work – as was best heard in their first album *Weather Report*. Later issues from *c.* 1975 onward gave more scope to soloists and the overall results were often more lyrical in effect.

Weird see **Crazy**

West Coast jazz Around 1950/1 a number of mainly white modern jazz musicians began to attract attention on the Pacific coast of America in the cities and towns of California; many of them were involved in the lucrative Hollywood studios musical activities. The main centre of activities was the Lighthouse, a Hermosa Beach club opened and run by ex-Kenton bass-player Howard Rumsey in 1950. Pioneering groups were the Gerry Mulligan Quartet (formed in 1952) and those led by trumpeter Shorty Rogers and drummer Shelly Manne. Other early West Coasters were Jimmy Giuffre, Bob Cooper and Wardell Gray. The style that was dubbed 'West Coast' was essentially cool, intellectual and controlled. Occasionally used of the contemporaneous West Coast revivalists, such as Lu Watters, and other traditionalists who based their activities on San Francisco. The modernists operated mainly in Los Angeles.

As a category of modern jazz it has to be approached with caution since many jazz commentators believe that the differences between West and East Coast jazz – i.e. the verbal distinctions that first came to be made in the 50s – were more apparent than real. Many West Coast performers, as typified by saxophonist/ flautist Bud Shank, claim that West Coast jazz began when the Californian players, whose background tended to include more formal musical education, started to refine the bebop innovations of Parker, Gillespie, Monk and Clarke. The result was a lighter-textured, more transparent sound than that achieved by the New York-based musicians. This led many to believe that West Coast jazz was a matter of head rather than heart. But in some cases this can prove a somewhat hasty judgment, especially with regard to the undeniably passionate playing of a musician such as alto-saxophonist Art Pepper.

Others associated with West Coast geographically or in spirit include Conte and Pete Candoli, Leroy Vinnegar and Mel Lewis, many members of Stan Kenton's early bands, Bill Holman, Lou Levy and Dave Brubeck.

West End Resort with a marina at the western end of the lakeside area of Lake Pontchartrain on the northern fringes of New Orleans. Its cafés and nightspots were a popular area for jazz activities and probably many early jazz developments took place there. Celebrated in the Oliver *West End blues* (1925) that Louis Armstrong used for one of his finest recordings in 1928.

Western The jazz style that developed in Chicago *c*. 1925–35 was sometimes referred to as Western Style, differentiating it from its similar derivative New Orleans style, 'more open . . . open horns, running chords and changes' (Gold). In boogie-woogie, the driving, train-imitative, rapid bass style was referred to as 'fast Western', again probably from its development in Chicago.

Western swing A cheerful, extrovert music played in Texas and the Middle West between mid-30s and mid-40s by small bands which combined some of the elements of hillbilly music with much of the spirit of swing. The Light Crust Doughboys, with their Fats Wallerish pianist Knocky Parker, were typical of these invigorating little outfits.

White One of the many names for cocaine, current from the 1940s, derived from 'the white stuff'. Also name for gin or the clear alcohol used for making bootleg whisky in the Prohibition period. A cheap, inferior bootleg corn whisky made from this source was known as 'white lightning' or 'white line'.

Whiteman, Paul The Paul Whiteman band and its leader have come in for considerable stick in jazz histories – what Max Harrison has aptly described as 'aggressive uninterest' – the sort of lofty derision that jazz fanatics reserve for anything which does not suit their tastes. Primarily, of course, this is a largely justified resentment at Whiteman's assumption, in the 1920s, of the title 'King of Jazz' which was purely a commercial gimmick.

Whiteman considered it one of his aims in life to make jazz respectable, and either he or someone closely connected with him coined the term 'symphonic jazz' for some of the music which his very large orchestra often played. Symphonic it might have been, but it swung not at all. The whole business is clouded by the fact that it was at a Whiteman concert in

1924 that George Gershwin's *Rhapsody in Blue* was premiered. This composition, now appreciated as a piece of American music in its own right, was widely misunderstood for a long time, rejected by jazz *aficionados* and classical devotees alike. None of this, of course, made a scrap of difference to Whiteman's popularity.

Whiteman has often been accused of restricting good jazz musicians within the ranks of the band and causing much artistic frustration. This is somewhat unfair as he offered a good living to many musicians, including Bix Beiderbecke, who would not otherwise have been so well off. By the time Bix joined the Whiteman band he was a fair reader of music and seems to have enjoyed the challenge of playing in such things as Gershwin's *Piano Concerto in F* where he handled the demanding cornet part well. He was one of the top salaried people in the band and was kept on the pay-roll through periods of illness. In further defence of Whiteman, it must be said that he generated a great deal of interest in jazz by his fringe activities and his wide appeal to a non-specialist public. Whiteman (1890–1967) formed his first band in 1918 and was well established by 1924 when he organized that famous New York Aeolian Hall concert which introduced *Rhapsody in Blue*.
Book: *Pops: Paul Whiteman, King of Jazz* by Thomas A. DeLong. Piscataway, J. J., 1983.

Wig (1) A general American slang term in the 1930s for the intellect or brain, as in *c*. 1935 'don't blow your wig', it became in the 1940s applied to an intellectual or academic sort of person. Thence, in the 1950s, it crept into jazz talk as the name for a musician of that kind, a progressive musician of a cerebral bent, 'cool and far out' (W & F). Also used as a verb, to play cool or way-out jazz.
(2) Black slang for a white person, i.e. one who has straight hair.

Wild see **Crazy**

Windy City Popular name for the city of

Chicago, bestowed, not because of the excessive blowing of jazz that went on there, but because of the cold winds that continuously blow off Lake Michigan in the winter season.

Wingy Nickname of Joseph Matthews Manone (1900–82), trumpet player and vocalist. At the age of ten he was badly injured when he got caught between two streetcars and had to have his right arm amputated above the elbow. The nickname 'Wingy' was bestowed upon him sometime thereafter. The accident also ensured that in the fullness of time he would become the victim of Joe Venuti's most celebrated practical joke. As a birthday present one year, Venuti gave him one cufflink.
Book: *Trumpet on the Wing* by Wingy Manone & Paul Vandervoort. New York: Doubleday, 1948; London: Jazz Book Club, 1964.

Wining boy Jelly Roll Morton's own explanation of this term (which he got round to recording as a title, *Winin' boy blues*, in 1939) was that it was bestowed upon him as a name when he was working at Hilma Burt's sporting-house next door to Tom Anderson's Saloon. 'When the place was closing down it was my habit to pour the partly finished bottles of wine (actually, champagne) together and make up a new bottle from the mixture'. This uncharacteristically modest account is in marked contrast to the claim made by practically every other printed source to the effect that a 'winding' or 'wining' boy was a man – usually a young one – whom women considered to be a particularly satisfying sexual partner. That ties in with Morton's main nickname, 'jelly roll' being common slang for the sexual act or anything associated with it. Furthermore, the opening words, as sung by Morton, make little sense in the wine-dregs context: 'I'm the winin' boy, and I don't deny my name'.

Winnetka Town in Illinois and the shores of Lake Michigan, population *c*. 15 000, to the north of Chicago. Remembered because of the important person from there who breezed into Chicago and was immortalized in the shape of an imaginative double bass and drum duet (with a little whistling) by Bob Haggart and Ray Bauduc in *The big noise from Winnetka* (1938).

Wire, The This influential magazine, published in London, was started in Summer 1982 by enthusiast and promoter Anthony Wood. To indicate its intentions, it carried the sub-billing: 'Jazz, Improvised Music, And . . .', and in the beginning its founder was not at all sure that he could even make the modest quarterly schedule he had planned. By 1984 it was clear that this stubborn periodical had it in it to survive, and in the summer of that year it moved into the shelter of the Namara publishing group (which includes Quartet Books), enabling it to go monthly, starting with the October 1984 issue, and to achieve national distribution. In mid-1985 Richard Cook took over as editor, and *The Wire* now appears to be firmly established. The 'Jazz, Improvised Music, And . . .' line has vanished and *The Wire* stands or falls on its name alone.

Wolverines Jelly Roll Morton said that he wrote *The Wolverines* in Detroit 'in the early days'. 'It was just one of those things that float around in my head and one day, when I sit down at the piano, it comes out of my fingers.'

The Wolverines that he possibly had in mind were not of animal origin, but from the name of a barber's shop in Lansing, Michigan (which is nicknamed the Wolverine State) owned by a friend of his. He was 'not sore but hot' about the way that, when the tune had got to be famous and popular in Chicago and the Melrose Brothers had offered him a $3000 advance on publication, the lyric-writing Spikes Brothers, Ben and John, muscled in and wrote some words for it. It was then put out as a rather cheapened song, copyright Spikes and Morton, and furthermore as *Wolverine blues* which Morton objected to because it was not a

blues at all. It appeared in this form on 14 February 1923. It was, as Morton said, already known as a jazz number in Chicago where it had first been played by the King Oliver Creole Jazz Band. It was recorded by the New Orleans Rhythm Kings in March 1923. Morton arrived in Chicago in May and had the original lyrics suppressed and the music republished, now with an original second strain in E-flat removed but with new lyrics also by the Spikes Brothers. Following the NORK recording, the number became such a popular item in the repertoire of a group of young college jazz musicians that one disenchanted member, Dud Mear, sarcastically suggested that they ought to call themselves the Wolverine Band.

Thus the Wolverine Orchestra (commonly referred to as The Wolverines) came into being. They were a group of college students, including after a time Bix Beiderbecke, fresh from Lake Forest Academy, who joined together and had their first engagement at a roadhouse in Hamilton, Ohio in 1923. The group were particularly influenced by the playing of the New Orleans Rhythm Kings at the Friars Inn in Chicago. They grew in fame and went to New York in the autumn of 1923. Beiderbecke left the group to stay with Charlie Straight's orchestra in Chicago. The Wolverine Orchestra first recorded for Gennett in Richmond, Indiana on Monday, 18 February 1924.

Women in jazz The reasons why, for most of its history, jazz has not been graced by very many female performers, are too much involved with social attitudes, longstanding male prejudices and other, subtler, factors to make them easy to pin down in a work of reference. All we can do is to take note of the fact that jazz has commonly been a male world, and to mention some of the growing numbers of women who are taking their places alongside male colleagues. We refer, of course, to instrumentalists, not to lady singers, who have always been active on the jazz scene. Female pianists have been accepted in jazz in a way that women playing other instruments have not – at least until very recent times. Lil Hardin (1898–1971) worked with King Oliver, married Louis Armstrong and later made some records under her own name. Mary Lou Williams (1910–81) was an extremely important jazz pianist and an essential part of Andy Kirk's band from 1931 to 1942, acting also as arranger and composer. The bandleader and vibraphone player Terry Gibbs has employed several women as pianists: Alice McLeod (b. 1937), who later became Alice Coltrane on her marriage to John Coltrane, and who also plays the harp; Pat Moran (originally Helen Mudgett, b. 1934); and Terry Pollard (b. 1931) also an excellent vibraphonist. Sarah Vaughan (b. 1924) started her career as vocalist and second pianist in the Earl Hines Band, in 1943. Cleo Brown (b. 1909) made a number of records in the middle and late 1930s, and became particularly well known as a boogie-woogie exponent.

In more recent times, Toshiko Akiyoshi, who was born (1929) in Manchuria, went first to Japan, then to the USA. In 1972, together with her husband Lew Tabakin, Toshiko formed a big band in California, for which she writes and arranges and which she conducts. Joanne Brackeen (originally Joanne Grogan, b. 1938) is a very powerful post-bop soloist who has also worked with Woody Shaw, Joe Farrell, Stan Getz and many others.

In some ways the most remarkable of the female pianists in jazz has been Marian McPartland, who was born Marian Turner, in Windsor, England in 1920. She came into jazz when, while entertaining troops in Belgium in 1944, she met American Dixieland cornettist Jimmy McPartland. After their marriage she lived in America and worked mainly with Jimmy. But her style rapidly outgrew his, and by the early 1950s she was striking out on her own. Now internationally known and hostess of a highly acclaimed show broadcast by public radio in New York, in which she interviews, and performs with, fellow pianists.

Marian has been quietly busy for some years on behalf of women in jazz, and she helped in the late 1970s to bring forward a fine young alto saxophonist, then called Mary Fettig Park but later billed simply as Mary Fettig (b. 1953, California). Other saxophonists have included Vi Redd (b. 1928, Los Angeles, California); Kathy Stobart (b. 1925, South Shields, England); Barbara Thompson (born in London), wife of drummer Jon Hiseman and leader, until 1985, of a jazz/rock band, wittily called Paraphernalia; Gail Thompson (b. 1958, London), leader of several groups.

Female trombonists do not abound but they include Melba Liston (b. 1926) also well-known as an arranger; and Annie Whitehead (b. 1955, England), an extremely powerful player. Among the few trumpet players, Valaida Snow (1900–1956) was one of the most remarkable and best known, especially to British audiences, to whom she was introduced in 1934 in the all-black revue *Blackbirds of 1934*. Billie Rogers played trumpet and sang with Woody Herman in the 1940s and later ran a band of her own. Laurie Frink not so far known as a soloist, is a very powerful lead trumpeter in America, constantly in demand for studio work, and seen at least once in Britain in Gerry Mulligan's 1980 Concert Jazz Band.

On drums, Sue Evans has appeared with Gil Evans (not related) both on tour and on record. Vibraphonist Margie Hyams (b. 1923) worked very successfully with Woody Herman in 1944–6, and in the late 1940s with George Shearing.

Books: *Women in Jazz: a Discography of Instrumental Music 1913–1968* by Jan Leder. 310p. Westport: Greenwood Press, 1985; *Jazz Women: 1900 to the Present* by Sally Placksin. 352p. 1985; *Stormy Weather* by Linda Dahl. 371p. London: Quartet 1984.

Wood block A open-ended, wooden box, used as a percussive rhythm feature in many early jazz and dance bands. Frequently used in spasm bands where other percussion was not available. Effect similar to using sticks on the rim of a side drum. Jimmy Bertrand (1900–1960) is frequently listed as a leading wood-blockist. Their prominent use in early jazz recordings may not reflect their true musical status. The bass drum was hard to record and wood blocks, being more amenable to the recording process, may have been given an artificial prominence.

Woodshed To play or practise music on one's own, in quiet and solitude; from the traditional use of woodsheds as havens for solitary sinfulness, such as boyhood smoking. The quiet rehearsal and 'one-night' times of a band between engagements.

Work song The kind of chanting song with a repetitive, rhythmic chorus that would have been ad-libbed by the slave workers on the plantations of the South or by the chain-gangs working on roads and railways. Forerunners of the spiritual and the blues. Exact equivalent of the capstan shanties, and other work shanties, used by old-time sailors for the co-ordination of effort in a communal physical task.

Xylophone The more percussive tones of the xylophone have largely been replaced by the vibraphone in jazz. In the early days a few drummers such as Jimmy Bertrand (1900–1960) and Jasper Taylor (1894–1964) would occasionally play and record on the instrument as would their classical counterparts. The vibraphone mainly took over *c.* 1935 but Lionel Hampton (b. 1909) would occasionally use the xylophone and Red Norvo (b. 1908) remained faithful to it until well into the 1940s and some time after.

Yardbird see **Bird**

Yas Yas Girl Stage name of blues singer Merline Johnson (b. 1915) who worked and recorded in Chicago *c.* 1935–42. Yas is a synonym for 'ass' or 'arse' so it suggests she was a provocative performer.

Yellow Dog Familiar name for the Yazoo Delta Railroad in Mississippi, USA, running across the state from east to west. The Yazoo Delta is a low-lying plain, liable to floods, some 200 miles (300 km) long and between 60 and 70 miles (96–113 km) wide through which the Yazoo River flows south in the area between Memphis and Vicksburg, where it joins the Mississippi; a very rich cotton-growing area. Immortalized in W. C. Handy's *Yellow Dog blues* – the line 'goin'' where the Southern cross the Yellow Dog' referring to the point at Moorhead, Mississippi where the Southern Railroad crossed the Yazoo Delta Railroad (now a part of the Illinois Central network), in the centre of the area.

Yerba Buena Literally meaning Good Herb in Mexican Spanish. It was an early name for the San Francisco area where many herbs grew. An earthy sounding name for the band which revived the New Orleans style and the Oliver two-trumpet lead formula on the West Coast of America in 1940. The band was formed and led by cornettist Lu Watters (b. 1911), who had organized his first band in 1926 and led an eleven-piece at Sweet's Ball-room in Oakland in 1938-9, specifically to make appearances at the Dawn Club, off Lower Market Street in San Francisco. It had a very strong influence on the traditional revival of the 40s with its robust, down-to-earth style and righteous roughness. Some sides recorded for the Jazzman label helped to spread the gospel before the group disbanded in 1942. Watters served in the Navy from 1942 to 1945 (leading a 20-piece band in Hawaii) then reformed the Yerba Buena Jazz Band in 1946; it broke up in 1951 but had temporary revivals in the 1950s.

The two-cornet lead in the original band was shared by Bob Scobey (1916–63), who later led similar San Francisco revivalist bands of his own.

Young Man With a Horn Title of a jazz-oriented novel by Dorothy Baker, published in 1938, and loosely based on the story of cornettist Bix Beiderbecke (1903–31). Filmed in 1949 with Kirk Douglas loosely cast as Bix and his playing loosely imitated by Harry James. Definitely legendary.

Z, ZZs A Z is the slang name for an ounce of narcotics. ZZs means drugs. To be on the ZZs.

It has another completely innocent meaning, deriving from one of the ingenious conventions of the comic strip. In strip cartoons, a sleeping figure is always shown emitting a string of ZZZZZs, to indicate snoring. 'Sleep' thus becomes 'zeez' in American pronunciation, not by any means restricted to use by musicians, but much favoured by them since it appeals to their sense of humour. It has been projected beyond musical circles in a witty song by pianist/singer/songwriter Dave Frishberg; entitled *Zeez* it extols the delights of sleep, finishing with the key line 'I'm gonna get me some zeez', a phrase which he heard used by a member of Stan Kenton's band in the 1940s.

'Zeds' for sleep, and 'racking up the zeds' for getting some sleep are quite well known in English slang.

Zero cool As cool as you can possibly get. Has superseded 'real cool' as the ultimate expression of admiration.

Zoot (1) One who is well dressed, attractive and in the fashion. Hence Zootie, Zooty or Zutty – a with-it, dressy person. Came into use by *c.* 1935 but had become out-dated by the 1950s. A dude (which itself comes from 'duds', meaning clothes). The name arose from the slightly earlier 'zoot suit' – a style of dress in the fashion of the 1930s and 40s with padded shoulders, large lapels, drape jacket, high-waisted pants full-cut and sharply pleated.
(2) Zoot! – a shout of encouragement to jive, swing, get hep, *c.* 1935–40.

Zutty see **Zoot** (above)

Zydeco This is the name generally given to the black counterpart of the white cajun music of south-west Louisiana. The word is said to be a corruption of part of the title *Les haricots sont pas sale* (the beans are not salty), one of the French songs widely known in this still largely cajun French-speaking area. The lead instrument is generally the accordion, but played in such a way as strongly to resemble the sound achieved by blues harmonica players. The rhythm instruments often include a washboard, or rubboard, and triangle, there is usually a guitar or two, while some bands also favour a tenor saxophone, giving the whole thing something of a rhythm and blues feel. Among the zydeco bands which have achieved a degree of international recognition are those of Rockin' Dopsie (sometimes spelled Dupsee, and almost invariably pronounced Doopsie), Clifton Chenier and Fernest Arceneaux (whose band is usually billed as 'Fernest and the Thunderers').

Jazz Musicians and Singers

a selective list and index

* indicates those mentioned in the book and indexed

Abbreviations

arr – arranger
as – alto-saxophone
b – banjo
bs – baritone-saxophone
bss – bass-saxophone
c – cornet
clo – cello
co – composer
cs – C-melody saxophone
cl – clarinet
d – drums
db – double-bass
f – flute
fh – flugelhorn
g – guitar
h – harp
hm – harmonica
k – kazoo
l – leader
o – organ
ob – oboe
p – piano
s – saxophone
ss – soprano-saxophone
tb – trombone
tp – trumpet
ts – tenor-saxophone
tu – tuba
v – violin
vib – vibraphone
vo – vocalist
w – washboard
x – xylophone